PRACTICAL SOFTWARE ENGINEERING SERIES

SOFTWARE IMPLEMENTATION

MICHAEL MARCOTTY

General Motors Research Laboratories

PRENTICE HALL

NEW YORK LONDON TORONTO SYDNEY TOKYO SINGAPORE

First published 1991 by
Prentice Hall International (UK) Ltd
66 Wood Lane End, Hemel Hempstead
Hertfordshire HP2 4RG
A division of
Simon & Schuster International Group

Typeset in 9½/12 pt Times Roman
by Keyset Composition, Colchester, Essex

Printed and bound in the United States of America

Library of Congress Cataloging-in-Publication Data is available
from the publisher.

British Library Cataloguing in Publication Data

Marcotty, Michael, *1931–*
    Software implementation. – (Prentice Hall international
    series in practical software engineering)
    1. Computer systems. Programming
    I. Title
    005.1
    ISBN 0-13-823493-0

1 2 3 4 5 95 94 93 92 91

CONTENTS

PART TWO   THE PRINCIPLES OF PROGRAMMING

PART THREE   THE PRACTICE OF PROGRAMMING

PART FOUR   THE ENVIRONMENT FOR PROGRAMMING

PART FIVE   APPENDICES

EDITOR'S PREFACE

The 'PSE series', five volumes on practical software engineering topics, is intended for several purposes, and their appropriate audiences.

First, as a whole, the series is intended as a basis for guidelines in software engineering practice, for people who engage directly in programming computers at a non-trivial level, as the whole or part of their work. Typically, this list will include software engineers of greater or lesser experience, amateur programmers who are generally of little (or intermittent) experience, and computer scientists. They will, by and large, be involved in some or all of the activities that make up software development such as system specification, software requirements, definition and design, implementation, testing and quality assurance.

Second, the series is intended for the comprehension of others involved in software development. In this category are managers of software engineers and the managers of these managers (and so on), commercial staff who buy or sell software, or contract for services to provide it, quality assurance people, personnel officers and operatives in associated disciplines – such as mechanical, electronic and production engineering – who may work with software development staff on composite systems.

Third, the series is intended as a text for courses in software engineering, both for academic-level and industrial/business courses in continuing education.

The breadth of this address may possibly invoke reaction, if not disfavor, for it is not immediately apparent that the third objective is compatible with the other two, certainly concerning the academic component of education as distinct from practical training courses.

A prevailing sentiment in business and industry, as we have found, seems to be that academic material is pretty irrelevant to real everyday problems of software development. It teaches (the argument goes) computer science; it does not provide (the argument continues) for good practices in software engineering to be learned. On the other hand, academics might repost – with some justification – that software engineering in the big wide world is in a state of such glorious shambles that the kindliest and most socially useful act that they can commit is to refrain from enabling it to be learned, and some may even opt for its prevention.

It is a lamentable state of affairs to summarize the problem as a gap between two deficiencies, for that makes three problems of it. Yet, that is the case and, seen that way, it goes some way to justify the stated aims of this series. Whether they eventuate is another matter altogether.

We have set the series out as five, monograph-length volumes. Four of these correspond to the main activities in software development:

1. Specification and feasibility.
2. Design.
3. Implementation.
4. Software estimating and technical quality.

These are Volumes 2–5 respectively, and their authors are Michael Marcotty (Volume 4 – *Software Implementation*), Wayne Stevens (Volume 3 – *Software Design*), and Allen Macro (Volumes 2 and 5).

There is also a volume whose subjects cover matters intrinsic to all four other volumes: in that sense it is the 'orthogonal' title in the series, and is called Volume 1; it covers:

5. Software engineering: concepts and management.

The impetus to read books of this sort usually arises from some recognized need; the disincentives to do so, merits of the work apart, include a misjudgment by people of what they need to know, and what they may be likely to understand. For example, it is commonplace to find software development staff, at the programming level, who think and say that they have no need to interest themselves in management matters, no wish to, and no facility anyway. Nothing could be more unwise. Practitioners may prevent good management practice, by others, if they are unaware of the scope and modalities concerned in it. Equally, it is commonplace to find managers – and others not especially knowledgeable in the subject, but involved one way or another – for whom 'software' is an uncharted territory (of the 'here be dragons' sort) and to whom 'software engineering' is an arcane – perhaps profane – art, conducted in some hermetic ritual by its initiates. To some degree, this attitude is understandable, if not justified. The terminology of software and its development may seem more alien to non-practitioners than that of any other subject, and apparently changes too rapidly for a start to be made in understanding it. In fact, this conclusion is only true up to a point. A basic method in cognition is that of classification and, once the basic classes are identified in this subject, as in any other, the problems of volatile terminology are lessened.

With this understanding, and in order to be helpful (with a modest reservation about the merits of books in this series, for it is the province of readers and critics to judge), we recommend that software *practitioners* and participants on courses offering software engineering modules, should read Volumes 1 and 5 as well as their rather narrow, subject-interest topics in Volumes 3 and 4. Chapter 1 of Volume 1, being elementary, may be read for passing interest only by these populations, and for an understanding of the basic problems in comprehension that many managers, and others, have, Volume 5 (*Quality*) should be read with especial care.

The *managers* and 'others' referred to should – in our view – start with Volume 1, progress to Volume 2 and then read Volume 5 with particular acuity. Anyone in these categories who also wishes to achieve some insight into the 'arcana' of software engineering should attempt Volume 3 (*Software Design*); Volume 4 requires some preliminary grasp of computer programming considerably beyond the level of Basic on a person computer – which is about the limit for many people in this class.

Students (in, for example, computer science) may benefit from a close acquaintance with Volumes 3 and 4. An interesting question, of considerable topicality, is what should be read by students in schools of business management or by undergraduates in the cognate disciplines of software engineering such as electronic engineering. In the first case, we would recommend 'the management volume' 1, and Volume 5; for the cognate disciplines such as electronic, production or mechanical engineering we would recommend the whole series, to be read in sequence, with the reservation that Volumes 3 and 4 may be beyond the detailed study of many in this class, and beyond their need to do so.

One other point of our policy might give rise to speculation or adverse comment, and an explanation is owed. The examples in each volume are not harmonized across volumes nor, necessarily, even within volumes. The reason is really quite simple. No one application of reasonable size would incorporate an example set sufficient for all purposes; the priority is to demonstrate points in the text in the best way for that issue, not necessarily the most harmonized way. Also, obviously, a thematic example across volumes might be seen as counter to the modular approach of this series if, for example, one had to get Volume 2 in order to understand the examples in Volumes 3 and 4. One would not want to attract accusations of sharp commercial practice.

In this volume, Michael Marcotty describes the implementation stage of software development – what, in the stone age of our trade, twenty-odd years ago, was known as the 'coding', and was undertaken in many places by a subspecies called 'coders'. Today, we recognize (or should recognize) that, between the purposive act of design and the existence of code, there occurs a variety of technical activities that make up more than just the 'coding'. To describe this in a single word, we have resurrected an old and honorable name, thirty years old at least: 'programming'.

Nowadays, there are few programmers in the strict and sectoral sense of people engaged only at the implementation stage of software engineering – but there are many 'amateur programmers', people whose inexperience may lead them to commit the ancient sins of programming, and some not so ancient.

This book is, in parts, a polemic against amateur programming of this sort, but not against amateur programmers. For the question confronts us all: 'How did you start, Mr ——?' And the answer must be: 'As an amateur programmer!' The sin, if there is one, is for how long one *stays* an amateur programmer, given the opportunity to become the Real Thing – which, in this case, means 'a software engineer'. Marcotty's book urges the view on us that programming is an expository act within software engineering. It is up to him, as author, to aspire for similar ends.

I shall leave further exposition to him . . .

Allen Macro FBCS
Rotterdam, 1990

INTRODUCTION

My client and I sat back to back. I was the 'duty programmer' charged with the job of assisting my company's clients to run their programs on our computer. My client worked for a government department and had written a large program in machine language – no mnemonics, no symbols, no comments. That's all we had available in 1958. We sat back to back to debug his program because it was classified and I was not allowed to look at it. He could only read little snippets of code to me and answer specific questions about values in registers and so on. It was rather like playing blindfold chess. This was debugging at its most elemental.

Since then, I have spent many hours debugging other people's programs as well as my own. As time went on, the programming languages became less cryptic, but there was always a tinge of blindfold chess in the task, even when I was allowed to look at the code. For quite a long period, my clients would come to me armed with a listing of their program and a hexadecimal dump that purported to represent the contents of the machine immediately after their program crashed. I became quite skilled in reading the traces. I knew that if I looked in location 000016 I would find a key pointer. This would lead me to a table of pointers and at offset 3C – hexadecimal arithmetic became another of my skills – there would be a pointer to the start of the deceased program's dynamic storage. From then on, it was only a matter of following pointers, doing hexadecimal arithmetic, consulting reference manuals to find the layout of control blocks, and applying hard-won intuition before the cause of death was established and the post-mortem complete. But this only established the cause of death, not the manner in which the disease was contracted.

After a while, I realized that debugging from storage dumps was not a fit human activity. In retrospect, I am not proud of how long it took me to come to this conclusion, but then no high priest likes to give up the power of being able to interpret the arcane for the laity. I then turned to helping my clients by showing them how to debug their programs from the listing itself. I rapidly discovered that the programmers had little idea of what went on in their own programs. Sometimes the program appeared to behave completely irrationally. Values would change without apparent cause, or the termination message from the system would have even less connection with reality than usual. After I had managed to persuade the programmer that the cause was not likely to be due to a hardware malfunction or to a compiler error, though neither of these could be completely ruled out, I would ask: 'Is it possible that you have used a subscript value that is outside the bounds of an array?' I soon learned to ignore programmers' avowals that their program did not use any arrays, or at least not in this part of the program, and sent them away to rerun the program with subscript range checking enabled. About 80 per cent of them never came back to report the results of that experiment. Sometime later, I would meet them in the corridor and they would admit with embarrassment: 'I had completely forgotten that I *did* use an array . . .'. The more I looked at their programs, the less I was surprised that they forgot what their programs used or did. The terms 'spaghetti' and 'rat's nest' have been quite popular for describing the programming style used. Some of them were so cryptic that deciphering hexadecimal dumps seemed easy. At least hexadecimal dumps do not try to show off with coding tricks. As time went on, helping others to debug their programs became less a part of my job and more an act of kindness. I was able to take a much more cavalier attitude and treated them to hell-fire and brimstone sermons on the sins of writing unreadable programs. I refused to look at their programs until they had rewritten them in readable fashion. Some of my colleagues still remind me of the diatribes they received. Most are grateful – at least those who still talk to me.

The problem of unreadable programs only starts with getting the program to work. If programs, once written, were never changed, it would not be quite so bad. Old programs never die, they are modified, and modified, and modified again until it becomes too difficult to change them any further and they gradually fall into disuse. In many cases, the problem stems from the original authors of the programs. Their programming style was so obscure that the modifiers, who may have been the original authors, could only guess at what was meant and made changes in a tentative *ad hoc* manner, hoping that the altered program would achieve the desired result. If it appeared to work, the modification was left, ungainly as it was, because the effort of going back and understanding enough to be able to tidy it up was too daunting, the work unattractive, and, as always, there was never enough time.

These days, the work of many brilliant people becomes embodied in a program. These people do not consider themselves programmers but scientists, engineers, accountants, teachers, . . . who use computers and write programs as an adjunct to their work. These are some of what we call *amateur programmers*, not in the sense that they do it for the pure love of programming but that programming is not their major life's work. Most programmers, in this sense, are amateurs. They make an advance in their field, write a program that implements it, and would like to make it available to others. Understandably, once the programs are written and demonstrated, the authors want to move on and pass the responsibility for repairing newly discovered errors and incorporating enhancements to others, who themselves may also be amateur programmers. Unfortunately, much of this valuable work is lost because the programs are so difficult to understand that nobody is prepared to take on this responsibility. In fact, the work is doubly lost, it is also lost because the procedure – *algorithm* is the more scholarly sounding term – that is the essence of the work cannot be understood and used by others. It is as if it were written in a lost language like Etruscan.

Many think that a program is a private communication between the programmer and the computer. It is the thesis of this book that:

> A program is a communication between programmers; it is a technical exposition describing information and how it is processed.

Consequently, the program must be written so that it can be understood and the process it describes be used and modified. As for other forms of expository writing, there are techniques that must be used to attain clarity. To demonstrate the idea that a program is an exposition, I have had groups of students work together to produce a single program of non-trivial size. They very rapidly discovered that they needed to be able to understand the programs written by the other members of the group and that the project was more an exercise in communication than in programming.

This book is one volume of a series that presents the complete process of producing a program from requirements analysis to maintenance. The coverage of the other members of the series is discussed in the Editor's Preface. This volume deals with what is probably the most discussed stage of the process, implementation – writing and testing the actual program. To those who would complain that there is nothing new here, I would reply that old unheeded lessons demand repeating. In fact, the principal justification of this book is that the techniques described here have yet to be applied in a consistent, disciplined manner.

This book is addressed to amateur programmers, that is, those who need to write programs but do not look on programming as an end in itself. It is also addressed to the professional software engineer who is working as a member of a team to produce a program that is larger than one person can handle and will eventually be passed on to another group of programmers for maintenance. Both groups are engaged in what I call *expository programming*, writing programs that are *technical communications* between programmers. Here, 'technical' refers to the form rather than the content of the communication. The program application may or may not be technical.

It is assumed that the reader understands the mechanics of programming and has reasonable facility with a high-level programming language, just as the reader of a book on technical writing is assumed to know how to write grammatical sentences in the language being used. Both professional and amateur programmers write their programs in order to satisfy an *external specification*, a description of what the program does when viewed from outside, that is, what process it performs. The specification may be informally expressed in the mind of the programmer or formalized using one of the notations described in the preceding volumes in this series. Where the description comes from is not important. What is important is that the program is being written to match a prescribed behavior. This book can thus be read in isolation or as one of a sequence. Although reference is made to other volumes in the series, knowledge of their contents is not assumed. In fact, those who have read the other volumes in the series may find some things restated among the new material. They are worthy of repetition. As it says in *The Hunting of the Snark*, 'What I tell you three times is true'.

The paradigm that this book follows is that of writing a program to carry out a defined procedure. This procedure may be intended to serve as part of a much larger program or it may be a complete program in its own right. The principles of expository programming apply to all sizes and types of program. This book deals explicitly only with sequential procedural programs because nearly all programs fall into this class. Other styles, such as *functional* or *applicative programming* (using, for example, the Lisp language, where the program consists of the evaluation of a function that uses the input data as parameters and whose value is the result of the computation) and *logic programming* (using, for example, the Prolog language, where the problem description is given in some logical formalism, such as predicate calculus, from which the system infers a solution), differ from the sequential style discussed here only to a degree and the rules and principles of expository programming can easily be extrapolated to them.

Concurrent programs are not dealt with explicitly; however, since they consist of sequential programs that socialize concurrent programs they are covered implicitly since all the homilies and exhortations to good programming practice in this text also apply to them. In this context, the 'socialization' of programs means that they interact asynchronously to any time basis in the software system. In fact, programs that may interact with each other concurrently need to be like Caesar's wife, above blame in the very basic respects. There is a whole subject known as 'concurrent programming' but the problems of concurrent software systems arise more through faulty design. What is required is a clarity of view at the design level of how four main problems – all concerned with programs 'socializing' – may be avoided. These problems – Macro (1990, p. 199) who describes them fully, refers to them as the 'fearsome foursome' – are:

1. *Deadlock*, when competition among programs causes the execution of the software to come to a shuddering halt.
2. *Deadly embrace*, where a pattern of program's socialization is repeated *ad infinitum*, as caricatured by courteous comedians insisting that the other go through a door first.
3. *Inaccessible topology*, where parts of a software system can never be executed by any combination of events occurring in the behavior space.
4. *Asynchronous updates* by different programs, resulting in the admixing of versions (or generations) of the data.

These problems, being principally concerns of design, are beyond our scope here. However, one implementation-level device does exist – Dijkstra's semaphore approach – for detecting the condition of deadlock. Again, readers interested in this will find a description in Macro (1990), while the topic of real-time design is treated in Allworth and Zobel (1987) and Ullman (1982). Beyond this, it suffices to repeat that in competent design for a software system in which programs execute concurrently, and 'socialize' while doing so, and in the use of good programming practices as extolled here, are the best approaches to a most exacting domain of computer applications.

So that the programming process can be seen in context, the book starts with a short history of programming showing how the principles and techniques came about. This is followed by a thorough discussion of these principles, such as abstraction, information hiding, cohesion between parts, and unity of purpose. Part Three shows how these principles are applied in practice. In order to illustrate the techniques, a complete example, 'The Running Example' is carried through several chapters. This example is implemented in Modula-2; since this is a widely known language based on another well-known language, Pascal, it should be readily understandable to most readers. For those unfamiliar with Modula-2, a synopsis of those parts of the language used in the Running Example is contained in Appendix A. This is followed, in Appendix B, by a listing of an implementation in Modula-2 of the Running Example. Unfortunately, the Running Example does not cover all the points that I wish to illustrate; consequently, other examples, separate from the Running Example, are used at various points in the text. These extra examples are marked as being separate from the Running Example. The final part of the book consists of a discussion of the need for *software tools* to help the programmer in the task of writing the program. Several examples of such tools are described from the very simplest to elaborate *programming environments*.

As the preceding paragraph shows, two classes of information are presented: the 'flesh' and the 'bones'. The skeletal material is contextual information serving as a support for the detailed matter that is the meat of the book. The skeleton is delineated sufficiently for the reader to understand the position occupied by the software implementation process in the general life-cycle. The other volumes in this series provide a full description of areas that are only sketched here.

You cannot learn to ride a bicycle by reading about it. Once you have learned the general principles, you must practice. So it is with programming; skill with writing readable programs comes only with putting the principles to task by actually writing. To quote Tony Wasserman: 'Software engineering can be caught but not taught.' The reader is encouraged to apply the techniques and discipline described here as soon as possible. Many of the ideas can be applied alone without waiting for the chance to do everything in one big bang. They are even worth doing for short throwaway programs that will only be run once – it is only practice that makes the technique become automatic. You cannot really say that you know how to ride a bicycle until you can do it without thinking. Once this level of skill has been achieved, you can use the bicycle purposefully.

No technical book springs unaided from the author's mind. The most that an author can claim as original is modest extension of the work of others and a different presentation. The boundaries between one's extensions and others' work often becomes blurred by familiarity. I have tried to acknowledge the sources of my material by means of references, but there will be many who are unmentioned inadvertently. I thank them and apologize for leaving them anonymous. For the invitation to start this book, technical advice, encouragement, and sedulous reviewing with detailed commentary, I acknowledge my debt to the series editor, Allen Macro. He provided me with so many helpful sentences and paragraphs that I hope he will accept this pan-acknowledgement for all the places where he recognizes one of his brain's offspring. I am grateful for the large number of very thoughtful comments that I received from the publishers' reviewers, in particular, Dr H. C. Johnston of The Queen's University of Belfast, who provided me with 250 detailed and helpful annotations. I am also grateful to Kurt Godden, Linda Means, Kent Quander, and Wayne Stevens for their many corrections and suggestions. Since I did not always heed their advice, they bear no responsibility for the errors that remain.

For a supportive work environment, I am grateful to the management of the General

Motors Research Laboratories, particularly the Executive Director, Nils L. Muench, and the two Department Heads, Donald E. Hart and George G. Dodd, under whom I have worked.

For love, support and patience well beyond the scope of the marriage vow 'to love and to cherish', I thank Tania Marcotty.

Michael Marcotty
Troy, Michigan, USA, 1990

ACKNOWLEDGEMENT

We are grateful for permission to include the following copyright material: extract on p. 103 from Frederick P. Brooks *The Mythical Man Month* Copyright 1975 Addison-Wesley Publishing Company reprinted by permission of Addison-Wesley Publishing Company Inc., Reading, Massachusetts.

PART ONE

THE BUSINESS
OF PROGRAMMING

CHAPTER ONE
THE PROGRAMMING SUB-CULTURE

A brief review of the history of programming shows that in the early years programmers were more concerned with having working hardware than with ease of programming. The early successes with programming led to a euphoric belief that larger programs could be built with a simple linear scaling-up of the effort. This did not take into account the non-linear increase in complexity that soon became beyond the programmer's mental control. The severe problems with the production of software were first publicly recognized at conferences organized by NATO. A number of new programming techniques emerged at the conferences and, in the years immediately following, were adopted by programmers, in varying degrees depending on their goals and motivations. A review of the different aims of programmers leads to the conclusion that those whose interest in producing programs goes beyond temporary mental recreation must regard a program as a form of communication with those who share common professional interests. This leads to the theme of this volume: a program is a form of expository writing and the same rules apply to its composition.

1.1 INTRODUCTION

To the outsider, computer programmers seem to belong to a closed society. They have their own intimidating jargon. When talking to each other, even on a social level, the speech of programmers is so interlarded with technical terms and computer-based metaphors as to be incomprehensible to the lay listener. In fact, it goes beyond just speech patterns; programmers share a set of beliefs and activities that shape their daily lives. It is a sub-culture within the larger culture into which they were born. The big-bang theory does not apply to the genesis of this sub-culture; it took several years. It has a history.

My grammar school education led me to believe that history was merely a succession of battles. The most important thing about a battle was its date, and the most important date was 1066, the Battle of Hastings. Since then I have learned that history does much more than chronicle one bloodletting after another. It provides a web of context in which we

3

can enmesh any subject that we study. This context is essential to its understanding. History shows us how important ideas were born, how the 'human element' entered into each development, and what progress has been made. This is especially striking in the case of programming, using the term in the narrower sense of 'writing the instructions that will be executed by the computer'. In passing, few of us realize the tremendous progress in notation that has grown up in this activity. In this chapter, we take a brief look at where we have been, where we are now, and at the programmers' objectives.

1.2 WE WERE GLAD WHEN THE HARDWARE WORKED

1.2.1 Machine language programming

In a sense, we can trace 'programming' back to the Babylonians of around 2000 BC. As described by Knuth (1972), their algebraic notation was not as powerful as ours and they represented a formula by a list of steps for its evaluation, that is, by an algorithm for computing the formula. Although algorithms have existed for more than 4000 years, it was not until the nineteenth century that an attempt was made to invent a notation for dynamic processes. Even that work was very limited, with a *machine language* developed by Lady Ada Lovelace, the world's first programmer, and Charles Babbage for his Calculating Engine. The most elaborate program developed by these two was a routine for calculating Bernoulli numbers, described in Morrison and Morrison (1961). Although there were many other attempts in this area, chronicled in Knuth and Pardo (1976), it was not until the advent of the electronic computer that could execute a stored program that the real task of developing a program had to be faced.

Figure 1.1 shows a revised version of the world's first working electronic computer program that ran on the morning of 21 June 1948 on the Manchester University Mark I computer (see Lavington 1975). That this program found the highest proper factor of a number using a process of repetitive subtraction to achieve the effect of division is not obvious. In those days, the programmer was just glad if the machine worked long enough to produce the results. The program shown ran for 52 minutes, which was viewed as a great success. Although great improvements were made in reliability, it was not until June 1949 that an uninterrupted run of nine hours was recorded.

Instructions for the Manchester University Mark I had to be written in binary notation, split into groups of five bits, and then translated into teleprinter code so that they could be entered into the machine. The resulting instructions looked like this:

```
E  @  H  O
X  E  /  :
V  E  /  :
@  @  H  B
I  @  T  /
I  @  /  C
@  @  /  N
T  C  T  A
```

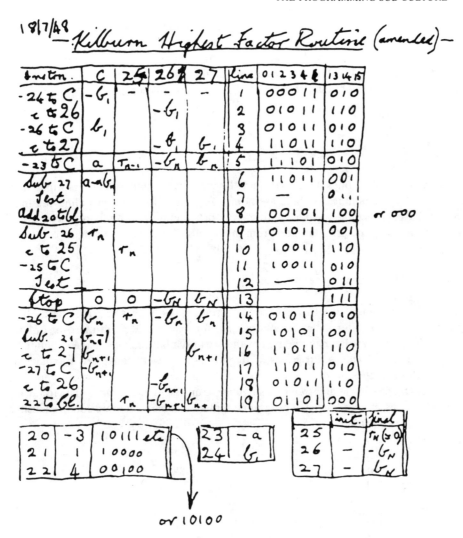

FIGURE 1.1 The world's first working program reproduced from Lavington (1975).

Writing a program in this form was a time-consuming task. It was also very error-prone since all sequences of bits were interpreted by the machine as having a meaning, and there could be no automatic checking for consistency. Nevertheless, it was possible to write programs in this way to perform serious computations, such as those for the engineering calculations used to design the St Lawrence Seaway. Almost all early programs concerned engineering and applied scientific computations.

A first improvement in making machine language comprehensible was to separate the bits functionally, making divisions between the bits that defined what the computer was to do from the groups of bits that defined the addresses containing the data to be operated on. These groups of bits were then represented by numbers, generally expressed in base eight (*octal*) numbers, but sometimes in base ten. Numbers of both bases could even appear in the same instruction representation. Separations between the groups were marked by blanks or decimal points in a further attempt to increase readability. Instructions expressed in this way were marginally more readable, for example, the following machine code fragment from the Ferranti Pegasus computer:

```
5.1 6 00
5.2 6 21
5.0 6 01
5.3 6 10
```

In this example, the groups 00, 21, 01, and 10 specify the functions load, multiply, add, and store. The remaining numbers are addresses. All processors, including the most modern, have a machine language. Progress in programming technology has consisted largely in shielding the programmers from the details of the machine language.

1.2.2 Assembler language programming

The next improvement was to provide the programmer with some mnemonic help through the use of letter codes for operations, for example MPY in place of 021 for multiply. This help was later augmented by the use of symbolic names instead of numeric addresses to refer to values. Programs written in this form were converted into machine language through the use of a program called an *assembler*. This form of expressing programs is referred to as an *assembler language* or an *assembly language*. The following example of an assembler language program fragment is somewhat more comprehensible than the previous examples:

```
          LDY  #0
          LDA  $60
CHBIT     BPL  CHKZ
          INY
CHKZ      ASL  A
          BNE  CHBIT
          BRK
```

The kind of work involved in writing programs in both these forms is illustrated by the fact that the actual writing of the instructions was called *coding* rather than *programming*. Programming implies a broader activity that not only includes coding but also the intellectually more difficult but less tedious task of designing algorithms.

The problems with expressing algorithms in these forms were:

• With programs written in binary notation, almost any sequence of characters could be translated into bit patterns that could be interpreted by the computer as valid instructions, sometimes with extravagant effects on the machine. Although assembler languages allowed for more mechanical checking, for example, the instruction BNE

CHBIT was only acceptable if some instruction had the label CHBIT, it was still possible to make many simple errors that could not be detected automatically. To tie the execution errors back to the faulty code was difficult and time-consuming.

- The programs had to be tailored to the particular characteristics of the available computer. Much effort was devoted to overcoming deficiencies of the computer's architecture, for example, no index registers, lack of built-in floating point operations, and restricted instruction sets.

- The close association between a program and a particular machine design not only permitted but also encouraged the invention of all kinds of tricks to wring maximum performance from the computer. Such tricks included modifying instructions during execution, and storing characters to be printed as text in a coded form that could also be usefully executed in some other part of the computation in order to save storage space. In fact there was a paper published in the proceedings of an important conference entitled 'Trickology', which described some of the tricks that were used. It was very difficult to validate that programs constructed in this way were correct, that is, that they did what they were supposed to do. It was also practically impossible to discover the algorithm behind a program coded by a colleague.

- When a new computer replaced the old one, all this inventiveness was wasted; the old programs had to be thrown away and the process of building a new library started again.

1.2.3 Higher-level languages

These shortcomings led to the development of so-called *automatic programming systems*. These systems generally provided operations such as floating point addition and trigonometric functions, together with either fixed or variable operands, through software subroutines that simulated the kind of operations now often performed by hardware. Usually, the programmer had to write statements in a rigid format that did not allow mathematical expressions to be written in anything resembling mathematical notation. However, it was a step forward in making programs more readable and thus easing the task of finding errors.

Automatic programming systems used software simulation to give the programmer a synthetic 'computer' with an instruction set that was different from that of a real machine. In particular, the synthetic machine generally had floating point operations, index registers, and improved input and output commands. It was much easier to program than its hardware counterpart. The programmer was able to think of a floating point addition as just that, and ignore the details of carrying it out in the hardware. The synthetic machine was thus an *abstract machine*, that is to say, a simulation of a computer that did not exist in hardware. The abstraction simplified the programming of complex operations by reducing the number of details that had to be directly controlled by the programmer (the topic of abstraction is discussed in greater detail in Section 2.5.1). The programmer was given the illusion of programming a machine that was beyond the creative capabilities of the hardware engineers.

The early automatic programming systems were costly to use since they slowed the actual machine down by a factor of five or more. Much of this time was spent in the subroutines that performed floating point arithmetic with hardware that could only do fixed point computations. Such subroutines are still required on many microprocessors. The programmers' familiarity with coding tricks coupled with their experience with these rather slow automatic programming systems, convinced them that any mechanical coding method would fail to apply the proper devious ingenuity that they believed was constantly needed in their work. Backus (1980) recalls this viewpoint:

> Just as freewheeling westerners developed a chauvinistic pride in their frontiers-manship and a corresponding conservatism, so many programmers of the freewheeling 1950s began to regard themselves as members of a priesthood guarding skills and mysteries far too complex for ordinary mortals . . . they regarded with hostility and derision more ambitious plans to make programming accessible to a larger population. To them, it was obviously a foolish and arrogant dream to imagine any mechanical process could possibly perform the mysterious feats of invention required to write an efficient program. Only the priests could do that. They were thus unalterably opposed to those mad revolutionaries who wanted to make programming so easy that anyone could do it.

The advent of computers with built-in indexing and floating point operations further increased the skepticism. By speeding up the floating point computations by a factor of ten, a common source of inefficiency in handwritten programs was removed. Consequently, the automatic generation of programs that were efficient, by comparison with handwritten ones, became more difficult. Those who wanted to simplify programming could only gain acceptance for their system if they could demonstrate that it could produce programs that were nearly as efficient as hand-coded ones in almost every case. It is out of this environment of close concern with questions of efficiency that we have inherited a feeling common among many programmers that efficiency is the one yardstick against which all programming must be measured, even at the expense of clarity. It has been rightly said that there are more programming sins committed in the name of efficiency, without actually achieving it, than for any other reason – including plain stupidity. In this atmosphere John Backus formed a group in 1954 to develop the Fortran (*FOR*mula *TRAN*slator) compiler. This project was aimed at the automatic translation of mathematical formulas into machine instructions. The group hoped to bring about a radical change in the economics of scientific computing by making programming much cheaper through a drastic reduction in the time it took for a working program to be prepared. Because of the atmosphere of skepticism, the group's emphasis was on the efficiency of the translated program rather than on language design. This view is expressed by Backus and Heising (1964):

> [Our development group] had one primary fear. After working long and hard to produce a good translator program, an important application might promptly turn up which would confirm the views of the skeptics: . . . its [translated] program would run at half the speed of the hand-coded version. It was felt that such an

occurrence, or several of them, would almost completely block acceptance of the system.

The Fortran programming system was viewed as applying to just one machine, and very little thought was given to the implications of making a machine-independent programming language. As a result, certain characteristics of the machine on which Fortran was first implemented became part of the language; for example, the naming of output channels was determined by the numbering of the tape units on the IBM 704 computer.

An example of a program in the original version of Fortran, taken from Knuth and Pardo (1976) is:

```
      DIMENSION A(11)
      READ A
   2 DO 3,8,11 J=1,11
   3 I=1-J
      Y=SQRT(ABS(A(I+1)))+5*A(I+1)**3
      IF (400.>=Y) 8,4
   4 PRINT I,999
      GO TO 2
   8 PRINT I,Y
  11 STOP
```

Fortran was just one of several programming languages that appeared in 1956 and 1957. This period was the beginning of a programming revolution. It seemed that each new computer, and even each programming group, was spawning its own algebraic language or its favorite dialect of an existing one. Most of these languages were for the scientific programmer and were restricted to a particular machine. Their designers were generally a small group of implementers, rather than users, drawn from a single company. A primary design objective was to produce efficient machine code, even if it meant sacrificing some clarity of expression in the language.

The objectives of the designers of Cobol (*Common Business Oriented Language*) were different. In 1959, a committee of representatives from several organizations was established to design a machine-independent programming language suitable for use by the business community. The committee decided that the language should make the maximum use of simple English so that managers who had no programming experience would be able to understand the programs and even write programs themselves. Many committee members felt that arithmetic operations should be specified by words like ADD and MULTIPLY rather than by the symbols + and * because these words would be more readily understood. Sammet (1969) puts it this way:

> COBOL is definitely *not* a succinct language; its objective was to be natural, where natural was defined as being *English-like*. This led to the introduction of certain concepts in the language designed specifically to permit this type of naturalness . . .
> COBOL does not permit minimal writing; on the contrary, it encourages a certain

amount of verbosity. The benefit gained from this, however, is increased readability and understandability in looking at programs.

The important thing is not whether the committee was right in its conclusions, but that a serious effort was being made to design a programming language for communication between people as well as with computers. Although the major thrust was to make communication with the machine easier, the secondary objective of making programs a medium of communication between programmers – and between programmers and their managers, if the latter stooped to reading them – was also achieved. Because the members of the committee represented competing computer companies, considerable effort was expended in making the language independent of the hardware. The hope was to avoid any manufacturer having an unfair advantage over the competition.

Cobol was only successful in certain respects. It achieved better machine independence than almost all other languages and was heavily used for business data processing; but on a really large scale, it failed to produce programs that could be readily maintained. At the time of its design too little was known about the theory of software design and many of the language structures required for the construction of large, simple to understand programs were missing. The first users were the amateur programmers of the period, $c.1959$–64, as was intended by the designers; they were swamped by the empirical professional, the 'coder/programmers', in the period $c.1965$–70. Amateur programmers reappeared after 1970, as electronic engineers, when miniaturization made it possible to regard the computer as a component – but this set high-level languages *back* by at least a decade since the mini- and micro-processors were (and largely still are) bereft of language support above assembler languages – in which class I include the language C.

The next major language development started in the late 1950s and culminated in 1960 as Algol 60. This language was designed by an international committee; its major objective was to be a language for the *communication* of algorithms. This was a major advance in the idea of a program being a description of a process. Algol 60 was also notable for other innovations, in particular the precise definition of its grammar through the use of rules expressed in Backus–Naur Form (BNF), which has now become an almost *de facto* standard for the specification of syntax. The linguistic genes of Algol 60 can be seen in its descendants, PL/I, Simula, Pascal, Modula, and Ada.

Fortran, Cobol, and Algol 60 are only three examples of the many programming languages that have been developed. Languages like these are referred to as 'high-level languages' since they achieve a higher level of abstraction than machine or assembler languages by suppressing many of the complicating details. They assist greatly with writing of clear understandable programs; but because of the obsession with efficiency, it was some time before they found acceptance. Although these two languages were among the first invented, it is still true that more programs written in these languages are used on a daily basis than all other languages put together.

A wonderful account of the early development of programming languages by one of the major protagonists can be found in Hopper (1981). Indeed, the book that contains this account, Wexelblat (1981), contains many other first-hand stories of the development of early high-level programming languages.

1.3 WE WERE AFRAID TO ADMIT THAT THE SOFTWARE DID NOT WORK

In the early 1960s, there were no big software problems. There was no big software. While the programs that were written then seemed big to the writers, they were made by one-person teams and were not more than a single brain-load, that is, the author could comprehend the whole program. Our minds concentrated on the unreliability of the hardware. In 1961, the released software for the IBM 709 consisted of about 100K words of program. The authors were small groups of highly qualified people. The software industry had many of the aspects of the cottage industries that flourished with small groups of craftsmen just before the industrial revolution. However, the seeds of problems were germinating. Software was generally undocumented and errors could only be corrected by the original author.

While higher level languages were being invented and programs had the potential of becoming more intelligible, the practice of programming was not keeping pace. There was a widening gap between the ambitions and achievements of the producers of software. It was a multi-dimensioned gap:

- between the promises that had been made to the users and the performance achieved by the software;
- between what seemed to be ultimately possible and what was actually achieved with the available technology;
- between estimates of software costs and actual expenditures.

During the 1960s, it became publicly evident that the reliability of software could literally be a matter of life and death. With the use of computers in air traffic control, the safety of passengers in an aircraft depended in some degree on the software's reliability. As technology advanced, so the dependence increased to the point of being total, as in an individual with a pacemaker controlled by a microprocessor. The conventional wisdom became that there were always 'bugs' in programs. In fact, the very use of the term 'bugs' is perhaps a form of psychological self-defence; everybody knows that the world is full of bugs and that little can be done about them except swat them on sight. Calling them bugs does much less damage to our egos than referring to them as what they really are – errors. US Navy Commodore Grace Hopper, one of the very first programmers of modern computers, relates in Hopper (1981) how the term 'bug' came about. In 1945 she was working as a programmer on the Mark II, a pre-electronic computer that used electromechanical relays as its switching units. One day, when the computer failed, the cause was found to be one of the relays:

> Inside the relay – and these were large relays – was a moth that had been beaten to death by the relay . . . Commander Howard Aiken had a habit of coming into the room and saying, "Are you making any numbers?" We had to have an excuse when we weren't making any numbers. From then on if we weren't making any numbers, we told him that we were debugging the computer. To the best of my knowledge that's where it started.

Despite the verbal ego defence, the seemingly unavoidable fallibility of large software was becoming a matter of great concern. It was only when manufacturers started writing large operating systems that were beyond the comprehension of any one individual and required hundreds of programmers that our sins started to become public.

1.3.1 Grand predictions

The programming community as a whole became guilty of the sin of hubris on a grand scale. Since computers had been programmed to perform all sorts of wonderful things, it was assumed that there was no limit to our mental capacity to manage complexity.

Programmers fell into the same trap as other technologists: assuming that complexity scales up linearly with the size of the project. Systems evolved in an unbounded ramified form, with complexity built on complexity. It is not surprising that this happened as, before the end of the 50s, well-respected scientists such as Herbert Simon and Alan Newell (1958) were making predictions about artificial intelligence programs such as this:

> There are now in the world machines that think, that learn and that create. Moreover, their ability to do these things is going to increase rapidly until – in the visible future – the range of problems they can handle will be coextensive with the range to which the human mind has been applied.

They also went on to predict:

1. That within ten years a digital computer will be the world's chess champion, unless the rules bar it from competition.
2. That within ten years a digital computer will discover and prove an important new mathematical theorem.
3. That within ten years most theories in psychology will take the form of computer programs, or of qualitative statements about the characteristics of computer programs.

It seemed as though we only had to think of it for it to be possible. In fact, it was twenty years before chess programs ascended into the category below master's level, impressive but not world's champion. In 1963 W. Ross Ashby announced:

> Gelernter's theorem-proving program has discovered a new proof of the *pons asinorum* that demands no construction . . . . [This theorem is one that] the greatest mathematicians of 200 years have failed to notice.

This is heady stuff. However, a closer study shows that the *pons asinorum* is the elementary theorem of Euclidian geometry stating that angles opposite the equal sides of an isosceles triangle are equal and that the proof, far from being a great discovery of the computer age, is attributed to Pappus in 300 BC. All this is not to diminish the great achievements of chess programs and theorem provers but to illustrate the climate of unwarranted belief in our ability to master any degree of complexity.

1.3.2 The scourge of complexity

Sometimes the complexity of programs came about through some of the same obsession with efficiency that was mentioned in the previous section. One company had a large application program written in PL/I. Because it was believed that procedure invocation was costly of machine cycles, the whole program had been written as a single procedure, 30 000 lines long. Among the workers, the program was known as 'Big Bertha'. In order to make a single change, all 30 000 lines had to be recompiled, requiring an elapsed time of several hours. If there was an error in the change, the whole process had to be redone. Since Big Bertha was so large and complicated, there was nobody who could understand it and it was almost impossible to make a change without introducing one or more errors. This process also took yet more machine cycles. This is a terrible example of short-term optimization of machine time. If the goal of such efficiency considerations is to save machine cycles, then the cycles saved by not having procedure invocations must be offset against those taken by the compiler to compile 30 000 lines every time a change is made. When I heard about Big Bertha, the company was well aware that the program contained errors but had decided that it was too expensive to correct. Consequently, every time it was run, a crew of people had to spend the following day hand-correcting the incorrect data that had been introduced into the database by Big Bertha.

There was no real escape for the company. There was, of course, no written specification for Big Bertha other than the program, which was incomprehensible. Nobody really knew what the program did or how it did it. Management knew, or assumed, that what it did was essential to the operation of the company. Here was a failure of communication on the grand scale – the equivalent of 6000 pages of incomprehensible technical document. In theory, a small crew of competent programmers could, in time, decipher the document and convert it to a manageable program, but this required a larger investment than the company was prepared to make. As Doug McIlroy of Bell Labs once put it, 'When you're up to your waist in alligators, you don't have time to think about draining the swamp.'

The early 1960s saw the introduction of the first comprehensive families of machines that ranged in size from tiny to elephantine and had a functional span across computing that covered data processing, through scientific applications, to the boundaries of real-time control of machines. All of this had to be managed by an operating system that offered compatible functions at all levels. Probably the best known of these operating systems was IBM's OS/360; but Exec 8, Scope 6600, Multics, TSS, Sage, . . . are also members of the same class.

One consequence of scaling up from the cottage industry was known as the 'human wave' approach. At the peak of the OS/360 effort there were over 1000 people involved – including programmers, writers, machine operators, clerks, secretaries, managers, and support groups. Brooks (1975) estimates that from 1963 to 1966 about 5000 man-years went into its design, construction, and documentation. The lesson that became abundantly clear was that the sheer number of minds that had to be coordinated had an overwhelming effect on the cost.

Communication is the Achilles' heel of the programming project. This is as true of programming on a Lilliputian scale as it is on the Brobdignagian scale of OS/360. Communication is not only *a* factor, it is *the* factor by which everything else stands or falls. Some measure of the communication problem during the development of OS/360 is given by Brooks (1975). He records that it was decided that there should be a well-structured workbook and that *each* programmer should see *all* information, i.e., have a personal copy of the workbook in the office and that this should be updated daily.

> Our project had not been under way six months before we hit a problem. The workbook was about five feet thick! If we had stacked up the 100 copies serving programmers in our offices in Manhattan's Time-Life Building, they would have towered above the building itself. Furthermore, the daily change distribution averaged two inches, some 150 pages to be interfiled in the whole. Maintenance of the workbook began to take a significant time from each workday.

Inevitably, there were errors in the maintenance of the workbook that resulted in miscommunication between the members of the team. The ill effects of miscommunication were later system debugging.

Although there are probably more stories about the many bugs in OS/360 than any of the other operating systems, it should be remembered that it was being used by more programmers throughout the world than the other systems and thus it was being more thoroughly tested. However, from the user's point of view, attempting to use the system could be particularly frustrating, and the reward for one's efforts was frequently a hexadecimal dump of store together with a message that was of little help:

    PROBABLE USER ERROR, CORRECT AND RESUBMIT JOB

which did little to inspire confidence in the system.

The overconfidence in our ability to handle complexity was not the only cause of software problems. Users as a whole were not really interested in correctness and its effect on safety. The problems of software reliability occurred at all levels. Mathematical software also had its problems. Rice (1983) writes:

> It is sobering to recall that, in the 13th release of the IBM 7090 system, the double precision trigonometric functions were correct only to single precision for 25 per cent of the arguments. That release included perhaps the fifth or sixth attempt to get those functions correct over a period of several years. You can hope that things have improved since then but the anecdotes that I hear make me suspect that such library functions are, on the average, less reliable now than they were 15 years ago.

In fact, some users were against revisions to the mathematical routines because when their programs were rerun with the new versions they produced different results. It did not matter that the results were more accurate, the fact that they were different was a problem. I sometimes think of this as I fly in an airplane or drive under a bridge designed on a computer.

Many of the errors that we saw during this period, and still see, were due to laziness on the part of programmers. Sometimes this laziness was enshrined in the design of the very tools that were to help the programmer write programs with fewer errors. Fortran was designed so that the programmer did not have to write a declaration for the most common variables – this saved time. This followed the practice adopted in mathematics, where the expression

$$\sum_{i=1}^{n} A_i$$

contains an implicit declaration of the variable i. Fortran was also designed so that blanks could be ignored at all points in the program. The idea was laudable; it was hoped that this would encourage programmers to insert blanks into names to make them more meaningful and readable. Alas, the tendency went completely in the other direction: programmers produced programs with almost no white space. A consequence of these two design principles was that the two statements:

```
DO 13 K = 1,3
```

and

```
DO 13 K = 1.3
```

are both valid. The first is the start of an iterative statement that loops with the variable K having the successive values 1, 2 and 3. The second is an assignment statement that assigns 1.3 to the variable named DO13K. Anybody who has done any proof reading knows that the eye sees only what it wants to, and detecting the period in place of a comma in a long program is almost impossible.

The fact that the programmer does not need to declare a variable before using it means that the compiler accepts this assignment to DO13K; that the value is never referenced again makes no difference. Although this slip of the finger has been blamed for the loss of a Venus probe, we should not blame Fortran too much. A search of the cross-reference listing produced by the compiler would show this strange variable DO13K that only appeared once. However the program probably had many different variables and such a search with human eyes would not have been very reliable. Nevertheless, it would not have been difficult for the programmer to write a software tool to perform the search and to report any variables that were only referenced once. Such a tool could have been made part of the project's standard compilation procedure so that it would not be forgotten. As we shall see:

Software tools are an important part of the programmer's armory.

1.3.3 The NATO software engineering conferences

Towards the end of the 1960s, there was a growing realization that the production of software left a great deal to be desired. The perceived problems were as follows:

- Software was unreliable.
- Software was difficult to modify.

- Software was delivered behind schedule.
- Software was too expensive to produce.
- Software was unpleasant to use.

By 1967 it was commonly agreed that there was a general problem with software. In October of 1968, the NATO Science Committee sponsored a *Working Conference on Software Engineering* attended by more than fifty people from eleven different countries. This was followed in 1969 by a second conference, *Software Engineering Techniques*. These two conferences are reported in Naur *et al.* (1976).

The participants of the first conference were all professionally concerned with software, either as users, manufacturers, or university teachers. The term 'software engineering' was deliberately chosen as the conference title, to imply the need for the production of software to be based on the types of theoretical foundations and practical disciplines that are traditional in the established branches of engineering. The conference created something of a sensation because it constituted the first open admission of the 'software crisis'. Previously, to talk about the problems of software as a crisis was akin to blasphemy. It was, after all, a realization of our human limitation in dealing with complexity, 'our human ability to do much', as Dijkstra put it. It was not really the complexity of the programs we had created that caused the crisis, but our failure to comprehend it.

> If we really understood a program, we would know why it was incorrect and how it should be modified to become correct.

1.4 A PALETTE OF PANACEAS

The discussions at the two NATO software engineering conferences covered all aspects of software production including its relation to the computer hardware and its design, implementation, distribution, and maintenance. A number of very powerful techniques for improving the production of software were described. Following the conferences, these were picked up, developed, amplified, and extolled in the literature so that one might gain the impression that each one of them was a kind of elixir that would allow us to produce flawless programs that would be maintenance free for ever. The ten main miracle cures offered over the past decade and a half have been the following – each one of which has been a vogue topic for an epoch, attracting great attention and generating excitement enough to lead the unwary to a view that here at last was 'The Answer':

1. Top-down development (Linger *et al.* 1979).
2. Modular programming, including the concepts of single decision code segments, coupling of structures, and information hiding (Parnas 1971, 1972; Stevens *et al.* 1974; Myers 1975; Yourdon and Constantine 1979; Stevens 1981).
3. Structured programming (Dijkstra 1969, Mills 1972, Naur *et al.* 1976).
4. Other design approaches, techniques and their notations (Warnier 1974, Jackson 1975, Orr 1977, Ross 1977).

5. Life-cycle management of software development (Boehm 1976).
6. Chief programmer team structures and practices, for software team organization (Baker 1972, Mills and Baker 1973).
7. Software tools such as Programming Support Environments (PSEs), and Integrated Project Support Environments (Ipses).
8. Formal methods (Dijkstra 1976, Gries 1981, Jones 1980).
9. Prototyping.
10. Other programming paradigms – such as concurrent programs, object oriented, executable specification languages, 'Fourth Generation Languages' and the use of Expert Systems technology in software development.

Some of these techniques are well established now, within the limits of their usefulness, such as the first six on the list; others, such as software development environments, are programmer tools constantly in development by major software firms; others again, such as formal methods and other programming paradigms, are the objects of research and limited attempts at serious usage. However, the reader should be warned, early and often that:

- *None of them constitutes a genuine panacea* in the sense that its use alone will, like the elusive philosopher's stone, transmute the base-metal into gold.
- *None of them will make sure that you will write beautiful, easily understood and modifiable programs.* For example, if modular design is used without the control flow simplicity of structured programming, you are likely to finish up with a set of modular rat's nests instead of one large rat's nest.

and above all

- *None is a substitute for thinking.*

However, they all have their part in the task of writing programs.

Some, notably items 2 to 7 on the list, have become a part of what constitutes good software engineering practice. Each one requires an extensive treatment, and all are dealt with at appropriate parts of this series. For the present, the following short skeletal definitions of items appropriate to this volume are offered. A more extensive treatment is given later.

1.4.1 Structured programming

One of the major barriers to the understanding of a program is that there are really two forms of the program. There is the fixed one, that is, the one that we see when we read the program where we take the statements in the order in which they are written. This is the *static form* of the program. There is also the actual sequence in which these statements are executed by the computer, the *dynamic form*. This sequence of statements is called the *flow of control*. The action of *software* is the effect of executing the dynamic form of a program on the hardware for which it was intended. The major part of the power of computers is their ability to follow different control flow paths depending upon the value of some data and to perform iterations. These very valuable constructions cause the dynamic form to be different from the written static form. In order to understand what a program does, we must read the written form of the program and from that build a mental image of the dynamic form. The greater the disparity between the static and dynamic forms, the greater the difficulty in building this mental image from the static form.

Structured programming aims to minimize this difference through the use of a restricted set of *control structures*, which can be shown to be sufficient for all programming. This restricted set also corresponds to those that occur in the real world. Thus, a more general definition of structured programming is:

> Basing the structure of the program on the structure of the part of the real world it models.

Since real-world processes involve sequencing, selection, iteration, and parallelism, using simple programming language facilities that model these is important to the understandability of the program. Structured programming thus brings the three forms of the process closer, the real-world form, the static form of the program, and the dynamic form of the program, so that their correspondence can be more easily understood.

The most famous of the control flow constructs that structured programming seeks to avoid is the unconditional transfer as exemplified by the GOTO statement, which allows control flow to be transferred to some arbitrary point in the program chosen by the programmer. Irresponsible use of this statement can lead to a great difference between the two forms of the program and consequent difficulty in understanding it.

It should not be thought that structured programming is just programming without the GOTO statement. What is really involved is a conscious effort to make the flow of control follow a path that is simple and obvious to the reader. The use of the restricted set of control structures of itself does not necessarily lead to easy-to-read programs. However, by bringing the static and dynamic forms of the program closer, other components of program complexity will become apparent from reading the text. In addition, the simpler control structure makes for an easier-to-understand relationship between programming errors and their symptoms. With very convoluted control paths, even simple errors can lead to extravagant effects that are difficult to explain even after the error has been discovered. Structured programming is a very important tool in the fight against complexity and is discussed in detail in Chapter 10.

1.4.2 Modular programming

In the previous section we described the monstrous program Big Bertha, which was a single 30 000 statement monolithic PL/I procedure. Modular programming is a consequence of functional decomposition by implementing each of the functions as a separate entity. These functional components communicate with each other through defined interfaces. Some and almost all of the modern, programming languages permit the separate compilation of the function entities for their later combination to form the complete program. (Exceptions include standard Pascal and some, though not all, interpreter-based languages.) The ability of programmers to combine these components depends upon the availability of two software tools: compilers that provide for separate compilation of integrands, and linkers that meld the integrands with library routines to form a single executable unit. There is a great difference between a programming language that allows a program to consist of *separately compiled* components that are linked later and one that requires that the components all be compiled together. The latter language design does not really promote modular programming and restricts the realm of application to what can be handled by one programmer. Standard Pascal is an example of this philosophy and this was adequate for its original purpose of teaching the principles of programming through small examples. When its use was expanded to larger projects, a need was found for separately compiled components. However, even if the programming language does not permit separate compilation, the division into functional parts is of great advantage.

In much of the literature, each of the parts is termed a *module*, hence the terms modular design and modular programming. However, the word module has become so over-used with different meanings to different authors that we have in this series preferred to use the term *integrand*, meaning a part of a program that is to be integrated with other parts to form the complete program. Had modular design been used in the construction of Big Bertha, instead of having to recompile all 30 000 statements each time a change was made, only that part of the program that contained the change would have had to be recompiled. Further, since each integrand would be of an intellectually manageable size, the whole program would have been much easier to understand and correct. Just splitting Big Bertha into 300 integrands of 100 statements would not have made the program into a modular one. Each integrand must have a clearly defined function, and its interface with the other integrands must be carefully designed so as to ensure that changing some specific function in the program does not require changes to all 300 integrands or even 50 of them.

> The crux of modular design is the principle upon which the separation into integrands is based.

1.4.3 Life-cycle management and prototype development

A common model of the life-cycle of software is that it passes through the successive phases of identifying the application, feasibility study, requirements definition, system design, implementation, systems test and acceptance, and finally, operation and maintenance. Between each of these phases there is an evaluation, and the next step is not started until the evaluation is satisfactory. A consequence of the evaluation may be that the cycle reverts to an earlier phase as though it were a game of snakes and ladders. The idea of life-cycle management is to recognize these stages and to provide appropriate procedures for each of them. A more detailed overview of the phases of software lifecycles is given in Chapter 2 of this volume and a detailed discussion is to be found in Volume 1 of this series (Macro 1990).

A problem with evaluating a requirements definition document is that it is very difficult for the users, who, after all, are the people who are going to be most affected by the product, to know whether the requirements specification actually describes software that will meet their needs. They will not really know how well it will suit their purposes until they are able to try it. It is rather like evaluating the drivability of a car by reading its engineering specifications. We need to take it for a test drive. By the time the users can test drive the software, it is too late to start again with a new design, too much money has been spent. This difficulty has led to the idea of building a coarse software model of the final product – a *prototype*. There are two kinds of prototype to be distinguished:

1. *Specification prototype*. This is a rough-and-ready working model of the defined requirements. The model simulates the external interface of the specified software so that the intended users can evaluate the requirements definition and the 'human factors' aspects of its use.
2. *Technical or feasibility prototype*. This is an experimental implementation intended to test the adequacy of a proposed algorithm or software design without, it is hoped, investing the large programming resources required for a properly engineered implementation.

After a specification prototype shows that the requirements specification is satisfactory, it may either become an adjunct to the requirements definition or replace it.

> This is extremely dangerous for reasons that concern quality issues in both the economic and technical domains.

These reasons are discussed in Section 2.3.7.

1.4.4 Chief programmer teams

One of the early success stories of the application of the techniques described above was the *New York Times* project described in Baker (1972). This was a project to automate the newspaper clipping library of the *New York Times* so that the staff could search for and view clippings on a display workstation. This project required a marriage of IBM equipment and other hardware made by separate companies, and the production of software to run it. The original IBM team fell behind schedule and the *Times* threatened to cancel the project. A new team under the direction of Terry Baker moved in and applied an entirely new programming management plan conceived by Harlan Mills of IBM. The failing project was turned into an extraordinary success. The chief programmer team replaced the traditional idea of having a pool of programmers, all of similar abilities and training, with the use of a team of skilled personnel, each of whom was trained in a particular area and performed a separate task. This team was under the direction of a chief programmer who managed the technical activities of the team. The specialists of the team included the deputy chief programmer, who was the chief programmer's shadow, waiting in the wings to take over should anything happen to the chief, the program librarian, programmers, testers, software tool makers, documentation experts, and support personnel. A comparison of the traditional way of programming with the chief programmer team has been likened to a comparison between a rural swine butchering party where everybody hacks along with the neighbors, and a surgical team consisting of a group of specialists, each with an assigned task. The success of a chief programmer team depends critically on the availability of a chief programmer who has both excellent programming and management skills. Such individuals are indeed rare. Attempts to form such teams without an adequate chief programmer lead to alienation of the programmers and management alike. Macro and Buxton (1987), in their discussion of Chief Programmer Teams, conclude:

> The fact is, however, that at the present time, some one and a half decades after its inception as a set of ideas, the concept of the Chief Programmer Team is established (although somewhat modified, as we describe), and looks set to become the norm rather than the exception in many companies.

The current form of the chief programmer team is a small task force whose composition is determined by the structure of the job. This arrangement is described in the next chapter and Macro (1990), who gives guidelines for the management of such a team.

1.4.5 Software languages, tools and environment

With the recognition that programming languages were the major tool of the programmer, a great deal of language development and experimentation took place. It became fashionable to develop a programming language. Some tried to give the impression that they designed a new language before breakfast as a way of starting the day right. Many languages looked as though this was exactly what had been done. Gradually, it was realized that if a language was to fill its intended purpose of helping the programmer write an error-free program, it must be designed with that purpose in mind. It was realized that different applications made different demands on the kind of programming required. A scientific numerical computation had different requirements from an application that was almost entirely devoted to the logical manipulation of records from a file. In Chapter 8, we discuss the various program paradigms and how languages fit them.

Both Fortran and Cobol are *typed* languages. That is to say, each variable has a type associated with it and this determines the range of values that can be assigned to it.

Originally, Fortran had just two types, floating point and integer. As new languages were developed during the 1960s, the set of built-in types was increased until the maximum was reached with the gargantuan language PL/I. The meaning of type has been extended beyond defining the set of values to defining the set of operations that can be performed on them. The introduction of built-in types brings two major benefits to programming:

1. The hardware representation is hidden from the programmer. This helps to make the program more easily portable from one machine to another since the program does not depend upon a particular configuration of bits to represent a value. (Clever

manipulation of the bit patterns used by the hardware was a popular trick used by early programmers to show how well they understood the underlying hardware and how clever they were.)

2. Type errors often referred to as 'adding apples to oranges' are detected by the compiler, thus saving much debugging time later.

PL/I, in its effort to make life as easy for the programmer as possible, defined an elaborate range of conversions between values of different types so that almost anything could be assigned to anything and the value would be converted automatically. ('Almost' because it was recognized that it did not make any sense to attempt a conversion between certain types. Label and pointer values only had a significance within a program and thus could not meaningfully be converted into a numeric value that had meaning in the outside world. Such conversions were considered to be type errors.) Thus, for example, a complex value could be assigned to a floating point scalar and the effect would be that the real part of the complex value would be assigned to the scalar. While in theory this made life easier for the programmer, it was really a mixed blessing. In particular, adding automatic conversions between complex and other types dramatically increased the complexity of the language by doubling the number of conversions for the benefit of the few programmers who used complex variables. Defining about 180 different conversions made the language much more complicated than it already was. Nobody could remember exactly how all the conversions were performed, or, if they could remember a particular conversion, they could not be sure that a reader of the program would remember it. It was always possible that one did not remember correctly how the conversion was performed and thus the results would not be what was expected. In retrospect, the inclusion of automatic type conversion was not a good idea. Nevertheless, PL/I was a first attempt to replace *both* Fortran and Cobol and thus remove the separation between scientific and commercial programming.

> The reason that it did not succeed in this was that it was perceived as being too big and complex, a judgement that is being repeated now with the Ada language.

Another facet of the type structure of PL/I is that there is a fixed set of built-in types with no facility for defining new types to match the problem being solved. All program data has to be forced into the mould of the primitive types and the fit is not always felicitous. The operations that are available for the primitive types do not correspond to operations that are natural to perform on the quantities being represented. This reduces the communicative power of the language and makes the programs more difficult to understand.

The programming languages that followed PL/I, such as Algol 68 and Pascal, went beyond a fixed set of built-in types by providing a facility for defining a new type name. In Pascal the improvement was essentially restricted to defining record types and scalar types through a set of values. For example the declaration

```
TYPE Day = (Mon, Tue, Wed, Thu, Fri, Sat, Sun);
```

introduces a new data type Day, called an *enumeration type* that is defined by the enumeration of its possible values Mon, Tue, Wed, Thu, Fri, Sat, and Sun. One important abstraction to note is that the actual representation of these values is not defined – that detail is the compiler's private business. While the new types could be used in parameters to subroutines and functions, there was no means of defining operations between the new types. Algol 68 provided this ability. This led to a different view of type. Instead of considering type as defining a set of values that can be assigned to a variable, type was looked on as defining a set of operations that could be performed on a set of values. In fact, the set of operations was used to define the type and the representation became of secondary importance. In other words, the objects of computations became classified according to their expected behavior rather than the structure of their representation. This behavior was expressed through operations that are meaningful in terms of the real-world objects being represented, and the operations are the only means of creating, modifying, and accessing the objects.

An important step in the development of this idea was the language Simula 67, described in Dahl *et al.* (1969). Simula 67 is a general-purpose programming language that is an extension of Algol 60 designed particularly for simulation. Its major contribution is the concept of *class*, which allowed the encapsulation of the structure of the data objects belonging to the class together with the operations that can be performed on the objects. This laid the ground for the view of a type being defined purely in terms of its operations. As the development of programming languages progressed through Pascal, Modula-2, and Ada, this view became more dominant. Modula-2 allows the definition of *opaque types* where the actual representation is hidden in the implementation module and not available to the user. In Ada it is also possible for the programmer to define *packages* where the operations were defined so that other programmers could make use of them without being able to find out how the values were represented. These are known as *abstract data types*. This had the great advantage that it was possible to change the representation without having to recompile all the programs that make use of the operations.

The theory of abstract data types led to so-called *object-oriented* languages in which data elements are active and have some of the characteristics normally associated with processes. This is in contrast to traditional languages where data elements are strictly passive and have operations performed on them by processes. The active data elements, *objects*, of object-oriented languages, respond to messages that cause them to act on their internal data, possibly returning objects or messages to other data elements. An object consists of some memory and a set of operations. Objects may contain representations of numbers, queues, dictionaries, programs, or other kinds of data. The nature of an object's operations depends on the kind of thing that it represents. An object that represents a number would have operations that compute arithmetic functions.

A message is a request for an object to perform one of its functions. The message specifies the operation to be performed, but not how the operation should be carried out. It is up to the receiver of the message to determine how the operation is to be performed. The set of messages to which an object can respond is its *interface*. The *packages* of Ada can be used to define objects in this sense since they provide the *only* way in which the data can be manipulated. Object-oriented programming languages provide data abstraction through objects.

Probably the best known example of an object-oriented programming language is Smalltalk (see Goldberg and Robson 1983). Variables in Smalltalk are references to objects, which are instances of a *class* – the Smalltalk equivalent of type. However, unlike Pascal, Modula-2, or Ada, the references are not statically bound to a class, but can refer to any object. Thus type checking is carried out during execution. The dynamic association of a variable with a type makes it easy to write overloaded operators, that is, operators that will work with operators of different types. Overloading is very common for the mathematical operations. For example, in the expression A + B, the + operator is floating point addition if the variables A and B refer to floating point values. (In some languages, for example, Fortran, Pascal, and Ada, floating point values are said to be of type *real*.) This is probably an unfortunate choice of name since the behavior of the floating point arithmetic of computers is considerably different from that of the arithmetic of real numbers of mathematics. In particular, there are only a finite set of floating point values and they are not uniformly distributed. Using the term *real* baits a trap for unwary programmers, and is integer addition if the variables refer to integers. In Smalltalk, it is, for example, possible to define a class that implements the mathematical concept of a Set, with the operations Insert, Delete, and IsMember. Then, it is possible to build sets of objects of some other class C by sending a message like Insert C1, where C1 is an object of the class C, to an object, S1, of the class Set. The only requirement of the class C is that an equality test operator be defined for it. S1 then uses the equality test operator that C1 brings with it to determine whether the set S1 already contains an instance of C1 before adding it to the set. Thus, the class Set could be defined before the data types of the members have been defined. The ability to write operators that do not depend upon the data type of the items involved and to 'generate' type-specific instances of the operations by 'passing' the type of an object to them makes the concept of *reusable code* a reality.

Another distinguishing feature of Smalltalk is that it is embedded in a consistent user environment. In conventional interactive environments, the syntax and semantics of commands to the document editor and to the command language interpreter are different. This is not true of the Smalltalk system.

As generally conceived, the purpose of a programming environment is to *support the programmer* in software development or maintenance. The simplest, and most common, form of a programming environment is a collection of *software tools*, programs to help people do things by computer instead of manually. The traditional tools of a programmer have been an editor (since the advent of the terminal) and a compiler and linker. These were used long before the term 'software tools' was first introduced in Kernighan and Plauger (1976). The programmer would prepare the integrand using one of a range of editors and then submit the text of the integrand, the *source integrand*, to the compiler for generation of the executable form, the *object integrand*. The object integrand would then be linked with any other object integrands and the elements of the support library that are needed for execution, to form an executable program. The idea of software tools is that the other work of writing and developing a program, beyond editing, compiling, and linking, can be greatly assisted by special programs constructed for the purpose. These programs would perform such tasks as checking the results produced by a test run, generating test data, and verifying that the documentation matches the source program. In other words, all of the many tasks that are involved with programming were traditionally done by hand, very inexactly. My experience is that I spend about 10 per cent of my time writing special-purpose software tools, some of which are so specialized that I will only use them once and then delete them, and others that are of more general use and will be shared among the other members of the project.

Generally, in using software tools, the programmer has to interact with the computer's operating system. Operating systems such as Unix™* have provided other software tools, some with strange names like grep, which extracts from a file those lines that contain a sequence of characters that match a given pattern. Unix provides a compendium of software tools for use as and when the programmer feels the need. Systems where the tools are integrated into a subsystem under which the programmer does all the work connected with program development, without requiring direct interaction with the operating system are known as *programming support environments*, generally referred to as 'PSE,' and are introduced later in this chapter with a more thorough discussion in Chapter 16.

The idea of a programming support environment existed long before it was given such an impressive title. Examples of three early environments are APL, described in Falkoff and Iverson (1978), Basic (see Kurtz 1978), and Lisp described in McCarthy (1978). The dates on these papers may give a very wrong impression of when these languages first came on the scene. The three 1978 papers recount the history of these languages. APL was first defined in Iverson (1962), Basic in Kemeny and Kurtz (1964), and Lisp in McCarthy (1963). Each of these systems provided a self-contained environment in which the programmer was able to develop programs without having to interact directly with the host operating system provided by the hardware manufacturer. The system thus catered to the user who wanted to solve a problem on the computer and did not want to learn to use the hostile user interface provided by the system's indigenous operating system. The user was able to work in an inner operating system that was consistent with the programming language in which the problem was being solved. The principles behind the design of Basic were motivated towards bringing a knowledge of computers and programming to non-technical students at Dartmouth College, New Hampshire. The use of punched cards was felt not to be suitable for this class of student. The system had to be friendly, easy to learn and use, and not require that the students learn about the intricacies of using a normal operating system. The design of the language and the operating system went hand in hand with a common set of goals. Kurtz (1963) states that an early memorandum of this project states:

> The Time Sharing System should be externally simple and easy to use for the casual programmer . . .

The final design was a system that provided a complete programming environment for its users. It was possible to go from program composition using an editor to execution without having direct interaction with the host operating system. The popularity of this

*Unix is a trademark of Bell Laboratories.

system is evident from the fact that there is a version of Basic available on almost all personal computer systems. For millions of students worldwide, including those in the Soviet Union, the first introduction to computer programming is through Basic. The success of Lisp in the area of artificial intelligence is probably largely due to the integrated environment that it provides. The fact that APL, Basic, and Lisp have enjoyed such continued success attests well to the appeal of a single environment in which a programmer can work without having to use the host operating system. It would be difficult to argue that the success of these three languages is due to their wonderfully clear language structure!

Two more modern examples are UCSD-Pascal^{TM} (Overgaard 1980) and Turbo-Pascal^{TM}*, where there is a close integration of editor and compiler. The programming environment provided by this combination stops the compiler when it detects the first syntax error and transfers control to the editor with the cursor on the error so that the user can make a correction and then recompile. The use of a fast compiler that communicates with the editor allows the programmer to work very fast.

Although there is a close link between the TurboPascal compiler and the editor, the editor is still a general-purpose editor that provides the programmer with no direct help in writing correct Pascal programs. An early example of an editor that provided help of this sort is contained in the Cornell Program Synthesizer, described in Teitelbaum and Reps (1981). The Program Synthesizer is an interactive programming environment with integrated facilities to create, edit, execute, and debug programs. The design of the editor was based on the syntax of the programming language by including a collection of *templates* that defined the form of all but the simplest of language statements. A template can be inserted into the program at the cursor's position with a single key stroke. It is impossible for the programmer to make errors in the templates because they are predefined and the editor prevents changes to them. Errors in user-typed text, for example expressions, are detected immediately by invoking a syntax checker on a phrase-by-phrase basis. The editor is really an electronic form of the language Newspeak described by George Orwell in his novel *1984*:

> The purpose of Newspeak was not only to provide a medium of expression for the worldview and mental habits proper to the devotees of Ingsoc, but to make all other modes of thought impossible.

By preventing the creation of syntactically incorrect programs, the Program Synthesizer lets the user focus on the intellectually challenging aspects of programming.

> However, this may be a mixed blessing; living professionally in a 'Newspeak' electronic environment seems likely to deplete the software engineer's communication abilities so needed in other parts of the software life cycle.

Taylor *et al*. (1987) suggest that an environment consists of two parts: fixed and variant. The fixed part contains all the mechanisms required to interpret the process programs. It thus consists of the language used for writing the process programs and an interpreter for

---

*TurboPascal is a registered trademark of Borland International, Inc.

this language. Also included in the fixed part is the data object manager and the user interface manager. The variant part contains those components of the environment that are prone to change; these include data objects representing, for example, specifications, source code, executable integrands obtained by compiling the source code, test data, management data, symbol tables, programs consisting of combinations of executable integrands, and so on. The variant part also contains detailed descriptions of development or maintenance activities. These are generally referred to as *process programs* and in the normal operating system environment correspond to command procedures. Process programs are defined in terms of specific operators such as are found in normal collections of software tools. Typical operators are parsers, code generators, debuggers, specification and design language processors.

A major difference between the implementations of design and specification methods, such as the Jackson System Development system described in Cameron (1986), and a programming support environment is that in the earlier systems there was more contained in the fixed part, thus it was difficult to tailor the system to meet a user's special requirements. We can make the analogy with programming languages. The early programming languages such as Fortran, Cobol, or PL/I had a fixed set of types and all application-specific data had to be represented though values of these types, as already discussed in Section 1.4.5. It was not possible to have user-defined types as are available in later languages such as Pascal, Ada, or Modula-2. In programming support environments it is possible to create data objects of new or different types or to follow development procedures that differ from those that are intrinsic to the design and specification support environments.

Some programming support environments are aimed at assisting in the development of code in a specific language. The structuring of the common activities such as editing, parsing, debugging, and documentation assumes that the user's activities can be integrated by viewing them as examination and transformation of a single representation of one thing, code. In Interlisp (Teitelman and Masinter 1981) all data objects as well as the procedures and tools used to create them are considered to be instances of lists. In Arcturus (Standish and Taylor 1984) both the software products and the process programs are written in the Ada language. Environments such as these thus provide only limited support, and the effectiveness is drastically reduced when the process that the user wishes to perform is not anticipated during the design of the environment.

Subsequent developments of programming environments have included more help to the user to prevent the creation of errors. The basic problem of programming is the modification and extension of programs while maintaining consistency with what has already been done. The more recent programming environments, in addition to providing the immediate syntax checking described in the previous paragraph, also provide inter-integrand checking as the program is being created. Some of these developments are described in the last part of this book. A major difference in the tools provided in a system like Unix and those in a programming environment like that of Smalltalk, a small single user environment, is that the programmer has no option but to use the tools in the programming environment. A more extensive exposition on the PSE/Ipse situation is to be found in Chapter 8 of Volume I of this series (Macro 1990).

1.4.6 Formal methods

The goal of formal methods of program construction is the production of programs that are correct because they have been derived from formal specifications in the same way as mathematical theorems are obtained from formally defined premises. As expressed by Reynolds (1981):

> I believe that a programmer should be able to specify the behavior of his program precisely, and to give a rigorous argument that the program meets its specifications. Of course, such an argument might not be a formal proof in the sense of logic, but it must be an adequate guideline for a formal proof. In other words, an adequately commented program should enable a competent reader to fill in the details of a formal proof in a straightforward manner.

On the surface, this seems to be unassailable. However, as we shall discuss in Chapter 7, there is great danger in giving too much obeisance to mathematical proofs – they are just as fallible as programs. Most of the currently developed software was produced without any use of formal methods of program verification. Most practicing programmers are not formally oriented and consequently the present limitations of formal methods, discussed in Chapter 7, will mean that these techniques will be slow in adoption and their application limited.

1.4.7 Other programming paradigms

Conventional languages like Cobol, Fortran, Modula-2, and Ada provide the programmer with an abstract machine that hides the details of the underlying hardware. However, they still leave programming as a matter of translating the requirements specification into a set of operations to be performed by a computer, a simulated computer, but nevertheless a computer.

The language of the requirements specification and its equivalent program are very different. In the early days and generally today, requirements are written in English and are thus imprecise and open to misinterpretation. The attempt to avoid this led to verbiage that reads like a government regulation where the meaning is so hidden that it is impossible to tell if it is imprecise or has been misinterpreted. As a consequence a new type of language began to emerge, specification languages. These took a variety of forms, some of which are mentioned in Chapter 4 and are discussed in Volume 1, Chapter 3, of this series.

Specification languages can be divided into three classes:

- *Executable specification languages*. These are application dependent and usually based on existing high-level languages, for example, the use of an APL-like (see Iverson 1962) notation in the Paisley specification language described in Zave (1982).
- *Languages for rapid prototyping*. These may be any programming language, the rapidity depending on the language, and lead to models that range between executable specifications and simulations of the intended software. Rapid prototypes attack the

problem of making sure that the specifications actually match the intentions of their writers or their writers' clients.

- *Non-procedural or declarative languages*. These differ from the procedural forms of the previous two classes in that they describe *what* has to be done rather than *how* it is to be done. These packages are sometimes given the title 'Fourth Generation Language' or '4GL'; however these terms have been so much over-used in sales hyperbole as to have become essentially meaningless.

Although a broad enough definition of the term would place the use of these languages within the scope of 'programming', from the point of view of this book, it is not programming in the sense of algorithm and data design, coding and validation. They will therefore not be discussed further.

Although the above 'programming' lies outside the scope of this book, we come now to a vogue topic for improving the software engineer's practice at several stages in the life-cycle – including implementation. This development, which has received much coverage in the press, is the use of 'expert systems'. Again, the term has been so over-used as to become nearly meaningless. It has been applied to almost any program that has any form of heuristic. In its strict sense, the input data to an expert system represent indications of some condition that is to be diagnosed, for example, the symptoms experienced by a medical patient; or they may represent some desired condition, for example, housing a specific set of computer hardware in a room of a certain shape. The expert system applies logical rules of deduction, sometimes with probability values attached, to these data. The objective of the deductions is to establish a probable cause for the symptoms, to suggest how the condition might be achieved, or to require further information before continuing. The contention is that the expert system will arrive at the same conclusion as would an expert in the area of application. There are current research projects that aim to apply such systems to the assistance of program-mers, for example, in the area of debugging. While there are certainly expert systems that have achieved good results, I am very skeptical of their achieving the ability of a genuine expert, and agree with Dreyfus and Dreyfus (1986) who write:

> we can understand why knowledge engineers . . . have had such trouble getting the expert to articulate the rules he is using. The expert is simply not following any rules. He is . . . [instead] recognizing thousands of special cases . . . That in turn explains why expert systems are never as good as experts.

Expert system specialists contest this assertion and maintain that there are documented cases of expert systems that *outperform* any individual expert and point to the Mycin system described by Shortliffe (1976) and Buchanan and Shortliffe (1984).

1.5 PROGRAMMERS

In 1971, Gerry Weinberg produced a book, *The Psychology of Computer Programming* (Weinberg 1971), that was a landmark since it was the first book to look at the way in which programmers think and behave. In a review of this book, Weiss (1972) concluded:

> Every manager of programmers should have his own copy. He should read it, take it to heart, act on the precepts, and leave the copy on his desk to be stolen by his programmers. He should continue replacing the stolen copies until equilibrium is established. The message, 'Programmers are human', is not only addressed to managers. It is addressed to programmers too.

Although this book was published almost twenty years ago, these comments still stand. To my knowledge, the book has not been superseded.

Weinberg distinguishes between professional and amateur programmers; however at the time he wrote his book, almost everybody who worked with a computer did so for serious work. Since then, the personal computer has burst onto the scene and we can distinguish a third class of programmer, *hobbyists and hackers*. In this section, we discuss these three classes of programmers.

1.5.1 Professional programmers

Professional programmers are those whose life's work is the creation and modification of programs and whose education, training, aspirations, and mental discipline make them fit for the task. When computers were first developed, it was thought that all programs would be written by professional programmers. It was expected that scientists and engineers would bring their problems to the professional programmer to have a program solution created, in much the same way as they might take a problem to a draftsman to have a blueprint created. This was at a time when conventional wisdom was that computers would only be used for numerical computation and that fewer than ten large computers could provide the world's computational needs to the end of the century. Even Thomas J. Watson, Senior, the founder of IBM thought at one time that there was no future in the manufacture of computers and that it would not be profitable for his company to go into that business.

It was quickly realized that there would never be enough professional programmers to write all the programs that would be required. It was also understood that there was always a loss of information in the transfer of the problem statement to the professional programmer. This was because the scientist would take certain facts for granted as being common knowledge and therefore not specify them to the programmer. The programmer, to whom the knowledge was not common, would neglect to take account of these facts and the program would fail. It was out of these realizations, among other things, that the push for higher-level programming languages came about. Although it was hard for the then professional programmers to understand, there were many people who wanted to use computers but were not interested in how they worked. Through the use of these higher-level languages, the scientists and engineers were able to write and develop their own programs.

There was, however, still plenty of work for the professional programmer. As the idea of operating systems and supporting software came to be understood as a requirement for the use of a computer, so the role of the professional programmer took on more meaning. We saw in an earlier section that the result of over-confidence on the part of the professional programmers was the software crisis. As a consequence of the 'software revolution' stemming from the NATO software engineering conferences in 1968 and 1969, programming became much more of a professional activity in the sense that the term 'professional' is used to describe a professional engineer. Nowadays, the professional programmer is well aware that a program, once created, will have to be maintained for many years and cannot be neglected once it is working. Therefore the design and implementation must be done with modification in mind. The fact that 'the professional programmer is well aware of this' does not necessarily mean that programs are written in that way. There is still a great deal of room for improvement in the standards used by those who ought to be considered professional programmers. I have seen source codes for operating system software produced by reputable vendors that are almost impossible to understand. I conclude that the reason why these vendors take so long to correct the all too frequent errors in their software is that they find it very expensive to modify it.

1.5.2 Amateur programmers

Amateur programmers are those whose major work is not the writing of programs or are professional programmers who have yet to achieve enlightenment. The amateur programmer writes programs as a way of expressing work done in another field. The ranks of amateur programmers consist of scientists, engineers, financial analysts, lawyers, doctors, in fact, anybody who can use a computer to help in their work. The problem with these programmers is that they regard programming as a necessary chore, to be got through as quickly as possible so that they can progress to the next step in the work in their own field. Consequently, they tend to take short cuts that the professional programmer knows should be avoided.

Ledgard (1987) describes an amateur programmer as one who writes programs that have only a very limited application for a small user population; usually one where only the author needs to be able to read and debug the program and there is no need for documentation. The advent of the micro-computer has changed this. Amateur programmers are now writing programs for micro-computers and these find their way into microwave ovens, washing machines and a host of other machines that are controlled by 'embedded' microprocessors. This is not to suggest that all such microprocessor programs are written by amateurs; on the contrary, I know of many such programs that are created by very skilled professionals. However, I do suggest that there are many amateur programmers who write programs for embedded systems. What I am worried about is that we shall see a repeat of the debacle caused by scaling up from small successes to large disasters. Allen Macro has suggested the following definition: 'An amateur programmer is one who, being usually an intermittent programmer on a small scale, never consolidates experience into a framework of good practice'. It is a category containing very many electronic engineers, nearly all computer scientists, and lots of others – including many very experienced software engineers who have never *bothered* to consolidate their experience into a 'canonical practice'.

In contrast, the professional usually writes programs for others to use and does so in the full knowledge that they will. Of course there are many times when professional programmers will write programs for their own use – to generate test data or to check the correctness of the output of a test run, to name just two examples of such *software tools*. Nevertheless, the main thrust of the professional programmer's work is to write programs to be used by other people, and this fact conditions the work in a number of ways.

Probably the most obvious difference is the way in which the program interacts with its user. The amateur's quadratic root program is likely to obtain the equation's three coefficients A, B and C through the statements

```
ReadReal(input, A);
ReadReal(input, B);
ReadReal(input, C);
```

Because the author and user of the program are the same person, when the terminal pauses in request for data, there will be no need for prompting about what data are expected. The professional programmer does not have this close a relationship with the user. The user must therefore be prompted.

```
WriteString(output, "Enter coefficient of x squared:");
ReadReal(input, A);
WriteString(output, "Enter coefficient of x        :");
ReadReal(input, B);
WriteString(output, "Enter constant coefficient    :");
ReadReal(input, C);
```

Note that the data entered by the user will appear aligned in a column for easy checking. Similarly, when the amateur programmer presents the output of the computation to the user, they are likely to be numbers unadorned with explanatory text since the user knows exactly the sequence of the printed answers. As a result, it is rather like a sports broadcaster who announces 'Here are the football results, 4-0, 3-2, 1-1' The problem is not that amateur programmers write programs for themselves alone but that they act as though they do.

For the professional programmer to provide a user interface in the style of the amateur would probably lead to a failure of the product. Users would find that the program was very difficult to use and would search for other more congenial solutions to their problem and the program would die for lack of users.

Another crucial difference between professional and amateur programmers lies in the style in which the program is written. The amateur's program is strictly a one-person effort; no one else will modify it or read it. Such a program is really a private memorandum belonging to the author, like a shopping list. And, like the shopping list, a year later even the author will often find the program to be inscrutably cryptic. It is here, probably more than in the user interface, that the amateur approach is likely to be the reason for failure of an implementation. The work of an amateur programmer that is embodied in programs can only be used by others if they can understand it, otherwise it will be wasted.

1.5.3 Hobbyists and hackers

The remaining class of programmers, *hobbyists and hackers*, comprises, as its name suggests, two sub-classes. Members of both groups share a joy in playing with computers, however, they differ in the arenas in which their interactions are played out. Hobbyists use computers through software written by others, spread sheets, word processors, games, etc. If hobbyists actually do any programming, it is in a recognized language such as Basic, Fortran, or, perhaps for the real enthusiast, C. Hackers find that for them there is insufficient intimacy in the man–machine relationship. For them 'twiddling-bits' is the whole thing, they have a desire to prove to themselves how clever they are, how powerful is their understanding of the inner workings of the computer. Some achieve this by making the machine perform in strange ways. Others, with a more sinister bent, boost their egos by breaking into computer systems where they may divert money to their own profit or vandalize files. From the point of view of this book, hobbyists and hackers, benign and malign, are lumped together because they have no interest in others reading their programs or in programs that are more than transitory objects.

Throughout their working lives, programmers may move from one of these classes to another. Figure 1.2 shows a diagram, created by Allen Macro, of the possible movements. The shaded part of the diagram shows those for whom this book is intended.

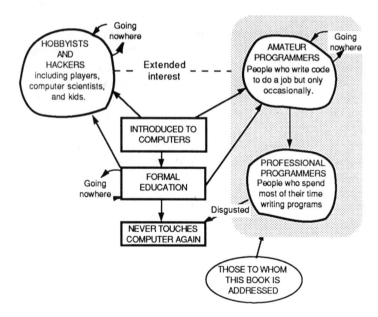

FIGURE 1.2 The migatory flight paths of programmers.

1.6 PRODUCTIVITY

Often, the first question on a manager's lips is 'How do these techniques improve programmer productivity?' Answering this question poses a problem. Productivity statistics are difficult to obtain and are very often meaningless.

First, there is the question of exactly what should be measured. The problem is that the measurement of programmer productivity is not just one of counting lines of code produced. Quite apart from the subjective decision of what constitute a 'line-of-code' – does it include comments, declarations . . . ? – the lines-of-code measurement penalizes high-level languages since they 'do more' per line of code. As a consequence, such measures tend to move in the wrong direction as productivity increases. Another popular measure is cost per defect. Cost per defect is always lowest where the number of defects found is greatest and always highest where the number of defects found is least. In fact, if there are no defects, the cost is infinite! Thus, what must be measured is the sum of all costs. We really want to measure the cost of developing the program initially, *plus the cost of maintaining it over its entire life*, say five or ten years. It serves us little if the program, when produced, is correct, though this is a *requirement*, if it is impossible to modify later without reducing its reliability – that is its tendency to go on running correctly.

This leads to the difficult problem of estimating programming costs for a program's life time. Cost figures are often used as a cloak of objectivity under which is hidden much shaky subjectivity. Cost figures are often derived in much the same way that, I am told, pigs are weighed in rural Texas. The pig is lashed to one end of a see-saw and a rock is placed on the other so that the two are in balance. Then the workers gather round and guess the weight of the rock.

The only chance of arriving at valid productivity and cost figures is to keep records for a particular working environment over a number of years and then make a change in the procedures and gather more statistics over a similar period. With the rate at which technology changes, by the time the productivity and cost measurements are completed, there will be new techniques available for which new miracles will be claimed. The whole question of productivity measurement is too complex for this volume and the reader is referred to Jones (1986) for a full treatment of the subject.

The question may, however, be academic. Measurements of individual productivity rates have shown considerable variation in the ability of individuals. Sackman *et al.* (1968) measured the performances of a group of experienced programmers. Within just this group, productivity ratios of 10:1 between best and worst performances were observed. Weinberg (1971) observed ratios of 4:1 for the same kind of measures. Since both samples were small, there is nothing inherently inconsistent about this. Any attempt to measure improvement in programmer productivity through the use of a particular technique must take into account the variabilities between different languages, problems, and errors. To do this probably requires the running of a controlled experiment on a non-trivial problem, which is a very expensive enterprise. Even if this is done, Sackman's results suggest that any changes in productivity measured are likely to be submerged in the individual variations between programmers.

Without meaningful data on productivity improvement, this book has to rely on the common sense of its readers for the support of its theme of programming as a form of expository writing. However, most *software engineers* would point not so much at simple productivity (however measured) as at the factors that might most radically *attenuate* productivity if insufficiently provided as the object of greatest interest in this area. On most lists, the following would rank highly as productivity modifiers:

1. Specifications, which must be unambiguous, complete, and stable.
2. Exponents; the software staff must be adequate for the task and available when required.
3. Adequate technical environment for software development (PSE) relative to the task.
4. Sufficient time to do the job.

It is with these potential modifiers in mind, as well as others not listed perhaps, that we continue our discussion.

1.7 EXPOSITORY PROGRAMMING

In the early years of programming, a program was regarded as the private property of the programmer. One would no more think of reading a colleague's program unbidden than of picking up a love letter and reading it. This is essentially what a program was, a love letter from the programmer to the hardware, full of the intimate details known only to partners in an affair. Consequently, programs became larded with the pet names and verbal shorthand so popular with lovers who live in the blissful abstraction that assumes that theirs is the only existence in the universe. Such programs are unintelligible to those outside the partnership.

Programs written as private communications between author and computer are 'owned' by the programmer. What is wrong with that? Artists 'own' paintings, choreographers 'own' dances, sculptors 'own' statues, and composers 'own' concerti. The difference is in the extent to which the programmer's ego is attached to the program. For conventional artists there is no objective test of the quality of their work. Critics who denigrate the work can be dismissed as not having the necessary insight. The programmer finds it more difficult to dismiss the computer's halt on division by zero as mere subjective bias. Programs that are kept as pillow talk between programmer and computer are unlikely to be as fully tested as those that have public exposure. After all, lovers are not noted for concentration on the hard facts of the real world but more for the dreams of the 'all is for the best in the best of possible worlds' philosophy. When the text of a program is made public, it is likely that it will be looked on with a more critical eye. After all, what greater joy is there than to find that *somebody else* has made a stupid blunder? Before a program is released for public scrutiny, it is almost a certainty that the author will look at it carefully.

There is another reason why programs should be made public. A program that remains as the private property of the programmer hangs like an albatross around the neck. There is no getting rid of it! Its users are always wanting errors repaired and extensions made.

The alternative is to write a program and have nobody use it. That, however, is dispiriting, like organizing a party to which no guests come. The great satisfaction in writing a program is to have lots of users, and to pass it on to somebody else to maintain. Another satisfaction is to take a program written by somebody else, improve it, increase its usefulness, and pass it on to another to continue with the work. But nobody wants to take on a program that they cannot understand and modify easily.

The major theme of this book is that a program is the description of a process and is a form of communication between programmers. It is just as much a form of expository writing as is a technical report, which relies on its clarity and understandability for success. For a program to be successful as a medium of communication, it must follow the same style of rules as are recommended for the more usual forms of expository writing. The term *expository programming* is used to describe the writing of programs that are easily understood by others. A program's structure should allow the reader to follow the logic of the program and to assure oneself that it correctly performs its function without error. However, being able to follow the program's logic is not sufficient; the program is not a piece of abstract 'thought stuff', it exists in the context of the real world and therefore its structure must reflect the structures of the part of the real world to which it applies. Recall the remarks on structured programming in Section 1.4.2.

While readability is a subjective criterion that depends to some degree on matters of taste and style, it is possible to define general rules that improve readability. Kernighan and Plauger (1978), *The Elements of Programming Style*, make a deliberate parallel with the book much used in the United States, *The Elements of Style* (Strunk and White 1979). The original version of this book appeared in 1919 and has been revised since. Both books offer short commandments that should be followed by writers who wish to have their words understood. For example, compare Strunk and White's

> Do not take shortcuts at the cost of clarity.

with Kernighan and Plauger's

> Write clearly – don't sacrifice clarity for 'efficiency'.

A more complete set of aphorisms of style is contained in Section 10.7.5.

More important than the aphorisms offered by manuals of style are principles of program design, which are really rules of style applied in a much broader context. These aphorisms define how the program can be split into parts that are each of an intellectually manageable size and how the parts are to fit together to form the complete program. Again, these pieces must have analogies in the program's real-world context. If these principles are followed, it is possible to construct a very large program that can be understood by programmers who were not involved with its implementation. A large program, for example an airline reservation system, makes stringent requirements of the implementation:

- It must function correctly despite errors by users and communication devices. Errors in such systems can be extremely costly.
- It must be long-lived. The cost of producing a large program is so high that it is totally uneconomical to replace it until after many years.

- It must undergo considerable modification. This is a requirement of being long-lived since its requirements will change due to changing regulations, technology, and market conditions.
- Many programmers, possibly hundreds, will be involved in its implementation and maintenance. These populations will not stay constant over time, neither in the development phase nor during service.

All of these requirements put a premium on the ability of the programmers to understand the program, not necessarily the whole program at once, which may be beyond anybody's capability, but the section currently being worked on. Since the context of a section must be understood for the detailed working of the section to be appreciated, the overall design of a program is also an essential part of expository programming.

At the other end of the programming scale, the presentation of the actual statements in the program is also of importance. That is to say, the way in which the statements are arranged and laid out also have an important effect on the readability of the programs. Expository documents have developed some techniques of layout that make it easier for the reader to understand. While stream of consciousness writing and breathless prose without punctuation may be sufficient for occasional letters retelling family news, they make for difficult reading and rapidly exhaust the concentration of the reader. Such things as proper paragraphing, the indenting of lists and the inclusion of white space are essential for rapid and complete understanding. This too is part of expository programming.

The work of many scientists and engineers has become embodied in programs. In many cases this work has been lost because the programs could not be understood. The physicist Erwin Schrödinger put it this way:

> If you cannot – in the long run – tell everyone what you have been doing, your doing has been worthless.

It is to prevent this terrible waste of one of our most precious resources, good ideas, that the principles of expository programming are recommended.

CHAPTER TWO
THE TASK OF PROGRAMMING

Implementation is the task of replacing the design with computer instructions that can be executed on a computer to do what the requirements definition calls for. After the life-cycle model of the computer program has been sketched as a context for the implementation phase, some preliminary definitions of the way in which a program models the real world are introduced. This is followed by a review of the tasks performed by the members of a programming team. The low-level stages of software design include several of the same methods as are involved during implementation; these are described, in particular the concepts of abstraction, information hiding, modularity, coupling and unity of purpose. This is followed by a discussion of what is actually involved in the task of programming. This is not so much an answer to the child's question 'What do you do at the office?' but a look beyond the superficial activities to what are the basic precepts in a programmer's work. Much of what a programmer does can be summarized as a *fight to maintain consistency*. Finally, the subject of program correctness is introduced.

2.1 INTRODUCTION

The programming phase of a software project, often referred to as the *implementation* phase, is where the rather abstract architecture or design of the software is turned into the concrete reality of a program. As Blaauw (1970) puts it, 'Where architecture tells *what* happens, implementation tells *how* it is made to happen.' To use his simple example, the architecture of a clock describes the face, hands, and winding knob. A user can learn from the architecture how to tell the time from any clock built according to this architecture. In contrast, the implementation defines the mechanism that makes the hands move from energy obtained through the winding knob and the way in which accuracy is controlled. Different implementations of the same architecture lead to steeple clocks and wrist watches.

The purpose of this book is to describe competent implementation. The subject of software structures is the proper province of the volume on design. However, some of the basic principles of software design carry over into implementation, and these concepts are introduced in this section and expanded in later parts of the book.

There are differing views of implementation. To some, it is the fun part of the whole project. After all, this is the point where there is going to be really creative contact with the computer to produce the new system and that's what this programming business is all about! To others, it is the manual laborer's work of a software project; as they see it, the implementors just do what they are told by the designers who are the real aristocracy of the business. Such people believe that there is no creativity in the task of implementation. This volume shows that there is room for a great deal of creativity in implementation, however it is a different kind of creativity from that required in other phases of program development.

2.2 THE LIFE-CYCLE MODEL

Old programs never die. As long as they continue to model reliably some real-world process that needs to be performed, they will continue to be used; their usefulness depends upon the accuracy of the model. However, the real world is constantly changing, and consequently the program must be frequently modified to maintain the fidelity of the model. This is the Law of Continuing Change as stated by Belady and Lehman (1979):

> A system that is used undergoes continuing change until it is judged more cost-effective to freeze and recreate it.

Just as a butterfly goes through the stages of egg, larva, chrysalis, butterfly, reproduction, and death, so the program goes through a similar cycle. The Law of Continuing Change summarizes the life-cycle of a program as birth, modification, death, and reincarnation. Different authors have identified various sequences of stages. In this section, we examine a sequence of eight phases of a program's life-cycle, and examine in particular where programming fits into the life-cycle and how the methods used in design and implementation can affect the longevity of the program. As with the butterfly, the results of each phase are passed on as the starting point of the next phase. The term often used in discussions is *deliverables*, a usage that I find unpleasant; I shall refer to the *outcome of the phase*. Figure 2.1 shows a depiction of the life-cycle taken from Volume 1 of this series. The implementation phase is shown in the shaded area.

2.2.1 Feasibility study

The object of this first stage is to take the utopian idea of the proposed program and see whether it is practical. This requires a careful formulation of the user's requirements so that the problem to be solved is well specified and the properties of the desired solution and the constraints on the final program are thoroughly understood by both the user and the system developer. In some cases, the construction of a technical prototype might be

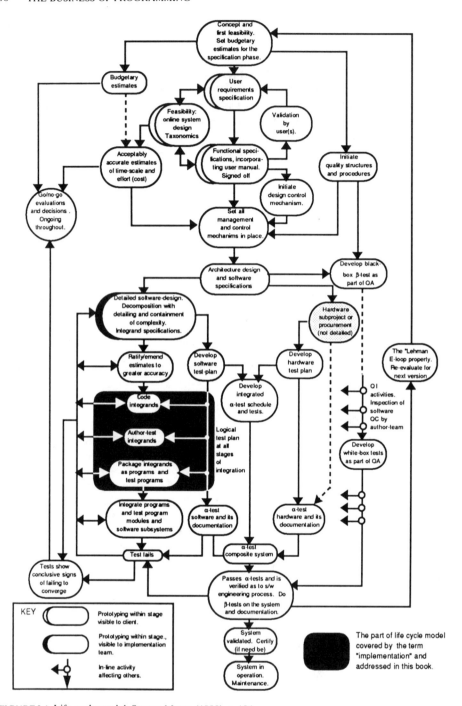

FIGURE 2.1 Life-cycle model. Source Macro (1990), p. 106.

required if the design of hardware or algorithms are not standard. A typical instance of this need was the development of software for image reconstruction in tomography. At the outset, the algorithms were unknown and there was no suitable hardware available. Both had to be developed before it was known whether tomography was even possible. These studies resulted in bit-slice architecture and software-based image reconstruction.

The feasibility study must include an examination of the economics of the project; that is, a comparison of the expected financial savings from the program with a gross estimate of the project costs. Great care is required in estimating the project costs. Other questions that should be addressed by the feasibility study include the following:

- Does the available hardware have sufficient power to handle the projected load and throughput?
- Can all portability requirements, see Section 2.6.1 below, be handled?
- How are the security and integrity, including reliability, requirements to be met?

Programmers are incurable optimists. Ask a programmer how long it will take to write a given program and you will get an answer that is tacitly based on everything always going right all the time. The algorithms will be correct, there will be no surprises in the numerical analysis, the terminals and supporting computer will always work, the compiler will produce no incomprehensible messages, the interfaces with the system will be clear, and so on. The strange thing is that programmers often do not *sound like* optimists – 'this will be a problem!', 'that cannot possibly work!', 'the new release of the software will be full of bugs!', and so on. However, when an estimate or a situation report is required, they have this romantic view of themselves as Saint George slaying the dragon or Joan of Arc giving the English their just deserts, fighting through these many problems to produce a working program in almost no time at all. Allen Macro points out that programmers are obviously romantics for taking the rotten job on in the first place.

How long it will actually take will depend on a large number of factors. Some of these 'productivity modifiers' are listed below in approximate order of magnitude of effect, according to Walston and Felix (1977):

- *Complexity of the user interface.* Programs that deal with human interactions become very rapidly more complicated as the scope of the human interface becomes wider.
- *Degree of user participation during design.* User participation in the definition of requirements can greatly shorten the implementation time.
- *Programmer experience.* Experience and qualification of programmers and designers can have a great effect on the time it takes to produce the program, particularly if the previous experience was with a project of similar or greater size and complexity. As we saw in the previous chapter, it is easy to fall into the trap of extrapolating from success with a small project into assuming only linear expansion of complexity with a larger one.
- *Choice of programming language.* It is not so much a question of which programming language is best for the particular problem as a question of which language do the programmers feel most comfortable with. There may, of course, be certain require- ments that the language must meet, for example the ability to handle concurrent processes. Apart from these kinds of requirements, familiarity of the programmers

with the language is probably the most important consideration, provided that they are prepared to follow the proper amount of discipline to write readable programs. Given good discipline, clear programs can be written in any language, even assembler language.

- *Complexity of application.* What is perhaps surprising is not that this appears in the list of factors contributing to cost but that there are so many other items that have a larger effect.
- *Previous experience with hardware.* A consequence of this is that the hardware is already working and is not being developed at the same time as the software, which would give a new level of uncertainty to program testing.
- *Access to the development computer.* Early testing of the program is essential to orderly building of the program.

While many of these factors will only come into effect during later stages of the project, they need to be identified during the feasibility study.

The outcome of the feasibility study is as follows:

- The decision whether to continue with the project. If it were not possible to abandon the project at the end of the feasibility study, there would be no point in doing a feasibility study, the feasibility having already been decreed.
- A brief description of the proposed system.
- An estimated schedule for the completion of key items in the project. This schedule must be tied to specific things that can be seen or certain performance that can be demonstrated. An item 'programming 90 per cent complete' is useless as it is impossible to show that the programming has reached this point. Whether the programming was in fact 90 per cent complete on the scheduled day will only be known when the programming is 100 per cent complete, by which time the information is only of value as history.

2.2.2 Requirements definition

During this phase, the early description of the proposed program developed during the feasibility study is expanded into an accurate and complete set of requirements. This requires a detailed study of the real-world system that is to be modeled. If the new system is to replace an existing system, there must be a clear understanding of what parts of the previous system are to be duplicated and what is to be different. In addition, the set of conditions to be met before the new system can be considered complete and working should be described. This is probably the most frequently forgotten requirement. Where a formal contract is drawn up on the basis of the requirements definition, this is often called the *acceptance test*.

Several years ago I was involved in installing a new stock exchange quotation system, consisting of both hardware and software, to replace one that had been in use for several years. The acceptance test required several days of running the new and old systems in parallel and that, at the end of each day, the two systems should agree. When the time came for the acceptance tests, discrepancies were discovered between the two systems. It took many days of acrimonious discussion and detective work to discover that the old system was all too fallible and had been inaccurate for many years without our clients noticing. Both parties to the contract had fallen into the trap of assuming that the system that was being replaced had been giving correct results. This gives pause to wonder how much accuracy is actually required and how much is good enough to run the business of this world. The lesson to be drawn here is that the criteria for acceptance need careful scrutiny to make sure that they are attainable.

The outcome of the requirements definition phase is:

- A detailed description of the user requirements for the new system.
- A summary of the proposed new system.
- A definition of what constitutes acceptable performance by the new system: 'How shall we know when we've finished?'

2.2.3 System design

The objective of this phase is to design a system that will meet all the requirements developed in the previous phase. There are two particularly important goals that require great skill by the designer during this phase:

1. The creation of a system that will meet all the requirements of the proposed system in a reliable manner.
2. The system will be such that, when the real world changes or, what amounts to the same thing, the client decides on new extended requirements, these changes and extensions can be incorporated easily.

Both goals are important. The first one is only the *short-term goal*. The second goal is very much more important in the long run. It can be restated as one of giving the program as long a life as possible and of minimizing the amount of effort that will be expended on it during its lifetime.

As we shall see later in our examination of the life-cycle, adaptability is the key to longevity. An organism or system that is not adaptable to a changing environment is doomed. Unless a program can be easily modified, its life is destined to be short and undignified. A favorite analogy for this is the dinosaur; however, we would do well to temper our smugness by remembering that if the human race is to match the 140 million years of the dinosaur's reign it still has at least 130 million to go!

To achieve this adaptability, the designer must always keep in mind that the new program will be frequently modified in ways that cannot be foreseen at the time of design. The wise designer will therefore create the program so that the subsequent modification process will be as painless as possible. The recognition of a program's operational lifetime of continuous modification provides some guidelines that can be applied during the program design phase.

To illustrate the principles of designing for change, I have run several Software Engineering classes based on Horning and Wortman (1977) where the students were grouped into 'Software Cottages' of three or four members. Each Cottage was given the same informal specification for a piece of software, for example, a text formatting program. The completed software and documentation, including user documentation, had to be produced by mid-semester. At that time, each Cottage presented its product to the other Cottages, who were at liberty to examine the programs and documentation. Each Cottage then had to decide which of the other products they would use during the rest of the semester as a basis for producing a product that would meet as yet unknown extensions to the specification.

After this decision had been made by all Cottages, modifications to the specification were announced and each Cottage had to change their chosen product to meet the new specification. The key point here was that each Cottage had to design its own product and to judge the ease with which the other products could be modified in ignorance of exactly how the specification would change. As in real life, all that was known was that the specification would change and modifications would have to be made. In addition to points being given for program and documentation quality, bonus points were given based on the 'sales' achieved by a Cottage for its initial product. There was thus considerable incentive to design a product that could be easily modified and be seen to be easily modified. This required special care during the system design phase.

The process of splitting a program into a number of integrands during the design phase is an important part of making later modification easy. A good analogy is the construction of a seaworthy ship, where the hull is divided into watertight compartments separated by bulkheads with limited access between the compartments. Thus, if the ship is holed, the flooding of the hull will be limited to just those compartments that are damaged. The Titanic's hull was divided, however each compartment went across the entire width of the ship so that when an iceberg scraped down the side, most of the hull flooded.

The integrands form the watertight compartments of a program with bulkheads consisting of interfaces that provide limited data access between the integrands. They embody the principles of modular programming: localization, information hiding, functional unity, which are discussed in Sections 2.5.3 and 2.5.4 below. If these principles are followed in the design, then when the program must be modified, the changes will be limited to a few integrands. In addition, it should be a *consequence* of the design that the other integrands will not even need to be examined to see if they need changing. The more successful the design, the more localized the changes will be, even though the particular alterations in the program's specifications are unknown at the time of the design.

The skill of the designer lies particularly in defining the boundaries of the integrands so that each has a clear purpose and is not intertwined with the others in such a complex way that one cannot be understood without comprehending them all.

By the end of the *software* design phase, the following should have been established:

- A set of external interface specifications, being the outcome of design, consisting of definitions of the algorithms, interfaces for each integrand, a program structure design, where this is possible, indicating how integrands invoke each other and, where the software consists of several programs, a specification of program composition showing how the integrands are grouped into programs. These are referred to again in Section 2.3.2.

- The definition of project programming standards. That is a specification of the format and coding conventions that will be used in the writing of the integrands. It is probable that the organization will already have established conventions but it is nevertheless important that it be stated that the project will adhere to these standards and any exceptions or modifications are defined. These standards should be laid down earlier rather than later in the software design phase.
- The definition of project procedures for management of the project data base of documentation, source code, object code, test data, etc. The statement about reaffirming existing standards given in the previous item also applies here.
- The definition of any special software tools that will be required for the project.

An example of a full software design is contained in Chapter 3.

2.2.4 Implementation

There is some overlap between the lowest levels of the work described in the previous section and the implementation phase described here. Coding of the individual integrands is done in this phase. As the integrands are completed, they need to be tested and integrated into a complete executable program, which must be tested. Experience has shown that integration and testing must be done in parallel with the implementation of the integrands. If testing is deferred until all the integrands have been completed, there are three approaches to testing:

1. *Big bang*. Link all the integrands together and test the whole program as a single unit. The major disadvantage with the big-bang approach is that the behavior space of a complete program is so large that it is very difficult to track an error to its source. The next two approaches avoid this problem.
2. *Bottom-up incremental*. Start with the lowest-level integrands, those that do not invoke any other integrands, link them with specially written test harnesses, and validate the lowest integrands. Testing continues by linking together low-level, already tested, integrands with higher-level untested integrands until the whole program has been tested.
3. *Top-down incremental*. Start with the top-level integrand, link it with 'stub' integrands that are place holders for all the integrands that it invokes, and test the top integrand. Testing continues by replacing stub integrands with actual integrands linked with their own lower-level stubs and testing successively larger and larger portions of the complete program.

In all three cases, delaying testing until all integrands have been written is likely to delay the finish of the project considerably. Inevitably, it will be found that there have been misunderstandings on the part of the developers of different integrands. This will be reflected in errors in the transfer of information between the integrands and needs to be found and corrected as early as possible, which will require recoding of already written integrands.

The usual way of overcoming this problem is to use the strategy of top-down development as formulated by Mills and Baker (1973), in which the integrands that are highest in the organization of the program are completed first and integrated into the program as soon as they are completed. Since the lower-level integrands that are to be invoked by those just completed have not yet been implemented, their place is taken by a *stub integrand* whose function is that of place-holder and may also report that it has been invoked so that the logic of the completed integrands can be checked. Starting in this way, complete (though mere skeletons in terms of function) versions of the entire program are executed from the very beginning. It is possible to use the strategy of incremental delivery in which the sequence of completion of integrands is arranged so that partially complete systems that already deliver some small but usable portion of the entire function are delivered to the client for use and experience. Even though the users have been involved closely at the early stages of analysis and have read and agreed to the external interface specification for the new system, there are bound to be some surprises for them when they actually start using even an abbreviated form of it. There will be some cries of 'That's not what I meant!' and the discovery that, with the passage of time since the original design was made and partial implementation completed, the real world has changed and the actual requirements for the system are now somewhat different.

It is easily forgotten that implemented integrands are not the only outcome of this phase; so too is documentation. In fact the implementation phase probably has more to do with communication than it does with the traditional idea of programming. Students in my Software Cottage project often reported that they learned more about communication through working closely with the other members of the Cottage and having to write readable programs and documentation than they learned about programming. At the beginning of the class, I always warned them that communication difficulties of various forms would be the major problem of the project. I told them that I guaranteed that there would be technical discussions that degenerated into shouting matches and tears, and this always came true. Since they had to convince other Cottages that their programs were easy to understand and modify, they were under considerable pressure to write programs that communicated just as clearly as the documentation that they had to produce.

The outcome of the implementation phase comprises:

- Source code for the integrands. If it is desired, printed listings can be produced from source code but it is not essential provided that it is readily available. One of the major problems with paper listings is filing them. They are only worth keeping if the latest listing can be found quickly and reliably. A possible solution is to use microfiche, if the necessary equipment is available. A system can be built that maintains an up-to-date directory that allows the programmer to carry the complete listings for a very large project in a single binder.
- A fully linked suite of executable programs that embody the system being produced.
- Command procedures for controlling the execution of the program.
- User documentation including training and reference manuals, operator guide, and an installation manual that describes how the new system is to be installed into the computer.

- Test data together with expected output that demonstrate that the program passes all the tests.

2.2.5 System test and acceptance

This phase is intended to provide a complete test of the full system against its original specifications. During implementation of the integrands, the system will have been tested as already described. The system test is really the acceptance test defined in the requirements definition phase and should be run under the control of the user. Of course, the test will have been run at least once before under the developers' control. This test should be designed so that it will simulate as closely as possible the actual usage of the system both in manner and volume. Particularly important in the design of the test are the ideas of verifiability and repeatability. That is, at the end of the test, there must be clear evidence that the test was performed according to plan and that the system functioned correctly. At this point in the saga of producing the system, when passions and stresses may well be running high, there is no room for doubts as to whether the test was administered correctly. To avoid finger pointing and discussions that lack the normal civilities of the culture, the system must maintain a proper audit trail that can be examined afterwards. Similarly, the test must be precisely repeatable; in systems that are interactive, this requirement may need very careful thought and design. For reasons of recovery after hardware failure, it may be prudent for such systems to maintain a journal record of user actions that can serve as a repeatable script for the acceptance test.

A test of the documentation is often forgotten. The people who will use the documentation, system users (including operators), maintenance programmers, and anyone involved in system evolution, must assure themselves that the documentation is accurate, readable, and provides the information that their staff need to use the system. Generally, this can only be done by readers who have no more than the same level of knowledge as the expected users of the documentation will have.

The outcome of system test and acceptance phase is determined by the criteria of software quality: compliance with requirements, and ease of modifiability. The outcome most frequently comprises:

- A set of test results. These need to be preserved to serve as the basis for ensuring that no regression has taken place when new versions of the system are produced later.
- A certificate of acceptance by the user. The exact form of this will depend upon contractual requirements and can thus vary greatly in level of formality.

2.2.6 Operation and maintenance

During this phase the objective is to execute the program in a production mode and to keep it operational. 'Maintenance' is a somewhat misleading term here. The work that is done during this phase is not like the maintenance that a homeowner has to do on the house. Computer instructions do not need repainting and bits do not rot. There are two reasons why work needs to be done on the program during this phase:

1. The correction of errors that were not discovered during testing.
2. Modifying the program to meet changing user needs. As we have already seen, a program's usefulness depends upon the accuracy with which it mimics the underlying real-world process. Since this is always changing, the user will want modifications to track these changes and keep the model faithful. In addition, no program ever does enough. The user will always have a wish list.

There are two major problems with maintenance work encountered in many organizations:

1. The program to be maintained may not have been designed with maintenance in mind. It is an axiom that is self-evident in its value that proper splitting into integrands can localize the work that is required to modify the program. Although this early investment will be amply repaid during the maintenance phase, the budget planning for the company may discourage it. Frequently a new piece of software is budgeted for its first version only and then it is transferred to a maintenance department, which is budgeted separately. Since the development group's manager is judged solely on the cost of producing the first version of the program, extra expense that helps the maintenance phase is not likely to be favored. Consequently, the maintenance programmers are often faced with programs that have not been designed with a view to maintenance. A good way for an organization to avoid this is to institute reviews during the system design and implementation phases at which representatives from the maintenance group have power of veto if they do not feel that the program will be maintainable without great effort.
2. Software maintenance is seldom performed by the original authors. Once a program has been written, its authors often move on to 'better things' – new programming challenges, punk rock singing, navel contemplation, etc. It is not easy to find properly qualified and motivated maintenance staff. Within the social hierarchy of programmers, maintenance is regarded as a rather lowly occupation. It does not have the glamor of writing new programs or, even greater, of designing them. The thought prevails that maintenance offers few opportunities for exercising creativity; maintenance is felt to be 'just straightening out somebody else's mess'. The fact that, in many organizations, the maintenance group is responsible not only for correcting errors, but also adding enhancements is often ignored. This view of the maintenance task is actually encouraged by management treating the maintenance group as the training ground for newly recruited staff. In fact, the differences between the skills required for development and maintenance are not really significant.

Development requires no more 'superior' or creative skills than does maintenance.

Successful maintenance requires the application of discipline in making the changes and this must be supported by adequate tools in the technical environment so that a proper audit trail can be maintained. These will ensure that no integrand can be changed by more than one worker concurrently, that a proper log of the changes is maintained, and it is possible to 'undo' a change and return to a previous level of modification. An example of a tool that can help support such management procedures is the Source Code Control System, SCCS, described by Rochkind (1975). Such tools are discussed in Chapter 16.

The results of the operation and maintenance phase are as follows:

- A program that continues to have the user's confidence that it meets requirements reliably. This is an amalgam of two quality criteria: compliance and modifiability.
- A compilation of known but unimplemented improvements (or even non-critical corrections), that might predicate a new version.
- An insight, where needed, of how software may be better 'engineered' next time, in terms of any of the life-cycle phases, in order to improve the operations and maintenance phase itself.

Actually, this phase is different from all the previous phases because its outcome is not usually passed on to the *next* phase but is fed back to the *previous* phase so that it can be revalidated and accepted by the user. In fact, the third of the results is not only fed back into the previous phase but all phases and into all life-cycle phases of future software developments by the same group of software engineers – it becomes part of their 'group intelligence'.

As each new version of the software is produced, it is essential to reapply the tests that were used in the previous phase (modified to match the changing requirements where necessary) to ensure that, in modifying the program to change one thing, something else has not been broken. This is why it is important to retain the test data for future tests to ensure that new versions of the system have not regressed.

2.3 SOME DEFINITIONS

2.3.1 Program

One view of a program is shown in Figure 2.2. A program consists of a computer model of some process that exists outside the computer. This process could be the generation of checks to pay workers, the control of inventory in a warehouse, the calculation of stresses in a bridge due to traffic and windage, microprocessor control of a washing machine, the prediction of the weather for 24 hours ahead, or the Running Example to be introduced in the next chapter. These will be referred to throughout as 'real-world processes' even though they could be as abstract as a theory in the mind of a mathematician. The usefulness of the program depends upon the accuracy with which it mimics the real-world process in both operation and results. The computer model of the real-world process manipulates representations of real-world objects such as names, hours worked, salaries, quantities of parts on hand, traffic volume, wind speed, signals to mechanical actuators, meteorological data, or prime numbers.

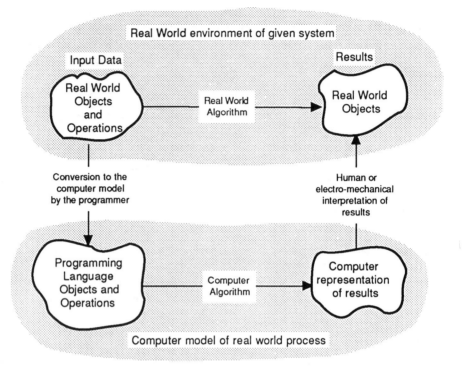

FIGURE 2.2 A program is a model of a real-world process.

2.3.2 External interface specification

The external interface specification for a program, which is *not* the same as the requirement specification (discussed in Section 2.2.2 above), defines the real-world process that the program is to model. The adjective *external* is used because it defines the behavior of the program from the outside. Thus it describes *what* a program does rather than *how* it does it. The specification may be defined in terms of real-world objects or, if it is describing part of a larger program, it may reference computer representations of real-world objects. In particular, the specification describes:

- The *set of inputs* to the program: files of data, tables of constants, user actions on terminals, signals from other equipment or computers, etc.
- The *set of outputs* from the program: files of results, displays on terminals, signals to other equipment or computers, etc.
- The *function*, in the mathematical sense, that maps the set of inputs into the set of outputs.

Thus, the external interface specification of an integrand will *define* the algorithm and internal data structures, and will define external data accesses. The form of this algorithm specification may be abstract or may depict its low-level design (e.g. flowchart or pseudocode). If in prose, the integrand's design will not be evident. For example, the function SquareRoot may have its input defined as the positive REAL value X and its output defined as a REAL value. In an abstract form, its function could be defined as $\sqrt{x}$ to some specified accuracy. Alternatively, its function could be described by a flowchart showing the Newton–Raphson iterative process.

The program's external interface specifications differ from the user's requirement specifications in that they have passed through high- and medium-level design (see Volume 1, Chapter 7, and Volume 3 of this series). The specification may be expressed with great formality with a notation that is based on mathematics or it may be given informally in prose. In both cases, it may contradict itself, have ambiguities, or be incomplete in that there are situations or conditions that are omitted. Anyway, as it was created by humans, it is more rather than less likely to contain errors.

2.3.3 Implementation

The implementation of a program or integrand is the process by which its external interface specification becomes realized in an executable form. That is, the programmer must choose a computer representation for the real-world objects described in the specification and one or more sequences of steps, or *algorithms*, that will model the real-world process. Generally, except for trivial cases, a program is not implemented as a single monolithic entity but is constructed from a number of separately implemented pieces, which we refer to as *integrands*, that are combined or *integrated* to form a complete version of the program that can be executed on the computer.

2.3.4 Integrand

An integrand has the following properties:

- It consists of an algorithm that manipulates data structures, some of which may be stored outside the computer as files.
- During execution, it may make use of data passed to it through data structures and it produces output that can be passed to other parts of the program through data structures, or to an output device.
- It can invoke other integrands.
- It can be invoked by its name, for instance, in a call statement.
- It can be separately implemented, compiled, and stored in a library.
- It can be integrated as a component of a program, hence the name *integrand*.

Although an integrand is, in general, only a part of a program, the basic paradigm of this volume is the implementation of a single integrand. Thus, our definition of implementation is refined to: the process by which the external interface specification of an integrand is transformed into executable form. The process of constructing a complete program from a set of separately implemented integrands will only be touched on; it will be covered in full in Volume 5 of this series.

2.3.5 Interface

In a program consisting of several integrands, data are passed between the integrands and also between the integrands and the outside world. The kind of values and the way in which they are passed constitutes the *interface* of an integrand. The specification of the interface is very important since both the user and implementor of the integrand must use the same definition, otherwise the communication is garbled. The design of the interface is also important because much of the understandability of the program as a whole depends upon the simplicity of the interface.

2.3.6 Obsolescence

This is not strictly a phase but is a stage in the life of a program. Instead of describing what should be done in this phase, I will describe the causes of obsolescence and what can be done to postpone it.

Obsolescence is really a by-product of change. Change is a way of life in programming; the challenge is to keep it under control. In physics, the Second Law of Thermodynamics states that disorder, or lack of structure (entropy), in a system will inevitably increase when a change is made to the system unless work is performed to prevent it. That this also applies to systems and programs was stated by Belady and Lehman (1979) as the Law of Increasing Unstructuredness.

> The entropy of a system increases with time unless specific work is executed to maintain it.

Another connection between programs and entropy was made by Augustine (1983) with the statement:

> Software is like entropy. It is difficult to grasp, weighs nothing, and obeys the Second Law of Thermodynamics; i.e., it always increases.

Belady and Lehman (1979) went on to say:

> What is fundamental to achievement of better software management and minimal life-cycle costs is the *recognition* that complexity grows *unless* and *until* effort is invested in restructuring. Some part of one's resources *must* be invested in restructuring periodically or continuously. The alternative is to reach such a level of complexity that further evolutionary progress can only be made through re-creation; total abandonment of the system and its replacement by a new system, redesigned and implemented to satisfy the most recent operational requirements.

To put this firmly into the context of maintenance requires that changes are only inserted into a program with a *clear understanding* of what the integrand is doing and a *conscious preservation of its structure*. The first requirement is the clear understanding. Unless the program is written so that it can be easily understood, there will be a strong temptation for the fixer to make a guess and try it with the expectation that it will work and thus only test the fix half-heartedly. Proper testing requires understanding. Fixes without understanding are also dangerous because they are likely to do violence to the structure of the program.

While changes without understanding are dangerous, informal changes, *quick fixes*, are doubly dangerous. Weinberg (1983) recounts that the three most expensive programming errors known to him, costing their organizations an average of more than $900 million *each*, were caused by the change of a *single digit* in a previously correct program. These changes were so trivial that they were made informally. He goes on to say that the chances of error are much greater for small changes because they are not taken seriously. Thus, quick fixes couple a lack of proper understanding with absence of controls and proper testing.

2.3.7 Discussion

It will be obvious from this description of the life-cycle that implementation is only a small part of the total task. Figure 2.3 shows a pie chart that represents the amount of time and

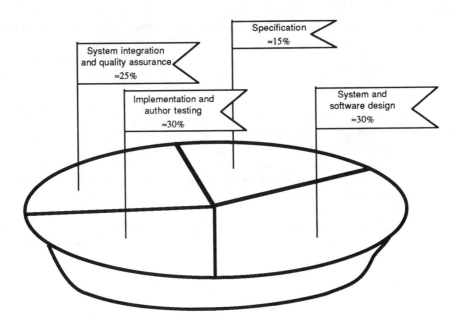

FIGURE 2.3 A pie chart showing activity distribution during software life-cycle, based on Macro (1990), Fig 8.1.

effort that is typically spent in actual implementation by expressing it as a percentage of the total project. On average over different applications and types of software, about 30 per cent of software engineering effort during the first pass through the life-cycle might be spent in implementation and all quality control activities up to alpha-test. This would comprise the creation of the integrands and testing them by careful inspection and reading of the code, and execution in a test environment by the author. Experience described by other authors (Boehm 1979, Brooks 1975) has shown that about 30–40 per cent of the total effort should be spent in specification and design, 14–20 per cent in implementation, and 40–50 per cent in testing. The trend is towards spending more effort at the front of the cycle and less at the end. Detailed methods for estimation of effort and time required for programming are beyond the scope of this book and are discussed in great detail in Boehm (1981).

The life-cycle just described has strictly followed the pattern that the outcome of one phase is 'income' to the next. This is even true when prototyping seems to obscure a strict and clear phase distinction of the life-cycle form. Each of the phases is necessary and must be gone through and can only be omitted at the risk of compromising the final product. This is true too on small projects, even where the whole project is in the hands of one person. In such cases, the form of the outcome passed from phase to phase is likely to be less formal than in large projects, or may even be a few neural wave patterns. However, the steps must be executed in order, with possibly some backtracking.

There is a strong temptation, with projects of all sizes, to start the implementation early. If this is done before enough of the design phase has been properly completed, the work of implementation can create a competitor to the design. It is a common perception that, unless the workers are actually engaged in the writing and testing of computer programs, no real work is being done. Brooks (1975) discusses this in a section entitled 'What Does the Implementer Do While Waiting?' in which he relates an example from his experience with IBM:

> It is a very humbling experience to make a multimillion-dollar mistake, but it is also very memorable. I vividly recall the night we decided how to organize the actual writing of external specifications for OS/360. The manager of architecture, the manager of control program implementation and I were threshing out the plan, schedule, and division of responsibilities.
>
> The architecture manager had 10 good men. He asserted that they could write the specifications and do it right. It would take ten months, three more than the schedule allowed.
>
> The control program manager had 150 men. He asserted that they could prepare the specifications, with the architecture team coordinating; it would be well-done and practical, and he could do it on schedule. Furthermore, if the architecture team did it, his 150 men would sit twiddling their thumbs for ten months.
>
> To this the architecture manager responded that if I gave the control program team the responsibility, the result would *not* in fact be on time, but would also be three months late, and of much lower quality. I did and it was. He was right on both counts. Moreover, the lack of conceptual integrity made the system far more costly

to build and change, and I would estimate that it added a year to the debugging time.

If the implementors start the implementation process before the fundamentals of the design are complete, the two processes become fused.

If design is created by implementation instead of the other way round, an unmaintainable system is the likely outcome.

Design should be performed at a more abstract level than implementation. To put it another way, to create an implementation requires the specification and fixing of many details that are left open by design (this is an example of *level of abstraction*, which will be discussed later). Thus, to create a design by implementation is to invest so much effort that it becomes difficult to discard should it be found unsatisfactory. An implementation is not a rough copy. Once there is actually functioning code, the resistance to change is enormous. The implemented design, with its deficiencies, is seen as if it were cast in stone. The attempt will be to patch over the problems rather than throwing it away and starting again. There is too much ego and resource investment woven into it to discard it. These are the deadly rocks to which the siren specter of idle implementors lures passing managers. In fact it is indeed a specter, something without real substance. There is plenty for the implementors to do. Long before the external interface specifications are complete, there will be sufficient information available for the design of data structures and their operators, algorithms, style conventions, and all kinds of software tools. They will also be able to plan, based on the same specification as that used as the basis for the design, how the system will be tested when it is completed. Such tests are likely to be more thorough than those developed after the design is known.

Brooks (1975) also offers the sage advice of 'building one to throw away'. The idea here is to make a quick and dirty working model of the final program. The more academic but less evocative name for this is *rapid prototyping*, which has been mentioned before. The early working model, built as part of the feasibility study or the requirements definition, allows the human interface to be checked with the actual users: users find it difficult to imagine the skeleton of the requirement specifications covered with the flesh of implementation and working. Having a prototype that can actually be tried out avoids the problem of users discovering, when the new program finally arrives, that it does not work the way they expected. Even with the best of modifiable designs, some major changes to the requirements are bound to be very expensive. In addition, Zave (1982) maintains that prototypes help with the design process. Building one to throw away is not an instance of premature implementation provided that:

- this is the announced intention at the beginning and not a *post hoc* rationalization for discarding a failed implementation and
- it is in fact thrown away.

This is a situation where many of the techniques of making a program modifiable can and should be discarded. 'Can' because the prototype by definition is not intended to have a long life and therefore will only be modified to a very limited extent. 'Should' because making the prototype difficult to modify will reduce the chances of an attempt being made to patch it into producthood.

2.4 THE PROGRAMMING TEAM

In the previous chapter, we gave a brief description of a chief programmer team, consisting of a small group of specialists under the direct control of the chief programmer. The members of the team were each skilled in a particular area of program development. Although I will discuss the particular tasks within the context of the chief programmer team, the set of skills required are common to all team arrangements, from the most autocratic to the most democratic. If the team consists of just one member, that member must have all the skills and be prepared to work in all areas. In addition, objective self-examination being foreign to human nature, a single author team will not have the benefit of the constructive criticism produced in design reviews and code reading. Such quality control activities must be obtained from an external source acting intermittently as the adversary. Some idea of the range of skills required for developing a program can be gained from the following list of specialists that are usually recruited to work on a chief programmer team of the traditional form. However, it must be understood that just because a task is given the pomp of a sub-section to itself does not mean that it defines a person's entire task in the team – although in the case of Tester this is likely. This part of the discussion is based largely upon Brooks (1975). Before discussing the different jobs, we will look at more conventional ways of organizing programming teams.

2.4.1 Team organizations

Programming was not always a team sport. Initially, the programmer worked alone as a kind of knight errant performing heroic deeds single-handedly against incredible odds. There are still many lone programmers who see themselves in this role. This view of the programmer as derring dooer is captured in an unfortunately unpublished essay by Martin Hopkins, *The Programmer as Hero*, from which the following is excerpted:

> Programmers tend to view their profession in heroic terms and they are the heroes. An understanding of this deep rooted and usually unconscious belief explains much about the choices programmers make and the way they behave . . . There are many parallels between the hero and the programmer. The hero steps into the unknown in quest of something, perhaps the Holy Grail (a working program). He overcomes many difficulties, slaying monsters (bugs), before returning to give his priceless treasure (Prometheus' fire or the working program) to a grateful world. No matter how much they may protest, the vast majority of programmers view programming and debugging to be a heroic quest. This explains the desire to make a new start on a program rather than modify an old one, like the Arthurian Knights who refused to begin their search for the Grail on the beaten path. Each selected a portion of the

wood to begin their search where there was no path, because it would be dishonorable to follow in another's footsteps.

A paradox of the heroic view, whether in programming or elsewhere, is the ambivalence toward technological assistance. Classical Greece considered their iron age culture to be crueler and less heroic than the bronze age when Achilles and Hector battled on the plains of Troy. So too the programmer with a heroic view, which means any programmer worth his salt, looks back to those halcyon times when he hand optimized for the IBM 650 and mentally rejects the whole baggage of operating systems and compilers. Certain technology is permissible such as bronze swords, IBM 001 pure numeric key punches with no printer, one card loaders and hopelessly slow paper tape readers with a waste basket for a wind-up reel. Such pieces of technology are like King Arthur's sword Excalibur and it is beside the point to argue that a more modern device such as a graphic display is better.

One of the most striking similarities between programming and heroic adventure is that both are basically solitary endeavors. However, in the past, heroes and programmers have sometimes congregated. Programmers call this a *project* while the ancients seem to have had no term to describe a group of heroes such as the Argonauts. But every programmer remembers that great adventure of a project in which all voyagers on his Argo were possessed of heroic qualities and all performed superhuman feats of coding and checkout like Jason and Hercules competing at the oars. This is an ideal world of camaraderie among the chosen.

Both programmers and heroes rely on trickery. Odysseus used it on many occasions as did Perseus to slay the Gorgon. One may doubt whether reliance on such trickery was ever statistically a good strategy, for the cleverness which will fix the last bug seems to cause programmers more than their share of grief. Completing a program can be as endless an endeavor as the task of Sisyphus, who was doomed to push a rock up a hill only to have it roll to the bottom just before it reached the top. A program which has that sort of quality can clearly only be saved by some unexpected good fortune bestowed by the gods. Programmers seem to hope that like Oedipus, they will solve the riddle of the Sphinx – the last bug.

The myth of Sisyphus can also serve as a metaphor for maintaining any large system like MVS or VMS, but it is only one of numerous metaphors for the programming process. The Labyrinth, a maze, created by the legendary craftsman Daedalus, is surely a description of any large operating system, not only because of its complexity, but because there lurked within it the savage Minotaur, ever ready to destroy the adventurer who attempted to penetrate the maze. The programmer who is debugging a large system environment can hardly help but feel himself to be a successor to Theseus who slew the Minotaur after solving the secret of the labyrinth. Ariadne's thread is surely a chain of control blocks. The Hydra, with her snake-like heads which grow back when cut off, is a compelling metaphor for debugging a program. There are hundreds of appropriate myths from many cultures so a programmer cannot avoid knowing about some heroes. As the heroic legends have basic similarities a programmer will inevitably conclude that he is engaged in a heroic activity.

The knight-errant approach to programming was replaced by the human tide of programmers, who trampled the problem to death leaving a landscape that users could not make productive – there were always hidden pitfalls and booby traps. Now we have the specialized programming task force constituted to carry out a particular mission, and bonded with a strong *esprit de corps*.

The chief programmer team stands between the horde and the task force. In organization, it represents one end of the team spectrum; its most autocratic end. The chief programmer is the ultimate authority in the team who must make all decisions and through whom all information must be funnelled. In political terms, it would be called a totalitarian regime. As we have already pointed out, there is a great difficulty in finding a capable chief programmer and there is a danger that the team's leader will become overloaded by the myriad decisions that must be made. The strict definition of the chief programmer team organization does not allow for any delegation of responsibility – everything must be done by the leader. Returning to the political metaphor, it is difficult to find a truly benevolent dictator, but, when one can be found, the dictatorship makes a worthy adversary for other systems both in the political and programming arena.

At the other end of the spectrum of team organizations is the 'democratic team', first described by Weinberg (1971) as the 'egoless team'. Egoless is probably a misnomer – the team members will still have egos, but, for the good of the project, they will keep them tightly leashed. In this kind of team organization the goals and major technical decisions are made by group consensus, though often a leader is named. The position of leader may rotate through the members of the team according to the requirements of the project. Actually, a democratic team is not quite the same as an egoless team in that, in the democratic team, one member is named as leader and remains in that position for the duration of the project. Among the advantages of this kind of organization is the ability of each team member to learn from the others and to contribute to the decisions of the group. Mantei (1981) suggests that the democratic team is well suited to long-term research and development projects and that the team members may remain together for many years. I have worked with a colleague for nearly fifteen years, most of the time as a two-person team where we attempted to make our roles interchangeable. Each one of us could do any job involved with the project and there was the tacit agreement between us that we would each take the next job that needed to be done, be it administrative or technical. Needless to say, each of us had our specialities but most of these were historical in origin. Because one of us worked on a particular part of a project, he naturally became more experienced in that area; however if one of us had to venture into the other's area of expertise in pursuit of a bug or extension, this was done without hesitation. When one was on vacation, the other was able to work on any part of the project as required. Our decisions were arrived at by consensus, generally involving little discussion. Over this period, we never had a major disagreement. We were very lucky; many partnerships do not have this good fortune. This experience has certainly been an example of an egoless team that has worked.

A mid position between the autocratic team and the democratic team is the hierarchical structure. Such a team has a project leader and a number of senior programmers as subordinates. Each of the senior programmers is responsible for a specific part of the project and the detailed work is carried out by junior programmers. The major disadvantage of this organization is that the senior programmers tend to be functioning more as administrators than as technical leaders. This leads to the difficulties, already discussed, of managers no longer performing technical work despite their experience and ability.

The particular choice of team organization must depend upon the corporate environment and the type of project being undertaken. Mantei (1981) suggests that the chief programmer team is the best for relatively simple projects, particularly where there are severe time constraints. As the programming tasks increase in size, the egoless team is no longer suitable because of the large number of communication paths that must be established between the members of a large team all at the same level where all members need to communicate with all other members.

A compromise position between the extremes is based on the following:

- A small team, three to six members is optimal.
- A chief programmer who is marginally more than less 'autocratic', and the most experienced member of the team being a contender for a chief programmer position when one became available.
- A deputy programmer.
- A mix of specializations and job descriptions that is appropriate to the task and designed to expedite team competence.
- A discipline of quality control practices such as peer review of design and code reading.
- A dedication to 'good software engineering' methods and a willingness to abide by the discipline that this requires.

This recipe will not work without properly qualified, experienced, and motivated team members, adequate technical support in the form of a programming environment, and an administration that is more interested in producing a product of first quality than in rearguard defenses. If the task is breaking new ground, then it is understood that pioneers suffer arrow wounds – that is part of the job description; if the task is run of the mill, then there should be no danger of failure. Such a force can handle jobs requiring about ten person-years. Above that size, the job should be split into multiple task forces with another level of management hierarchy. What must be avoided, outside a research department (and even there it is highly questionable), is a large, democratic, unstructured, apparently homogeneous team where everybody has to communicate with everybody else. This requires $\frac{1}{2}n(n-1)$ lines of communication, which rapidly exceeds manageable bounds. This is another example of the dangers of assuming that scaling up small successes will produce big successes. This was how we got into the software debacle. Programming teams are discussed in Volume 1 (Macro 1990).

Before continuing with the discussion of the members of the chief programmer team, there is another, unfortunately rather common, team organization to be mentioned, the 'relay team'. This consists of specialized groups, 'specifiers', 'designers', 'coders', 'testers', . . . who take on the job in turn, work on it and pass it to the next group. This is ineffective because, in practice, the job does not flow evenly from one phase to the next. There is always some eddying back to a previous phase because a later phase has discovered something that was not done perfectly upstream. If the job has to be passed back to another group, there will be delays because they are by now involved on another job and there will be much time wasted in bureaucratic wrangling.

2.4.2 Chief programmer

A chief programmer is a senior-level programmer who is completely responsible for the implementation of a program. In addition, the chief programmer is involved in the development of the requirements specification and feasibility study and also provides valuable input to the estimation process. All other members of the team report directly to the chief programmer who is the technical manager. In addition to these managerial functions, the chief programmer performs a number of technical tasks:

- writing and testing the critical nucleus of the program,
- specifying and integrating all design and programming tasks for the project,
- checking the quality of the work of the members of the team by reading a large amount of the code written by them.

Two of the major problems with chief programmer teams are related to the chief programmer: finding a suitably qualified person who has the necessary skills in both the technical and administrative areas is very difficult, and, since the chief programmer must make all decisions, there is a considerable danger of saturation at the top level. This can lead to the second problem, namely poor information flow, which can be detrimental to the work at the lower levels.

2.4.3 Deputy chief programmer

The deputy chief programmer is the chief programmer's shadow – able to do any part of the job, but less experienced. One of the main jobs for the deputy chief programmer is to act as devil's advocate in technical discussions with the chief programmer. As the term 'deputy chief programmer' implies, the function also serves as insurance against losing the chief programmer. In any important project no member should be indispensable; the chief programmer is no exception to this rule.

2.4.4 Administrator

A chief programmer team is under the direction of the chief programmer, whose main concern is the technical leadership of the team. In order to assist the chief programmer with the administrative details of running the team, the services of a professional administrator will be used. Since the chief programmer teams are generally small (three to six people typically), administrative tasks will not require all of the administrator's time which will often be shared between several such teams. The use of the services of an administrator is a departure from the industrial norm where it is more usual for the administrator to command the team even though the project is very technical in nature and the administrator has little or no technical experience. It is assumed that the administrator will seek technical advice from competent people before making the decisions. When the job is very large, requiring several chief programmer teams, it is possible that the teams will be under the management of a senior administrator. However, each of the teams will be under the direction of the chief programmer. If the person in charge of the team is an administrator to whom the chief programmer is responsible then it is no longer a chief programmer team.

2.4.5 Editor

One of the components of the outcome of the implementation phase is documentation. While it is reasonable to expect that all programmers have good if not excellent communication skills, Dijkstra once said that the most important language for a programmer to know was his native language; however, the production of good training materials and reference manuals require experience beyond that of the average programmer. The editor takes the draft manuscript produced by the chief programmer and the programmers on the team, edits, reworks it, passes it through several versions with input coming both from the editor and the original authors, and oversees the mechanics of production. As with the administrator, the services of a full-time editor are not usually required and the editor's time is shared between several teams.

2.4.6 Secretary

In a project of any size, there is bound to be a need for secretarial help. Both the administrator and the editor will certainly have correspondence that needs handling. On projects requiring large implementation teams – above twenty say, suitably arranged into small three to six person teams – a project secretary is often assigned.

2.4.7 Librarian

The librarian is responsible for all the technical records of the project generically known as *the archive* and fully discussed in Volume 1, Chapter 11. In order to protect these records, certain procedures must be followed by the librarian. To some extent the librarian's function is similar to that of a divisional financial controller in a large corporation. There are certain accounting procedures that must be followed and the divisional controller is responsible for ensuring that they are. In this, the controller is responsible to the corporation's central management and not to the division's management. Thus, the local management cannot instruct the divisional controller to ignore some of the standard procedures. Similarly, the chief programmer cannot instruct the librarian to circumvent some of the procedures designed to protect the project's records. In the same vein, some organizations have a quality control team, outside the individual project teams, to help ensure that this, and other agreed procedures, are followed correctly.

Nowadays, with the almost universal use of terminals and various software tools, much of the manual component of the librarian's function has been taken over by the computer. However, the *function is still required* since the project's records are a vital part of the project. Hence, when the librarian's function is subsumed into software tools, care must be taken through the use of access control and logs that no one, not even the chief programmer, can interfere with their proper operation.

2.4.8 Tester

The function of the tester is to test for and demonstrate errors in the program. These tests are devised from the program's specifications and by studying the actual code looking for any error or weakness where, for example, a division-by-zero could conceivably occur.

A good general rule is that the person who tests an integrand or program should be different from the person who wrote it. Indeed, this should be generalized to separating the group that does the testing from the group that develops the program. In both cases, the authors know or think they know too much about the program and therefore will make assumptions about what does not need testing. The mindset of a good tester must be somewhat different from that of the normal project manager. Myers (1979) summarizes it this way:

> Most project managers call a test case that did not find an error a 'successful test run', whereas a test that discovers a new error is usually called 'unsuccessful'. This is often a sign that the wrong definition of testing is being used, for the word 'successful' denotes an achievement and the word 'unsuccessful' denotes something undesirable or disappointing. However, since a test case that does not find an error is largely a waste of time and money, the descriptor 'successful' seems inappropriate . . . Program testing is more properly viewed as the destructive process of trying to find the errors (whose presence is assumed) in a program. A successful test case is one that furthers progress in this direction by causing the program to fail.

One might characterize a successful tester as one who has the unfortunately common human trait of being able to find errors committed by others developed to an above average extent. Coupled to this must be an ingenious and devious mind that can search for tests that will expose errors in the program.

2.4.9 Toolsmith

In addition to the normal software tools, which are nowadays called the *Programming Support Environment*, PSE, comprising editor, language, linker, word processor, and so on, there is always a need for software tools that are not included as part of the system. For example, a utility that takes two lists, List1 and List2 and constructs three lists whose names are InList1AndNotList2, InList2AndNotList1, and InList1AndList2 is not generally available yet is very useful for managing lists of files. As well as tools of general use, a project often has need for special-purpose tools that embody the standard procedures used by the project, for example, those discussed as automating much of the project librarian function. If the project consists of implementing a program that will run on special-purpose hardware or make use of unusual peripherals, there will certainly be a need for special tools to help debug the program. The programmer who specializes in building tools has a rather special view of programs. Most tools are interactive and therefore must be written to make their use as easy as possible. A tool that is difficult to use will not be used because it will be felt that the service it offers is not worth the trouble of using it. One could make the analogy to a screwdriver with a handle of triangular cross-section – if it is gripped tightly enough to turn the screw, it hurts the hand. Tools are also a particular example of programs that are being constantly improved and extended and must be designed and implemented accordingly. In any team of more than ten programmers, there will be a need for at least one full-time toolmaker. These tools can, for example, enshrine the project's procedures for managing the project library or build tables of data to be used by the program.

The major tool of a programmer is the programming language itself. Some programmers pride themselves on knowing all the details of the programming language; others have to use the reference manual. There are always details that are not covered by the manual. Sometimes the question to be answered requires a combination of knowing what should happen in the language versus what actually happens in a particular implementation. This may be a question of the difference between an error in the compiler or an error in the reference manual. In either case, the problem must be discussed with the suppliers of the compiler and resolved, either by modifying the compiler or the reference manual. If it is a compiler error, work may need to be done to find a way of working around the problem so that the function can still be used while waiting for the compiler to be fixed. In all these cases, the programmer with a special interest and knowledge of the language is critically useful to the project. This also falls into the province of the toolsmiths, together with a knowledge of the hardware, requirements, standards (for project management, documentation, and acceptance) and other tools provided by the PSE are also involved here. They must not only make new tools but must be thoroughly knowledgeable about all aspects of the programming process.

2.4.10 Programmer

The programmer too is a specialist. The major difference between the team member working as a specialist and the other team members with more impressive titles is that of experience. Every specialist must *start off* as a generalist otherwise the view of the wider context will be missing and decisions will be made on the basis of too limited a scope. To take the analogy back to the world of medicine, a specialist of diseases of the left big toe will see the entire body as an appendage of the left big toe. All symptoms will be seen as results of some disorder of the left big toe. A programming project needs programmers who can take a general view of the system. Ultimately, it is the programmers of the project who are going to do the bulk of the work.

2.5 THE DESIGN PROCESS

The aim of design is to produce a structure; something that has strength and the ability to sustain loads, to be *robust*. The great cathedrals of Europe are structures that show an elegance of design and strength to resist the forces of nature. Occasionally, the unity of design has not been carried through, as in the cathedral at Chartres where the two towers are designed differently; when this happens, the mismatch stands out. Most large programs show little of the unity of design of the cathedrals. The symptoms stand out just as starkly as the difference between the towers at Chartres.

Where there is lack of proper fit between the units of the structure, fragility and instability result. When we were young and built structures of wooden blocks, try as we might, there was always a limit to the height to which we could build. It was not the strength of the blocks but the imperfections in the junctions between the bricks that led to instability and eventual collapse. Or perhaps, we built houses out of playing cards; where the boundaries between the units were very tenuous and if we tried to modify the shape of a room at one end of the house, we were likely to see a collapse at the other end. The analogy between these two fragile structures of our youth and many computer programs is uncomfortably close.

The task of the software designer is to produce software that, *if competently implemented*, will withstand the buffeting of the elements and will allow modification without the collapse of apparently unrelated sections. To achieve this, the whole of the software structure must have a design where the components fit each other. To pursue the architectural metaphor a little further, the pyramids have withstood the elements, even though the basic unit of their construction is a simple block without mortar, because the blocks fitted to each other so well. The software design has to define the integrands that are to form the program so that their boundaries, *interfaces*, are simple and match perfectly.

2.5.1 Abstraction

One of the most daunting things about computer programs is the myriad details that are involved. The only escape from this is through *abstraction*, the art of discarding the inessential. First, we must distinguish between two kinds of abstraction: *abstraction of form* and *abstraction of content*. As an illustration of the difference, consider the abstraction of form which might have been obtained from the following description;

The cat, Fred, which ate six mice and a parrot every day and existed only in the mind of Erwin Schrödinger, sat on the once pink and now badly stained mat licking its paws like lollipops.

which is an abstraction of content since there are many details that have been suppressed, for example, the number of hairs on the cat's tail. A further abstraction of content of that sentence is

The cat sat on the mat.

A more formal abstraction of form is

$[c]$ s $[m]$

which is expressed in a syntax that the reader can guess.

Computers are basically such simple devices that every action must be broken down into a sequence of baby steps for execution. We can think of sorting as a single action without considering a specific method for sorting. Indeed, the verb *to sort* represents a number of different techniques with varying characteristics such as time to carry out the operation. The command sort allows us to represent any of these methods without specifying exactly which one; it is an *abstraction*, a method of conceptual simplification through the suppression of details. Note that, contrary to popular belief, the process of abstraction does not necessarily require an abstract notation – sort is very near to natural language.

Abstraction assists us in software design chiefly through *process abstraction* and *data abstraction*. When performed in natural language, these abstractions are for *verbs* and *nouns* respectively. Process abstraction affords a powerful simplification by allowing us to designate a process without specifying the details. The power of this mechanism is further enhanced through the use of parameters, which permit different parameter values to be bound to the process on different invocations. Sometimes, it is possible to group similar processes under a single name, with automatic selection between the members of the group based on the type of the parameter values. This is called *overloading* and is described in Section 1.4.5. To be able to use overloading for user-defined processes is another powerful abstraction mechanism.

Data abstraction allows the programmer to define a data type by specifying the operations that can be performed on values of that type without defining the specific representation. For example, the data type Stack can be defined abstractly through the operations NewStack, Top, Pop, Push, and IsEmpty. Such data types are abstract in the sense that the details of the representation and how the operations are carried out are hidden inside the actual processes that perform the operations.

These abstraction mechanisms allow algorithms to be written in a simple manner. They are therefore able to serve the essential purpose of communicating a description of the process to the reader without burying it in a welter of detail. The reader can thus appreciate the forest without being distracted by a description of every leaf. If too much is specified, we rapidly suffer from overload and abandon any attempt at understanding – the role of program as communicator has then failed. It is only through abstraction that it can succeed.

2.5.2 Modularity

A program that is *modular* is one that consists of well-defined integrands, each of a manageable size and complexity and with properly specified interfaces between them. The opposite of a modular program is a monolithic program like Big Bertha described in Section 1.3.2. Each of the integrands constitutes an abstraction that localizes some aspect of the total problem being solved. In a well-designed system, the integrands are such that:

1. Each integrand has a single, well-defined purpose. Since there is only a single purpose, everything contained in the integrand is part of the implementation of this purpose. This makes the integrand easier to understand.
2. The integrands can be organized in a hierarchically dependent way, that is, higher members of the hierarchy invoke lower ones. Such an arrangement constitutes a sub-system that is potentially useful in other applications. A hierarchical organization improves information hiding and makes understanding, implementation, debugging, testing, integration, and modification easier.

Splitting programs in this way is one of the keys to clarity. Since the integrands are of an intellectually manageable size, the way in which they implement their interface can be understood. This understanding may be made easier through the use of abstractions implemented by other integrands. The next sub-section introduces the two principal criteria used for separating a program into integrands.

2.5.3 Coupling and unity of purpose

Two integrands that could function completely without each other's presence are said to be *independent*. There would be no interconnections of any sort between these integrands. Since there are no interconnections between them, modifying one of them could not affect the execution of the other. Since the integrands of a program must communicate with each other in order to perform their function, it is inevitable that there are interconnections between the integrands. The greater the number of interconnections, the greater the difficulty of modifying one without having to make compensating changes in the other. The term *coupling* was introduced in Stevens *et al.* (1974) as a measure of the degree of interconnection between integrands. If two integrands are highly coupled, there is a strong probability that a change to one will require a change to the other.

The term *interconnection* needs some explanation. An interconnection is an assumption made in one integrand about another. Such an interconnection can be obvious and explicit like the data that are passed from one to another through the argument–parameter relationship. It can be less explicit like the sharing of a global variable, or it can be subtle like the assumption that execution of one integrand will leave a file on a particular disk. Generally, the fewer the interconnections the lower the coupling between a pair of integrands and the more explicit the interconnection the lower the coupling.

Choosing a design that keeps the coupling low will give integrands that are more independent and hence easier to understand because there is less knowledge required about the other integrands. This makes the task of modification easier and more likely to be successful. Thus the aim of good software design should be to minimize the coupling. Coupling refers to the relation between integrands, it is an *inter*-integrand quality. There is a companion measure that concerns the elements within an integrand; this is an *intra*-integrand measure. If all the elements of an integrand are concerned with the performance of a single function, we can say that the integrand has *unity of purpose*. Stevens *et al.* (1974) use the term *cohesion*; other terms used to denote the same concept are *modular strength*, *binding*, and *functionality*.

The terms *coupling* and *unity of purpose* can be illustrated through analogy with a hi-fi system, which consists of several integrands: an amplifier, a tape-deck, a record player, a compact disk player, a radio tuner, and, depending on the degree to which the owner's ears or passing bats are to be flattered, one or more loudspeakers. The coupling between these integrands is through co-axial cables carrying the sound signal and through the power lines that are connected to a single on–off switch on the amplifier. Each of these channels has a well-defined protocol, a.c. current at the appropriate voltage and frequency and sound waves within a defined band-width and voltage variation. The integrands have good unity of purpose, each of their functions is fully contained within the integrand – there is, for example, no element of control of the laser used to read the compact disk contained in the tape-deck and the details of the encoding of the audio signal on the compact disk are all hidden in the player. Because of this, adjustment to new technology is possible. If compact disks with a different encoding are made available, replacement of only the player will bring the system up to date.

Both coupling and unity of purpose have considerable effect on the maintainability of a program. If an integrand has high unity of purpose then it is only likely to require modification if the function that it performs has to be changed. It would be less likely to require modification when functions that are the responsibility of other integrands are changed. If the signal encoding for compact disks is changed, nothing in the tape-deck needs to be modified. Further, the more true it is that all elements of an integrand are concerned with a single function, the more likely it is that the integrand will perform all parts of the function. Thus a change to the function is likely to be concentrated entirely within the single module.

2.5.4 Information hiding

The Stack data type discussed above could be represented in a number of ways, for example, as a linked list or as an array. If the routines that perform the operations NewStack, Top, Pop, Push, and IsEmpty are the only places where the actual method of representation of the Stack is recorded, then we can say that this information is 'hidden' in these routines. To do this would require that other integrands can make use of the operations without making use of the representation information. Within these integrands, a Stack value would be represented by a pointer. (This assumes untyped pointers or, at least, dynamically typed pointers, as in PL/I. Languages like Pascal, Modula, and Ada, require the use of variant records; however, this reduces the information hiding. The approach of object-oriented languages, discussed in Section 1.4.5, also achieves information hiding in this application.) Doing this allows the freedom to change the representation of Stack values without modifying the integrands that use them. Provided the interfaces with the operations are maintained, only the routines that perform the operations need to be changed.

This is the principle of *information hiding* first formulated in Parnas (1971). Parnas' principle was that the design phase should be begun with the most difficult design decisions and the ones that are most likely to change. The results of these decisions should be hidden inside an integrand; this will localize the scope of the modifications should the decisions be changed later. The example of hiding the representation of the Stack data type is a typical instance of information hiding.

In the early operating systems, the layout of control blocks such as those that managed files was 'public' and programmers who needed access to the information contained in these blocks referenced them through standard definitions. However, the layout of these blocks was changed frequently, which required consequent changes or at least recompilation of all the integrands that referenced these blocks. A small change then became a bookkeeping job of identifying all the integrands that required recompilation – a task that could be automated but too often was, and still is, not.

One of the great schisms of computer hardware is the internal representation of characters. One might have expected some consistency in this area within a single natural language but this is not so. Neither the actual bit patterns used to represent the characters nor their ordering is always consistent. While it is true that the sequence of letters in the alphabet is ordered consistently and the sequence of digits is as one might expect, everything else is arbitrary. The two most popular character encodings are the ASCII set, which is a standard in Europe and the United States and the EBCDIC scheme of IBM. In the ASCII code, the digits precede the letters; in EBCDIC, the letters come first. (An even more awkward property is that the '~' has been defined into a gap in the middle of the letters – which was there because the physical strength of punched cards made it prudent to avoid holes punched in neighboring rows!) A consequence of this is that if a program that involves the sorting of textual information is to be made available on different hardware, the details of the character set used must be hidden.

Coupling and unity of purpose are not independent though the relationship is a complex one. A monolithic program has the lowest possible coupling and has the lowest

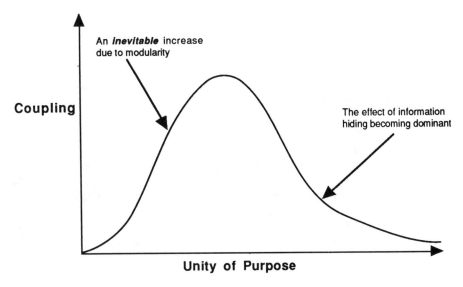

FIGURE 2.4 Notional relationship between unity of purpose and cohesion under strict information hiding.

unity of purpose unless we define 'purpose' as 'performing the whole requirement' instead of making a single decision. In the absence of strict information hiding, the relationship between unity of purpose and coupling seems likely to be non-linear, monotonically *increasing*. With strict information hiding, the relationship may be like the graph shown in Figure 2.4. After the increase due to modularity, the decrease in coupling as unity of purpose increases reflects the fact that the integrands have less need for them to make assumptions about each other.

From the practical point of view, the software designer should pose the questions 'Do these things belong together?' and 'Does the function performed by this integrand make sense in the context of the real-world process being modeled?' This second question is particularly important since the designer must never lose sight of the fact that it is a real-world process that is being modeled. To forget the relationship between the model and the real-world process is a sure step to speedy obsolescence because, as the real world changes, there will be no corresponding part of the model to be changed.

2.5.5 Aesthetics

The design of software, for all its abstraction, has many points in common with the design of buildings, bridges, and other structures. In particular, simplicity, elegance, and clarity of purpose are important. These qualities fall under the general title of aesthetics. There is a strong connection between software design and mathematics. In many universities, the study of computers started as an offshoot of the mathematics department, and there is a great deal of mathematical theory that applies to the study of programs and algorithms. This connection extends to the aesthetic considerations of programs.

The aesthetic appeal of mathematics has been the subject of many authors. The English mathematician G. H. Hardy wrote that 'The mathematician's patterns, like the painter's or the poet's, must be beautiful'. The term *mathematical elegance* is sometimes used to describe equations and proofs. Later in this book, I shall discuss 'style' and 'clarity' in writing programs. We shall see that attempts, though to my mind not very credible ones, have been made to quantify these attributes, almost as if something that cannot be measured does not exist. Nevertheless, we can recognize what we feel to be beauty when we see it, though we may not agree that a particular item is beautiful. Well written programs, even if they are incorrect, please good programmers, because they show evidence of craftsmanship. Not only are such programs less likely to contain errors than poorly written ones, but any errors that they contain will be more obvious and easily corrected. Beauty and comprehensibility in software are strongly correlated and the designer should apply aesthetic considerations to the design of software.

2.6 THE CRAFT OF PROGRAMMING

2.6.1 What the programmer does

Since 1958, I have spent by far the largest part of my working hours programming, yet I find it very difficult to describe to those of my family and friends who have not spent some part of their lives programming what it is exactly that I do. The statement 'write programs' is so trite as to merit unpleasant retribution.

As I see it, the programmer's function is to compose sequences of computer instructions that will cause a computer to solve a given problem. In addition, the objectives of programming are to cause the software to have the following properties, keeping in mind that software is the dynamic behavior of programs on the computer and associated equipment for which they were intended:

- *Software must behave reliably.* That is, under all circumstances short of genuine hardware malfunction, the computer will produce correct results or, if the input data are nonsensical, provide a response informing the user of this. This is the aim to which I aspire but which I do not always achieve. This implies that I will not knowingly pass on to the users a program with errors. If it is incomplete, then the points at which there is more to be implemented will be protected with messages to the invoker. (Throughout this paragraph, the term 'invoker' refers to the process, human or machine, that invokes the program. The style and syntax of the messages will vary with the type of invoker.) The view, seen in some systems, that it is acceptable for the program to terminate in disarray, 'crash', if the invoker provides invalid data is not good enough. There should be no input that the invoker can provide that will cause the system to crash. This means that the program must be designed so that reasonableness checks are made on all input and helpful diagnostic messages are given if the data fail the test.

- *Software must be usable*. This requirement implies that a program does not exist by itself but must be accompanied by some documentation that describes how it is to be used. Without the documentation, the program is not usable. This documentation is not necessarily in printed form but may be provided to the user interactively.
- *Software must treat the user with courtesy*. This does not mean giving saccharined little messages like 'Thank you and have a nice day!' which become grating after the twentieth time. It means giving messages that are helpful rather than guilt-inducing. I recently attempted to use an interactive system on which I had a valid account. I entered my identifier and I immediately got the message

```
LOGON FAILED
```

and nothing more. This was a level beyond the already aggressive

```
ILLEGAL USER ID
```

which commonly happened if I mistyped my identifier or password. This time, it did not even get as far as asking me for my password before rejecting me. The message LOGON FAILED seemed to mean 'You've failed the first test of userhood so badly we're not even going to tell you what was wrong!' There was no way that I could ask the system for help or for an explanation. This was the final verdict and there was no appeal. One immediately felt transferred to the world of Franz Kafka where the bureaucrats, on principle, do not tell the ordinary citizen anything. It might be argued that such boorish behavior was a deliberate attempt to deter illegal trespassing by hackers; however, such attackers are by definition thick-skinned and persistent. Politeness need not compromise security. Messages must be in language that the user understands. This implies that the user should have some say in choosing the messages and that they should be defined in the Requirements Definition. Unpleasant messages from computers are not limited to interactive terminals. I receive statements from medical insurance companies that I am unable to parse and bills from a credit card organization that have

```
110110100111000101010100010001110100100101001
```

printed across the foot of the page. I have no idea what this means. Clearly it is intended only for the administrators of the system. It might mean 'Watch out for this client, he always pays his bills late' or something equally derogatory. I was always taught that it was bad manners to whisper in public and this is a sort of electronic whispering in public. A good guide in designing what messages and output is sent to the users is that they should obey the standard rules of etiquette. Be courteous – for example:

```
I could not understand that input
```

is better than

```
Invalid input
```

Unfortunately, there is an attitude among some programmers that unpleasant human interfaces are a fundamental characteristic of computers caused by the limitations of the hardware. This is not true. They are the result of bad design and poor programming practice. The subject of the interface with the users is part of the discipline of *human factors* and is beyond the scope of this book, however; two good references are Mehlmann (1981) and Rubinstein and Hersh (1985).

- *Software must be relatively easy to modify*. We have already seen that programs have to be modified if they are to continue to be useful. The programmer must therefore aim to produce programs that can be changed relatively easily. I use the term 'relatively easily' here because all code is trivially easy to change – just change a statement! The much more difficult task is to make the change *correctly*, in such a way that the change also preserves the program's good structure (assuming that it had good structure to start with – changing programs that are poorly structured is a separate subject taken up in Chapter 14). In previous sections, we have discussed some of the design considerations that are required for ease of modification, in particular the splitting of the program into integrands and the principle of information hiding.

  Ease of modification also requires that the programmer who is making the changes should feel sure that the changes are correct. While any changes must be followed by careful testing, this does not mean that programming is an experimental science except when the user is unable to understand the documentation for some software and must make some experiments to discover what should have been apparent from the documentation. A program is *like* a hypothesis undergoing demonstration (alpha-testing of a benevolent if exacting sort), and falsification (beta-testing, which must – for one aspect of quality, *compliance* – be exhaustive).

  The programmer, generally not the original author, who modifies a program, must be able to understand the program and build a good mental image of how the program works before starting to make a modification. The outline of this mental image should generally be obtained from some good documentation of the design. When the code has been studied, it should be clear how it corresponds to the design and should complete the mental image. Without this mental image, we are unlikely to make successful modifications. Thus, the requirement for ease of modification also requires the programmer to produce programs that can be easily understood. This emphasizes the communication role of programs and the need for the programmer to keep this in mind during the creation of the program.

- *Software should be reuseable*. One of the most wasteful aspects of programming is that we are constantly rewriting the same program with only minor variations. This is because we have not, in the past, made the effort to design programs to be useable in more than one context. One of the major advances in industrialization was the idea of standard parts, for example, nuts and bolts, that could be used in many different contexts without having to be made especially for a particular application. Without standard parts, the modern production line would be almost impossible. Responsibility for achieving reuseability lies with a number of phases of the life-cycle:

  1. *During the specification phase*, the specifier can define common features over requirements. This has to be done very skillfully otherwise it results in large (allegedly reusable) programs that create problems at the design and implementa-

tion level – such as efficiency of use and efficiency of execution. Spotting such 'specification commonality' is a management problem.

2. *During the design phase*, the designer can design utilities. These are usually small software packages or subroutines. Here, there is less difficulty in identifying the commonality and using the result.

3. *During the implementation phase*, the programmer will often make use of small chunks of reusable code that can be easily adopted or adapted for other purposes. I frequently use the editor to make use of parts of other integrands in the construction of a new integrand.

Because of the many levels of responsibility, true reuseability may be elusive. Managers expect reuseability at the specification level, programmers produce it at the implementation level. Nevertheless, when a programmer implements an integrand, it is important to consider how it could be generalized. Good structured programming practice helps up to a point – unity of purpose, as in mathematical routines such as LogFunction or SquareRoot, and makes reuse easy to identify and implement with minimal coupling.

- *Should execute efficiently*. There are two types of efficiency: time and space (that is, execution time and object space), which *may not be independent*. There are two approaches to attaining efficiency, which we may term *macro-efficiency*, which treats the system globally, and *micro-efficiency*, which has a local view.

  In optimization for time, macro-efficiency is concerned with the choice of the proper algorithm so that the process is performed efficiently; for example, choosing the appropriate sort routine depending upon the number of items that are expected to be sorted or arranging a list so that it can be searched efficiently. This is the proper realm of the programmer. Micro-efficiency is concerned with making minor optimizations in the belief that the saving of a few machine cycles here and there will be advantageous even at the risk of loss of program clarity and modifiability. Often these local optimizations inhibit larger-scale optimizations that can be performed automatically by the compiler. 'Micro-optimization' is often the misplaced dominant interest of the amateur programmer. When it is, it prevents – or, at best, undermines – good program design practice. Such optimization must *follow*, not lead, the creation of well-structured programs, that is, optimizing from strength, or 'tuning'.

  Efficient execution may be only one aspect of the efficiency issue; in some applications program and data space may be important. In the world of large mainframes, space is usually plentiful. At the other end of the computer size range, the microprocessor embedded in a dishwasher or microprocessor may be desperately short of space. There, every byte saved is magnified by the number of replications of the device – in an appliance that sells very well, each byte is the equivalent of a megabyte! Conventional wisdom has it that run-time efficiency can be traded-off against space and 'modularity'. While this can occur in some cases, it is impossible to generalize and each situation must be evaluated according to accurate measurements. This question will be returned to in Section 10.4.4.

- *Software may have to be portable*. This means that the program should be written in such a way that it can be moved to another machine and produce the same result. True portability, that is when the program, without modification, performs identically on two machines, is very difficult to achieve because the virtual machines represented by their compilers are unlikely to match due to hardware differences – for example, in the way in which floating point arithmetic is performed. Many years ago, I had an assembler language program that executed to normal completion on one model of the IBM 360 and terminated abnormally on another. It turned out that I had unwittingly made use of some effects that were not part of the 360's behavior, as defined in its Principles of Operation. In order to make the transfer of a program to another machine as easy as possible:

1. Avoid dependence upon particular features of the underlying virtual computer, for example, specific floating point, or character representations. Where such dependencies are inevitable, for instance, in arithmetic precision, or timing, there should be some easy way in which the dependencies can be identified mechanically and, if it is not possible to automate the modifications, lead the programmer through the places that need to be changed to the new requirements.
2. Adopt a popular language that is likely to have a compiler on other machines. Unfortunately, some widely implemented languages do not support good software engineering practices very well; for example, the language C is widely implemented but does not have adequate type checking.
3. Make sure that the program is well specified and documented.
4. Separate I/O and logic into different integrands – the logic is likely to be unchanged in the move whereas the I/O is very likely to be rewritten.

2.6.2 There is more to programming than writing programs

It is easy to think that all that a programmer does is write programs. I realize that many organizations reserve the term *programmer* strictly for someone whose function is to code programs and test them. Jackson (1975) takes a broader and more realistic view when he says:

> Traditionally, programming is distinct from system design. The system designer, usually called 'systems analyst', decides what files and programs are needed in the system, and specifies these for the programmer; the programmer then writes his programs according to the designer's specifications. This traditional division of labour is absurd: it has had several damaging effects on our understanding of computer systems and on the way we build them . . . it has helped to perpetuate the primitive idea, derived from the earliest batch-processing systems, that there is a hard boundary between the tasks of system design and program design. We expect to apply different techniques and different design criteria, and to use different tools, when the elements of our design are programs and files from those we apply and use when the elements are subroutines, machine instructions and core storage.

Most often forgotten is a sizeable non-technical component to the job. This might be described as 'Manage and be managed'. All programmers have to *administer* their own work – if only by organizing an archive for their working documents, making activities plans, etc. They also have to *coordinate* with co-workers, and to make reports to their management. This is an essential aspect of the programming task and an understanding of this fact is what often separates professional programmers from amateurs.

As can be seen from the set of requirements that a program must satisfy before it passes from the programmer's hands, there are many other facets to the task. Depending upon the environment in which the programmer works, the job may include the following elements:

1. *Designing*. This may involve the low-level design of a complete program, using the principles of system design as discussed in Section 2.2.3, or it may require the design of an individual integrand, which may need to be split into several lower-level integrands. In both cases, the same principles are used, the difference is one of scale. The continuum of design may be, and very often is, done by the same individual.
2. *Writing code*. I use the term 'writing code' to mean the actual task of writing the specific programming language statements that are to form the integrand. As we shall see later in the book, this part of the job is very much like writing any kind of expository text. It involves choosing the proper sequence for the steps and expressing them in as clear a manner as possible.

   All forms of communication depend upon protocol; that is, a set of rules that define the signals that are to be used and their meaning. Without this protocol the communication is formless and is impossible to understand. The protocol may not be explicitly defined; it may be implicit in the context of the communication. For example, the choice of language for written text is usually determined by the nationalities of the author and intended readers. Beyond the rules of grammar imposed by the language, there is generally a set of additional rules designed to assure consistency of spelling, capitalization, punctuation, and abbreviation in the text. For text, these rules are contained in a Style Book, for example, *'The New York Times' Style Book for Writers and Editors*. Unfortunately, there is no equivalent generally accepted manual of style for programmers.

   The requirement for an agreed-upon set of style rules is particularly important in writing programs. Among other things, these rules will define the programming language to be used, the way in which the program is to be set out, and how the names for variables are to be chosen. A comprehensive set of style rules will be invaluable in the production of readable programs. It will also help produce correct programs, because familiarity with a consistent style will make it easier for programmers to read and check the programs produced by their co-workers. Some of the rules, like the number of characters to indent for the body of a loop are essentially arbitrary. It is more important that there be a rule than what the details of the rule are. It will be almost impossible to get consensus on this kind of rule and there should be no attempt at trying to achieve it. Style rules are best established by fiat of a benevolent dictator or by taking them from somebody outside the project, so that no one project member is a butt for complaints, which will die down fairly quickly.

   There is no point in having a set of style rules unless they are followed. This requires *discipline*. There is a commonly held misconception that creativity is stifled by constraining it to a set of rules. In fact, the opposite seems to be true – Bach managed very well with the limited-form cantata, and Shakespeare produced some wonders within the tight metrical and rhyme constraints of the sonnet. The maintenance of a discipline of programming style can have an enormous effect on the success of a software project.

3. *Testing*. Once the code is written, it must be tested. It is the programmer's responsibility to ensure that every path in the integrand has been traversed and produces correct results. This does not mean that the integrand is fully tested, it defines a minimum level of testing before the integrand is passed on to somebody else for complete testing.

4. *Documenting*. Every integrand in a program requires some documentation beyond the source program itself. The very least requirement is that the integrand's interface is specified. Other levels of documentation that may be required from a programmer include the documentation for the user, specifications of the overall implementation design, and data structures. For a programmer, it is not sufficient to know the programming language; facility with the people language is also essential – this means an ability to write clearly in whatever language is used for communication with co-workers and management.

5. *Building tools*. There are always small jobs where the programmer can be assisted by the computer and so part of the programming task is to make small software tools to do these jobs. The habit of building tools is one that needs to be acquired. Once this habit has been acquired, one wonders how one managed before.

6. *Task management*. Despite the fact that programmers are reluctant to think of themselves as 'managers', to complete the job of programming they must always perform some tasks that can only be described as administrative in nature. These include making plans and estimates, preparing reports, organizing structured walkthroughs, scheduling their own time, etc. There are also tasks that are technical in content but none the less administrative in nature; for example, establishing and maintaining archives, installing new versions of software on the computer being used, setting up communication links, designing procedures, which may be purely paperwork or may be implemented in an executable form, for the handling of errors reported by testers or users, and so on. A more complete and detailed list of these tasks is contained in Macro (1990). Conversely, it is also essential that the programmer who is working as part of a team be amenable to *being administered*. Unless the programmer acknowledges the need for both the active and passive forms of administration, the process of producing software will become fixated on the actual artefacts of the task and the expositoriness of the process will be skimped.

7. *Miscellaneous*. Finally, there are always tasks that are difficult to categorize and are generally left off any list. They are so much part of the everyday round of activities that it is hard to bring examples to mind; none the less, they are essential to the programming process. They include such things as helping move equipment, fetching reference books from the library, going to a store to get some needed part or piece of software. I have found that one should approach the profession of programmer with

the willingness to do whatever task is needed to get the job done. No task should be beneath one.

The components of the programmer's function that I have just listed define the job of programming as I see it.

2.6.3 The work environment for the programmer

First, the programmer needs a work environment that allows for great mental concentration. The task of writing a program is one of the most mentally complex jobs that there is. As we have said before, a program is a model of a real-world process; however, it is a completely abstract model. It is made of 'thought stuff', you cannot touch it, feel it, weigh it. It does not really exist except in the mind of the programmer or the reader of the program. It is possible to draw diagrams and flowcharts or to write a program on paper or on the screen of a terminal but these are imperfect depictions of the true program. Any representation that shows all the linkages, control and data flow, becomes so hopelessly complicated that the eye is lost. For true understanding, the programmer must rely on mental images. Consequently, a noisy office with many interruptions is unlikely to produce correct programs.

Managers, unless they have had direct experience of programming *real* programs, generally have no conception of the mental concentration that is required. Often they are sent on *management introductions* to computers during which they use a terminal to write a simple program. From the point of view of the programmers under their direction, such a class may do more harm than good. The managers, fresh from their experience of having *written a computer program*, feel that if they could write a program after only a few hours of introduction, why do their programmers say that it is so difficult? This is another example of the error of assuming that complexity and task size can both be scaled up linearly. Without having had the actual experience of writing a program of some complexity, it is difficult to understand the degree of concentration that is required. As a result, managers often assume that a 'bull pen' environment with many desks separated by low partitions, with no sound deadening, provides an adequate workplace.

Both specification and feasibility prototyping are now commonly accepted as development techniques. Cheap workstations to main hosts make the prototyping possible and the professional programmer should expect no less for preparing programs. With the current level of technology this implies the need for at *least* ready access to a terminal. The terminal should be connected to a computer on which the program will be created. This need not be the computer on which the program is to be executed, but there should be a means of obtaining easy access to it for testing purposes. The computer on which the program is to be created should provide good response. What constitutes 'good' response time is much debated, see for example Miller (1968), but my experience, which accords with Doherty and Kelisky (1979), is that if the delay after a trivial editing action is more than half a second, my train of thought is severely disrupted and my productivity slows down. It is generally agreed that consistent response is important, that is, the delay should be roughly proportional to the complexity of the action required by the computer.

The programmer depends upon software tools to assist in the production of programs. The most fundamental of these is the compiler, often taken for granted. Beyond the compiler there should be many others, for example, editors, linkers, source code management systems, and text processors.

More recently, there has been a growing awareness of the important part played by software tools beyond compilers, editors, and linkers in the daily work of the programmer. The book *Software Tools* (Kernighan and Plauger 1976), makes this very clear and operating systems such as Unix™* provide the programmer with many tools. They serve to perform the mechanical detailed jobs and leave the programmer able to concentrate on the creative aspects of the task, an area where the human brain is at its best. This is where the computer's ability to perform repetitive trivial tasks with consistent accuracy, something that the human brain is *not* good at, can be harnessed. The human brain is very poorly adapted for doing this monotonous detailed work. Very soon, it wanders from the task and goes in search of more interesting thoughts. As soon as that happens, details are missed and the work no longer is trustworthy. Take for example the very simple task of paying full attention to the movement of the second hand or to every change of the digital display of a watch. It is a very rare person who can do this while being aware of breathing and without thinking of anything else for five minutes. Once a software tool is made to function correctly it will continue to do so without further deflecting the concentration of its users.

If the proper selection of tools is made available to the programmer it is probable that many more checks to ensure the consistency of a program's components will be made and the program will be more likely to function correctly. Many implementations have failed because of inadequate technical support at the software tool level. The subject of tools is returned to in Chapter 16. It is also addressed in Volume I, Chapter 8.

2.6.4 The character attributes and skills the programmer needs

I distinguish between attributes, which are inherited, and skills, which can be acquired. The major required attributes are:

- Intelligence, to be able to grasp requirements and virtual computer details, and to adapt this knowledge as they both change.
- Patience, to live, without damage to one's health, through those inevitable days in programming where nothing goes right and everything one touches seems blighted.
- Modesty, to admit error without sacrifice of self-worth. Programming is a job that will require this over and over again. Modesty is also requi· :d to realize our limitations to handle complexity. This implies the need to use all the help of notation and disciplined thinking to master the complexities of the problems that we are asked to solve.

---

*Unix is a trademark of Bell Laboratories.

Because a program is a communication medium, the single most important skill a programmer can have may well be ability in his native language – in reading and, particularly, writing. All the other useful skills, for example, the ability to think logically, follow from this.

Programmers come from a wide variety of educational backgrounds. Although nowadays many have studied computer science at university, there are a large number who did not start with a scientific background. Physicists and mathematicians often like to think that they are the only people who can understand and manipulate abstract representations of the real world, but this is far from true. I have a certificate that tells the world that I was trained in mathematics and, given sufficient motivation, I can remember enough of what was covered in the course to surprise myself. Most of the detailed mathematics that I have used in the intervening years has been to help my children with calculus homework. Yet, a major aspect of the mathematics that I did learn, and which I continue to use every time I write a program, is the ability to use symbols to represent abstract objects. This is the basis of mathematical notation. However, this is not to imply that I could not have obtained the same ability through many other disciplines, the formal study of music, for example.

Ultimately, all notations, including natural language, are symbols that can represent abstract objects. However, in addition to the communication skills that come from facility with a native language, the programmer needs the ability to use formal notations, one that has a set of rules that are much more restrictive than the grammar of a natural language. It was this discipline that I retained and used from my mathematical training. The skills that the programmer needs include the following:

- Communication. The importance of written communication has already been mentioned. Oral communication is also important for the successful working of a team of programmers.
- Ability to abstract content.
- Ability to abstract form. This is the ability to deal with symbols and codified operations.
- Ability to work with others without alienating them.
- Meticulous attention to detail. In any large program, there will be many tasks to be performed, some exciting, some menial. Euclid told Ptolemy I: 'There is no "royal road" to geometry.' Neither is there to programming.

2.7 THE FIGHT FOR CONSISTENCY

A complete suite of programs consists of several interrelated sets of files, for example:

1. The source code for the individual integrands.
2. The fragments of source code that are common to several integrands and are to be automatically copied into the integrand's source code during compilation. These will be referred to as the *include files*.

3. The object code obtained by compiling the source code for the individual integrands.
4. Executable programs consisting of the object code for several integrands linked together possibly with object code segments from a support library.
5. The standard command language procedures used by the suite of programs.
6. The documentation text for both users and maintainers of the suite of programs.
7. The test data.

In some cases, a suite of programs may have integrands written in different programming languages, for example, there may be some integrands in Modula-2 and others in Fortran or Assembler. Generally, the source programs in the different languages will be kept in separate sets of files.

These sets of files are not mutually independent. There are some obvious relationships, for example, the object integrands must be generated from the current versions of the source integrands, the documentation must match the programs being described, and the executable programs must be generated from the proper set of object integrands. There are also some less obvious relationships, for instance, the object codes for a particular language must all be generated with the same version of the compiler. In other words, the data sets that comprise a suite of programs *must be consistent* – they constitute a data base.

As we have already seen, a program undergoes frequent modification throughout its useful life. It is this fact that poses *the* major problem of programming – *maintaining consistency in the face of change*. This is true at all levels, both between integrands and within individual integrands. Failure to maintain consistency between the file sets leads to the following:

• New versions of programs that contain incompatibilities that cause wasted effort by the users.
• The documentation text no longer properly reflects the program that it describes. It is thus unreliable as an aid to understanding the software system.

The root cause of these problems is the difficulty in maintaining consistency between the elements of the sets of files.

A suite of programs, being a collection of data with relationships linking the basic entities together, has the characteristics of a database; however, very often, much of the information is duplicated because of the difficulty of extracting and organizing it. Duplicated information compounds the problems of maintaining consistency, since all copies must be updated when any one of them is changed. This is the concept behind the second set of files, the include files, mentioned above that contain fragments of source code that are common to several integrands. Some compilers are able to copy these fragments into the source code being translated during the compilation process. Thus a change to the single copy of one of these code fragments followed by recompilation of *all* the integrands that use the fragment applies the change to all the integrands concerned. This is an application of the principle of reducing the number of places that must be changed in order to make a consistent modification.

In the description of the process of automatically incorporating copies of code fragments into an integrand during compilation, the phrase 'followed by recompilation of *all* the integrands that use the fragment . . .' was used. This provides an example of the type of support that is required to maintain the consistency of a program database. If we leave the bookkeeping to human resources, using what might be termed 'back of envelope technology', inconsistencies are bound to creep into the database.

Database errors are much more pernicious than program errors and very much more difficult to eradicate once detected. This is because some parts of a database are often derived from others, thus propagating the error like the spread of a virus. Consequently, the management of a program database requires the use of automated processes to ensure the consistent integrity of all files.

An important part of this support is the automatic verification of the consistency following each modification or period of modification. The following are typical examples of the relationships that would be verified:

- The entry descriptions of integrands used for invoking them must match the descriptions obtained from the integrands themselves.
- The set of object integrands is complete and corresponds to the latest versions of the source code.
- In each compilation, the latest version of include files has been used.
- The latest version of source code for an integrand represents an update of the previous version and not an update of some earlier version.
- The latest version of each load integrand must contain only object integrands obtained from the latest version of source code and there must be no regressions from previous versions of the program.

Some of these verifications would require the use of some source code control system that would track successive versions of source code automatically, for example SCCS (Rochkind 1975). In addition to such a system, there would have to be additional software tools to track version dates from included source to compiled integrands.

In addition to the implementation related consistency items discussed above, there is also a need for consistency within and between specification and design documents and between design documents and the code. The support needed to maintain such a database will be considered in much greater detail later in this book.

2.8 CORRECTNESS

Before we can define an incorrect program, we need to say what we mean by a correct program. How can we define correctness? The programmer and the user are likely to have different perspectives but the same objective. The differing perspectives may lead to a failure of quality in the sense of the software's compliance with the users' intent. The following is a list of various interpretations of correctness in order of increasing difficulty of attainment:

1. The program contains no syntax errors that are detected by the compiler. That is, the program can be compiled without any error messages.

2. The program contains no compiler-detected errors or operation errors that can be automatically detected during execution. In other words, it executes to normal termination for some set of input data.

3. The program contains no compiler-detected errors and there exists some set of input data for which the program executes to normal termination to yield the correct result.

4. The program contains no compiler-detected errors and, for a typical set of input data, executes to normal termination to yield the correct results.

5. The program contains no compiler-detected errors and, for deliberately difficult sets of input data, executes to normal termination to yield the correct results.

6. The program contains no compiler-detected errors and, for all possible sets of input data that are valid according to the program specification, executes to normal termination to yield the correct results.

7. The program contains no compiler-detected errors and, for all possible sets of input data, executes to normal termination to yield the correct or reasonable results.

The beginning programmer may, for a short while, be content with levels 1 or 2. Programs that satisfy these levels are said to be *valid*, that is acceptable to the compiler, capable of doing something. Eventually, the programmer will generally be satisfied with level 5. The user, of course, would like to see all programs at level 7 but must come to realize that this may be prohibitively expensive. How many operating systems or compilers can you confidently place at level 7? How could you know whether your compiler is at level 7 – is the description of the programming language sufficiently clear for you to be able to tell? How can we set about approaching level 7?

'Correctness' concerns the compliance of the software as it works with the requirements as specified, provided that the specifications are *adequate* for the compliance to be demonstrated. That the requirements specification is 'correct', that it defines a system that will satisfy the users, is a separate issue and has nothing to do with the correctness of the implementation. It is important to realize that this rather narrow use of 'correctness' not only concerns what is expedient for our treatment of implementation but is often the ineluctable meaning for programmers – say, in cases when a client has been responsible for the specification and has delegated by contract the design and implementation of software to meet the specification. Then, a perfectly 'correct' implementation may be only of limited use or of none at all if the basis – that is, the specification – was wrong.

There is a great deal of semantic fog surrounding the terms 'validate' and 'verify' as applied to a program. These terms reflect two fundamentally different approaches to determining the correctness of a program. In software engineering, 'validating' software is the process of demonstrating its compliance with the specifications by testing and demonstration and is thus applied to the software in its *dynamic* state. Section 12.5 discusses this process further. In contrast, 'verification' is a static affair. In software engineering, verification is the Quality Inspection task of determining that the software engineering process has been adequately performed. This is often done by peer review as described in Section 12.4. Computer scientists also use the term 'verification' as applying to the static form of the program. They treat the program as a mathematical theorem and seek to provide a proof of its correctness as we did in high-school geometry. Chapter 7 treats this subject in considerable detail.

Attempting to verify the correctness of a program in the formal sense may be shutting the stable door after the horse has bolted. Earlier in the history of programming, correctness was more or less taken for granted. It was assumed that it would happen naturally without any special steps being taken. Many programmers still live in the dream world where programming errors, like traffic accidents, only occur to others. We now recognize this as a simplistic view; correctness does not come about without special care and planning. It is difficult to add correctness to a program after it has been written; correctness is not like a coat of paint that can be applied after the structure has been built. There are three different approaches to producing a correct program:

1. *Error prevention* consists in adopting design and implementation techniques that will lessen the risk of committing errors during the implementation process. Their rehearsal summarizes what has gone before:
   - Use good design decomposition into integrands.
   - The integrands have unity of purpose, are designed according to the principles of information hiding, and have low coupling with each other.
   - Adequate documentation.
   - Incremental testing to alphatest.
   - Exhaustive black box betatests.
2. *Error detection* consists of the implementation of a defensive design incorporating self-validation checks to whatever point can be afforded. It must be recognized that even systematically designed programs can have errors and therefore the implementation design must contain a plan for diagnosing and finding the errors. This means that there will be reasonableness and self-consistency checks on the input data, proper error reporting and logging, and error recovery procedures.
3. *Error correction* consists of modifying the program whenever the symptoms of an error are encountered during the testing process. Before this can be done, the cause of the error must be located. This can be a long and painful process, especially if the program has been written with an overly complex structure, but can be much eased if approach 2 above has been properly followed. Error correction involves changing the program and this requires the expenditure of effort to preserve the program's structure, as was discussed in Section 2.3.7.

In this book, we recommend this three-layer approach to errors: i.e., to reduce the chance of error commission during implementation, to imbue the program with defensive behavior during execution to limit the damage caused by any errors, and to increase the relative ease of correction of any errors that may still occur.

CHAPTER THREE

THE RUNNING EXAMPLE

A requirement specification for an example program, used as a vehicle to illustrate some of the points in the later chapters, is presented. This is followed by a discussion of the design steps that must be undertaken before the implementation phase is begun.

3.1 INTRODUCTION

Many of the concepts discussed in this book seem very abstract unless demonstrated with an example. As a vehicle for such demonstrations, we will rely mainly on the use of a single 'Running Example'. The choice of such an example has to lie on a narrow middle ground between examples that are too trivial to illustrate the techniques and those that are so complex that the reader will be unable to see the techniques clearly. This chapter contains the requirements specification for the example. The design of the solution will be presented in Chapter 5 and its implementation in Chapters 9–10. As our Running Example we will use a problem discussed in Parnas (1972).

3.2 THE REQUIREMENTS

Suppose we were interested in programming languages and looking for books or papers on the subject. It would be easy to find promising titles in a listing, provided that the authors have been considerate enough to put the words *Programming Language* at the beginning of the title. Thus the book *Programming Language Concepts* will be in its expected place in the alphabetical ordering. However, the paper *A Comparative Study of Programming Languages* will be in another part of the listing and, unless we think of looking under *Comparative*, we will be unlikely to find it without a sequential scan through the catalogue – an act that rapidly exceeds our attention span making us very likely to miss items.

The Key Word in Context (Kwic) index tries to solve this problem by listing each title several times, once for each of its keywords – 'noise words' such as *a*, *the*, *and*, *of*, and so on are not counted as keywords. We might define a Kwic index as being produced by taking each title, generating *circularly shifted* copies, each with a different keyword at the beginning and then sorting the newly generated list alphabetically. A circularly shifted copy is formed by moving one or more words from the beginning of the title to the end.

The title 'A Comparative Study of Programming Languages' would appear four times as:

```
Comparative Study of Programming Languages. A
Study of Programming Languages. A Comparative
Programming Languages. A Comparative Study of
Languages. A Comparative Study of Programming
```

This is not very easy to read and in its final form of the index, part of the listing might be rearranged as:

```
   A comparative study of   programming langauges
                            Programming language concepts
                            Programming language landscape:...
                            Programming language structures
        A comparison of     programming languages for softw...
                            Programming languages: design a...
         Principles of      programming languages: design, ...
...ion to the study of      programming languages
        Concepts of         programming languages
     Concurrency and        Programming Languages
     Fundamentals of        programming languages
...cture and design of      programming languages
```

where the titles have been aligned on the word that is being used for the alphabetical ordering and sufficient other words are provided to give some context. Also appearing would be a citation to allow the reader to find the work.

The Running Example will consist of producing a program to generate a Kwic index. The following informal problem description is adapted from Parnas (1972):

> The Kwic program accepts an ordered set of lines, each line is an ordered set of words, and each word is an ordered set of characters. Each line consists of two parts, a Title-Part and a Reference-Part. The Reference-Part is enclosed in brackets. It is assumed that brackets never occur in either the Title-Part or the Reference-Part. A segment of the input data, derived from the Bibliography in this book, is:

```
Software Engineering with Ada [Booch 1983]
The Mythical Man Month [Brooks 1975]
An Overview of JSD [Cameron 1986]
Nesting in Ada is for the Birds [Clark et al. 1980]
```

```
Object Oriented Programming [Cox 1986]
Social Processes and Proofs of Theorems and Programs
                                      [DeMillo et al. 1979]
Programming Considered as a Human Activity [Dijkstra 1965]
```

A Title-Part may be *circularly shifted* by removing the first word and appending it at the end of the line to form a new Title-Part. From each line in the input data, new lines are constructed by appending a copy of the Reference-Part from the original line to all distinct circularly shifted Title-Parts. The first word of each such line is the *keyword*. Those Title-Parts that begin with the keywords: a, an, and, as, be, by, for, from, in, is, not, of, on, or, that, the, to, with, and without are ignored. The output of the Kwic program is a listing of all the titles constructed in this way and presented so that the title is presented with its original word ordering with all keywords lined up vertically in the center of the page. Where a line must be truncated at the beginning or end in order to fit on the printed line with the keyword aligned the truncation is shown with an ellipsis, (. . .).

In the course of later chapters, the outline of a programming solution to this problem will be developed. The particular points of consideration will be the following:

- How easy will it be to modify the program that is produced?
- What must be done during the design and implementation processes to assist in the validation and debugging of the program?
- How can the program be written so that it is easy to understand?
- What documentation is required for the product?

The proposed solutions are not presented as the 'best' solution but as one that avoids some of the pitfalls that often ensnare programmers.

The language chosen for the exposition will be Modula-2, since this provides the ability to split a program into integrands in an easy way with well-defined interfaces. It is also a language that can be understood by programmers who do not have direct experience of the language but have experience of another high-level language.

3.3 DESIGN DISCUSSION

The specification of requirements is found in the previous section. The design of the software to meet these requirements serves as input to the implementation phase and is not properly the subject of this book, however in this section, I will discuss some of the design decisions since they have a profound effect on the implementation. I am indebted to Allen Macro for his design, and discussion (most of which is reproduced verbatim).

It should be noted that the supporting text *and* requirements in Section 3.2 contain typographical errors in book titles – for example, langauges for languages and Brooch for Booch. This illustrates that index entries may contain errors. How to deal with these is an issue in design, dealt with later.

3.3.1 Design decisions

There are several design decisions, which must be made explicit at the outset, whose initiators are concealed in the specifications. These are:

1. *Identification of 'noise' words*. There are two options to consider, both legitimate questions of design.
   (a) The title entries are marked for keywords by the operator librarian, for example, Software engineering with Ada [Booch 1983], and provisions are made for identifying marked characters, and for increasing their extent in a title at some later stage, for example, Software engineering with Ada [Booch 1983].
   (b) The title is stored as an unmarked character string of any length and the program matches this against a lexicon of 'noise words', which it has available.
   Either scheme could be made to work, probably with equivalent characteristics of user perceived flexibility and ease, and efficiency. Macro proposes the first alternative, on consideration that a lexicon of 'noise words' might be difficult to define adequately and also the possibility that the title might consist of words contained in the lexicon. For example, H. Rider Haggard's *She* might fall into this category. However, the 'client', to whom the choice was put, opted for the lexicon and deliberately made the assumption that all titles will contain words that are not noise words. Further, the creation and modification of the lexicon is outside the scope of the Running Example.
2. *Title discrimination and word distinction*. These will be required in the store of saved titles. Spaces (the character blank) are a dangerous mechanism for this, as it is too easy to omit them (for example, Software engineeringwith Ada . . .) or to enter too many spaces by keystroke error (for example, Software   engineeringwithAda . . .). In a real application, the designer would design a proper mechanism for a keyboard-to-file section for the program. This would allow the user to make interactive checking for the correct entering of data. Here, in order to keep the size of the Running Example within bounds, it is assumed that the input data is correct and that all words in titles are separated by exactly one space character and that there will be exactly one space character between the last word of the title and the '[' that introduces the reference part.
   To surmount these problems, the following procedure is proposed for systems design, keyboard-to-file features:

Step 1: A character-string submitted for entry to the title store will require a special keystroke to indicate Endstring if an intermediate storage device is in use (for example, key-to-disk equipment), or *Endstringandenter* if direct updating is possible. In both cases, this special character will be **. This is really two keystrokes treated as a single character as is done, for instance, in Fortran for the exponent operator.

Step 2: When ** appears, either in reading an intermediate disk of title character strings, or in direct access, the operator will receive a prompt message to check the title carefully before signifying continuation. These messages are:

   Output: Error check on title required
   Input: then press 'Return' to enter title

Beyond this point, titles are presumed checked and correct in all respects – including stringend and word delimiting – which latter will be by the normal method of one or more spaces between characters. Thus: So ftware engi neering withAda** will denote a string of five words. The importance of this operator input checking is clear. Errors in character strings cannot be detected. Kwic will process gibberish as faithfully as correct text. A better system *could* be designed but the client seems to want it this way.

Step 3:   When 'Return' is pressed to instruct Kwic to enter the character string to store, it will arrange the entry in Titlestore with word and string discrimina-tors transparent to operator use.

Step 4:   The lexicon will be compiled in the same way as Step 2 for the list of titles, the distinguishing input commands being:

```
Enter Title
Enter Lexicon
```

3. *Building the Printfile.* Once the Titlestore and Lexicon have been built as described above, the Printfile may be built. The command:

```
Build Printfile
```

achieves this. The external specification for the program BuildPrintfile is thus:

Input: *Titlestore:* an ordered set of character strings consisting of words separated by blanks. Each string consists of two parts, a Title-Part and a Reference-Part. The Reference-Part is enclosed in brackets.
Lexicon: an ordered set of character strings, each string consists of a single word.

Output: *Printfile:* an ordered set of representations of the elements of Titlestore, separated into 26 parts, see Function below.

Function: Build Printfile from the data contained in Titlestore and Lexicon. Each Title-Part of Titlestore contains keywords, that is words that are not contained in Lexicon. For each keyword in the Title-Parts there will be an element in Printfile with a designation of the keyword. The elements of Printfile are ordered alphabetically by designated keyword, the complete file being split into 26 parts according to the initial letter of the designated keyword, there being one part for each letter of the alphabet.

After the Printfile has been built, it may be printed or searched as described below.

4. *Use of Kwic.* The system may be invoked, and then used by the following operator commands:

```
Call: KWIC
```

which causes the complete Keyword in Context index to be printed.

```
Search: ...(keyword/endkeywordcharacter(**))
Search: etc.
```

An example of a search command would be

```
Search: Software engineering **
```

Use of Kwic in the search mode produces messages at a screen. Message length will be 80 characters maximum, including special tags and spaces. A maximum of 22 titles will be displayed, and if more exist under the keyword(s), a right justified message at the lower edge of the screen will read:

```
Overflow - press 'Return' to show more
```

Each overflow screen will show the caption at the top right:

```
Continuation - press $ to go back to previous screen.
```

and the overflow message will be shown, at the bottom right, if more overflow exists.

5. *Searching.* The search algorithm will operate as follows:

   5.1 All entries in the title store will be searched to match the keyword/key-phrase. However, it is taken as an objective that as soon as a full screen can be presented, it should be. Thus, when enough entries have been found, they will be displayed, plus the message at the lower right of the screen

   ```
   Search continuing
   ```

   When the next screenful has been identified, the Search continuing message will be supplemented to read:

   ```
   Search continuing: Overflow - press 'Return' to show more
   ```

   this message will be replaced with

   ```
   Overflow - press 'Return' to show more
   ```

   as soon as the search terminated. This message will persist only as long as a next (or residual) screen exists. Browsing over continuation screens can be effected by the provisions of 1.2/Step 6.

   5.2 To expedite the first response under 2.1, the search will begin under the initial of the keyword (e.g. p if the keyword programming is being searched for). Thereafter, searching is done down the complete keyword or keyphrase.

6. Organization of the screen display:

   6.1 A count of matched titles will be held (Find) for each Kwic search. This number will be displayed at the top left of the screen. If Find = 0,

   ```
   No Entries
   ```

   will be displayed centrally on the screen.

   6.2 The print file will hold the formatted titles of found entries matching the keyword/keyphrase.

   6.3 The selected titles will be displayed as shown in Figure 3.1.

   6.4 When the screen is first displayed, the first title shown is highlighted to denote that it is the selected title. The user can move the selection from the current line to the

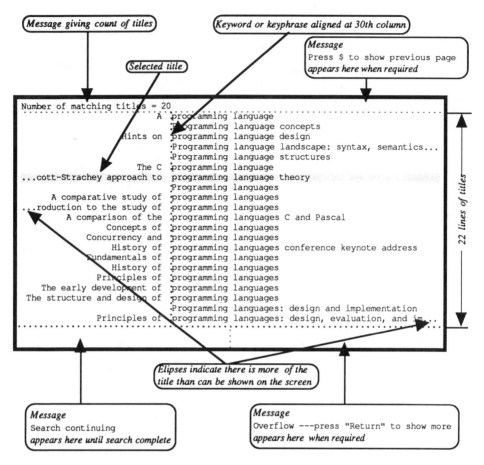

FIGURE 3.1   Display of titles selected by keyphrase programming language.

next by the 'Down-arrow' key and from the current line to the previous one by the
'Up-arrow' key. If the 'Select' key is pressed, the complete title and reference is
displayed. Thus, if the 'Select' key were depressed when the screen was as shown
in Figure 3.1, the display would be replaced by:

```
[Stoy 1977]
Denotational semantics: the Scott-Strachey approach
to programming language theory

Press "Return" to go back to previous display
```

6.5 It follows from the requirement that the screen display the matched titles as soon
as possible that it will not be acceptable for the entire list of titles to be searched
for the keyword or keyphrase. The printfile must be maintained so that it is
possible to find all matches of keywords and keyphrases already grouped. There

should be a directory into the file with 26 entries corresponding to the first letters of the keywords so that the search time can be shortened even further. The actual form of storage is left to the implementor.

7. *Design as a diagrammatic depiction*. Algorithms, those are the elements of design, and they are presented for Kwic, pictorially as Figures 3.2 and 3.3 as logic flowgraphs. Datastores are depicted as open files whose regime is regulated by the operating system or programming languages involved. An organization for the printfile is shown in Figure 3.4.

As a coda to the earlier point on input error and its need for sedulous checking at that stage, it will be noted that minor errors of inversion (for example, langauge) do not disqualify a title or a keyword, but major lacunae (for example, Brooch) would, if in keyword or keyword-in-title, lead to exclusion. Tough! The client wants cheap, the client gets cheap . . . and commensurately nasty.

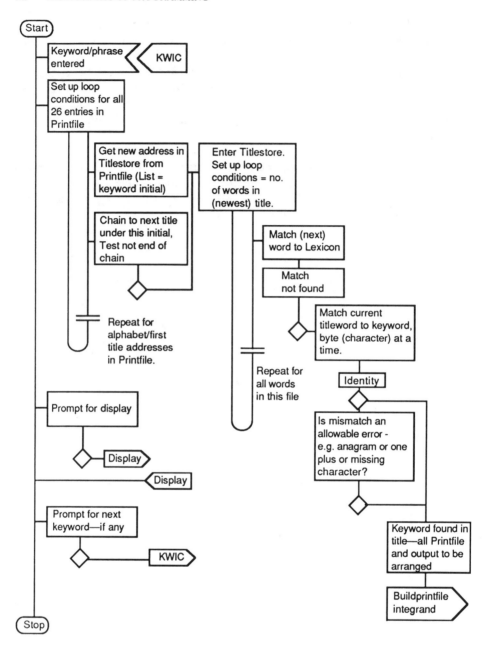

FIGURE 3.2 Intermediate level design for Kwic – BS 6224 notation.

<u>Entered:</u> from KWIC Main-routine, and returns.
<u>Calls:</u>   Display with a screen image in SCREEN
<u>Input:</u>   No parameter input from KWIC-Main, merely the latest found title saved, in its
             entirety, in Printfile.

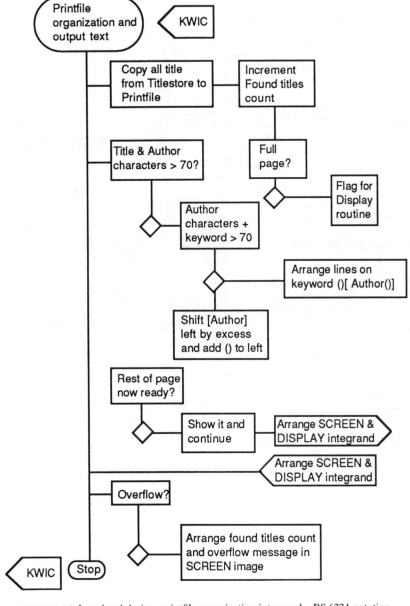

FIGURE 3.3 Low-level design, printfile organization integrand – BS 6224 notation.

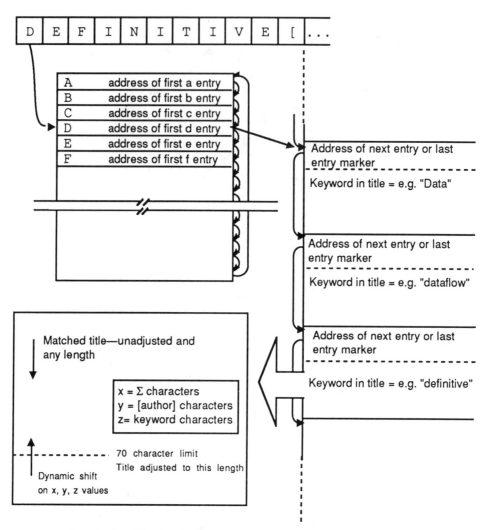

FIGURE 3.4 Organization of data in printfile.

PART TWO

THE PRINCIPLES
OF PROGRAMMING

CHAPTER FOUR
ABSTRACTION

A program is an abstraction whose implementation starts from a specification, which is another abstraction. Integrand specifications are needed to describe the integrand's data interface, for communication between implementors, to limit the amount that the programmer needs to know, and to permit program portability. Specifications must be complete and precise. There are several notations varying from informal to formal, each with its particular difficulties. A common form is an operational specification, which is really a description of how the program *might* work. The problem with an operational specification is that the boundary between what is actually required and what is an incidental feature of the method of specification is sometimes hard to determine. This problem is avoided through an abstract specification where the product is defined by a set of assertions that must be satisfied by the program. This kind of specification is difficult to produce and difficult to understand. A brief description of some of the common notations used for specifications leads to a discussion of notations in general and their function. For a notation to be effective, it must, by allowing the mind to concentrate on what is important, help the designer's journey towards 'algorithms and data' definition at the lowest design level (= highest level of *solution detail*). At different stages in the implementation of a program, various levels of detail are appropriate, corresponding to differing levels of abstraction. The external interface to an integrand represents the highest level of abstraction for the integrand. The programming of the integrand consists of filling in the details until everything is specified. A program where the details have yet to be completed is an abstract program; a data type that is characterized by its operations and whose representation is unspecified is an abstract data type. Part of the skill of a programmer lies in maintaining a level of abstraction that is appropriate to the progress of the implementation. If this discipline is not followed, there is a great danger that some decisions will be made too early and will either have to be remade later or will contort the implementation so as to reduce its maintainability.

4.1 INTRODUCTION

As we saw in Section 2.3.1, a computer program is a model or abstraction of some real-world or conceptual process. The genesis of the program is its specification, whether it exists on paper or only in someone's mind. The specification is an abstraction of the executable program in that it does not contain all the details that are required in order for it to be executed. Thus, abstraction lies at the very heart of programming and is discussed in this chapter.

4.2 SPECIFICATIONS

In the context of implementation, *specifications* are taken to mean integrand and program specifications that are the outcome of the design phase. These comprise the definitions of the data and the algorithms that are to manipulate them. Earlier in the life cycle there are other specifications: the user requirements that lead to the functional specifications, which, in turn, are the input to the design process. It is important to realize that although the mapping from the functional specifications to the implementation specifications may be obvious, the reverse is often not true. This is because the functional specifications are generally organized according to the externally perceived functions of the complete function and the implementation specifications are organized according to data and, possibly, control flow considerations. This tendency towards unidirectional mapping may have severe consequences for the ease with which the program can be modified to accommodate changes in the functional specifications. Thus the designer should aim to make the isomorphism between the two specifications as strong as possible, however this may give problems with the design. As with most things, there must be a compromise between the two positions. This tug-of-war is addressed in much more detail in Volume 1, Chapter 7 and in Volume 3 of this series.

4.2.1 Why we need them

In Section 2.2.3, we defined the Software Implementation to be the process by which the *external specification* for a program or integrand is transformed into executable form. Ideally, this external specification is a precise statement of what is required of the integrand from the outside, this is its 'interface' with all sources and destinations of data or signals that lie outside its bounds. These can include other integrands, files, electronic devices, and human users. This external interface specification, it will be remembered, was an outcome of the design process.

Although to many the need for specifications is so obvious that no justification is required, it is useful to review some of the reasons why the implementor needs specifications. A fuller discussion of this subject is given by Parnas (1977).

TO DESCRIBE THE INTEGRAND'S DATA INTERFACE
Unless the programmer knows the function of the integrand precisely, it is unlikely that it will satisfy its users. This leads to an era of finger pointing and mutual recrimination and little positive will be accomplished. What is true for each separate integrand is also true for the program as a whole. For an integrand, the 'user' is generally a programmer who

writes code that invokes the integrand. The features of the program or integrand described by the specifications are the effects that can be observed from outside. These must be demonstrable because they will be used as the basis of testing.

FOR COMMUNICATION BETWEEN THE IMPLEMENTORS

For all but very small projects, the implementation will be a cooperative effort of a team of programmers. Unless they have some standard work of reference on which to base their discussions, the essential communication between the programmers will have no solid foundation. This too can lead to acrimonious loss of time and a product that will satisfy neither the users nor the creators.

TO REDUCE THE AMOUNT THAT THE PROGRAMMER NEEDS TO KNOW

With most large software systems, it is impossible for any one individual to understand the entire system. A set of specifications allows the programming task to be split into integrands, each of which will be implemented by one programmer, who will probably work on many such integrands during the course of the project. Each of these integrands will have well-defined boundaries and communication protocols with other integrands. To implement one of these integrands requires only a knowledge of the boundaries and protocols. The programmer does not need to know the contents of any of the other integrands. Indeed, this would be dangerous knowledge since it might be unwittingly woven into the implementation of another integrand, making a connection between the two integrands that is not documented in their interface specifications. Not only does this introduce an inconsistency between the specifications and the source code, it also increases the interconnectivity between integrands making modification of either, without introducing inconsistency, harder. Inevitably, since a programmer will implement several integrands, there will be a danger that the programmer carries some of this information across unconsciously. On a large project this danger can be reduced by careful task assignment.

FOR PROGRAM PORTABILITY

This may be a requirement. Without specifications a program becomes defined by its first implementation and will be tied to a specific machine with little chance of being moved to a different kind of computer system. Once the first implementation has been completed, it is too late to separate the real requirements of the program from the incidental effects of being implemented on a particular hardware configuration. The fact that program portability is to be a goal of the program must be recognized *before* the integrand specifications are produced so that it is clear what the behavior of the integrand is to be, irrespective of the machine and operating system on which it is implemented.

4.2.2 Completeness and precision

Even though many programming team organizations make no separation of staff according to development stage and so designers and implementors may be the same, we will, for the moment, employ the imagery of such a separation. We may then say that the external interface specifications for an integrand serve as a contract between the designer and the implementor. It provides a clearly defined boundary between the two areas of responsibility. Like legal contracts, there are two major requirements of the external interface specifications:

- Precision
- Completeness.

When a lawyer draws up a client's last will and testament, what is being created is a contract between the client and the executor. The lawyer will spend a great deal of time ensuring that the document is both precise and complete. In this case, it is particularly important since one of the parties will not be available to answer questions of intent during the performance of the contract.

In the case of external interface specifications, it is to be hoped that the designer will still be available during the implementation phase, however the need for precision and completeness is still crucial. In the previous section, we gave some reasons why specifications are needed. Matching these reasons, we need to be precise:

- to avoid the implemented integrand behaving in a different way from that intended by the designer, due to the implementor interpreting the specifications differently from the designer's intention;
- to avoid misunderstandings about the division of responsibility between the implementors with the result that communication between the integrands will fail;
- to avoid the necessity for programmers to study each other's programs to understand what is required, with the possible result that the integrands will depend on each other in undocumented ways, making subsequent modification very difficult. If an integrand needs to be studied in this way, it serves as a model upon which others are built and essentially becomes part of the specifications.

The property of completeness is also essential because none of the integrand's external properties should be left to the programmer's choice. Thus, the specification must include at least the following:

- The data that will be passed to the integrand. This definition includes format, value ranges, and passing mechanism. Input may include data obtained from external sources.
- The output that will be produced by the integrand. This definition includes format, value ranges, as well as passing mechanism of the output and what error indications are to be generated. Output may include data written to external devices.
- The relationship between input and output. How the output is to be mathematically or logically derived from the input, including what consistency tests are to be applied to the input data.

To some extent the distinction between the effects of lack of precision and lack of completeness is arbitrary and the cause of a particular effect could arguably be ascribed to either. Although the requirement for specification completeness and precision are identical with those at higher levels in the life-cycle, that is, functional specification, the issues are far more tractable at the implementation level. Lehman's classification of S-programs, defined in Macro (1990) – totally and invariantly specifiable and proveable – applies here, in terms of the life-cycle, with the previously noted reservations on 'proof' and 'correct', as formal objectives. As we shall see, the nearer one takes an external interface specification to its objectives of completeness and precision, the closer it becomes to being an equivalent of the program to be produced.

4.3 NOTATIONS

A specification requires a notation – a language in which it can be expressed. The completeness and precision of the definition depend heavily on the adequacy of the language used. In this section, we first discuss the role of a notation and then describe various notations that are used to express specifications. These are:

- Natural or structured natural language
- Abstract notations
- Graphical notations.

4.3.1 The function of a notation

The choice of a notation is all important. A notation should be a semantic expression, rapidly conveying meaning to the reader. In addition to speed, the transfer of meaning should be clear, precise, and complete. Further, it should be obvious if any of these conditions is not met, for example, if the message has been corrupted in some way. With all of this, the notation should require little learning for the user to become fluent.

A notation is also a mental beast of burden that serves to relieve the brain of unnecessary work by reducing the perceived complexity of what is being described. Since we all have a limit to the amount of complexity we can handle, a good notation sets us free to concentrate on more advanced problems. As an example of the way in which a notation can reduce complexity consider how our positional notation for numbers assists us in arithmetic. Compare calculating the product $63 \times 7 = 441$ using Hindu-Arabic numerals and using Roman numerals:

$$
\begin{array}{ll}
\begin{array}{r} 63 \\ \underline{\times 7} \\ 441 \end{array} & \textit{versus}
\end{array}
$$

$$
\begin{aligned}
\text{LXIII} \times \text{VII} &= \text{L} \times \text{V} + \text{L} + \text{L} + \\
&\quad \text{X} \times \text{V} + \text{X} + \text{X} + \\
&\quad \text{V} + \text{I} + \text{I} + \text{V} + \text{I} + \text{I} + \text{V} + \text{I} + \text{I} \\
&= \text{L} + \text{L} + \text{L} + \text{L} + \text{L} + \text{L} + \text{L} + \\
&\quad \text{X} + \text{X} + \text{X} + \text{X} + \text{X} + \text{X} + \text{X} + \\
&\quad \text{V} + \text{V} + \text{V} \\
&\quad \text{I} + \text{I} + \text{I} + \text{I} + \text{I} + \text{I} \\
&= \text{C} + \text{C} + \text{C} + \text{L} + \text{L} + \text{X} + \text{X} + \text{X} + \\
&\quad \text{V} + \text{V} + \text{I} \\
&= \text{C} + \text{C} + \text{C} + \text{C} + \text{X} + \text{X} + \text{X} + \text{X} + \text{I} \\
&= \text{CDXLI}
\end{aligned}
$$

Similarly, within the Hindu-Arabic scheme, the number

1340000000000000

is more difficult to read and understand than

1 340 000 000 000 000

which in turn is less apprehensible than

1.34×10^{15}

Each of these improvements is a notation that better helps us to count the zeros in the number.

It has been suggested by McLuhan and Logan (1977) that the use of the phonetic alphabet in the West was pivotal in encouraging abstract, logical and systematic thought and explains why science began in the West and not the East, despite the much earlier technological achievements of the Chinese. They conclude that the concrete nature of Chinese ideograms makes them less conducive to abstract scientific thinking than an alphabetic script. If their conclusions are correct, this is an extreme example of the importance of a notation. It should also be pointed out that the Chinese ideograms have an important advantage over the Western phonetic alphabets, in that they enable those whose speech is mutually unintelligible to converse using the writing brush instead of the tongue. This whole topic is investigated in detail by Logan (1986).

> To use a notation we have to make the investment of time and mental effort to master it.

A poor notation does not produce an adequate return on this investment. Therefore, when choosing a notation, it is essential to take into account the amount of mental investment that will have to be made by all the users for it to become useful.

4.3.2 Natural or structured natural language

Some form of natural language is probably the most common notation that is used for specifications. In this section, we will see that it is almost impossible to make a precise definition in a natural language. An attempt to overcome this by adding more structure to the language so that the specification becomes more 'program like' runs the danger of overspecification. When no particular structuring is applied to it, it is often called an 'informal specification'.

As an example consider (which is not part of the Running Example) the following informal external specification for the implementation of a stack. It is 'informal' because normal everyday language is used. The stack is defined through the operations that are to be available for manipulating it. There are to be five operations:

NewStack: creates a new stack that is empty.
Push: puts an element on the top of the stack.

Top: returns the top of the stack.
Pop: deletes the top element from the stack.
IsEmpty: returns TRUE if the stack is empty, otherwise returns FALSE.

This specification fails both the precision and completeness criteria. For example, in the definition of the Top operation, 'returns the top of the stack' leaves it unclear whether it is the value at the top of the stack that is returned or a pointer to that value. Apparently the implementor is left to make the decision. This same definition is incomplete since it does not say what is to be the result of the operation if the stack is empty.

Unfortunately, in most cases, it is very difficult to write the part of the external interface specification that defines the relationship between the input data and the output results. It requires great care to make sure that everything is covered exactly. The trouble is that it is only when the specifications are interpreted with the thoroughness that is required to make an implementation, that all the nooks and crannies are investigated, and one is sure that the specification is complete. It is for this reason that a common way of defining this relationship between input and output is by describing a hypothetical implementation either in natural language or some more formal notation. This is known as an *operational specification*.

An operational specification is really an *equivalent program* to the one being defined. This equivalent program is purely to show the way that the output is to be derived from the input and is not to serve as a model for an implementation. It does not matter if the specification implementation is inefficient. The implementor is asked to produce a program 'to do the same thing' except for a few 'irrelevancies' that are connected with the way in which the specification program is implemented. The problem is for the implementor to separate what is to be considered a requirement and what is an irrelevancy. It is somewhat like the question of program portability again. This time the implementor will be trying to transport the program from the operational specification to a real machine where it will become a real program. This portage may be even harder than moving a real program because there is no guarantee that the operational specification would actually work – it has never been implemented and the implied operating system consists of hand waving.

The ultimate example of an operational specification – one done in 'some more formal notation' – is an actual correct implementation. An example of this is the specification of a programming language by the behavior of a specific compiler. It is complete and precise, all questions can be answered definitely and unambiguously by experiment. There can be no debate about the answers or appeals to some higher authority. The implementation is the last word. I can remember several occasions when I have complained to a vendor that there was an error in their compiler because it did not conform to the definition in the programming language reference manual only to receive the response that they would modify the reference manual. Brooks (1975) describes the disadvantages:

> The implementation may over-prescribe even the externals. Invalid syntax always produces some result; in a policed system that result is an invalidity indication *and nothing more*. In an unpoliced system all kinds of side effects may appear, and these may have been used by the programmers. When we undertook to emulate the IBM

1401 on System/360, for example, it developed that there were 30 different 'curios' – side effects of supposedly invalid operations – that had come into widespread use and had to be considered as part of the definition. The implementation as a definition overprescribed; it not only said what the machine must do, it also said a great deal about how it had to do it . . . For example, some machines leave trash in the multiplicand register after a multiplication. The precise nature of this trash turns out to be part of the *de facto* definition, yet duplicating it may preclude the use of a faster multiplication algorithm.

An operational specification for the stack described informally in the previous section might be given as shown in Figure 4.1, using the style, but not the strict syntax, of Modula-2. Each of the operations is defined as a separate 'PROCEDURE', the first line of which defines the protocol of its interface – that is, the type, in the sense of Section 1.4.5,

```
MODULE StackOps;
    TYPE Stack: RECORD
                    Sp:     CARDINAL [0..StackSize];
                    StArr: ARRAY [0..StackSize] OF Element;
                END;
    VAR  OuterSt: Stack;

    PROCEDURE NewStack(): Stack;
        OuterSt.Sp := 0;
        Return OuterSt
    END NewStack;

    PROCEDURE Push(El: Element; St: Stack): Stack;
        IF St.Sp < StackSize THEN
            St.StArr[Sp] := El;
        ELSE
            Error
        END;
        St.Sp := St.Sp + 1;
        Return St
    END Push;

    PROCEDURE Top(St: Stack): POINTER TO Element;
        IF Sp = 0 THEN
            Error;
        ELSE
            RETURN ADR(St[Sp-1])
        END;
    END Top;

    PROCEDURE Pop(St: Stack): Stack;
        IF St.Sp > 0 THEN
            St.Sp := St.Sp - 1
        END;
        RETURN St
    END Pop;

    PROCEDURE IsEmpty(St: Stack): BOOLEAN;
        IF Sp = 0 THEN
            RETURN TRUE;
        ELSE
            RETURN FALSE
        END;
    END IsEmpty
END StackOps.
```

FIGURE 4.1 Operational specifications for the operations of Stack.

of the data flowing across the interface. This provides some information that was not available in the original informal definition. For example, the first line of the definition of the function Top:

```
PROCEDURE Top(St: Stack): POINTER TO Element;
```

tells us that it is not the actual value of the stack's top element that is returned but a pointer to it. (This may seem a rather strange way of defining these operations but some artificiality has to be introduced to present a small example.) The part that follows the first line of a procedure definition is an operational definition of the relationship between the operation's input and its result. These definitions answer many questions that were left open by the informal definition. We now know that to attempt to apply Top to an empty stack causes the value 'Error' to be returned. The notation Error in the operational specification means the application of the operation in these circumstances is an error and what happens next is undefined. It is meaningless for the program to continue. The situation is analogous to the application of the function SquareRoot to a negative value. What should the function return? Should it return anything or should it just commit suicide, bequeathing a helpful note to the user? Generally, this decision is left to the implementor although a more complete definition might call for a specific action that is independent of the implementation. In contrast, the definition of the Pop operation specifies that, if the operation is applied to an empty stack, it has no effect but it is not an error.

The specification in Figure 4.1 also contains too much information. The model chosen for the 'definition implementation' is that of an array. This has the property that if we Pop the stack, the top element, although not available through the stack operations, still exists and can be accessed through a pointer value that was obtained from Top before the Pop operation. This element will retain its value until another element is pushed onto the stack. Was this intended or was it an incidental artefact of the operational specification? Suppose we implemented these operations using a linked list where popped elements would be destroyed, would this match the operational specification? With this kind of operational specification, there is no foolproof way of separating the important details from the incidental artefacts of the definition. Even though we do not have a real implementation serving as a definition we are in the same situation, as if it were.

An operational specification expressed in structured natural language, pseudo-code, is essentially a metaphor and, like all metaphors, has the danger of being taken too literally. If we say that somebody is 'a bear of a man', does that mean that he is covered with hair? No – we expect the reader to extract only the attributes of size and strength from the bear metaphor. This expectation is based on some unwritten protocol that is part of the writer's and reader's common database about the language. This database is built up by frequent usage in daily life. Unfortunately, operational specifications are not used sufficiently often for any such insight to build up. It can only be hoped that the reader is by intuition able to differentiate between meaning and mechanism.

In summary, the more precisely we attempt to define the function by saying *how* the results are to be produced, the more we drag in incidental details that are not essential to an implementation on a real machine in an actual programming language.

4.3.3 Abstract notations

If we are to escape from the dangers of an operational specification conveying unintended meaning, we must provide an abstraction from any real or imagined implementation mechanism. This we do by defining *what* relation the results have to the input instead of *how* they are to be derived from the input. This, in turn, requires an *abstract notation*.

As we saw in Section 2.5.1, we must distinguish between two kinds of abstraction: *abstraction of form* and *abstraction of content*. In this section, we deal with abstraction of form. Abstraction of content will be discussed in Section 4.4.

As we have seen, there is no objective test we can make to validate that an implementation satisfies an operational specification. An alternative to this kind of specification is to use a set of *axioms* or relations whose truth defines the operations. Such a set of axioms form an *axiomatic definition*. For the stack specification, the axiomatic definition would be as shown in Figure 4.2.

The test of the correctness of an implementation is to verify that it satisfies the axioms. Axioms like these refer only to the properties of the functions and do not suggest the way that they might be implemented. When we refer to an External Interface Specification, we use the adjectives *external interface* to mean that the specifications are defined solely in terms of effects that can be observed by the invoker of the integrand. The axioms shown here do exactly that. Unfortunately it is not easy to construct a set of rules like this though there are techniques that have been described, for example in Guttag and Horning (1978). Another problem with this type of specification is that it requires practice to get a mental picture of what the operations actually do from the axioms.

There is a fine distinction between a structured informal notation and an abstract notation. I have separated the 'informal' notation I used for the operational specification of Stack in the previous subsection from the almost identical notation used here for the axiomatic definition of Stack on two grounds:

1. The operational specification is based on a not very formal use of pseudo-code and hence can be termed 'informal'.
2. The axiomatic definition is rooted in the propositional calculus and is thus more of an abstract form.

4.3.4 Graphical notations

The use of graphical notations is a frequent adjunct to human communication. From a halting (or even fluent) exposition, we rapidly slip into, and out of, the world of pictures – for example, a quick sketch on the blackboard or gestures with the hands – as naturally as if we were grasping a handrail. As the much quoted Chinese proverb has it: 'one picture is worth a thousand words' with, of course, the corollary that an incorrect picture is the equivalent of a thousand wrong words.

It is in the design phase of the development life-cycle that graphical notations play their principal part, although they may also be used to enhance natural language in the

AXIOMS		Natural language equivalent of axioms (not part of abstract definition)
IsEmpty(NewStack())	= TRUE	The function IsEmpty when applied to the result of NewStack() always gives the boolean value TRUE.
IsEmpty(Push(St, El))	= FALSE	The function IsEmpty when applied to the result of Push(St, El), which pushes an element on to the stack, always gives the boolean value FALSE.
Pop(NewStack())	= NewStack()	The function Pop has no effect when applied to the result of NewStack()
Pop(Push(St, El))	= St	The function Pop applied to the result of Push(St, El) always leaves the stack unchanged, thus Pop and Push are defined as inverse operations.
Top(NewStack())	= ERROR	An attempt to apply the function Top to the result of NewStack() is an error and the result of the operation is undefined.
^Top(Push(St, El))	= El	The function Top applied to the result of Push(St, El) gives a pointer to the element just pushed onto the stack. It is to be understood that if Push(St, El) gives ERROR then the axiom becomes meaningless.

FIGURE 4.2 Axiomatic definition for definition of Stack.

functional specification of requirements, see Macro (1990). In general, graphical notations belong to generic 'methods' devised to assist, for certain application types, in the process of design decomposition with enrichment – where 'enrichment' is an unquantifiable concept conveying the notion of increasing the relevant detail of a solution while containing the complexity resulting from the increase in detail.

It is beyond the scope of a book on implementation to provide a detailed discussion of graphical notations, for which the reader is referred to Macro (1990) and Stevens (1991). However, some minimal clarity may be attempted by classification.

'Methods' generally comprise a procedure – rules for operation – and a notation, which is the pictorial language. If we separate them by usage, methods may be said to fall into roughly three categories:

- *Description:* for use in the requirements analysis part of the life-cycle. In addition to natural language, one may employ systems analysis methods such as Hipo, Jackson's

JSD , SADT™*, Entity Relationship Analysis, State Transition, and many others. The procedures of these methods tend to be more important than their notations – which are, in general, simple box and arrow schemes.

- *Architecture:* for use in design decomposition with detailing. Here the methods (including some already listed) tend to be application-relevant, that is more suited to certain types of requirement taken into solution design, than others. Here we find JSD, SADT, Data flow analysis, CCITT-SDL, Mascot, Petrinet simulation, DeWolf's method of abstract process characterization, Data transformation schema, and many others. At this level, it tends to be the notation that is more important than any of the procedures – with the exception of Petrinets, which can be executed, when adherence to the rules is essential.

In both the descriptive and the architecture cases, the reader will find abundant examples in the texts cited for detailed discussion of this subject, which we will not duplicate here since they concern mainly specification and design. Here, we are concerned with the parts of design leading to implementation, and with the use of graphical notations for that purpose.

The design process in software development may be seen as a stepwise process as shown in Figure 4.3. The use of graphical notations as the steps are descended culminates in the third classification:

- *Detail:* for use at and around the implementation level. Here, the 'methods' tend to be graphical notations only, with limited syntax. They include structured flowcharts, Nassi–Schneiderman charts, stylized flowcharts such as the *British Standards Institute BS 6224 Design Structure Diagrams*, and a variety of program structure and call hierarchy schema. In addition to these graphical notations, informal textual notations, semi-formal structured text such as pseudocode, and formal 'abstract' languages may be in use, at this level, for depicting detailed designs.

It is, perhaps, useful to revise what we are about at this point. Design is becoming sufficiently detailed, and common facilities are being identified, along with chunks of functionality that will probably result in program structures comprising generically or call-related hierarchies of integrands. All of these designs will comprise the definition of algorithms and accompanying data flows and logic relationships, and there will be (if this has not happened even earlier) a very strong impetus to define data formats and structures. This is the point at which design imperceptibly transforms into implementation.

As we said earlier, we can begin to consider the implementation stage from the time at which this rather uneven and fairly disordered state occurs; 'uneven' because all the detail design may not be equivalently defined; 'disordered' because there will still be a substantial amount of definition and organization work to do as implementation proceeds. The reader should understand that, while we may take the special case of a

---

*SADT is a trademark of SofTech Inc.

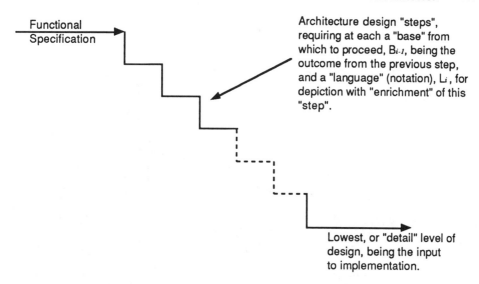

Functional Specification

Architecture design "steps", requiring at each a "base" from which to proceed, B_{i-1}, being the outcome from the previous step, and a "language" (notation), L_i, for depiction with "enrichment" of this "step".

Lowest, or "detail" level of design, being the input to implementation.

FIGURE 4.3 The software development staircase, as in Macro (1990).

single integrand for the purpose of discussion and illustration, real-life designs for substantial systems 'deliver' an amount of detailed information about all of the system-to-be.

As we have remarked elsewhere, we can take as typical of this input from design an external interface specification that may be, probably will be, still at too high a level of definition to be coded simply. Looked at *ex post facto*, we may find that our external interface specification results in a family of integrands, or in some integrands that socialize with common features elsewhere in the program-system. In any event, the external interface specification will probably be in a graphical notation – such as a structured flowchart. The Figures 3.2 and 3.3 in Chapter 3 depict this level of definition in BS 6224 notation. In addition, the reader will see in Figure 3.4 the result of the urge to define data structures and their relationships at this stage.

The next step is the intermediate one of defining an operational specification. This may further decompose the external specification down to the integrand level, but without the full rigor required to see it as the necessary and sufficient model for an implementation. Here, the notation may again be graphical, in any of the forms listed, or (perhaps more likely given the nature of implementors) it may be in pseudocode and this may lead to the notion of it being an equivalent (if inexact) program.

The integrand may then be coded in the language of choice, either with or without a formal, abstract-form definition of its purpose. When coding results from an operational specification, there will be some loss of isomorphism between the two, as the reality of the integrands supplants the metaphor of its specification; it is customary then to backtrack and redefine the integrand, graphically or textually, so that the documentation is exact. On the other hand, if a formal definition is attempted then it stands as the 'necessary and

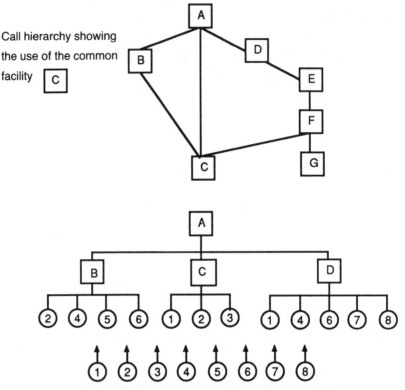

Call hierarchy showing the use of the common facility

Call hierarchy showing multiple use of integrands from a higher level program structure.

FIGURE 4.4 Graphical representation of call hierarchies.

sufficient' level for the purpose and may even be used for static proof that the program is 'correct' in the sense that a post-condition of the integrand will necessarily follow from a given pre-condition, or not if the intermediary code is incorrect. In the case of formal definition, the notation will be some derivate of predicate logic.

The use of graphical notations down to code level is, and has been since the inception of programming as we know it, ubiquitous – although the use of pseudocode has increased since the advent of modern PSEs with easy text-editing facilities for the syntax of one's favorite programming language, which is all that pseudocode is. An additional use of graphical notation, for documentation purposes rather than design, comes just before and just after coding. This concerns the call hierarchy of integrands and programs in systems where this can be prescribed or predicted. Thus, diagrams of the sort shown in Figure 4.4, which are not connected with the Running Example, may be seen.

By far the most common graphical notations in use at low level of design and in implementation, are flowcharts – either structured or stylized. The basic elements for structured flowcharts are discussed in Chapter 10, whilst of all the stylized schema BS 6224 is probably the most powerful (Macro 1990). Nassi–Schneiderman charts (Nassi and Schneiderman 1973), which Chapin (1974) refer to as 'Chapin charts', are self-limiting in two useful ways: only well-structured (see Section 10.3.2) control flows can be represented and the size of the algorithm that can be represented is self-limiting through one of its constructs:

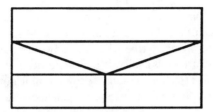

This shows the Nassi–Schneiderman convention for choices following an ordinary statement that does not affect control flow. The repetitive use of this on a page leads to microscopic or anyway increasing small elements as shown in the example in Figure 4.5. This has the advantage that the bounds of both visual acuity and mental ability to master complexity are reached at approximately the same time.

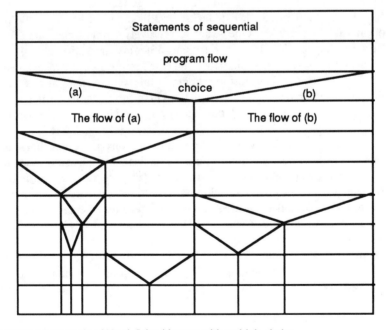

FIGURE 4.5 Example of Nassi–Schneiderman with multiple choice.

There has been little enthusiam for graphical notations at this level of the life-cycle, over the years, and for some good reasons:

1. Poverty-stricken malnourished little sketches, flowcharts and structure diagrams, are often cobbled together as *a posteriori* program documentation.
2. Historically, even when flowcharts were attempted as *a priori* designs, they represented an ill-structured and generally too high a level of definition to be adequate for the coding stage without the refinement of further decomposition and detailing or the creation of operational specifications.
3. The ratio of 1K words/picture is reduced at the implementation level and very often the *ex post facto* flowcharts said no more than the code-listing, even disregarding the comments. This was particularly true when the flowcharts were generated from the code by one of the software tools available for the purpose. All too often, the effect of these tools was to convert the fairly compact programming notation into a sprawl over many pages to meet the letter of the requirement that the documentation contain flowcharts. When the code was – as was common – an unstructured tangle, the corresponding flowchart was a horror of intersecting lines and boxes.

For these reasons, graphical notations had and have a bad reputation, quite wrongly in fact. Most of the notations described do have quite acute limits, being simple box and arrow, or bubble and line constructions, some combinations of these with the simplest grammar attaching to their use. In fact, graphical notations are neutral – neither good nor bad, even the maligned flowchart – and their virtues or vices lie in their use.

Some graphical notations are claimed to be of general use across the software development life-cycle. Thus, SADT or Jackson's JSD might be so considered, and for small applications of a particular type – such as relatively simple serial data processing, this may be a valid supposition. However, in many other instances, the general scheme of appropriateness for descriptive, architecture and detail purposes is the case, and one may find, say SADT and Entity relationship schema in the systems analysis and functional specification phase, Mascot and Petrinet depictions in the architecture design decomposition stage, BS 6224 and Pseudocode at the detail design and implementation level, and a call hierarchy chart made after the fact.

There is nothing against this state of affairs; all notations and other 'languages' are merely tools, and one would not think to employ a single tool to make a wooden table for example, but use a saw, plane, chisel, hammer, screwdriver, and so on, at appropriate stages. The same is true of software development – and the keyword is 'appropriate'. In some cases, to use a particular notation at a certain stage may be analogous to driving nails with the handle of the screwdriver – possible, perhaps, but silly and ineffectual if a hammer is at hand.

Until recently, one inhibition on the use of graphical notations was the lack of support tools, since the implementation of graphics in general requires particular features of the display hardware, and tends to consume computer processing power for image storage, retrieval and emendation. With the advent of improved screen displays in the early 1980s, and the development of PC-based workstations to more powerful host machines in the same epoch, the problems of implementing graphical notations within PSEs were reduced. These days many support environments have facilities for creating, storing, and emending a variety of graphical notations, such as SADT, JSD, finite state diagrams, Mascot, Dataflow, Petrinets, BS 6224, and elementary structured flowcharts.

Whereas before there was a reasonable inhibition in the use of graphical notations, much bad 'press' to support prejudice, and a relative ease of using pseudocode (plus an impetus to do so from advocates of formal methods and abstract languages), now the electronic environment of the designer and implementor permits far more options.

The notations mentioned above are graphical and need to be drawn and redrawn, and redrawn, . . . Until recently, all the drawing and redrawing has been by manual labor, and for this reason diagrams have generally lagged behind the evolution of thought. Gries (1981) refers to flowcharts as 'flawcharts'.

When choosing one of the graphical notations it is essential to have available a convenient software tool that will allow easy updating of the diagrams. Such a system should go beyond just drawing charts by providing proper restructuring so that they are always easy to read.

4.4 THE ABSTRACTION OF CONTENT

As described in Section 2.2.2, an external specification of an integrand consists of three parts: descriptions of the inputs, the outputs, and the function. The definition of the function should properly be a description of the essence, the Platonic ideal, of the integrand. That is, it should contain only the essential information that is required to implement the desired integrand.

4.4.1 Distilling the essence

Abstraction is the art of discarding the inessential. The skill in making an abstraction lies in deciding precisely what is inessential and may be discarded. If facts that are essential are omitted then there can be implementations that do not perform as required. If inessentials are included then some potential implementations are excluded and it may be more difficult to modify the implementation later.

4.4.2 Levels of abstraction

A program is an abstraction of a real-life process. The notation that is used to express the program, the programming language, is also an abstraction. A programming language provides abstractions in two ways:

- The programming language offers facilities that allow the programmer the ability to build abstractions that match the application being programmed. These abstractions form another level of virtual machine. The subroutine invocation:

  ```
  Sort(DataFile);
  ```

  appears as a direct instruction to a virtual machine that has a Sort operation.

- It provides the programmer with a virtual machine, one that exists only on a conceptual level, that is divorced from the often squalid realities of actual hardware with its compromises to what can actually be realized in silicon and mechanics. This virtual machine is almost always, if the language designer is worthy of the title, simpler to use and more powerful than the actual underlying computer hardware. This virtual machine is characterized as a useful set of abstractions that we think of as the 'features' of the machine. The beginning programmer is often convinced that the computer actually executes statements in Basic directly.

We always make use of abstractions. When we read a program written in a high-level language, we usually do so to understand its meaning without considering the machine instructions into which it will be translated for execution. Under some circumstances, for example, when we are developing a compiler, we may need to look at these machine instructions and understand how they will make the hardware behave. However, we generally do this without considering the binary form in which instructions will be represented in the machine and how they will cause the logical gates and flip-flops of the processor to act. If this last is the level of detail at which we must work then we will probably not need to consider the voltage changes on the individual transistors. At each level of detail, we are taking the next level of greater detail for granted and this can go on until we represent states by means of wave equations. Each of these levels is a *level of abstraction*.

Computer programs must handle many details. One of the keys to writing clear programs is to present these details hierarchically by dividing the program into sub-procedures. This division is analogous to the way that a book is divided into chapters, the chapters into sections, the sections into paragraphs, and the paragraphs into sentences. Each part of the hierarchy implies a degree of detail that defines a level of abstraction. A notation helps understanding by providing a level of abstraction.

Thus, successive levels of the hierarchy provide a sequence of abstractions, each following from the preceding one by adding more detail. To take an example closer to programming, suppose we are writing some software to interact with a disk drive. This device can be viewed at a number of levels starting at one that is very abstract:

- A collection of files referred to within an application program through logical names that are private to the program. These logical names contain no information about where in the system any particular file is stored; indeed, the correspondence between logical names and actual files can be changed easily. This is the utility of the logical names – they are built into the program instead of details about particular files. By changing the correspondence, the same program can be used to refer to different files. Within the program, the logical names are used as abstractions of the concept *file*.

- A collection of data sets (throughout this book, the term *file* will be used to refer to the abstract concept of a file as used in a program while *data set* will mean the actual collection of data recorded in the system) referred to in the system command language through names that are recorded in a directory together with other information such as version number, protection status, and organization.
- A mass storage organized by tracks and sectors with control blocks that specify the organization of the data on the device. System programs that are concerned with the allocation, freeing, and accounting for space on the devices work at this level.
- A collection of addressable bytes of data. The actual 'device driver' routines that send the control signals and data to the physical storage device, receive data from it, and respond to its status and interrupt signals, operate at this level of detail.
- A physical device that receives control signals and data, and that produces status and interrupt signals and data. The logical design of its controller electronics is concerned directly with these concepts.

Each of these views constitutes a level of abstraction. As we go down the list, the view becomes more detailed. In summary, abstraction allows us to view the sheep without being distracted by the wool fibers.

4.4.3 The abstract program

In the context of programming, the external specification for an integrand is the highest level of content abstraction for the integrand. (The highest level of abstraction of form for the integrand is the bit pattern of the translated program.) At this level, the integrand is defined without specifying any details that are not required to define the process to be performed by it. Only the input and output data and the way in which they are related are given. The actual algorithm that links the two is not defined. The specification is an *abstract program* in that it represents *all* possible programs that could be written to perform the integrand's task, from the simplest and most elegant to the most ridiculous. They are all valid implementations providing they meet the requirements of the external specification.

We can illustrate this idea by returning to the example of the SquareRoot integrand used in Section 2.2.2.

External specification:

$$\textbf{Input:}\ X: REAL, > 0$$
$$\textbf{Output:}\ Y: REAL$$
$$\textbf{Function:}\ \sqrt{x} - \varepsilon < y < \sqrt{x} + \varepsilon$$
$$\text{where } \varepsilon = x \times 10^{-6}$$

Equivalent program:

Pseudocode equivalent of flowchart

$$\text{SET } y_1 = x/2$$
$$\text{SET } k = 1$$
$$\text{REPEAT}$$
$$\quad \text{SET } y_{k-1} = (y_k^2 + x)/2y_k$$
$$\quad \text{INCREMENT } k \text{ by } 1$$
$$\text{UNTIL } |y_{k-1} - y_k| \leq x \times 10^{-6}$$

Operational specification:

Flowchart for Newton–Raphson square root algorithm

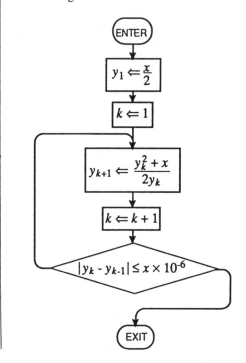

Note that the Function defined in the External specification leaves it to the implementor to decide on the algorithm, for example, interpolation from a stored table might be used, provided the specified accuracy could be guaranteed. The Operational specification, either as a flowchart or equivalent program, leaves no such choice.

The process of implementing an integrand from its specification consists of supplying details that are not contained in the specification. The sequence: external specification, operational specification, pseudocode, real program shows the addition of more and more details as the real program is approached. Each time a new piece of information is added, a new abstract program is constructed, forming a sequence of programs, each more detailed than its predecessor. The end of the sequence is a complete program with everything specified. Each of the abstract programs in the sequence represents an ever smaller class of possible programs until the class has only one member – the final complete program. For each possible program that satisfies the specification there is such a chain of abstractions.

It is sometimes forgotten that this principle of consistency within a level of abstraction works in both directions. At a particular level of abstraction, there must be no information about the context in which this level will be used. This is important so as to make the set of potential invocation contexts as broad as possible and the integrand as widely useful as can be.

4.4.4 Abstract data type

A major decision during program design concerns the representation of data. A program is a description of a computer model of some real-world process that manipulates real-world data such as names, salaries, taxes, and pensions, in a payroll process. The computer model represents these real-world data by sequences of bits that are interpreted as having some of the properties of their real-world counterparts. The choice of representation can have a great effect on the clarity and correctness of the computer model. For example, a telephone number is not really a number but is a sequence of digits that are used to identify a telephone line. Thus, an integer or a floating-point number would not be suitable representations for a telephone number, since we never perform arithmetic operations on it. It makes no sense to speak of the average telephone number of one's friends. Thus a character string would be better for storing a telephone number than a floating point number.

The actual hardware of a computer ordinarily includes no provision for restricting the operations that can be performed on an item of data. At that level, everything is viewed as a collection of bits, without any distinction. Once you have seen one bit, you have seen them all. The programmer supplies an interpretation for the bit patterns through the program. The first higher-level languages provided a set of basic *data types* such as *real*, *integer*, and *character string*. *Type checking* was provided to ensure that only reasonable operations are applied to data of a particular type. Thus it is not possible to add two telephone numbers represented as character strings. Although, through type checking, the set of operations on a variable of a particular type were limited, this set did not necessarily correspond to operations on the real-world counterpart of the data item. For example, if the real-world process manipulated dates, the computer model might represent these as integers, giving the number of days that have elapsed since the beginning of the Julian era, 1 January 4713 BC. Representing dates as integers means that all the operations that are available for integers can be performed on the modeled dates. The programmer faced with the task of finding a date mid-way between two given dates would be tempted to add the dates and divide by two. The compiler type-checking mechanism will raise no objections to this, because these are valid operations on integers. However, in doing this, the programmer is working at the wrong level of abstraction. In the real world, adding two dates has no meaning and writing an expression that does this fractures the abstraction. We can subtract one date from another to obtain a time interval – for example, 1989:September11 − 1989:April26 = 138 days – this can be divided in half to produce another time interval, which can be added to a date to produce a new date, that is, the date that is mid-way between the two original dates. The computer model of a real-world data item needs to model also the set of real-world operations that can be performed on that data item.

The early characterization of a data type was a *set of values* that a variable of that type might take. Languages such as Fortran, Cobol, and PL/I offered a limited set of *primitive types* each with its own set of fixed values. Pascal advanced from this by adding separate *type definitions*, which allowed the programmer to define data types, each with its own set of possible values, for example,

```
TYPE WeekDay = (Mon, Tue, Wed, Thu, Fri, Sat, Sun);
```

The next step in the evolution of the concept of data type lies in the understanding that a data type comprises not just a set of data objects but also a set of operations to manipulate those data objects. The set of operations NewStack, Push, Top, Pop, and IsEmpty described earlier in this chapter characterized the data type Stack. This was done without prescribing a particular representation. A type that is defined entirely by a set of operations is an *abstract data type*. There are two major advantages to defining a type as a set of operations:

1. The separation of operations from questions of representation results in data independence. The representation can be changed without corresponding changes in the parts of the program that manipulate the data through the operations.
2. The operations can be defined rigorously. In Section 4.3.3 we gave a set of axioms that define the stack operations. The implementor of a stack type defined in this way knows precisely what has to be implemented and knows precisely what must be tested to show that it has been accomplished.

At each level of abstraction, in the implementation of an abstract program, there may be a set of abstract data types each characterized by a set of values and a set of operations that can manipulate these values. For example, a database application may need to manipulate a set of logical files. One of its abstract data types will thus be a file and the operations that it will need to perform will be to open, close, read, and write these files. These operations will be used in the context of making logical decisions on which files to work with and what data to use from the files. It would make these decisions very much more complicated to have to handle the physical details of finding the proper track, controlling the read and write heads, and performing checksums and error recovery when required.

4.4.5 Constructive procrastination

It takes discipline to maintain a single level of abstraction throughout the final code for an integrand. This is not a discipline that we generally maintain in our daily lives. Listen to any conversation, technical or otherwise, and note how rapidly the level of abstraction changes, how easy it is to slip off into a discussion of some details that are not germane to the main subject level. There is mental safety in details, they are much easier to think about and visualize than abstractions. The mind can straphang on these details and get a more comfortable ride. However they are also dangerous, for once described, they tend to become fixed and wield a power of their own that can warp the proper development of the abstraction.

In the development of programs, postpone making any decisions as long as possible. Avoid making decisions about details before it is necessary. Very often, details decided upon too early will need to be changed when other higher-level decisions are made. This is one place where the fine and ancient art of procrastination that we all practice with strong feelings of guilt can be used to good advantage. This is not to say never make a decision but rather postpone making a decision until it is impossible to make further progress without it. This is the process of *constructive procrastination* and is practiced with a feeling of triumph rather than guilt.

An example of making a decision in the composition of a program is what is known as *binding*. The term is generally used in programming to mean the process of resolving or associating an identifier to a specific referent. At the time this is done, the abstraction represented by the identifier becomes concrete. The time-line of a program may be thought of as extending from the beginning of its requirements up to and including its execution. The point on this line at which a binding is made is the *binding time* of the association. Bindings can occur at various points along this line, for example:

- *During program composition:* the association of a value to be used with a named constant in an integrand.

```
CONST
    Rate = 1.20;
```

- *During compilation* of the source code: the identifiers for functions that are intrinsic to the language, for example Sin, become associated with specific library routines that evaluate the function with the appropriate precision.
- *During the linking* of integrands to form a complete executable program: At this time, the references between integrands are bound.
- *When execution of the program is initiated:* some constants are specified by means of parameters in command parameters.
- *During execution:* during the invocation of a sub-routine an argument becomes associated with a parameter, the parameter identifier is bound to the argument. The terms *argument* and *parameter* are used with various meanings in the literature. In this book, they are used as follows: the information that is *passed* to a subprogram by an invoker is an *argument*; the information that is *received from* an invoker by a subprogram is a *parameter*. The duration of this binding and its form depend upon the language being used.

The binding time of an identifier has a great effect upon the flexibility of the program in a way that is simple and direct: the later the binding, the greater the flexibility. However flexibility obtained by delayed binding time may come at a cost in execution time. We will discuss this in a later chapter.

From the point of view of developing an integrand, delaying the making of decisions until their proper time maintains the flexibility of the development process by preserving the abstraction, and avoids a great deal of backtracking if it is discovered that a decision was made early and badly.

In Chapter 9, we will discuss the abstract data types that are needed for the Running Example.

CHAPTER FIVE
FIGHTING THE TYRANNY
OF COMPLEXITY

There is a strong temptation to make things more complex than they need to be. We find safety in complexity and admire those who appear able to grasp it mentally. We constantly delude ourselves into believing that we can manage almost unbounded complexity. Even in a program consisting of many integrands, there can be a great deal of complexity stemming from the way information is passed between the constituent integrands through their interconnections. A first design for the Running Example shows that the interconnections are such that many of the possible changes in the program's specifications will require modifications to many of the integrands. In order to reduce the scope of such modifications, we introduce the idea of 'hiding' information in a specific integrand. A second design shows how this could be achieved. The complexity of interconnections depends upon the mechanism used for passing the data and this is illustrated by considering three methods: global variables, control blocks, and argument-parameters. The dangers of the first two methods are discussed. Finally, the concept of an integrand's unity of purpose is elaborated.

5.1 THE LURE OF COMPLEXITY

Some years ago, I was involved in the selection of new faculty staff for a university department. Each candidate was invited to visit the department for a day, be interviewed by members of the faculty, and present a lecture to the faculty and students. I noticed that, if the lecture material was presented in a manner that was difficult to understand with a notation that tended to obscure rather than illuminate, the reaction was, 'That candidate was great! There was real intelligence and mastery of subject there.' However, if material of the same complexity was presented in a clear and easily understood style, the reaction was, 'That candidate wasn't very good. Fancy insulting us in that way by giving a lecture on such trivial material!' We all seem to want to make things more complex than they really are so as to show our listeners or readers how wonderfully intelligent we are at being able to handle this great complexity. This is the root of the programming one-liner – 'Can you guess what this does?' – and the competitions that are run by some trade magazines for the most inscrutable program.

120

We can also slip into complexity unwittingly, through laziness or lack of proper knowledge about program construction. In the throes of creation, we continue to build a program, adding another bell here, another whistle there until finally we find that we have built a monster of complexity. By the time our brain child is working, we are under pressure to give it to our users, there is a new project waiting to be started, and there is a large part of ourselves invested in it. To start again is tantamount to infanticide. At no stage during the creation process did we stop to look at what we were producing and realize that the program had to be restructured. We have been verging on being what Weizenbaum (1976) calls a *compulsive programmer*:

> He knows that he can make the computer do anything he wants it to do . . . but the computer nevertheless reproaches him by misbehaving in a number of mysterious, apparently unrelated ways. It is then that the system the programmer has himself created gives every evidence of having taken on a life of its own and, certainly, of having slipped from his control. . . . Should he, however, find a deeply embedded error, one that actually does account for much of the program's misbehavior, his joy is unbounded. It *is* a thrill to see a hitherto moribund program suddenly come back to life; there is no other way to say it. . . . But the compulsive programmer's pride and elation are very brief. His success consists of his having shown the computer who its master is. And having demonstrated that he can make it do this much, he immediately sets out to make it do even more. . . . The act of modifying the then-existing program invariably causes some of its substructures to collapse; they constitute, after all, an amorphous collection of processes whose interactions with one another are virtually fortuitous.

Whether we create complexity deliberately or fall prey to it through laziness, we delude ourselves into believing that we can manage almost unbounded complexity. Jugglers have a limit to the number of balls they can keep in the air at once. A mental analog to this limit is the number of concepts we can keep in our mind at once. As a name for this bound, Booch (1983) introduces the term *Hrair limit* based on *Watership Down* (Adams 1972), where, on page 13, Adams determines this limit to be about four for rabbits and Miller (1956) estimates that for humans it is only seven, plus or minus two. It is likely that, if the concepts are complex, the number should be reduced. In any case, even if it is seven, we are strictly limited in what we can remember in the short term: how many mental balls we can keep in the air at once.

A consequence of the Hrair limit is our threshold of complexity. For each of us there is a limit to the complexity that we can understand, but it flatters our egos to ignore this limit and revel in the joy of our program's complexity and our imagined mastery of it. We can conjugate the imaginary irregular verb:

> I write clever programs.
> You write obscure programs.
> He writes unmaintainable programs.

Our delusion thus consists in denying the finiteness of our brain and making believe that we can in fact master almost unbounded complexity. In this chapter we will discuss the complexity of a complete program; the complexity of its constituent integrands is the subject for a later chapter.

5.2 INTERCONNECTIONS

In Section 2.3.6, we used the metaphor of the water-tight compartments of a ship to illustrate the way in which the scope of a change to a program can be limited to a few integrands. Two integrands that are mutually independent can each function completely without the presence of the other. Because there are no interconnections between the integrands either direct or indirect, a change can be made to one without requiring a consequential change to the other. However, for a set of integrands to be able to work together as a program they must be interconnected. The greater the number of interconnections, the more difficult it is to understand the working of the complete program. In this section we consider the question of the degree of interconnection of the integrands of a program.

The *degree of interconnection* between integrands is an abstract concept. The obvious measure involves the amount of information that passes between the integrands. However, the concept 'amount of information' is vague. It is easy to think of passing information between arguments and parameters but this is only part of the traffic. Information can also be passed through global variables and files. When we talk of information being passed, we generally think of data in the conventional sense. Suppose an integrand opens a file so that some other integrand may write to it. In this sense, the open state of the file is being passed from one integrand to another and thus constitutes an interconnection. It would perhaps be foolish to try to enumerate here all the possible ways of passing information. Instead, we characterize an interconnection as

> An assumption made by one integrand about another.

Such an assumption is really the passage of information. The key question is: How much information must be passed between the two integrands in order for them to work together? The terms 'how much' and 'passed between' are used in a very broad sense here; they cover the following:

- *The time at which the information is passed.* This can vary from program composition time to execution time, as with binding time. Information is 'passed' at program composition time when something is written in integrand A because of something that is written in integrand B. It is now impossible to change one of these two integrands without making a consequent change in the other. This is another booby trap in the road to consistency. As with any booby trap worthy of the title, its position is not advertised. Not only is its position undocumented, and here is where yet another metaphor fails, the setter of the trap is often not aware of having done so. The interconnection is recorded in the subconscious of the program's creator. At the other end of the scale, data that are passed through the argument-parameter connection are examples of information being passed at execution time. This is very much easier to manage because it is shown explicitly in the invocation statement.

- *The way in which the information is passed.* Information can be passed through global variables, parameters or other mechanisms. The particular mechanism used has an effect upon the degree of interconnectedness of the integrands. As in the free market, publicity is the road to success. Argument-parameter mechanisms are well publicized, global variables are documented but must be searched for to be discovered.
- *The complexity of the information that is passed.* This is really a measure of the number of different logical items passed. This need not have a direct relation to the amount of data passed. A number is a number irrespective of how many bits of precision are used to represent it. From the conceptual point of view, the abstraction of an item represented by a record with many fields counts as a single item. The same number of fields passed as individual items is much more complex, partially because they do not have the same degree of abstraction and therefore take more mental effort to understand.
- *The type of information that is passed.* There are two types of information that are passed between integrands, pure data, which will be processed by the receiving integrand, and control information, for example flags, which are used to affect the operation of the receiving integrand in a way *that is known by the user*. The passing of pure data provides less of a connection than the passing of control information. Control information is a stronger interconnection since the calling integrand influences the execution of the called integrand. Although the values of data that are passed can have an influence on the execution of the called integrand, the use of control information implies some knowledge of the internal processing of the called integrand – it is no longer a 'black box'. Thus a change to either of the partners is more likely to require a change to the other to maintain consistency.

5.3 THE RUNNING EXAMPLE

At this point we need to digest some of the definitions that we have introduced by taking the Running Example a stage further. Later subsections, Section 5.4 onwards, will develop further themes based on the development of the Running Example in this section. The specification of requirements and general software design is found in Chapter 3. Based on this software design, we may now look at some of the implementation decisions. In order to keep the size of the implementation of Running Example within bounds, only that part that generates the Printfile from Titlestore and Lexicon will be considered further.

5.3.1 First design for BuildPrintfile

The external specification for BuildPrintfile derived in Chapter 3 is:

Input: *Titlestore:* an ordered set of character strings consisting of words separated by blanks. Each string consists of two parts, a Title-Part and a Reference-Part. The Reference-Part is enclosed in brackets.

> *Lexicon:* an ordered set of character strings, each string consists of a single word.

Output: *Printfile:* an ordered set of representations of the elements of Titlestore, separated into 26 parts, see Function below.

Function: Build Printfile from the data contained in Titlestore and Lexicon. Each Title-Part of Titlestore contains keywords, that is words that are not contained in Lexicon. For each keyword in the Title-Parts there will be an element in Printfile with a designation of the keyword. The elements of Printfile are ordered alphabetically by designated keyword, the complete file being split into 26 parts according to the initial letter of the designated keyword, there being one part for each letter of the alphabet.

As an illustration of the interconnections that exist between integrands consider the simple dataflow design specification of the BuildPrintfile program shown in Figure 5.1 using the notation of Gane and Sarson (1977). This specification shows that outside the system is a source of data in the format given in the requirements, the 'Title File', a 'Noise Word Lexicon', which contains a list of noise words, and an output for the results, the 'Print File', which is such that it can be printed in the format defined in the requirements. This single BuildPrintfile process can be broken down into four sub-processes that transform the input into the output as shown in Figure 5.2.

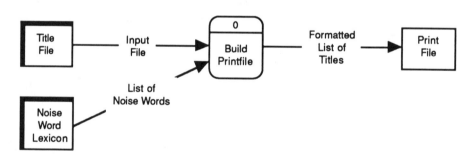

FIGURE 5.1 Dataflow design specification of BuildPrintfile program.

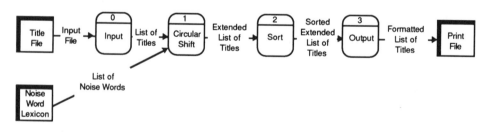

FIGURE 5.2 Dataflow design specification showing BuildPrintfile split into four sub-processes.

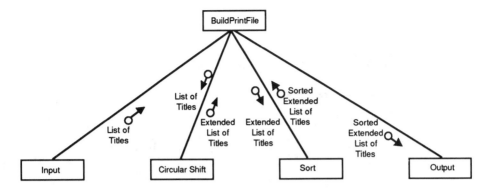

FIGURE 5.3 Structure diagram for first design of BuildPrintfile program.

The four processes are defined as follows:

- *Input*. This process takes the *Input file* in the format defined by the requirements and converts it into the *List of Titles and References* in an internal format, not yet defined.
- *Circular Shift*. This process takes each element in the *List of Titles* and for each word in the title that is not in the *Noise Word Lexicon*, a 'keyword' produces a circularly shifted copy of the title with the keyword at the beginning. To this circularly shifted title is associated the reference and the two are added to the *Extended List of Titles*.
- *Sort*. This process sorts into alphabetical order the *Extended List of Titles* to produce the *Sorted Extended List of Titles*.
- *Output*. This process takes the *Sorted Extended List of Titles* and converts it to the printing format given by the requirements and puts it into the *Formatted List of Titles*.

Obviously, there are many other solutions to the problem including those that use concurrent processes. The solution discussed here is adopted because it is simple and can be easily used as an illustration for the ideas discussed in this book.

This specification suggests a control flow organization that splits the BuildPrintfile program into four procedures invoked sequentially as shown in the structure chart shown in Figure 5.3 in the notation of Stevens *et al.* (1974). This outline of the program represents what might be an early step in the design process to be used for investigating its suitability for implementation. It will serve as a basis for our discussion of interconnections between modules. An outline of the program as it might be implemented in Modula-2 is shown in Figure 5.4. This could be thought of as an operational specification for the next stage in the implementation.

It would seem that we have managed to segment the problem into logically independent parts. However, a test of this is to see what would be involved if some likely changes had to be made to the program.

1. *Data and listing formats*. The item of the specifications that is most likely to change is the external representation of the data. It would be 'more convenient' to present the data differently or the output would be 'easier to use' if its format were rearranged.

```
MODULE BuildPrintfile;
    PROCEDURE Input;
    BEGIN
        (* Read the input data consisting of lines containing a Title-Part *)
        (* followed by the reference marker [ and a Reference-Part         *)
        (* terminated by ] and convert to internal format.                 *)
    END Input;

    PROCEDURE CircularShift;
    BEGIN
        (* From the Title-Part of each title in the list of titles,        *)
        (* construct all possible titles consisting of circularly shifted  *)
        (* Title-Parts followed by copies of the Reference-Part from the   *)
        (* original title. Constructed titles, and possibly the original   *)
        (* title, that start a word contained in the Noise Word Lexicon are*)
        (* discarded.                                                      *)
    END CircularShift;

    PROCEDURE Sort;
    BEGIN
        (* Sort the extended list of titles produced by CircularShift into *)
        (* alphabetical order.                                             *)
    END Sort;

    PROCEDURE Output;
    BEGIN
        (* Prepare the sorted data produced by Sort for printing.  The     *)
        (* Title-Part is shown in its original form and occupies           *)
        (* TitlePartLen characters with the first word of its circularly   *)
        (* shifted form starting at KeywordPosition characters from the    *)
        (* beginning of the printed line. Where a TitlePart must be        *)
        (* truncated at the beginning or end to fit into TitlePartLen after*)
        (* alignment, the truncation is shown by an ellipsis, (...). The   *)
        (* Reference-Part is listed on the same line as the TitlePart and  *)
        (* starts TitlePartLen + TitleRefGap characters from the beginning *)
        (* of the printed line.  If the Reference-Part is too long to be   *)
        (* printed on the line, it is truncated and this is marked with an *)
        (* ellipsis.                                                       *)
    END Output;
BEGIN
    Input;
    CircularShift;
    Sort;
    Output
END BuildPrintfile.
```

FIGURE 5.4 Skeleton of BuildPrintfile program version 1.

With the splitting shown in the skeleton, modifications to accommodate either of these format changes will be limited to either the Input or the Output procedures. Thus the scope of the program modifications will be limited and probably cannot be improved by some other arrangement.

2. *Where the data are stored.* Suppose that in the first version of the program, the data are stored in main memory, in an array for example. This may have been an early design decision based on the idea of minimizing execution time. However, if the program is successful, users will want to apply the program to increasingly large sets of data. Eventually, there will be too much to keep in main memory and some secondary storage medium will have to be used. As the design stands, no mention is made of where the data will be stored. Given the conventional wisdom current in most

programming environments, it is not mentioned because 'everybody knows that it is held in a globally defined array'. It is understood that each of the procedures makes direct reference to the data, probably with direct references to the array. The question 'Why is the data storage not explicitly mentioned?' would probably elicit the response 'To allow flexibility.' Unfortunately, the effect of this silence is to reduce rather than enhance flexibility. The conventional wisdom is spread throughout the program. The 'everybody knows' is implemented in each integrand. The change to the use of secondary storage will impact each of the procedures in a rather drastic way.

3. *How the data are represented.* There are several ways in which the data could be represented. The most obvious perhaps is for each title and circularly shifted title to be stored in a record, for example:

```
TYPE
    LongString  = ARRAY [0..120] OF CHAR;
    ShortString = ARRAY [0..40]  OF CHAR;
    Line        = RECORD
                        TitlePart:     LongString;
                        ReferencePart: ShortString;
                  END;
```

The end of the character string in each part is marked by a special character. While the simplicity of this scheme is attractive, it is very expensive in space since each Title Part and Reference Part is entirely repeated for each circularly shifted version. This will ensure an early need for secondary storage. An alternative would be to keep one array of these records, created during input. Each circularly shifted version could then be stored as an index into the array and a count of the number of characters to be shifted – a count of characters is preferable to a word count since this avoids scanning for word gaps during processing. However, we are not discussing the merits of various methods of storing data but demonstrating that there is more than one method. Again, a change in the form of the stored data would impact each one of the procedures. The form of the representation of the data is another interconnection between the integrands. Even though there is no direct interconnection between Input and Output, the data representation forms an implicit interconnection, which is none the less real.

We conclude from this analysis that the first design only appeared to be simple because all the interconnections were below the surface and only documented in the designer's mind. We need to make a clear distinction between the hidden details in the abstractions and those in this case. In an abstraction, the details are readily available and are comprehended as part of the abstraction. In the first design of the BuildPrintfile program, the detailed connections are buried deeply with no map by which to dig. It is not that the interconnections have been put out of sight to achieve mental clarity, as is done with abstractions, but rather that they have been ignored; possibly to the extent of being forgotten or unsuspected. There is no guarantee that the reader's mind would have the same documentation. The only part of the design that was explicitly stated was the flow of

```
MODULE BuildPrintfile;
    FROM TitleStore IMPORT Title, TitleIn, TitleOut;

    PROCEDURE Input;
    BEGIN
        (* Read the input data consisting of lines containing a Title- *)
        (* Part followed by the reference marker [ and a Reference-Part*)
        (* terminated by ] and convert to internal format.           *)
    END Input;

    PROCEDURE CircularShift;
    BEGIN
        (* From the Title-Part of each title in the list of titles    *)
        (* construct all possible titles consisting of circularly     *)
        (* Title-Parts followed by copies of the Reference Part from   *)
        (* the original entry. Constructed titles that start with a   *)
        (* word contained in the List of Noise Words are ignored.     *)
    END CircularShift;

    PROCEDURE Sort;
    BEGIN
        (* Sort the augmented data produced by CircularShift.         *)
    END Sort;

    PROCEDURE Output;
    BEGIN
        (* Prepare the sorted data produced by CircularShift for      *)
        (* printing in the format defined by the requirements.        *)
    END Output;
BEGIN
    Input;
    CircularShift;
    Sort;
    Output
END BuildPrintfile

DEFINITION MODULE TitleStore;
    TYPE       Title;
    PROCEDURE TitleIn(TitleForStore: Title): CARDINAL;
    PROCEDURE TitleOut(TitleKey: CARDINAL): Title;
END TitleStore.
```

FIGURE 5.5 Skeleton of BuildPrintfile program version 2.

control, which was simple; the data flow was complex and required implicit assumptions in each of the parts.

5.3.2 Introduction of explicit title storage

Our first attempt at a design for the BuildPrintfile program failed to provide a solution that would be stable under the kind of changes one might expect during its life. Its downfall was the question of storage of the data. Our next attempt at a design is shown in Figure 5.5. There, we have a separate integrand (*module* in Modula-2 parlance), TitleStore, that manages the storage of titles with two procedures TitleIn and TitleOut.

TitleStore stores each title separately, assigning a key that can be used for retrieval to each. TitleIn takes a title and returns a key, much like a cloakroom attendant gives a token to a patron in exchange for a coat. TitleOut takes a key and returns a title – the cloakroom analog still holds with the return of the coat in exchange for the token.

In Modula-2 integrands are defined in two parts, a *Definition Module* and an *Implementation Module*. The definition module contains all the information about the integrand that is to be made public, that is to say, that can be used by other modules. The definition module does not contain code but instead contains the interface needed to use the facilities provided by the implementation module part of the integrand. The interface definition attaches meanings to identifiers. It includes the identifiers for constants, types, and procedures. In the case of TitleStore, three identifiers are defined, the type Title and the two procedures TitleIn and TitleOut.

The main part of the program, BuildPrintfile makes explicit its intention to use the services of TitleStore through the IMPORT statement:

```
FROM TitleStore IMPORT Title, TitleIn, TitleOut;
```

BuildPrintfile can now use the three identifiers Title, TitleIn, and TitleOut with these meanings in its program.

Two other things to note about the definition module for TitleStore are concerned with what is specified and what is not specified. The identifier Title is defined as being a type but no details are given of the actual representation for a title. That information is hidden inside the implementation module for TitleStore. BuildPrintfile may declare variables to be of type Title but the only operations that can be performed on them will be provided through TitleStore. Two such operations are TitleIn and TitleOut. The definition module defines the interfaces to these procedures; TitleIn takes a data item of type Title and returns a **CARDINAL** key that be used to retrieve the title through TitleOut, which takes the key and returns the corresponding title.

At this stage in the elaboration of the example, nothing is said about how a Title value is constructed from the list of titles and citations contained in the input file. Since nothing is known about the structure of such values, additional operations will have to be provided to other integrands by TitleStore to do this. This will be discussed in Chapter 9. In addition, the interfaces of Input, CircularShift, Sort, and Output will be defined later.

The major point to note from this version is that the details of how titles are stored, how they are associated with keys, and where they are stored are *hidden* in one place inside the implementation module of the TitleStore integrand.

The design of the integrand TitleStore has been made on the basis of *information hiding*, a concept introduced in Parnas (1972) and discussed in Section 2.5.4 above. It may seem strange to use the hiding of information as a design principle. It would seem that if everything were made clear and public, it would be easier to understand the program and hence easier to modify it. However this runs counter to the need to contain all the details of a design decision in one place so that when the decision is changed, the scope of the modifications is restricted. With our second design for BuildPrintfile, a change in the way in which titles are stored only affects TitleStore because all the information about the storing of titles is contained in TitleStore.

5.4 WHY IS INFORMATION HIDING USEFUL IN THE RUNNING EXAMPLE?

We may summarize the purpose of information hiding as:

To make details that do not affect other parts of a system inaccessible.

Information hiding helps to enforce abstraction by enforcing the suppression of details that are not required at the level of abstraction used outside the integrand that hides the information. The identifiers Title, TitleIn, and TitleOut are abstractions; to surround them with the details of their implementation is to mar the clarity that they achieve. It thus forms the basis for the separation of an integrand into sub-components during design. By starting the design at the highest, most abstract level, the more detailed design decisions can be relegated to lower levels of abstraction hidden wholly within sub-components.

TitleStore is at a lower level of abstraction than the integrands that use it. As with many of the techniques discussed, the driving force behind the information hiding is the reduction in complexity.

5.4.1 Localization of change

A large measure of the skill of a system designer is to predict what changes to the program specification are most likely and to structure the abstractions and, consequently, the information hiding, accordingly. The students in the Software Cottage exercise had to make exactly this kind of prediction, both when they were designing their product and when they were choosing the product to use in the second part of the exercise. In the case of TitleStore, a change in the way in which titles are represented or stored requires only the modification and recompilation of TitleStore. After that has been done, the other parts of BuildPrintfile can be relinked and the program executed with the new implementation of the storage of titles.

Sometimes, a change to an integrand may have wider implications. In order of increasing severity they are:

1. Other integrands in the program need to be recompiled and relinked without modification. With suitable support software tools, it is possible for the appropriate integrands to be identified and recompiled automatically.
2. During the compilation of other integrands, the compiler flags parts of them that are no longer consistent with the newly modified integrand and require manual change. While this is serious and error prone because of the need for manual intervention, finding all the parts that need modification automatically is an important advantage. Manual searching, even if assisted with software, is a task that often surpasses our limited ability for concentration especially with interruptions like the telephone.
3. Many of the integrands can still be recompiled apparently successfully, yet on rerunning the program, it no longer works as it did before. This is the worst situation and recovery can take a long time.

Thus, the guiding principle in making design decisions is the containment of the consequences of the decision within as small an area as possible.

5.5 THE COMPLEXITY OF THE INTERFACE

The principle of information hiding gives a useful yardstick for examining the complexity of an interconnection between integrands based on the mechanism used for passing the information. Three such mechanisms will serve to show the application of the principle:

5.5.1 Global variables

Global variables can be referenced by name by any members of a group of integrands. They are available in some form in most programming languages. In Fortran the COMMON statement provides a central repository for data elements that are accessible to all parts of the program. All variables in Basic are global. In these languages, global really means universal, these variables have universal name recognition, a situation much prized by status seekers. In PL/I the EXTERNAL attribute provides access to a named data item by all procedures that declare the same name with this attribute. Block structured languages such as Algol 60, PL/I, Pascal, Modula-2, and Ada all allow access to a data item to be shared by several procedures.

```
MODULE Outer;
    VAR
        GlobalVariable: CARDINAL;

    PROCEDURE InnerOne;
    BEGIN
        GlobalVariable := GlobalVariable + 3;
    END InnerOne;

    PROCEDURE InnerTwo;
    BEGIN
        (* Does something that does not reference
                                    GlobalVariable )*
    END InnerTwo;

    PROCEDURE InnerThree;
    BEGIN
        GlobalVariable := GlobalVariable + 7;
    END InnerThree;
BEGIN
    GlobalVariable := 1;
    InnerOne;
    InnerTwo;
    InnerThree;
END Outer.
```

All three procedures InnerOne, InnerTwo, and InnerThree have access to the variable GlobalVariable. At the level of abstraction of the executable part of Outer we have the sequence of statements:

```
GlobalVariable := 1;
InnerOne;
InnerTwo;
InnerThree;
```

After the initialization of GlobalVariable the invocations of the three procedures provide abstract operations whose meaning ought, in the interests of clarity, to be clear in the context of the environment in which they are used. This environment contains the variable GlobalVariable but there is nothing to indicate that the invocations have any effect on the variable. In fact, in order to discover this we need either to look inside those procedures or to read the procedures' specifications. To some extent, the changes to GlobalVariable are going on behind our backs, out of sight of the reader of the executable part of Outer. The term generally used is *side-effects*. The example snippet of code that is shown here is really only a microcosm of the more usual situation. Each of the procedures InnerOne, InnerTwo and InnerThree may be many pages and contain deeply nested procedures. At any of the levels of nesting, there may be a reference to GlobalVariable. Such references cannot be found with any certainty by eye. The cross-reference listing produced by the compiler might be helpful but is not often available when one is reading a program and is seldom provided in a convenient format. The comments *should* describe references to global variables but may not be up to date. It is all too easy, when fixing a bug in a low-level procedure to insert a reference to a global variable with an 'I'll update the comments after I've tested the change'. In such a case one fix uncovers another bug and changing the comments is forgotten.

There are three major problems with this use of GlobalVariable:

1. There are unheralded changes to GlobalVariable; the invocation of InnerOne looks much as the invocation of InnerTwo yet one of them affects GlobalVariable and the other does not.
2. The procedures InnerOne and InnerThree depend upon the accessibility of a CARDINAL variable named GlobalVariable for their action and therefore cannot be used in other contexts.
3. It is difficult to manage access to GlobalVariable. The programmer of any procedure at the same level as or contained within these three who decides to reference GlobalVariable has access to it. In the situation where an entire program has access to a variable, it is very difficult to track down the culprit when the value of the variable has been corrupted.

The subject of the use of global variables has been much debated and the case against them is generally understood and supported. Yet their use continues on a widespread basis.

I believe that this comes about mainly through laziness and the making of modifications to programs without properly rethinking the design on the basis of the flow of

```
MODULE Outer;
   VAR
      I: CARDINAL;

   PROCEDURE Inner;
   BEGIN
      (*  beginning part of procedure *)
      I := 1;
      WHILE (I <= 10) DO
         (* Some computation *)
      END;
      (*  ending part of procedure    *)
   END Inner;

BEGIN
   I := 1;
   Inner;
   (* More of Outer *)
END Outer.
```

FIGURE 5.6 Possible inadvertent use of global variable.

information. It is so easy to add another global variable and avoid the rewriting that is required to add another parameter. Sometimes it is a deficiency of the design of the programming language that requires the programmer to use a global variable. We shall discover such a situation in our implementation of BuildPrintfile in Modula-2 later. The general rule that I advocate is

Never use a global variable unless the programming language design forces it.

If one is forced to use a global variable, special care must be taken to restrict its globality. The concept of block structure in a language is, I believe, contrary to the generally received wisdom, an idea that does more to reduce clarity than enhance it. Block structure is further discussed in Chapter 8.

As a general rule, a procedure should be such that it could be compiled successfully outside its block environment. This test avoids the possibility of the inadvertent use of a global variable, as illustrated in Figure 5.6. The writer of Inner had intended to declare I locally in the procedure but forgot. The compiler found I declared outside the block and thus did not signal any errors. The major advantage I can find for block structuring is that of restricting the access to identifiers by procedures outside. The inheritance of names to inner procedures is potentially very harmful.

On the subject of global variables Ledgard (1987) is particularly eloquent. Also of interest on global variables in general are Wulf and Shaw (1973) and on block structuring in particular are Clarke *et al.* (1980). Dunsmore and Gannon (1980) present evidence that suggests that it may not be detrimental to use global variables for data communication in program construction, however formal parameters make it easier to understand an unfamiliar program prior to modification.

5.5.2 Control blocks

Sometimes programmers attempt to escape from the problems of global variables discussed above by explicitly passing control blocks, that is, records containing status information, between integrands, generally through the use of pointers. These pointers are passed either as global variables or through the argument-parameter correspondence. This is particularly common in system software. Myers (1978) describes the situation in IBM's OS/360 in the following way:

> In OS/360 most of the operating system's data elements are contained in system control blocks. These control blocks are mapped, element by element, in mapping macros. Any module that references a data element must contain the mapping macro of the proper control block. Anyone familiar with the ongoing development of OS/360 knows that the "macro problem" is a very costly one. Since the mapping macros are constantly changing and since it is not feasible to recompile the many thousands of modules in the system whenever a macro changes, the modules always contain varying versions of the same macro. This has led to more bugs in OS and also to costly procedures to attempt to track and control this situation.

The problem here, beyond the mechanical bookkeeping ones mentioned by Myers is really another variant of the global variable problem that we just discussed. The information is being made too public. Every integrand that has access to one of these control blocks through a pointer or as a parameter contains a specification of the whole block even though it only references a few fields. This goes completely counter to the principle of information hiding. Knowledge of the other fields is available in areas that have no use for the information and a change to the definition of these fields will require, at the very least, recompilation of the integrand *even though it makes no reference to the changed fields*.

There is also the danger that a 'smart' programmer may decide to make an efficiency improvement by referencing one of the other fields, thus introducing another interconnection to the integrand, an undocumented one. Such programmers are dangerous. Since access to these fields is already defined, it is very easy for the programmer to reference them without updating the documentation. There is yet another similarity with the global variable problem and that is the difficulty of tracking an error that causes corrupted data to be put in a field. Since all integrands that reference even just one field in the block have access to the whole block, any one of them is a potential suspect.

5.5.3 Arguments and parameters

The safest and most explicit way of passing information between integrands is through the argument–parameter mechanism. This makes it quite clear to the reader of the program what information is being passed, nothing is being done out of sight, and such interfaces can be automatically checked by the compiler. Suppose that we have a subroutine Sub whose interface specification defines it as having three parameters, A, B, and C of types TypeA, TypeB, and TypeC, which are all input–output parameters. Its Modula-2 definition module will be

```
PROCEDURE Sub(VAR A: TypeA; VAR B: TypeB; VAR C: TypeC);
```

The invocation of Sub will be a statement of the form

```
Sub(X, Y, Z);
```

The compiler will check that the argument X is of type TypeA, Y is of type TypeB, and Z is of type TypeC. Since the parameters A, B, and C are defined to be the *complete* interface, it is clear that the execution of

```
Sub(X, Y, Z);
```

can change the values of X, Y, and Z and *no other variables*. The reader does not have to remember about other unmentioned variables being referenced or set.

Generally, software tools are available so that a change to the interface definition will lead to an investigation of all parties to the interface. Since procedure headings appear in the interface definitions, changes in them can be checked.

5.6 UNITY OF PURPOSE

As we described in Section 2.5.4, an integrand whose elements are concerned with the performance of a single function is said to have *unity of purpose*. The degree to which two integrands are connected is a measure of the *cohesion* between the integrands. The greater the cohesion, the less the unity of purpose. The two concepts of unity of purpose and cohesion form the basis of splitting a program into integrands.

In splitting a program into integrands, the aim is to make the data flow between them clear and to be handled by the argument–parameter mechanism, as just discussed. This criterion only dictates how information is to be passed across the interfaces between integrands. The next question is to decide *where* the interfaces are to occur. Crystals and logs split in preferred directions, those with minimum interconnections. Programs, like rocks and wood, should be split into integrands along the lines of minimum interconnection.

The principle of information hiding gives some guidance on splitting into integrands, however, by itself, it is not sufficiently restrictive. Many different kinds of information could be hidden within a single integrand. If these were mutually unrelated, hiding them together would run counter to the idea of unity of purpose, introduced in Chapter 2. Unity of purpose refers to the degree to which the elements of an integrand are united in a common goal. Coupling and unity of purpose are complementary principles that work together. The greater is the unity of purpose, the lower is the coupling.

An integrand has good unity of purpose if its function can be described fully in a simple, as opposed to compound, imperative sentence with a single transitive verb and specific object. Yourdon and Constantine (1979) use the single descriptive sentence as the basis for distinguishing different levels of unity of purpose. These are, in order of increasing unity:

- *Coincidental:* Little or no relation between the elements of the integrand. The descriptive sentence will show this by reading as a list of unrelated functions separated by commas. There is really no unity of purpose at all and it is often the result of blind panic by the designer or of slavish adherence to a management instruction to split up a program into integrands, each no longer than some number of statements. I have seen a program that had been given this treatment, almost as though it were being cut up like fire wood, with every piece being the same length. The programmer told me 'I modularized my program!'

- *Logical:* The elements of the procedure are *logically* associated in that one can think of them as falling into a class of similar or related functions. The procedure EditAllTransactions is likely to consist of logically related elements. This is an easy trap to fall into. The functions of a group of integrands are combined into a single integrand with the operation controlled by a set of logical switches. While this approach may save space, its execution will require additional time to interrogate the switches and maintenance is likely to be difficult. The exact function of the integrand is likely to be hard to understand because of the complex logic that will probably only become worse as a result of modifications.

- *Temporal:* The functions of the procedure are to be performed at a specific time in the whole process. This is similar to the procedure with logical unity where the logical relation between the parts are the time at which they are to be performed. Thus an initialization procedure that opens output files, resets counters, and clears totals would have temporal unity. The goals of information hiding and unity of purpose would be better achieved by splitting out each of the functions into a separate integrand, or possibly into an integrand that contains other operations on the same types or objects, and replacing the initialization integrand by a sequence of invocations. This new integrand could then rightly be called InitializationControl and would have good unity of purpose.

- *Communicational:* The elements of the procedure either reference the same set of data or pass data between themselves, for example, the output of one element might be the input of another element.

- *Functional:* All elements of the procedure are related to the performance of a single function. Such a procedure will contain only elements that contribute to accomplishing a single goal. Examples of such procedure are 'compute square root', 'obtain random number', or 'delete record from master file'. However, this does not mean that in order to have functional unity or purpose, a procedure must be primitive; it may be decomposable into a hierarchy of sub-functions and yet retain functional unity. A sorting procedure has functional unity but the procedure 'compute sine/cosine' probably does not.

According to Yourdon and Constantine (1979), a procedure does not have pure functional unity of purpose if the single sentence that describes the procedure's function has one of the following forms:

- It contains a comma or more than one verb, or is a compound sentence. Examples:
    Zero table and mount transaction tape.
    Plot graph and print report.

- It contains the word 'all' or a plural object implying a process applied to a *class* of things. Examples:
    Edit all data.
    Perform IO.
- It contains such time-oriented words as 'first', 'next', 'after', 'then', 'start', 'step', 'when', 'until', or 'for all'. Examples:
    Close file then print control totals.
    Write report for all delinquent accounts.
- It contains such words as 'initialize', 'clean-up', and 'housekeeping'. Examples:
    Initialize symbol table
    Clean-up database.
    Manage free space queue.

The procedure is then likely to have less unity than provided by purely functional procedures. The aim is to keep the procedures as close to functional as possible, however it is often not possible to make all procedures have strictly functional unity of purpose. A design that calls for procedures with less than functional unity should only be adopted after very careful consideration of the consequences.

Yourdon probably does not go far enough – he assumes without comment the literacy of the programmer where at best sub-literacy seems to be the current fashionable norm. Many programmers disdain the humble comma, and some disguise verbs so thoroughly that it is difficult to detect when multiple functionality is smuggled into an operational specification. Literacy, at the basic level, is essential in an expository act like programming; it is no less necessary for the practitioner to use it in pursuit of Yourdon's precepts. There is a distinct danger, in the modern world where a feeling of what constitutes correct usage is not nurtured by many national publications, that 'computer literate' people, such as those that program, may not be literate in the wider sense.

CHAPTER SIX

A PROGRAM AS
TECHNICAL EXPOSITION

A program is a form of technical exposition that describes a process to be used in transforming data. Such expositions are read by other programmers, the maintenance programmers, who need to understand the process before modifying it. The writer of a program needs to keep in mind the abilities and experience of the program's intended readership. This mental picture will help the author describe the process clearly and make it obvious to the reader that the process is performed correctly. The clarity of the program depends upon its writing style, which should be chosen to help the reader understand with the least mental effort. This requires that the author have the correct mental attitude for exposition, and continually verify the clarity and simplicity of the program. In addition, the program must have a general and sound method and an appropriate interface with its human users and other external devices.

6.1 INTRODUCTION

One of the definitions of 'program' given in *The Devil's DP Dictionary* (Kelly-Bootle 1981) is 'a sequence of detectable and undetectable errors aimed at coaxing some form of response from the system.' (The major definition is: 'A *programme* written in a lower-level language, such as American English'. *Programme* is defined as: 'A *program* written in English'.)

This agrees with the belief that was generally held until comparatively recently that a program is a private communication between a programmer and the computer. This despite the fact that one of the design aims of Cobol was to make the maximum use of simple English language so that programs could be read and understood by managers. To this end, it was decided that, in the initial version, the four arithmetic verbs, ADD, SUBTRACT, MULTIPLY, and DIVIDE would be included while the use of the mathematical symbols would be deferred until a later version (Sammet 1978). It was felt that symbolic expressions were 'too complicated for normal data processing use, and were unneeded in general'. We should not smile condescendingly at this assumption that managers of data processing operations suffer from mathematical dyslexia, but recognize that even in 1959 some thought was being given to the possibility that programs might be read by others. Though Cobol was the first language with an explicit design principle of communication, some recognition of the idea was also given in other languages. For example, Fortran was designed to accept blanks in identifiers so that they would be more readable. Algol was intended as a language for communicating algorithms.

Rather than take the Devil's definition, I prefer to think of a program as an *exposition* of the process to be used in transforming the input data into the output data using numerical and logical operations. Both the input and output data may be electrical signals. In a factory, a machine tool transforms the raw material into a finished product. The blueprint and description for that machine constitute an exposition of the process used for making the transformation between raw material and finished product. The engineer who wishes to modify or maintain the machine must know how it works and will read and need to understand this expository material before working on the machine.

In Section 1.5 we discussed programmers, in particular professional programmers, whose function was discussed in greater detail in Sections 2.4 and 2.6. Section 1.6 introduced the concept of expository programming. The link between the professional programmer and expository programming must now be discussed in greater detail.

6.2 WHO READS PROGRAMS?

Programming is a kind of writing. When we learn to write, we not only learn by writing but by reading examples of writing, good and bad. A course in writing, whether technical exposition or literature, will have required reading of examples, some will show how it should be done and some will show the opposite. When we learn to program, we do so almost exclusively by writing a program to solve a problem defined by the instructor. In the course of writing that program, we may consult a textbook to see how a similar problem is solved. Before we can modify the textbook solution to our own problem, we must understand it. If we define 'magic' as a technology that we do not understand, to attempt to apply the textbook's example without understanding it is akin to looking in a book of magic spells. Sometimes, as with the sorcerer's apprentice, the use of such spells in computer programs without proper understanding can lead to unpleasant and surprising results. Rarely do we read a complete program to see how it has been constructed by a master of the craft.

There have been some, very few, examples of programs presented as reading material. One such is a program that prints the first 1000 prime numbers, which is contained in a paper entitled 'Literate Programming' by Knuth (1984). That is, something that offers ideas of lasting interest expressed with clarity and elegance of expression. In addition, he has produced a literary form of a large program 'The WEB System of Structured Documentation' (Knuth 1983). Other shorter examples of this style of writing are in Bentley (1986b, 1986c) with further discussion in Bentley (1987). However, in general, programmers do not study examples of the work of the masters of their craft in the same way that architects study the work of LeCorbusier or Frank Lloyd Wright or structural engineers study beautiful bridges. Who reads programs?

6.2.1 Other programmers

In the world of professional programming, it is vanishingly rare that there is only one programmer involved in the implementation of a program. The program becomes a medium of communication between the programmers who write the program, though they will generally spend more time studying the external interface specifications of the integrands than the code of the integrands. It is the maintenance programmers, who are responsible for the continuing development of the program, who will spend the most time studying the details of an integrand. They are concerned with being able to modify the actual programming language statements of the integrand.

To the maintenance programmer, all documentation is suspect. The program's comments, though probably accurate at some time, are often not updated to reflect later changes. Flowcharts, if provided, are even less helpful. If they were generated automatically from the statements of the integrand, they are so detailed and devoid of abstraction as to be useless. Such flowcharts are generally produced to satisfy the letter rather than the intent of some documentation requirement of a software contract. Hand-generated flowcharts, especially if produced to satisfy similar contractual requirements, are even more suspect. Even if they originally accurately reflected the way that the program worked, the difficulty of modifying them makes it unlikely that they have been kept up to date.

I remember studying some operating system flowcharts furnished by the manufacturer. The charts were at a higher level than statements arranged on pages with inter-page links giving the page and coordinates to which control went next. In order to try to follow the flow of control through these charts, I found myself referring to so many pages at once that I was using almost all my fingers as page markers. This chart told me more about why there were so many errors in the system than it did about how the system worked.

The only solid basis from which the maintenance programmer can gain an understanding of the program is the programming language statements of the integrand itself. These statements form a technical exposition of a process that must be read and understood by the maintenance programmer. The fact that the program will also be used to cause a computer to carry out certain processes is almost incidental. The major effect of this need for a program to be read for understanding is to impose certain syntactic and stylistic restrictions on the mode of exposition. As a technical exposition, a program is subject to the same set of rules that are used for writing prose.

It is becoming more and more generally understood that programs should be readable. Kernighan and Plauger (1974) was one of the first books to discuss this. They presented excerpts from textbooks on programming to show that the examples of 'how to do it' given there were not always worthy of emulation. By the time they came to write their second edition (Kernighan and Plauger 1978) they were able to say in their preface:

> The practice of computer programming has changed since *The Elements of Programming Style* first appeared. Programming style has become a legitimate topic of discussion. After years of producing 'write-only code', students, teachers, and computing professionals now recognize the importance of readable programs.

A program serves the dual roles of communication between programmer and programmer and programmer and computer. As is common with expository text, the reader (maintenance programmer) will generally have no direct personal contact with the author (development programmer).

It is for the maintenance programmer that the development programmer is writing.

Note that 'maintenance' here goes beyond corrective maintenance and includes enhancement up to the extent of a complete rewrite. Of course, if the world was perfect, in the case of a complete rewrite, the clarity of the superseded version would not be important because the new requirement specifications and design specifications would have been developed from the previous versions. But things are not always perfect, and the previous version of the program may be needed in order to find out exactly what the previous version did. In that case, the clarity of the exposition will be very important.

It must also be remembered that two fundamental issues in maintenance are the preservation of compliance and maintainability. Lehman's Law of Increasing Unstructuredness, quoted in Section 2.3.6, that work must be done to preserve or improve structure, always applies. The maintenance programmer must be able to see and understand the structure of the program in order to want to and be able to preserve its structure.

6.2.2 Picture the maintenance programmer

A key to successful expository writing is to picture one's reader. For the development programmer it is essential to know several things about the maintenance programmer:

- *How much experience of software development of this type does the maintenance programmer have?* In particular, how well does the maintenance programmer understand the programming language being used, the operating system in which the application is embedded, and the use of subroutines drawn from specialized libraries, for example, graphics display routines? In addition, will the reader be equipped with what the development programmer may well regard as the normal armament of an 'educated' (like the development programmer) software engineer of standard algorithms for sorting, space management, queue and list management, and hashing techniques, to mention a few examples? Some of the interactions with the operating system may be very specialized and involve knowledge of the structure of control blocks and symbol tables; knowledge of these will not be common – even among experienced system programmers. If the system is a 'real-time' system involving concurrent programming techniques, how well aware is the maintenance programmer of the techniques involved and the special steps that must be taken to ensure reliability? Although we might assume that the author of an integrand is likely to be its best maintenance programmer, the detailed knowledge fades very rapidly. It is related that when Sir Thomas Beecham asked the composer Frederick Delius about playing one of his scores Delius replied: 'Damned if I know, play it how you want.'

- *How much specific experience of software development of this type does the maintenance programmer know about the application?* This is specialized knowledge that the general programmer will not have been able to acquire during the normal education of a software engineer. Depending on the application, topics such as statistical methods, numerical analysis, and graphic representation may be involved.
- *How much does the maintenance programmer know about the general system design and data structures?* Very often, before an understanding of a particular program can be obtained a knowledge of the context within which it is being invoked is required. In particular, there may be data structures that contain information that is required by the integrand. The description of these structures and the general layout of the system organization is not, in general, included in all integrands but must exist somewhere in the system documentation.
- *How much does the maintenance programmer know of the special terminology that the development programmers have developed?* Inevitably, during the evolution of a large program, the programmers will develop a specialized jargon that they use among themselves to discuss the program. This is almost never defined in a dictionary and becomes a kind of folklore that enters the collective unconscious of the project members. Unless the maintenance programmer has worked closely with the original project members it will be very difficult to obtain a knowledge of this vocabulary.
- *What does the maintenance programmer intend to accomplish by understanding the integrand?* The usual reason is to make modifications to it. There may, however, be other reasons such as understanding a particular algorithm for use in another application. Each different goal will bring with it a different mindset and way of understanding.
- *What does the maintenance programmer know about program modification?* The proper technique for controlled program modification avoids the old ideas of the 'quick fix', which chooses the shortest route to removing the symptoms. It also avoids the Rambo approach of solving the problem by firing patches into object-code or its bit-level representation with a 'zap' utility. Program modification requires understanding the working of the integrand from reading its current source code and realizing its place in the design of the program and how it satisfies the functional specifications.

All of these areas have a bearing on the degree of explanation that must be included through notes in the form of comments in the program. In the preceding sub-section, I disparaged comments because they can often be misleading. Comments are sometimes required and must be designed so as to reduce the possibility of becoming obsolete.

6.2.3 Expository programming

From the point of view of exposition, the integrand must be written with two major objects in view:

1. To present in language that is clear to the reader a description of the process performed by the integrand.

2. To make it obvious that the process is performed correctly in accordance with the specifications and that all cases have been handled.

To a very large extent, these two goals must be reached through the writing of the statements of the integrand itself without relying on additional comments. Comments can certainly be of help in clarifying the exposition but only to a limited extent. Since the comments do not affect the execution of the computer and there is no automatic verification that the meaning of the comments matches the meaning of the programming language statements, the action of the integrand must still be clear to the reader from the statements themselves. Thus, in writing the integrand, the programming language must be used in a way that will help the reader reason about, and deduce the correctness of, the integrand. I am not referring to 'formal proofs of correctness' here, a subject that will be discussed later, but to informal reasoning.

Later chapters will develop this view of programming as expository writing that also causes a computer to perform in a desired manner.

6.3 WHAT IS PROGRAMMING STYLE?

Style is the personality and character of writing, the mode of expressing thought in language. Its chief elements are the sequence and organization of paragraphs, sentence structure, and choice of words. In programming, the characteristics of style are analogous, the design of a program, the organization of a procedure, the flow of control, and the choice of data elements. Generally, when the term *style* is used, *good style* is implied.

Simplicity of style is one of the traits that distinguishes the professional programmer from the hacker. Hackers are so involved with building the program, making it increasingly complex, that they do not bother trying to make it understandable to others. Rather than using the clearest method, they enjoy condensing their solution into incomprehensibility. The principles of good programming style are aimed in the opposite direction. The idea is to make a program so easy to understand that the reader thinks of the program as being simple rather than complex.

The reader of your program, a maintenance programmer, is approaching from a very different direction. There is a vital need to understand the program because there is an unrealistically short time in which to modify the program and make it work again. Hence, the reader will continue to work at understanding the program until it is clear. Your reader will not think any the less of you because the program is simple to understand. Indeed, if after expending a sizeable amount of time, it is discovered that your program could have been written in a much more easily understood way, the reader is likely to hold your programming abilities in contempt for having wasted so much time.

6.3.1 Why is style important in programming?

Much has been made of what is termed the 'software crisis'; reflecting the fact that software is seldom produced on time, rarely meets performance goals, and is very prone to errors. Another aspect of the crisis, now being more frequently recognized, is the great difficulty, and hence expense, involved in making modifications to existing programs.

Although almost never measured, the cost of this continuing program development may greatly exceed the original development cost. Boehm (1973) documents a case where the cost of the continuing development of a program exceeded the cost of its original development by a factor of 100. On one aircraft computer reported on by Trainor (1979) the original development costs were roughly $75 per instruction, while the costs of all the continued development were $4000 per instruction. The generally accepted reason for this is *complexity*. Large programs are among the most complex creations of the human intellect.

There are two components to this complexity: the inherent and the gratuitous. The first is there because the real world process being modeled is itself complex. The second, we ourselves have created and added in the modeling process.

It is not the complexity itself that is at fault but the human limitation of our mental processes to deal with it. We are not able to deal simultaneously with a myriad of interrelated details; they get in the way of our understanding the program. If we really understood a program, we would know whether it was correct or incorrect, and how it should be modified to improve it. We will only be able to understand a program if we are able to reduce its *perceived complexity* to a level that matches our human limitations.

The term 'perceived complexity' was used deliberately to imply that the way in which written material is presented has a great effect on the ease with which it can be understood. If its apparent complexity can be reduced by suppressing the details that obscure the main ideas, its meaning will be much easier to assimilate. We are already familiar with this idea from our discussions of notation in an earlier chapter. The style in which a program is written constitutes a notation and the same concepts apply to it as to any other kind of notation. The inherent component of complexity is reduced by improving the abstraction of both form and content of the program. The gratuitous component is reduced by resisting the urge to show off by forcing the reader to repeat the original programmer's mental leaps without having had the benefit of that programmer's understanding of the problem being solved.

For programs, ease of understanding can only be achieved by reducing the perceived complexity of the only accurate description of the program, the source text itself. The question 'What makes a text understandable?' is a question that can be applied to all kinds of expository texts, including program texts. The answer is, universally, the style in which the text is written.

6.4 PRINCIPLES OF EXPOSITORY PROGRAMMING

We have introduced the term *expository programming* to describe the writing of programs as a medium of communication between programmers. The meaning of such programs will be *clear* to their readers. In this section, the basic principles of expository programming are listed. The first two will be described in this chapter and the remainder will be discussed separately in the subsequent chapters.

1. Proper mental attitude during writing – Section 6.4.1
2. Adequate program definition – Section 6.4.2
   - Generality
   - Soundness of method
   - Appropriateness of interface
3. Organization of the complete program – Chapter 9
   - Helpful choice of data representation
   - Suitable initialization and termination
   - Logical organization into processes
4. Organization of a process
   - Introductory comments – Section 10.1
   - Orderly definition of variables – Sections 9.3, 9.4
   - Division into paragraphs – Section 10.3
   - Exceptional conditions treated – Chapter 11
5. Organization and development of paragraphs
   - Unity of subject matter – Section 10.2
   - Simple flow of control – Sections 10.4, 10.5
   - Orderly arrangement of details – Section 10.7
   - Fullness of development – Section 10.9
6. Effective use of statements
   - Proper use of language – Section 10.6
   - Clarity of expression – Section 10.7
7. Presentation
   - Good layout – Section 10.8
8. Rereading and rewriting – Chapter 12

6.4.1 Proper mental attitude during writing

The decision to write a clear program must be a conscious one. It is a decision that must be made *before* the writing is started.

> Clarity is not something that can be put on a program later like a coat of paint.

The programmer must think of the program as a technical document that is addressed to a particular audience who will wish to be instructed by it. The reader of the program is likely to be a maintenance programmer who knows less and has thought less about the problem being solved than the original programmer. The maintenance programmer usually is responsible for the maintenance of many large programs and does not have the opportunity to study the theory of each application to the extent that the development programmer has. This means that the writer must take care to make explicit many things that may seem to be common knowledge, without drowning the reader with too much explanation. Knowing where to draw the line between parching and drowning requires that the writer has a mental image of the reader.

The mental image of the reader is something that the programmer must be prepared to draw on frequently while writing the program. There are two key questions that should be posed frequently while writing the program:

1. 'Will the reader be able to understand this?' An equivalent form that might help is 'Will I be able to understand this in a year's time?'
2. 'Could this be expressed more simply?'

6.4.2 Adequate program definition

We have already discussed the question of adequate external interface specification from the point of view of the specification itself – its precision and completeness. This is the starting-point for the writing of the program. Now we must consider some aspects of the content of the specification – the problem itself – and why the proposed solution will be satisfactory.

- *Generality*. We have an unfortunate habit in the world of programming of writing programs that solve only very narrowly defined problems. As a result, the program must be rewritten to be used in another, only slightly different, context. Later, when it is too late, we often discover that the problem statement could have been generalized to result in a program that is more widely applicable. Even though this may require changing the external interface, it is usually worth while considering and discussing a generalization. This is directly connected with the question of program reuse discussed in Section 2.6.1. However, generality is not free; there is program overhead in deciding which of the several uses afforded by generality is to be applied. While generality is the key to reuse, there is no guarantee that reuse will follow from generality.
- *Soundness of method*. Solution of the problem will call for an algorithm. The algorithm needs to be chosen with care to ensure that, for the given range of input data, the correct answer will be produced. The algorithm must not only do this when the input data are within range but it must also reject out-of-range data. The complete program must be so designed that no combination of incorrect input data can cause the program to crash – this is called *defensive programming*. A compiler that I was working with a few years ago had an unfortunate tendency to crash when programs containing certain syntactic errors were submitted. The response of the compiler's suppliers was 'User error, correct program and resubmit'. I felt this to be totally unsatisfactory as a response, particularly since the compiler gave no clues as to what was wrong with the program. Eventually I was able to convince them that it was their problem. Possibly, my program had an error but certainly, the compiler had one. In choosing a sound method, we must look for one that is proof against bad data. The method chosen must be such that reasonableness tests are made before accepting input data. It is almost always true that the set of possible incorrect input data is very much larger than the set of valid input data.

    Suppose we again use a compiler as an example. A program is a character string hence the set of all possible input data to the compiler is the set of all possible character strings. Many members of this set will be illegal because they contain characters outside the language's character set. Of the remainder, only a very small minority will be sequences of characters that satisfy the rules of the language. These must be processed correctly while the remainder are rejected gracefully with helpful messages of condolence to the errant programmer. The general rule of a program should be to take a skeptical view of data and not accept everything that is input unless it is absolutely impossible to check it, a very rare situation. Defensive programming at the micro-level, although essential, is not enough. The complete program design must be defensive so as to strive to protect the whole from all eventualities in its behavior space. This goal, though unattainable in the absolute sense, must always be attempted.

If the problem calls for a solution that involves concurrent processes that communicate, the choice of a sound method is particularly important. This is because testing where there are inter-process time dependencies is much more difficult than testing normal sequential programs. With the latter, it is simple to repeat a test and be able to get identical performance. It is a deterministic system. Where a program is interacting with some external real-time process, generally a mechanical or human process, repeatability is only attainable with accuracy measured in milliseconds, much larger than the granularity of time of the computer operations in the program. From the point of view of the programmer, the program must perform in a non-deterministic behavior space. We will return to this point later.

- *Appropriateness of interface.* In this case, we are referring to the human interface of the program. In an earlier chapter, we have discussed the data interface of an integrand and we will be returning to this in much greater detail later. The program really has two kinds of human interface. There is the interface with the users who view it as a black box, that is, data go in, results come out and what happens in between is unknown and there is no way of opening the box to find out. The black box view is covered in Volume 2, Software Specification. Failure in the design of a suitable outside for the black box can lead to early rejection of the program as being unusable. The other human interface is the white box view that the maintenance programmers have. Here the works are clearly visible and the visibility depends upon the programming style. Failure of the white box interface leads to a more lingering death due to unmaintainability. The task of expository programming is to make the white box transparent so that the structure can be seen.

CHAPTER SEVEN

CORRECTNESS IS NEXT TO GODLINESS

The first requirement of an implementation of a program is that it satisfy its requirements. This leaves the difficult question of how to establish a program's correctness. In all but the most trivial cases, exhaustive testing is impossible. Partial testing can never establish the full correctness of a program. Another approach is to treat the program as a mathematical theorem and to prove its correctness by the normal rules of proof. This technique is illustrated with a simple example that demonstrates that proving correctness is both difficult and complex. Next is a discussion of the role of proof in mathematics and the fallibility of proofs in general. The criticism of the complexity of formal proofs of programs is often answered by proposals that proofs be done by program. Unfortunately, there is not much hope in this direction either. The conclusion is that programs must be written so clearly that confidence in their correctness can be gained by reading them. When this is done, the structure of the program is apparent and guides the testing strategy for further validation.

7.1 INTRODUCTION

In previous chapters, we have limited ourselves to the area of implementation where 'specification' takes on a rather narrow meaning to do with external interface and operational definitions of algorithms. Here, we move, perhaps abruptly, from this micro-world, where the implementation of one integrand may be taken as a paradigm in good practice, to the macro-world, where we are concerned with Quality with a capital 'q' and the dynamic aspects of programs operating as software. 'Specification' now takes on a wider meaning, referring to system requirements unless otherwise noted.

Software quality has two components: *compliance* with its requirements, and *modifiability*. 'Compliance' means 'correct operation', given an adequate definition of what is correct. It is a clear-cut issue, either the software is in compliance or it is not. 'Modifiability' is more difficult to assess; it is closely associated with the attribute of clarity or understandability; however, as we shall see in Chapter 9, a program can be crystal clear and yet not modifiable in any meaningful sense. Compliance is associated with the black-box view of the program where tests are applied without any attention to the program's internal structure. Modifiability is strictly a white-box issue, which depends entirely on the program's structure.

Most programmers find some programs easier to understand than others. However, it is difficult to define this attribute of clarity. To use the words of St Augustine, 'If no one asks me, I know what it is. If I wish to explain it to him who asks, I do not know.' Although we can make subjective judgements about programs – 'This program is clearer than that one' – there seems to be no way to quantify the 'goodness' of a program. We do not have any algorithms that can analyze a program and report that it is 93.25 per cent clear. There has been much research aimed at finding such measures by investigating the 'complexity' of programs. One approach, known as *Software Metrics*, has been mostly based on the pioneering work done under the title of *Software Science* and described in Halstead (1974). Halstead observed that if one divided the basic elements of a program into operators and operands, counting led to values that could be hypothetically correlated with software engineering issues such as 'effort required to create'. It has been argued that these values are statistically consistent across a wide range of programs. There has been a great deal of controversy on these 'measures' with criticisms by Malengé (1980) of the statistical techniques applied and by Elshoff (1978) of the criteria used for separating operators and operands when making the counts. Other attempts at measuring complexity such as McCabe (1976) have led to considerable debate in the literature. Certainly, there is no generally acceptable objective measure of this kind of program complexity and hence of modifiability.

Despite the dual criteria of software quality, which also subsume the requirement for reliability, compliance tends to dominate. 'Get it working' comes long before 'make it modifiable' in importance. Correctness *is* next to godliness, but the also-ran status of modifiability has led to many of today's software problems.

The essential objective condition that one can apply to a program is:

Does the dynamic behavior of the program meet specifications?

This is what we mean when we say that the program 'works' – it gives the correct output for each possible input. A program that works correctly according to its specifications, but works slowly, is always better than one that does not work, unless specific performance characteristics are called for in the specifications. The latter is a program that does not meet its specifications any more than an incorrect one does. How can we assure ourselves that our program is correct? The traditional technique has been to test the program with test data and to compare the output with results that are known to be correct. Another method is to apply the rules of formal logic to the program and attempt to prove the correctness in a formal way.

Section 7.2 gives a brief description of the first of these options – 'exhaustive testing'. Chapter 12 treats the subject of testing in greater detail, though falling short of the level addressed in Volume 5 of this series, where quality is the main subject. In Sections 7.3 and 7.4 we discuss formal verification of programs and mathematical proof in general. Before embarking on these brief discussions, we need to explain the practice of testing a little further than we have done so far.

As will be described in greater detail in Section 12.5, there are several modes in which integrands can be tested. (Here I am using 'versus' in the sense of 'as distinct from'; a usage permitted by American but not by English dictionaries.)

- Static versus dynamic.
- In isolation versus in combination with others.
- Benevolently by the author versus adversarially by others.

What usually happens is that the integrand will be tested statically by its author reading the code and a quality control check on this will involve another team member or programmer also reading the code. Then, as complete programs are built up by adding more and more integrands, these partially complete programs are dynamically tested by their authors who attempt their execution under simulated test conditions. This is known as 'benevolent accretive testing'. The end point of this process is what is called an 'alpha-test', when the whole software suite is benevolently tested for its compliance with requirements, by its authors. We use the word 'benevolent' since authors have a vested interest and expectation in a positive result.

Benevolent testing is a necessary, but insufficient level of testing. It must therefore be followed by an adversarial test, quality assurance, comprising 'black-box' tests in which the system is tested as a whole for its dynamic behavior against the functional specification, and 'white-box' tests, in which the modifiability of the programs is assessed subjectively by static inspection and limited controlled damage experiments. These adversarial tests, black and white box, constitute the 'beta-tests' and serve as quality assurance.

In the following section, we consider only the dynamic testing of the software system as a whole – the black-box testing that goes on benevolently at alpha-test level and adversarially at beta-test level. The results of these tests form part of the 'deliverable documentation' as described in Sections 2.2.4 and 2.2.5.

We must now consider the question of how complete can black-box testing be.

7.2 EXHAUSTIVE TESTING OF PROGRAMS AND SOFTWARE

The term *behavior space* is used to refer to the set of all possible inputs to a program. Suppose that you were an electronics designer and had designed a new two's complement multiplier that took two 32-bit operands and produced a 64-bit result. The multiplier had been built and you now wished to test it. To be completely confident of the result, you planned to perform exhaustive dynamic testing, that is to say with all possible pairs of 32-bit operands. To perform this test you built an automatic tester that would generate the operands and would check the product computed by the multiplier. It could do this at the rate of one complete test cycle every microsecond. The behavior space for the multiplier consists of the 2^{64} possible pairs of 32-bit operands so the test will last 2^{64} μs. To get an estimate of this amount of time, we note that 2^{64} is greater than 1.6×10^{19} and that there are fewer than 3.2×10^{13} μs in a year. Thus the test would take longer than 500 000 years. The chance of completing the test without equipment failure seems remote.

Remember, this is a test of a simple thing like a 32-bit multiplier, which has a relatively restricted set of possible states. Relatively, that is, compared with a complete computer or a large program, such as a compiler. If it is impossible to consider exhaustive testing of this device, what of a compiler? This multiplier also differs from most programs in another way. For the multiplier, all possible sets of input were valid. For most programs, only a very restricted subset of the possible sets of input data is valid. However, in addition to producing correct answers for valid data, we expect the program to react 'reasonably' to all other sets of data. Defining what is a reasonable result of submitting incorrect data to a program is something that users and programmers argue about, however it is part of the behavior space of the program that needs to be specified.

Our test of the multiplier treated it as a *black-box*. That is to say, we test what comes out of the box when known data is input and this is *all that we do*. With this kind of testing, there is no looking inside the box and making use of information that we obtain that way. For example, this multiplier might have been designed as a combination of 16-bit multipliers and adders. Exhaustive testing of a 16-bit multiplier, using the same testing device, takes much less than a day and is certainly feasible. However, to achieve this reduction in time, we had to find out something of the structure of the device so that the individual multipliers and adders could be tested. In the case of a program, we must be able to see its structure and test individual parts. This kind of testing is known as *white-box* testing and implies that the structure of the device being tested can be understood and that it is possible to test sub-parts separately. Since exhaustive testing is almost always infeasible, an analysis of the structure is used to determine the correct set of test cases to be performed. Thus, this form of testing is partly static in that the structure of the multiplier is examined so that, from the results of a reduced number of dynamic tests, its performance throughout the behavior space can be inferred. From the point of view of programming, this makes requirements on the way in which the program is designed and constructed. It should be noted that the more complex a program is, the more difficult it is to test and correct. More difficult to test because its behavior space is larger and more elaborate. More difficult to modify because of the greater number of interrelations whose consistency must be maintained.

Even if we are able to understand the structure of the program, it is still many orders of magnitude more complicated than the multiplier. It is very unlikely that we shall be able to perform exhaustive testing. If we want to be sure that our program is correct, what alternatives do we have? If we are unable to try all possible combinations of input data, we must do the best we can with a subset. However, with only a subset, we can never attain the absolute certainty that exhaustive testing would provide. As Dijkstra (1972a) puts it:

> Program testing can be used to show the presence of bugs, but never to show their absence!

We will return to the subject of testing in Chapter 12, its treatment here being only to establish the practical impossibility of complete exhaustive testing of anything other than a trivial program. In fact the behavior of a real program over several years of actual use does not explore much of the 'accidental' regions of their behavior space – what happens when the unforeseen occurs? This fact is attested to almost daily by accounts of software errors in the press – and remember that only those that are sufficiently far reaching as to be newsworthy are reported. Dijkstra's epigram is correct in the sense that, if testing shows anything at all, then, by definition, it must be a fault, since any 'positive' results of testing must be qualified by the limitations placed on software testing by the inability to investigate its entire data space.

Those who advocate alternative approaches to verifying program correctness, particularly those involving mathematical means for 'proving programs', often use this as their *raison d'être*. We must now enter their territory to see if testing has a real alternative in 'formal verification', as has been propounded by its advocates.

7.3 FORMAL VERIFICATION OF A PROGRAM

The term 'verification' has widely different meanings in software development and computer science. In software development, one verifies the software engineering process for its quality, and one validates the artefact produced – the software system – for its compliance and modifiability. Computer scientists borrow the term 'verify' from the field of mathematical proof, where the demonstration of correctness of a theorem is said to be a verification of the theorem. The issue of formal verification can be considered at each of two levels:

- *Partial:* concerning parts of the entire program taken in isolation; or
- *Total:* the entire program.

As will be seen, the formal verification of an entire program is, except for trivial instances, impossible to achieve, and in practice the approach to formal verification requires the whole to be seen as parts; integrands or even logical parts of an integrand.

This decomposition of aims is brought about by the non-linearly increasing difficulties of establishing unequivocal 'proof' of programs, as program size and complexity increase. In practice, one considers what are called 'intermediate assertions' attaching to a part of program code, and these are conditions that must obtain before and after the execution of the segment of code. A proof of partial correctness follows if the code can be shown to be entirely consistent with its intermediate assertions. Thus, formal verification, as described here, is essentially a form of static testing because its subject is the code in its unexecuted form – i.e., as written down.

To form a basis for discussing formal verification of programs in general, we will present a small example, based closely on one given in Gries (1981). Although the example comes from David Gries, the presentation and, in particular, the discussion are mine. It must be pointed out that he would probably disagree strongly with my conclusions concerning the practicability of proving the correctness of real programs.

Imagine that a small part of a large program, separate from the Running Example, consists of the following code to calculate the values Quotient and Remainder obtained from dividing the non-negative integer Numerator by the positive integer Divisor.

```
    .   .   .
Remainder := Numerator;
Quotient  := 0;
WHILE (Remainder >= Divisor) DO
    Remainder := Remainder - Divisor;
    Quotient  := Quotient + 1
END;
    .   .   .
```

We would like to assure ourselves of the correctness of this code fragment. However, instead of executing the program and checking the results, we want to present a logical argument derived entirely from the program statements in the fragment. What can we assert about the program? Before executing the fragment we know from the specifications that

$$\{ (Numerator \geq 0) \wedge (Divisor > 0) \}$$

and, from the rules of arithmetic, after the fragment has executed we require

$$\{ (Remainder\} \geq 0) \wedge (Remainder < Divisor) \wedge$$
$$(Numerator = Divisor \times Quotient + Remainder) \}$$

These two logical expressions contained in braces are *assertions*. We assert that when execution reaches the beginning of this code fragment, the first assertion will be true and, when execution reaches the end of the fragment, the second one must also hold true if we have written the program correctly. If we were dealing with a complete program instead of just a fragment, the beginning and ending assertions might be obtained from the program's axioms described in Section 4.3.3. In order to help us understand what is going on, we can show the assertions included as part of the program.

```
{ (Numerator ≥ 0) ∧ (Divisor > 0) }
    Remainder := Numerator;
    Quotient  := 0;
    WHILE (Remainder >= Divisor) DO
        Remainder := Remainder - Divisor;
        Quotient  := Quotient + 1
    END;
{ (Remainder ≥ 0) ∧ (Remainder < Divisor) ∧
        (Numerator = Divisor × Quotient + Remainder) }
```

Indeed, there are some programming languages where assertions are taken as instructions to the compiler to generate code to check the validity of the assertion when execution reaches that point in the program. If the assertion does not hold, an error condition is raised.

Using assertions to check execution is really no different from printing partial results during debugging. It is only another form of testing, working with particular data values. It does not attempt to validate the assertions in a general manner. What we are doing here is to show through mathematical reasoning that, whatever the values of Numerator and Divisor, as long as they satisfy the *input assertion*, when execution of the fragment terminates, the *output assertion* will be true.

Given the input assertion,

```
{ (Numerator ≥ 0) ∧ (Divisor > 0) }
```

we know that, following execution of the two assignment statements,

```
Remainder := Numerator;
Quotient  := 0;
```

the following will be true:

1. The value of Remainder is equal to the value of Numerator and therefore

    {Remainder ≥ 0}.

2. The value of Quotient is zero.

Hence the assertion

```
{ (Numerator = Divisor × Quotient + Remainder) }
```

holds. The value of Divisor has not been changed and is still greater than zero. Taking this all together, we can add a new assertion to our program fragment.

```
{ (Numerator ≥ 0) ∧ (Divisor > 0) }
    Remainder := Numerator;
    Quotient  := 0;
    { (Remainder ≥ 0) ∧ (Divisor} > 0) ∧
    (Numerator = Divisor × Quotient + Remainder) }
    WHILE (Remainder >= Divisor) DO
        Remainder := Remainder - Divisor;
        Quotient  := Quotient + 1
    END;
{ (Remainder ≥ 0) ∧ (Remainder < Divisor) ∧
    (Numerator = Divisor × Quotient + Remainder) }
```

Comparing the assertion before starting the loop with the desired assertion at the termination of the loop, we see that part of it,

```
{ (Remainder ≥ 0) ∧ (Numerator = Divisor × Quotient + Remainder) }
```

is already true. What is required for completing the output assertion is that Remainder must be less than Divisor. From the condition on the WHILE statement, the loop will not terminate until this is true. If we can show that executing the body of the loop does not change the truth of the assertion

```
{ (Remainder ≥ 0) ∧ (Numerator = Divisor × Quotient + Remainder) }
```

in other words, that it is an *invariant* of the loop, then it will still be true when the loop terminates, *no matter how many iterations are made*. Finally, if we can show that the loop does indeed terminate, we have a proof of the correctness of this program fragment. In order to show that

```
{(Remainder ≥ 0) ∧ (Numerator = Divisor × Quotient + Remainder)}
```

is an invariant, we concentrate our attention on the loop body

```
Remainder := Remainder - Divisor;
Quotient  := Quotient + 1
```

Just before making the first assignment, the assertion

```
{(Remainder ≥ 0) ∧ (Divisor > 0) ∧ (Remainder ≥ Divisor) ∧
         (Numerator = Divisor × Quotient + Remainder)}
```

holds. This is obtained by adding to the assertion that was true before entering the loop the condition for executing the body of loop. Executing the first assignment has the following consequences:

1. It reduces the value of Remainder so that {Remainder ≥ Divisor} may no longer hold. In fact, since the value of Divisor is greater than zero and since no other statements in the loop modify Remainder, after some number of iterations this assertion will no longer be true and the loop *will* terminate. We thus know that the loop *will* terminate.
2. Since the condition for entry into the loop was {Remainder ≥ Divisor}, subtracting the value of Divisor from Remainder must leave {Remainder ≥ 0} intact.
3. It changes the assertion

   ```
   {Numerator = Divisor × Quotient + Remainder}
   ```

   to

   ```
   {Numerator = Divisor × Quotient+ (Remainder + Divisor)}
   ```

At this point, the relationship that we are trying to prove, the loop invariant, no longer holds. However, what we require to prove is that, *when the body of the loop has completely executed*, the invariant relation is still true. Once execution of the loop body has been started, it will continue until it has completed. There is no exit part way through the body. Considerations of loop invariants become very much more difficult if there are ways in which the loop can terminate without completing the execution of the body. Here, although the invariant relation does not hold after executing the first statement of the loop, we shall now show that executing the second statement restores its truth.

Executing the second assignment, Quotient = Quotient + 1, only affects the assertion

```
{Numerator = Divisor × Quotient + (Remainder + Divisor)}
```

by changing the value of Quotient. Taking account of the new value of Quotient, the assertion becomes

```
{Numerator = Divisor × (Quotient - 1) + (Remainder + Divisor)}
```

which, by simple algebra, reduces to

$\{$ Numerator = Divisor × Quotient + Remainder $\}$

The second assignment statement leaves

$\{($Remainder $\geq 0) \wedge ($Divisor $> 0)\}$

unchanged. The invariant relation of the loop is thus shown to be maintained after execution of the loop body. The required output assertion of the program fragment holds and we have demonstrated that the fragment achieves its desired purpose. That is to say, its dynamic performance for its *complete behavior space* has been inferred statically from the program itself. Of course, this demonstration shows only that the program's behavior matches the given assertions; it says nothing about whether the assertions match the user's expectations. The same thing is true of dynamic testing: if the test data are not representative of actual data, no validation takes place.

This exposition on formal verification has been more wordy than would have been the case had this been a paper written by an enthusiast for an audience already well versed in the subject. Then much of the text would have been omitted, and the demonstration would have taken on the form of a mathematical proof, which itself leads to a practical objection to formal verification. We will return to this at the end of this section and in the next.

First, we must return to the issue raised at the start; how does one demonstrate the proof of even partial correctness – leaving aside the question of totality – for a medium or large suite of programs? It has been suggested that the answer lies in 'automatic verification techniques', in which computers play the central role.

It is often argued that it does not matter that verifications of computer programs are unreadable because they are not really for people to read. With the current advances in writing automatic theorem provers, it is argued that program verification will be done by automatic verifiers. An automatic verifier would take the set of input assertions for the program and the desired output assertions and then analyze the program according to the set of axioms that define the behavior of the programming language. After the analysis, it would either certify that the program had been verified, a sort of electronic version of the ecclesiastical *nihil obstat*, or give guidance to the programmer in finding the errors in the program.

Of course, the verifier itself would be a program, both large and complicated, subject to all the errors and uncertainties of large programs. If we are to trust it with the vitally important task of verifying our software, we have to believe that it is correct. Our confidence in the verifier has to be much greater than our confidence in the compiler. In our normal mode of developing software, we go through a rigorous testing phase and errors in the machine code generated by the compiler are revealed in the same way as our own coding errors.

To be useful, a verifier must be good enough to allow us to do without much testing. How the correctness of the verifier is to be established is unclear. To put trust in a verifier establishing its own correctness makes the idea of employing foxes as security guards for geese seem conservative. However, if such a scheme is used *in conjunction with* dynamic testing, it can be very helpful in locating errors in the program. The Gypsy language (Good *et al*. 1978) is part of an integrated system for specifying and programming small-scale operational software of 1000–2000 lines of code and has been applied to the production of a verified communication processing system of this size.

Even if we set aside the problem of verifying the verifier, there is still the major problem of writing the input and output assertions. While it was fairly easy to generate them for the trivial programming fragment we discussed earlier, it was at least a problem that was related to mathematics. As can be seen in Gries (1976), specifying the input and output assertions for such a simple process as justifying a line of text by inserting extra blanks between the words, so that the last character of the last word appears in the last column of the line, becomes quite difficult. The level of difficulty will not increase linearly as we enlarge the scale of the problem from a toy example to a real-life application such as a compiler, inventory management system, or automatic verifier.

Automatic verifiers will require a formalized notation for the input and output assertions and this notation itself becomes the equivalent of a programming language. The specifications then become programs and automatic verification requires proving the equivalence of two programs. If we can write a program to do this, we can surely write software that will take the formalized specifications and convert them into an executable program. This leaves us with the problem of proving the correctness of the input and output specifications. Proving this correctness requires us to show that the specifications match the real-world process being modeled. We are left with the problem of verifying that we have made a correct translation from our mental image of the real-world process into the input and output specifications. What we achieve through automatic verification is similar to building a motorway into a city in order to relieve the traffic congestion at the city's outskirts: the only result is to move the traffic jam elsewhere. In fact, the motorway itself often becomes a long thin parking lot.

That, then, is the approach to formal verification and its automated apparatus for proofs of partial correctness. The largest 'lump' of program claimed to have been totally correct, to date, is about 1000 source statements of code, and the largest suite of programs whose proofs of partial correctness have been verified by automatic means is about 5000 source statements (Good *et al*. 1978).

As a substitute for testing, formal verification has the following drawbacks:

1. It concerns the static properties of parts of a totality, not the dynamic behavior of that totality. It serves therefore more to increase confidence in the status of programs than to establish categorical proof about the real software.
2. Where automatic verification tools or systems are concerned, the recursive question of establishing their own correctness occurs.

Formal verification is essentially partial where non-trivial program suites are involved, and therefore says nothing necessarily about the static properties of the whole. Software is dynamic, and its validity is always contingent on the virtual computer system on which it executes. These factors are beyond the means of formal verification. There is another drawback:

3. The highly abstract and abstruse nature of formal verification techniques stands as a barrier to many perfectly competent software engineers, or a major investment in their training.

These are not trivial drawbacks. Yet formal verification has an important role to play in the establishment of confidence in a program's compliance. Unfortunately, the subject tends to be – like many others in the computer business – over-sold, and presented as a future panacea for the ailments of software engineering, temptingly within reach for partial proofs for static properties of programs, seemingly just beyond our grasp (at the moment) for the jackpot of total proof. It is to this last subject that we now turn for, to paraphrase the most famous handwasher, 'What is proof?' (John 18:38).

7.4 ON MATHEMATICAL PROOF

Some computer scientists believe that once a mathematical verification of a program has been established, there is no need to test it dynamically. The implication is that there is something very absolute about a mathematical proof. Either something is provable and therefore *true* or not provable and therefore, forgetting Gödel for the moment, *false*.

There is ample evidence that mathematicians themselves do not regard mathematical proof with the same veneration. As far back as 1928, the British mathematician G. H. Hardy (1928) wrote:

> There is strictly speaking no such thing as mathematical proof; . . . proofs are what Littlewood and I call *gas*, rhetorical flourishes designed to affect psychology, pictures on the board in lectures, devices to stimulate the imagination of pupils.

In a more modern discussion of this topic, Kline (1980) writes:

> There is no rigorous definition of rigor. A proof is accepted if it obtains the endorsement of the leading specialists of the time or employs the principles that are fashionable at the moment. But no standard is universally acceptable today . . . Logic has all the fallibility and uncertainty that limit human minds.

In other words, a mathematical proof is correct if it convinces a sufficient number of mathematicians. If there were an absolute quality about mathematical proof, there would be no papers with titles of the form *Counter-example to X's Theorem*. If the proof of X's theorem had been correct, there could, by definition, be no counter-example. The mathematician Henri Lebesgue wrote in 1928, 'Logic can make us reject certain proofs but it cannot make us believe any proof.' This seems a precursor of Dijkstra's (1968b) 'Program testing can be used to show the presence of bugs, but never to show their absence!' Even Bertrand Russell, whose aim it was to formalize the proof of all mathematics wrote in Russell (1903) 'It is one of the chief merits of proofs that they instil a certain scepticism about the result proved.'

DeMillo *et al.* (1979) discussing the relation of mathematical proof to program verification wrote:

> Mathematical proofs increase our confidence in the trust of mathematical statements only after they have been subjected to the social mechanisms of the mathematical community. These same mechanisms doom the so-called proofs of software, the long formal verifications that correspond not to the working mathematical proof but to the imaginary logical structure that the mathematician conjures up to describe his feeling of belief. . . . Verifications cannot really be read; a reader can flay himself through one of the shorter ones by dint of heroic effort, but that's not reading. Being unreadable and – literally – unspeakable, verifications cannot be internalized, transformed, generalized, used, connected to other disciplines, and eventually incorporated into a community consciousness. They cannot acquire credibility gradually, as a mathematical theorem does; one either believes them blindly, as a pure act of faith, or not at all.

Thus, all 'proof' is seen as a social process involving adversarial review by subject peers. For programs the 'adversary' is, at first, the peer group of programmers in the context of quality control and assurance which may use testing or formal verification, or both. The American mathematician and philosopher Charles Sanders Peirce defined 'truth' as 'the opinion which is fated to be ultimately agreed to by all who investigate.' (See Russell 1945.) Ultimately, the real 'adversary' is the user who, before pronouncing on compliance, or 'correctness', will have to have been convinced in a social, practical, context where the program 'acquires credibility gradually, as a mathematical theorem does'.

The notion that mathematical proof is, in some way, uncertain disturbs the orthodoxy of many people's ideas about mathematics. As Tymoczko (1980) put it:

> The great tradition in philosophy of mathematics . . . proceeds as if mathematicians are infallible. (To assume infallibility one need not explicitly assume that mathematicians are infallible, one need only refrain from introducing the idea of mathematical mistake!) By 'great tradition' I mean the rather coherent line of thought on mathematics developed by the Greeks (Euclid, Plato), advanced by modern philosophy beginning with Descartes and Leibniz through Kant, and dramatically advanced by the founders of modern mathematics such as Dedekind, Cantor, Frege, Russell, Hilbert, and Heyting. This tradition either ignores error or consigns it to nonmathematical causes (e.g., in Descartes' philosophy, mathematical error turns out to be a species of sin). In either case the effect is the same. Error is an accident, not part of the essence of mathematics: the mathematician *qua* mathematician is treated by philosophy as infallible. My claim is 'checkable' – check the writings of the tradition for discussions of mathematical error!

In this century of relativity theory, uncertainty principle, and Gödel's demonstration, it is the idea that mathematical proof is absolute that seems the more counter intuitive.

In my view, a correctness proof of the totality of a suite of programs of non-trivial size through the use of an already 'proved' automatic verification system will never be a reality, for all the reasons already given. If large-scale total and categorical proof could be done, if the infinitely recursive question: 'how far proved are the means of proof?' could be answered satisfactorily, and if a suite of programs of 50 000 statements could be 'proved', even then, what would be known about the program would only apply to the *static* properties of the programs – not their dynamic properties as software executing on a virtual computer implemented in a real operating system on real hardware. As Gogol (1835) said at the end of his masterpiece of grotesque comedy, *The Tale of How Ivan Ivanovich Quarreled with Ivan Nikiforovich*:

> The damp pierced me through and through. The gloomy gate with the sentry box, in which a veteran was cleaning his gray equipment, slowly passed by. Again the same fields, in places black and furrowed and in places covered with green, the drenched cows and crows, the monotonous rain, the tearful sky without one gleam of light in it. – It is a dreary world, gentlemen.

7.5 WHERE DOES THIS LEAVE US?

The chain of reasoning in this chapter is listed below:

1. The single most important attribute of a program is correctness.
2. Exhaustive testing of a program is impossible.
3. Verifying a non-trivial program by mathematical proof is *at present* no more trustworthy than the programs themselves and I am not sure how much more reliable it can become for real programs. However, mathematical proofs can increase our confidence in the correctness of the program in the same way as adding a column of numbers from the bottom to the top can give us more confidence in the total we obtained earlier by adding them from top to bottom. However, the sum can still be wrong.
4. Automatic verification is not yet a practical proposition beyond its use as a special form of static testing on parts of code.

What are we to do to establish our confidence in the correctness of a program? The use of formal verification, like other kinds of static testing such as code reading *used in conjunction with* dynamic testing, all serve to increase our confidence. However, all forms of static testing require the ability to understand the program. Without understanding, we can do nothing. Unless we understand how the program works we will be unable to build any real belief in its correctness. Belief without understanding, while acceptable in a metaphysical context, should be excluded from the software engineering paradigm. The methods of expository programming are aimed at providing the required understanding by:

- Encouraging the writing of programs that can be read and understood as technical expositions. We achieve confidence in technical specifications in the same way, by proofreading them.

- Avoiding control flow constructs that would make the program difficult to prove. Earlier in this chapter, when we were discussing the proof of a loop, we remarked that loops that terminate part way through the execution of the body are much more difficult to prove. As Stoy (1977) says:

> Dijkstra has remarked that a formal proof of a program is in the same relation to the programmer's informal sense of its correctness as the text of an Act of Parliament is to one's sense of justice. In both cases there arise difficult situations where the rules are not clear; to resolve them recourse must be had to the formal text, and this is usually a job for professionals. But if these situations arise too frequently then something is wrong, either with the rules or with the upbringing or training of the people concerned. Our job as [language] designers is to frame the rules so that they are sufficiently simple and universally applicable that they may be faithfully followed even in informal argument.

The good expository writer will avoid grammatical language constructs that are difficult to understand, for example, the sentence

The tree the cat the dog chased climbed broke.

while logically correct, is so deeply nested as to make understanding difficult.
- Making sure that data flow between integrands is explicit. That is, nothing is passed through global variables whose existence has to be remembered by the reader without assistance from the executable code.
- Using the principle of information hiding so that the details of each programmed mechanism is contained within a closely circumscribed area and the reader does not have to wonder 'Where did I see that other part of this definition?'
- Reducing complexity through abstraction.

However, following the methods of expository programming assiduously does not excuse the writer from thoroughly testing the finished program. As pointed out by Abrahams (1978) in his review of Dijkstra (1976), even very careful program development by a very skilled practitioner of the art of formal development can make slips that would be detected by testing.

PART THREE

THE PRACTICE
OF PROGRAMMING

CHAPTER EIGHT
PROGRAMMING LANGUAGES

A programming language is the most important tool that a programmer can use to assist in the mastery of complexity. It does this by guiding the programmer's thoughts in the areas of program design, comprehension, and establishment of the correctness of the program. In order to do this, the design of the language must accord with a number of principles, which are reviewed. The applications of computers are varied but may be classified as following a few distinct paradigms. These are described and the languages Ada, Assembler-language, Basic, C, Cobol, Fortran, Lisp, and Modula-2 are compared in the context of these paradigms.

8.1 INTRODUCTION

For the amateur mechanic, the car repair problem of removing an axle hub can seem insoluble. Trying to lever it off always applies a force to one side of the hub and jams it even tighter onto the axle. Using a hammer only makes matters worse. There is a tool, a slide hammer, shown in Figure 8.1, that is designed exactly for this task. It consists of a shaft on which a metal weight slides but is prevented from coming off the shaft at one end by a stop. The other end of the shaft bolts on to the hub so that the shaft forms an extension to the axle. Sliding the weight on the shaft so that it hits the stop applies an axial shock to the hub sliding it off its axle. This tool is effective because its form fits its context of application. This is an example of what Alexander (1964) refers to as *fitness of form*. The form of this tool matches the context defined by the problem. The slide-hammer is effective because it guides the user's muscular effort so that it is applied axially and none of it is wasted.

Programming languages are the programmer's most important software tool for implementation. As with other tools, programming languages must have fitness of form to be effective. Just as the slide-hammer guides the mechanic's muscles, so an effective programming language guides the programmer's ideas so that they are applied in the proper direction. A good language can lead the programmer to the correct solution of a problem in a natural and easy manner. Conversely, a poor language may add so much

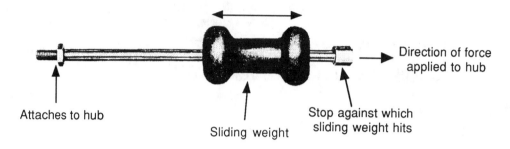

Direction of force
applied to hub

Attaches to hub

Sliding weight

Stop against which
sliding weight hits

FIGURE 8.1 A slide-hammer.

complexity to the programming solution that the programmer will have great difficulty in getting a clear enough understanding of the program to know that it is correct. Note that a 'poor language' may only be poor relative to a particular application. A slide hammer is a poor tool for inserting Phillips screws and Cobol is a poor language for finding the eigen values of a matrix, though both are excellent at their particular application. (Incidentally, Cobol may be better at the latter than a slide hammer is at the former.)

The linguist Benjamin Whorf has hypothesized in Whorf (1956) that one's language has a considerable effect on the way that one thinks; indeed on *what* one *can* think. Essentially, a language puts one into a mental strait-jacket. That is why the main design discussion should be taken and recorded in a richer notation than a programming language provides before thinking too much about implementation. Escaping from the language strait-jacket to another language is difficult. Even more difficult is to recognize exactly what are the bounds imposed by the language – one cannot say what one cannot say without saying it.

The language designer's task goes beyond programming itself and concerns itself with the symbolism that is used to express computations. Thus, if Whorf's hypothesis is correct, the skill of the designer will have a considerable effect on the range of problems that can realistically be solved in a language. I use the word 'realistically' because all programming languages are in theory equivalent in power, however we all have a threshold of complexity and if the solution of a problem exceeds that threshold, we are never able to reach that solution – we abandon the problem before we get there. The designer must survey the many attractive features that are available for inclusion in a language and choose the most powerful set of facilities that will constitute a harmonious assembly. The objective is sufficient power with *minimal* complexity. As Niklaus Wirth said, 'The most important decisions in language design concern what is to be left out.'

In this chapter, we examine the principles of programming language design and how these principles fit various programming applications. An understanding of these principles will help the programmer in choosing the right language for the problem.

8.2 THE LEVERAGE POINTS

The primary purpose of a programming language is to help in the task of programming by preventing the commission of trivial errors, such as mistyping the name of a variable or forgetting to mark the end of a loop, that are so easy to create and so time consuming to remove. Thus, it must aid at those points in the programming process, the *leverage points* that are the most difficult:

- *Program design.* Deciding and specifying what must be done and how the data are to be represented. In program design, the language must assist the programmer in specifying the process and the data clearly and naturally. It must be possible to construct abstractions that match the characteristics of the problem. This means that it must be possible to avoid extraneous detail that will clutter a solution. A common deficiency in this area is the inability of a language to manipulate abstract data objects other than the few primitive types supplied by the language. The details of this representation are likely to appear in the algorithm, making it more difficult to understand. Thus, it is most important for the ease and clarity of programming that the language be able to treat abstract objects that match the problem data. Languages that permit the definition of abstract data types are very helpful in making simplifying abstractions.
- *Understanding.* Explaining the working of the program to a reader. All too often documentation is added to a program as a chore after the program has been made to work. As a result, either too little or too much detail is supplied. If there is not enough, the programmer who wishes to modify the program later will not be able to do the job reliably. If there is too much detail, it usually repeats what is written in the code and serves to obscure rather than enlighten. A well-designed language will encourage the programmer to write so clearly that the program will be *self-documenting*, with only modest need for additional comments, such as are described in Section 9.6. Making the documentation an integral part of the program avoids the well-known trap of misleading documentation that occurs when a program is modified without corresponding changes in the separate documentation. For self-documentation to be possible, the language must allow the specification of operations and data to be made clearly and naturally. Note that 'self-documenting' only applies to the detailed information about a program that can be supplied by the source code, this does not obviate the need for other documentation, such as specification and design, to provide the context within which the source code can be understood.
- *Confidence.* Establishing confidence in the correctness of the program. We are not talking about formal verification of categorical correctness here, that is a subject that is discussed in Chapter 7 of this volume, but rather about giving the programmer a degree of belief that the program is correct. Thus, it must aid the programmer to obtain either formal or informal validation. Again, one of the best ways of achieving this is for the program to have been written with such crystal clarity that it is obviously correct. Since it is always probable that careless errors will be made, the notation of the

programming language should be designed to reduce the scope of such errors and allow the compiler to detect them.

8.3 THE PRINCIPLES OF PROGRAMMING LANGUAGE DESIGN

Based on the leverage points described in the previous section, we will now consider a number of principles of design that can be used as a basis on which to judge a programming language:

1. *Clarity of syntax*. The syntax of a language defines the way in which it will be written; it is the grammar of the language. This greatly affects the ease with which it can be written and read. A frequently applied principle in the design of languages is the minimization of keystrokes on the grounds that this will help the programmer. This may have been a problem at one time when programs were laboriously written, erased, and rewritten by hand on paper. Now that terminals and editors are generally available and most programmers have acquired the motor skills to use a keyboard efficiently, saving of keystrokes is no longer a proper consideration. Readability of programs is a much more important criterion than writability; after all, the program will probably only be written once, but read many times. Just as languages whose syntax is very terse can lead to programs that are difficult to read, the opposite, a verbose syntax, can have the same effect. It must be recognized, however, that, even though a language may be designed with the goal of program clarity, it does not follow that all programs written in that language will be clear. As Flon (1975) puts it:

> There does not now, nor will there ever, exist a programming language in which it is the least bit hard to write bad programs.

2. *Clarity of semantics*. The semantics of a language defines the meaning of the statements in the language. In Wexelblat (1976) the author discusses the various ways in which language designers *appear to* have made their languages as difficult to use as possible. Examples are:

   • Make a construct in a new language look like a construct in an old language – but make it behave differently. PL/I, which came after Fortran, has an iterative statement

   ```
   DO I = 1, 10;
   ```

   which resembles Fortran's

   ```
   DO 13 I = 1, 10
   ```

   however, the PL/I version only executes the body of the loop twice, once with I having the value 1 and once with the value 10.

   • Use unconventional operator precedence in expressions. The language APL (Iverson 1962), has right-to-left precedence modified by parentheses in the usual way. The microprocessor language PL-11 has expressions that are evaluated in the conventional left-to-right manner but parentheses are ignored.

Elsewhere, Wexelblat refers to this kind of language design as violating the *Principle of Least Astonishment*, which states that a language should be designed so that its effects will be so obvious from the way in which the language is written that they will surprise its users as infrequently as possible.

3. *Modularization and information hiding.* As we have seen, complexity control can be achieved through the division of a large program into a number of independent integrands. Each integrand is then like a small program that can be implemented independently of the other integrands. Information hiding depends upon the ability to split a program into independent integrands, each of which contains the result of each of the program's difficult design decisions. A language's support of these principles lies partially in the ability to split the program into separate integrands and partially in its support for abstraction, this is support in making routines have unity of purpose. Properties of a language can also affect coupling. For example, Fortran permits (perhaps one might say encourages) common coupling through the facility for defining COMMON. Algol, Pascal, and other block structured languages allow hierarchical references, perhaps the term 'block coupling' might be coined. The import–export control of Modula-2 and Ada also address this issue.

4. *Abstraction.* A traditional technique for abstraction is the subroutine. However, subroutines provide only algorithmic abstraction, data and control abstractions are also required. For data, this requires the programmer to be able to define new data representations and the operations that can manipulate them. For clarity of expression, it must be possible to attach these operations to standard operator symbols through the principle of *overloading*. If the programmer wishes to define a new data type, say matrices, it should be possible to define * so that, when it occurs between two matrix variables, it is understood to mean matrix multiplication using algorithms supplied by the programmer as part of the definition of the data type matrix.

5. *Orthogonality.* An important part of a simple design is that there should not be more than one way of expressing any action in the language, that is, each component of the language should be independent of the other components. The design is then said to be *orthogonal*. In a truly orthogonal design, there are a small number of separate, basic constructions, and these are combined according to regular and systematic rules without arbitrary restrictions. Many programming languages include composite data types, such as structures and arrays. They also allow functions, processes that map arguments into a result. A proper combination of these two orthogonal concepts, data types and functions, would permit functions to return results of any data type that is allowed as an argument. One restriction, for example, would allow arguments to be of a composite data type but permit only scalar results. However, there is a danger in removing all restrictions; the complexity of the language might be increased without a corresponding gain in facility.

6. *Portability.* For many projects it is important to be able to move the resulting programs from the machine on which they are developed to other computing

systems. Indeed, it frequently happens that, even if this were not thought important at the outset, once the program is running and the application is a success, suddenly it is important to make it run on another system. For this to be possible, the language should be widely available and have a definition that is independent of the features of a particular machine. True machine independence is very hard to achieve. Beyond the obvious dependencies on machine architecture that might be included in a language, such as references to particular registers, there are a number of subtle issues that need to be remembered. These include character sets and the representation of floating point numbers. This latter point is especially difficult since most languages and computer hardware do not follow any general standard for floating point operations. The programmer can mitigate these problems by isolating such hardware dependencies within special integrands and making sure that they stand out clearly to the reader.

> Portability should be viewed as portability of *design* rather than of *implementation*, since any code that is non-compliant when ported will have to be reviewed at the design level before the code 'can be tuned' to the new environment.

7. *Structure*. The problem of understanding a program is one of inferring the dynamic form of its execution from reading the written static form. This requires a mental leap. The greater the difference between the two forms, the greater the mental leap required. There are a number of areas of language design that affect the relationship between the two program forms:

- *Control flow:* The language should have a good set of control flow structures. The go to statement provides an open invitation to obscure the relation between the two forms. Statements that allow control to exit from the interior of a loop, usually called exit, leave, or break statements make determination of the effect of the loop and the computation state at termination difficult.
- *Name scope:* The scope of a name determines how a reference to a variable will be resolved to the declaration of that variable. This is of particular importance when the same name is used in more than one procedure. There are two main positions, *static scoping* where the resolution is made at compile time based on the program's static structure and remains constant during the execution of the program, and *dynamic scoping* where the resolution can only be made during execution and depends upon the dynamic structure of the program. Static scoping requires a smaller mental leap than dynamic scoping. Within static scoping, there are a number of different ways in which the rules may be applied. A common rule leads to what is known as *block structure*, which allows internal procedures to reference variables in containing procedures without any redeclaration. This can lead to great complication as described in Clarke *et al.* (1980). Hanson (1981) also argues against the inclusion of block structure in a language.
- *Typing:* Again there is a choice between static and dynamic forms. In static typing, a type is associated with a variable during compilation and only values of that type may be assigned to the variable. Under dynamic typing, types are associated with values and may be assigned to any variable. Thus, to understand what type of

value is stored in a variable with dynamic typing, the history of the computation must be understood.

In all these examples, it is a conflict between the added flexibility afforded by a dynamic philosophy and the added security that is available through defining relationships based on the static structure of the program.

8. *Degree of permissiveness*. This refers to the extent that the compiler can detect simple errors made by programmers through consistency checks. For this to be possible, the programmer must provide redundant information. The design issue is to balance the value of checking against the extra work of providing redundant information. Some languages allow the implicit declaration of variables. That is, variables do not have to be declared explicitly. The designers argued that this would save the programmer trouble in cases where the attributes assumed by the translator matched those required by the programmer. The penalty for this convenience is that the compiler can no longer detect simple spelling errors in the names of variables. The occurrence of a misspelled name constitutes an implicit declaration of that name as a new identifier. More importantly, the explicit declaration of variables does a great deal to establish the intent of the program in the reader's mind. The declarations may then be viewed as 'definitions' of program objects, and the executable statements as steps in the process of computing the result. Most modern programming languages require explicit declaration of names.

There are a number of areas in which permissiveness allows the programmer to indulge in dangerous programming practices:

- The ability to create aliases, that is, alternative names to access a given variable. For example, if it is possible to pass a variable by reference as an argument to a subroutine that can also reference the variable as a global variable, the same variable can be referenced through two different names, the global name of the variable and the parameter name. When aliases exist, it is possible to modify a variable in non-obvious ways. It also hinders compiler optimization.
- The ability to circumvent the language's type-checking mechanism.
- The ability of the programmer to make use of the run-time representation, for example, the value of pointers or the bit representation of characters.

9. *Efficiency*. The need for efficiency has been part of language design from the beginning. The atmosphere during the early development of Fortran in 1954, described by Backus and Heising (1964), was one where the only way in which acceptance of 'automatic programming' could be obtained was to demonstrate that it could produce programs that were almost as efficient as hand-coded ones in practically every case. The atmosphere has changed since then. Efficiency is no longer measured only by execution speed and space. The effort to produce a program initially and to maintain it are also viewed as components of efficiency. In addition, the language should be designed so that its programs can be 'optimized'. That means, that the compiler is able to perform efficiency-improving transformations on the program that *maintain its meaning*. While it may seem trite to say that the transformations do not change the effect of a program, it is really the nub of the question. The optimizer, part of the compiler, must make careful analysis of the

program to make sure that the proposed transformation will not change its meaning. If there is the slightest doubt, the program must be left unchanged. Thus, for example, if there is a possibility that the name X may be an alias for the variable Y, then it must be assumed that this is always the case and certain efficiency-improving transformations omitted. This means that saving a few cycles by maintaining the value of Y in a register, rather than storing it, cannot be done because the reference to X might also be a reference to Y and must access its latest value, which is in the register. The optimizer must work in a pessimistic manner. Thus, the design of the language has a considerable effect on the efficiency of its programs. In this regard, the existence of go to statements considerably complicates optimization. It should not be thought that optimization is intended to compensate for poor programming. Rather, it should be thought of as making the best use of a machine by making transformations that are not easily available to the programmer. Consider, for example, the checking of subscript ranges during execution. It is desirable to detect all attempts to reference outside the bounds of an array. A few machines check for this in the microcode so that there is no additional execution time penalty. However, on most machines, extra code must be generated to test subscript ranges and unfortunately, such range checks are expensive in execution time and are generally omitted although it is well understood that this is a dangerous sacrifice of safety. The analysis that is made as part of optimization can show that many of the range checks are superfluous. If the index has been shown to be correct at one point in the program there is no need to check it again unless its value has been changed. Again, the ability for the optimizer to perform such analyses depends greatly on the design of the language.

10. *Uniformity*. Basically, this means that the form of a particular construct should be independent of its context of use and that similar things should have similar meanings. As an example of a failure of syntactic uniformity, consider the two Fortran statements, both of which include a list of objects:

```
READ (5) A, B, C, D
GO TO K, (10, 20, 30, 40)
```

In one case there is a comma before the list, in the other none. In one case, the list is in parentheses, in the other, it is not. In general, the more exceptions there are to a rule, the harder it is to learn.

11. *Ability to deal with exceptions*. There are 'exception' conditions that can arise in every program. Input data may contain values that are out of range, a hardware unit may fail, a table may become full, or the wrong reel of tape may be mounted by an operator. Here, we refer to conditions that are associated with particular operations, they are *synchronous* in the sense that they can only occur at specific points in the program – a divide-by-zero condition can only arise during a division operation. The treatment of truly *asynchronous* events, that is, those associated with separate concurrent processes, is discussed in paragraph 12 below. To think of all exception conditions as errors is too limiting. Some exception conditions, though occurring rarely, are required for the proper termination of a program. For example, the end of

the input file may mark the end of the input phase of a program and the beginning of its computation phase. There is no general distinction that can be made between erroneous and normal exception conditions. What is normal in one context may be an error in another. We can define an exception condition as:

> A condition that prevents the completion of the operation that detects it, that cannot be resolved within the local context of the operation, and that must be brought to the attention of the invoker of the operation.

This means that either the operation's input parameters do not satisfy its requirements or that it is unable to produce a result that is within its range. In either case, the exception must be brought to the attention of the operation's invoker for resolution. The language must provide facilities for handling these exceptions in a manner that allow the program to make it clear that all such cases result in actions that are consistent with the specifications. We discuss the handling of exceptions in Chapter 11.

12. *Ability to handle concurrent processes*. Some applications require the coordination of mutually asynchronous processes. These processes may be taking place in separate machines, in a single machine but under the control of a system (multi-programming or time sharing) outside the application program, or involve the interaction of humans and machines. In order to coordinate the action of such processes, the programming language must provide special structures for handling the inter-communication of synchronizing signals or data between the processes. Data is passed between processes either through shared variables or through messages. The constructs that allow data to be passed through shared variables are generally such that they permit one process to have exclusive access to a shared variable for some finite period of time. During that time, any other process that requires access to the variable must wait. It must be possible to arrange this so that there is no possibility of *deadlock* where two or more processes are waiting for events that will never occur. Since processes are executed in parallel with unpredictable speeds, it must be possible for some applications to be able to synchronize the processes, possibly with a message being passed at the point of synchronization or *rendezvous*. For an excellent review of the language constructs required for concurrent processes the reader is referred to Andrews and Schneider (1983). A more detailed exposition is in Ben-Ari (1982).

13. *Programming environment*. The term 'programming environment' refers to a collection of hardware and software tools that a software engineer can use to develop a program. While this term can refer to tools that support all the activities that comprise the software development cycle, in this volume we are particularly concerned with those that support the implementation part of the cycle. A detailed discussion of these tools will be reserved for Part 4; for the moment we will mention that there are many tools that are now available that interact directly with a programming language. Such tools include particularly *language sensitive editors* where the editors have been particularized for a specific language and a detailed knowledge of the syntax of the language is built directly into the editor so that the

user can, for example, obtain immediate feedback on the syntactic correctness of the source programming without having to wait for compilation. Until recently, the idea of the programming environment has not been considered to be in the province of language design. However, it is becoming increasingly clear that the context in which the language appears is of great importance to the user and therefore must be considered at the time the language is designed *if* the tool-set within which the language is contained is to be properly integrated.

For more complete discussions of programming languages, the reader is referred to Barron (1977), Elson (1973), Ghezzi and Jazayeri (1987), Higman (1977), Horowitz (1984), MacLennan (1983), Marcotty and Ledgard (1986), Nichols (1975), Organick *et al.* (1978), Pratt (1984), and Tennent (1981).

8.4 CATEGORIES OF APPLICATION

The applications of computers are many and varied and each type of application makes different demands on a programming language. We may classify applications according to a number of paradigms:

- *The data processing paradigm (DP).* Applications in this class consisting of simple transformations on sequential records of information, with little time criticality and no concurrency. The requirements here are for record handling, logical decision making, and text manipulation. There is only a limited need for numerical computation, however what computation there is must generally be done exactly. Financial transactions are usually computed down to the smallest monetary denomination; thus, there is little call for floating point computation. In addition to the more traditional data processing applications, most software tools fall into this category.
- *The numerical computation paradigm (NC).* This class of applications involves high-order mathematical and logical transformations on aggregates of numerical data, with little time criticality and no inherent concurrency. (Nevertheless, for several years now, concurrency has been *very* important in numerical computation. Now that processors are running almost as fast as is possible, greater computation speed can only be achieved by using many processors in parallel. This subject is beyond the scope of this book and the reader is referred to Fox *et al.* (1988) for a fuller discussion.) There must be a good support library of mathematical functions and the programmer must have the ability to control the accuracy of computation and round-off.
- *The process-oriented paradigm (PO).* This is the class of applications generally known as 'real-time programming' and involves either or both record processing and computation, also time criticality and possibly asynchrony and concurrency of processes. Inter-process communication through shared data and the ability to synchronize processes is generally important. The processes may either be executing on one or more processors under the control of a single operating system or on separate processors and operating systems communicating through some inter-

processor protocol. This paradigm includes the transaction systems found, for example, in banks, airlines, or insurance companies, in addition to the real time control systems used in airplanes, chemical works, and nuclear power stations.

- *The system-programming paradigm (SP)*. In this class of application the requirement is for the programmer to be able to 'get close to the machine'. That is to say, the program must be able to reference specific addresses, control the use of registers, and execute the full range of machine instructions. Typically, in most higher-level languages, the compiler will never generate 'privileged instructions', which may only be executed when in *supervisor mode*. Programs written in this class of applications are often operating systems and execute in supervisor mode. There must be a way for the programmer to cause these special instructions to be generated. At the same time, the language must provide checking and generate object code of high efficiency.

- *The auto-adaptive process paradigm (AP)*. Applications in this class are generally given the description 'artificial intelligence'. Unfortunately, the term has been so over-used, particularly in the hyperbole that generally accompanies publicity, as to have lost almost all meaning. Nevertheless, there are many applications where the use of record processing, computation, asynchrony, and concurrency of processes, and their heuristic emendation, all yield excellent results. Probably, the greatest distinguishing characteristic of this paradigm is that the program evolves and undergoes modification during execution.

8.5 COMPARISON OF LANGUAGES

The following is a brief critique of a representative set of languages, taken in alphabetic order, based on their applicability to the various classes of application described in the previous section. Although it is a 'representative set' only, it is likely to cover well over 90 per cent of the use of programming languages – although the complete set of such languages is far larger. The reader will, no doubt, understand and forgive the omission of any personal favorite.

It must be recognized that all the languages discussed here are as powerful as a Turing Machine and thus can be programmed to calculate any computable function. There are examples of Fortran being used for a payroll and Cobol being applied to the solution of differential equations. However, these two languages are more suitable for applications in the numerical computation and data-processing paradigms respectively.

Although we may set up a set of ostensibly objective criteria for judging a language any critique such as this has a large subjective content. When programming languages are discussed between programmers, unless all parties agree (an unlikely occurrence), logic and rationality are often early casualties in the ensuing battle in which more heat than light will be shed. Analogously to the near impossibility of making a rational assessment of one's mother tongue, the programmer's view of programming languages is heavily conditioned by experience with various languages. The following comments will clearly be biased by my own experience of programming and software engineering.

8.5.1 Ada

This language was specifically designed for use throughout the United States Department of Defense. It was intended for all types of application DP, NC, and PO. In addition to these areas, its use in the SP class of applications is implied by its original specifications calling for its use in *embedded systems*. An embedded system is typically a microprocessor that is used to control some part of a larger system, for example the microprocessor that is used to control fuel and ignition in many modern cars. In these applications, there is generally no operating system in the conventional sense, the application program is itself 'the system'. It is not clear how the requirements of the SP paradigm can be achieved in Ada.

From the point of view of general software engineering principles, Ada is a very good language. It provides excellent capabilities for data abstraction through its *package* construct, interface checking between separately compiled parts of a program, type checking, and inter-process communication. The major complaints concern its size and complexity. It is a block-structured language with some additional scoping rules beyond what is normal for block-structured language.

8.5.2 Assembler-style languages

Although assembler languages may in general be scorned as leading to programs that are almost impossible to understand and maintain, this is not necessarily the case. I have seen very clear examples of assembler programs that were written for the microprocessors that control car engines and thus required a very high degree of reliability. In fact, they were far easier to understand than many programs written in high-level languages. A high level of discipline needs to be maintained throughout the writing process. Nevertheless, the great amount of work that is required to write and maintain assembler language programs precludes recommending their use. This is largely because of the low level of checking that is possible and the great exposure of detail required of the programmer. A consequence is that the testing and debugging process takes a long time. These languages are traditionally used for SP applications because of the access to the full range of hardware functions though their primacy in this area is starting to be eroded.

8.5.3 Basic

Basic was originally developed at Dartmouth College as a language for programming from interactive terminals. As a language, it has had a phenomenal success; it has been implemented on almost every personal computer made. Probably, Basic has been the first programming language learned by more students than all others combined. Almost every high-school student who takes a programming class will have been introduced to Basic. As suggested earlier, the reason for this popularity is that it is presented in a simple self-contained environment that shields the user from the more unfriendly interface with the host operating system. From the software engineering point of view, Basic is not a suitable language for writing easily maintainable programs. In the earlier dialects of Basic, the control structures are too limited and restrictive to allow the control flow to be organized simply; this however has been improved. As will be explained in a later chapter, it takes a great deal of discipline to produce well-structured programs, particularly when the language does not provide adequate support. In addition, all variables in Basic, except parameters, are global and there is almost no power for abstraction. Wexelblat (1981) has suggested that since one's first programming language has its effect on the way in which one programs for the rest of one's life, this loss of innocence through Basic may have a very bad effect on future generations of software engineers. Dijkstra (1972b) puts it even more strongly when he says 'It is practically impossible to teach good programming style to students that have had prior exposure to Basic; as potential programmers they are mentally mutilated beyond hope of regeneration.'

8.5.4 C

This is another widespread language, originally described in Kernighan and Ritchie (1978). It is a general-purpose programming language, not specialized to any particular area of application. It has been closely associated with the Unix system, however, it is not tied to any one system or machine. Although it has been called a 'system programming language' because it has been found useful for writing operating systems – Unix and its software are written in C – the language has been found useful to write major numerical, text-processing, and database programs. A superset of C, called C++, has been developed and is described in Stroustrup (1986).

C does little to hide the underlying hardware; in fact, it tries to provide a convenient way of controlling the machine. Although its instruction level is usually higher than that of the hardware, its data objects are very similar to those of the hardware. Its type checking is very limited, for example, it does not distinguish between Boolean and integer types, which leads to some unexpected results. Specific physical addresses can be referenced in C as can particular bits within a word.

The language treats almost everything as expressions, including assignments, which encourages side effects. Expressions can be extremely complex given that there are 46 operators that appear at 16 levels of precedence, some associating left-to-right and others right-to-left (Harbison and Steele 1984). This convention, if fully understood by the programmer, can lead to great economy of keystrokes and of readability. For example, the following statement reads characters into an array until end-of-file:

```
while((s[i++] = getchar()) != EOF);
```

The array s is indexed by the expression i++ which gives the current value of i and then increments it by 1. The standard library function getchar reads the next character from input. Thus, the complete expression obtains the next character from input, assigns to the ith location of s, increments i and then tests the character against the end-of-file marker with the symbolic name EOF. The loop continues until the end of file is detected. The equivalent construction in Modula-2 would be:

```
WHILE NOT EOF(InputFile) DO
   ReadByte(InputFile, S[I]);
   I := I + 1
END;
```

C's economy of expression encourages the writing of cryptic programs through linguistic braggadocio – a sin we are all sometimes guilty of. Programs written in this way generally have lower reliability and are difficult to modify. However, as is explained in Darnell and Margolis (1988), with discipline, it is possible to use C to produce well-engineered programs.

8.5.5 Cobol

Cobol (*Co*mmon *B*usiness-*O*riented *L*anguage) was designed in 1954 for writing non-numeric file-oriented applications. The original design philosophy explicitly considered the issue of program compatibility and portability between machines. The goals of portability were achieved and there is probably a better chance of taking a program written in Cobol that runs on one machine and moving it to another machine and having it work than for almost any other language. The designers intended programs written in Cobol to be readable by people without knowledge of the target computer. This was approached by making the language resemble English as much as possible. The designers had a far-sighted grasp of the great importance of program readability. However, the pseudo-English style hinders readability as much as it helps it. While the individual statements are readable, they tend to be verbose, which decreases the intelligibility. The language is defined in terms of a set of individual features, with each feature tailored to its own task with a syntax appropriate to that task. Consequently, each has its own syntax and the rules are not uniform across the features. The control flow constructs are very restrictive and it has been difficult to build well-structured programs, though this has been much improved in Cobol 85. The subroutine mechanism is weak since it does not permit parameters, so that all data must be passed through global variables. In contrast, the definition of data structures does allow powerful abstraction. For large DP applications, Cobol clearly has its place.

8.5.6 Fortran

Fortran was one of the earliest 'higher-level' languages for expressing applications of the computation set. It was developed in the mid-1950s in an environment where machine efficiency was the yardstick used to compare it with hand-written assembler programs. It is basically a single-level language with little nesting. There is a good subroutine facility with variable names local to a subroutine. Data are passed from one subroutine to another either by explicit parameter passing or through global variables. In the world of engineering computation, Fortran is certainly the most popular language and, in the United States at least, virtually all engineering students study Fortran. There are a large number of application programs for performing engineering calculations available. Thus, it is mainly used for applications of the NC paradigm.

The language has been considerably enhanced since it was originally designed and the more modern versions have good control structures for writing structured programs. The concept of type checking is weak and can easily be circumvented. The only data aggregate structure is the rectangular homogeneous array of scalar elements. Since pointers and records are not available, all non-array structures must be modeled in terms of arrays, for example, list structures would require array indexes to serve as pointers. Since there is no macro capability, there is little that can be done for abstraction and information hiding.

8.5.7 Lisp

Lisp, designed in 1961, is the most popular language for programs in the AP paradigm. It is basically an applicative language, that is, it achieves its primary effect by applying functions either recursively or through composition. For example, the Modula-2 expression

```
2 * X + Y * Z
```

might be written in Lisp as

```
(PLUS(TIMES 2 X) (TIMES Y Z))
```

In a purely applicative language, functions can only return values. However, Lisp does have the ability to have side-effects through global variables. It is usually an interpretive language. It has a single data-structure, the list, whose elements can themselves be lists. Since a Lisp program is itself constructed as a list, it is possible to make data structures that can be executed. This allows for powerful abstractions. The basic syntax of the language has the salient characteristic of embedded lists denoted by enclosing parentheses. However, through the use of special software tools, written themselves in Lisp, much of the original heavily parenthesized syntax can be hidden to make more easily readable programs.

8.5.8 Modula-2

Modula-2 is a descendant from Pascal. The defining document for the language, Wirth (1983), defines the major additions with regard to Standard Pascal as follows:

1. The *module* concept, and in particular the facility to split a module into a *definition part* and an *implementation part*. This is a particularly important feature since it helps in the design of modifiable programs through information hiding.

2. A more systematic syntax than Pascal's. This helps in learning the language. In particular, every structure that starts with a keyword also ends with a keyword, that is, is properly bracketed, with the first keyword acting as an opening bracket and the last keyword acting as a closing bracket.
3. *Low-level facilities* that make it possible to breach the rigid type consistency rules and allow unstructured storage to be mapped with a Modula-2 structure. In Pascal, breaches in type checking were achieved through manipulating the tag field in variant records; this permitted machine dependencies to occur in a way that could not be found mechanically through the use of search operations. In Modula-2 there are low-level functions that provide type transfers. It is possible to search source code for these to discover these machine dependencies.
4. The concept of *process* as the key to multiprogramming facilities.
5. The *procedure type* that allows procedures to be dynamically assigned to variables. This is a technique used in heuristic programming.

From the point of view of writing clear programs, I find that the two major shortcomings of Modula-2 are:

1. The treatment of character strings as arrays of characters. This makes the handling of variable length items of text, needed by text manipulation programs, very difficult. A particular consequence of this view of character strings is that since functions can only return scalar values, it is difficult to have a function that returns a character string. Concatenation and extraction thus must be procedure invocations, which makes programs more difficult to read.
2. Requiring constant bounds for arrays. Since the bounds of an array are built into the type structure, a pointer to an array has the bounds of the array built into its type. It is thus impossible to write general code that can create and manipulate an array whose size is only determined during execution.

Despite these problems, Modula-2 lends itself to writing clear well-structured programs.

8.5.9 Pascal

Pascal was originally designed by Niklaus Wirth (Wirth 1971) to satisfy two principal aims:

1. To make available a language suitable for teaching of disciplined programming based on concepts that were clearly expressed in the language.
2. To define a language whose implementations could be both reliable and efficient on the computers that were available at that time.

Its use has gone well beyond these original aims and there are now implementations on most machines including microprocessors.

The language is block structured with a limited set of control structures, a data definition facility, and strong typing, i.e., all conversions between data types must be explicitly defined through functions. These features have advantages and disadvantages:

- *Block structure*. A complete program is a single block. In the original definition and in the ANSI standard, (ANSI/IEEE 1983), there are no facilities defined for the separate compilation and subsequent linking of integrands. This makes the use of this language with a team of programmers very difficult. Several implementations have recognized this problem and provided such facilities. Another consequence of this is that for any program that is other than trivial, nesting is required and there is a strong temptation for the programmer to use global variables for passing data between procedures.
- *Control structures*. Although the control structures are limited, a goto statement is provided. Its use is discouraged by restrictions and using labels that are numbers, that compound the dangers of the goto statement with the obscurity of meaningless labels.
- *Typing*. Although the language claims to be strongly typed, the use of variant records with tag fields that can be changed dynamically provides an easy escape for the programmer who wishes to circumvent the rules. (A variant record is a data structure, sometimes called a *discriminated union*, that specifies that a choice is to be made between different alternative constructions. The particular construction that is chosen is defined by the value of the tag field in the record.) A particularly awkward feature is the language's use of arrays of characters to represent text strings. The manipulation of varying length strings, essential for the programming of serious text processing, is difficult. This is compounded by the fact that strings, because they are arrays, cannot be returned as values by functions. Consequently, all string manipulation must be performed by procedures.

Pascal is probably adequate for its original goals but its serious use for programs of the DP, NC, and SP paradigms is, in my opinion, unwise.

8.5.10 PL/I

By 1962, the development of Fortran had progressed to Fortran IV and, despite many improvements over its forebears, the language still lacked character handling and the ability to interact with modern equipment and operating systems. The IBM scientific users' group, Share, decided in 1963 that further improvements were required and, together with IBM, set up a task force to design a language that would cater to more users. The new language was intended to be suitable for both the DP and NC paradigms and thus was expected to draw on the experience of both Fortran and Cobol. Although the original name for the new language was to have been Fortran VI, it soon became clear that it would be impossible to meet the language's objectives and yet retain compatibility with Fortran, thus a new name had to be found. A major design departure from both Fortran and Cobol was that PL/I should be a block structured language. (A cartoon that appeared shortly after the first definition of the language showed doting parents labeled Fortran and Cobol looking at their PL/I child who bears a close resemblance to the milkman labeled Algol seen coming up the front path.)

PL/I attempted to be all things to all programmers. I used to tell my Principles of Programming Languages classes that PL/I contained an example of every major language concept, good or bad. One author likened it to a Swiss Army knife that had a blade for every purpose where some blades hindered the proper use of others. Consequently, it became fashionable to castigate the language, sometimes fairly, others not. The following is a review of some areas of contention:

- *Size*. PL/I is certainly a very large language and it is doubtful whether the complete language as defined in the ISO/ANSI Standard has ever been implemented in any compiler. At one stage, I thought that PL/I would be the last of the behemoths, yet from the point of view of complexity, it is simpler than Ada. A subset of the complete language has also been standardized and I have found this to be very satisfactory.
- *Defaults*. One design principle in the original language was that of minimizing the work of the programmer. One example of this was that variables did not have to be explicitly declared and undeclared variables acquired attributes according to a system of defaults. For example, undeclared variables whose names began with the letters in the range I to N were integers – an idea that came from Fortran. A consequence of this was that mistyping the name led to the creation of a new and unexpected variable. My own experience has been that one can stay out of too much trouble by adopting a strict discipline of declaring every variable with exactly the desired set of attributes.
- *Conversions*. Another example of the principle of minimizing the work that the programmer had to do was that almost all possible expressions were valid. Mixtures of types led in most cases to automatic conversion of values from one type to another. This too was dangerous and could cause the programmer many hours of debugging because the conversion rules were so complicated and numerous that the results were often unexpected. Again, these problems could be avoided by adopting a discipline of defining exactly what one wanted.
- *Pointers*. Reference variables in PL/I are pointers in that they can refer to space containing values of any type. The strict definition of the language says that it is an error to use a pointer to circumvent the type checking and conversion rules. This implied that pointer variables were dynamically typed and the rule could only be enforced through checking during execution. This exactly matches the situation that exists with Pascal through its variant records. The careful serious programmer will only use a variable to contain values of a single conceptual type and avoid, for example, using one numeric variable to contain values representing the real-world quantities hours and distance at different points in the program. The same principle applies to the use of pointers.

PL/I also had some features that have been forgotten in more 'modern' languages to their detriment. For example, its handling of exceptions, discussed in greater detail in Chapter 12, although not perfect, has much to commend it. It also has variable length text strings as an intrinsic scalar type so that it is possible to define functions that return string values, and text manipulation is much easier than it is in Pascal or Modula-2. I have probably written many more lines of program in PL/I than in all other languages combined and have found it to be a very workable language.

CHAPTER NINE

THE REPRESENTATION OF DATA

The model of the real world represented by a program must be faithful to the objects being modeled. Without this, it is likely that later attempts to modify the program to follow changes in the real world will be difficult or impossible. This principle is emphasized through an example of a small program that was unmodifiable because a key feature of the real world was missing from the model. A discussion of the influence of data representation on program complexity and hence readability follows. Abstract data types are described including the fact that they are characterized by the operations that can be performed on their objects, which in turn leads to improvement in program readability. The actual meaning of input and output data in the external interface specification of a procedure is discussed. This external interface specification provides a context in which the executable statements are to be understood and therefore must be contained in the integrand's introductory comments, which provide a synopsis of the actions performed by the executable statements of the integrand.

9.1 INTRODUCTION

Change dominates the universe. Without evolution and entropy, we would lack 'time's arrow', and the notions of decay and regeneration that are central to so many philosophies. At the human level, something is always happening, whether perceptible to our mere senses or not. That is why all human languages are built around verbs and nouns. The same can be said of programming languages. The early programming languages were very action oriented in the sense that they were concerned mainly with expressions and control. Later, language designers realized the importance of matching the data's structure to the real-world objects being represented. As this development continued, it became clear that an accurate representation of these objects and the operations that could be performed upon them was essential to a successful computer solution to a problem. Once the world objects have been modeled the design of the program will follow, or so it might be thought – and in some cases correctly, as we shall see . . .

9.2 A CAUTIONARY TALE

The program and its data (variables and constants) represent the problem data. For the program to be easily modified later as the problem changes, the data must be represented accurately. There are two areas to consider, changes in the information in the problem space and changes in the solution space, which imply functional changes to the program. In either case, an unwise choice of representation may act as a limiting, even prohibitive, factor. The division between the representation of information by specific values or by active components of the program is rather subtle; however, it is beyond the scope of this book, and the interested reader will find a discussion of isomorphism between program structure and the real world in Chapter 7 of Macro (1990). Functional-structured design decomposition de-emphasizes data considerations, leaving data structures to be determined after algorithm definition at low-level design. The result is easy to change functionally but not from the data view. Thus the approach is suitable for computation paradigm applications. The converse is data-structure driven design, which is more suitable for the data processing paradigm. The following cautionary tale based on an example, unconnected with our Running Example, in Jackson (1983) illustrates this choice:

> The Golden Hind Sailing Club rented sailing boats by the hour. Customers were able to sail the boats on the small lake adjoining the Club's facilities and were charged according to the amount of time that they took a boat out for a sailing session. Times were recorded by their timekeeper Joe, who sat in his little hut at the end of the pier and watched the boats come in and out.
>
> The management of the Club decided to keep up with the times and obtained a computer to help them manage their enterprise. The computer was attached to an input keyboard in Joe's hut so that he could enter starting and ending times for each session together with the boat number. They also hired a programmer Tom to write the program for the computer. Tom was intelligent and relied on this intelligence and a glib tongue to avoid the unpleasantness of hard work.
>
> The management told Tom that they wanted him to write a program that would accept Joe's input and, at the end of the day, print the total number of sessions and the average length of a session. In other words, the input would consist of a sequence of records of the form:
>
> $$S_a, S_b, E_b, S_c, E_c, E_a, \ldots$$
>
> where S_i records the starting time of the session with boat number i and E_i records the ending time of the session with boat number i.
>
> Tom very quickly noted that the total number of sessions was equal to the number of session starting times and that the average session time was computed from the formula,
>
> $$\left\{ \frac{(E_a - S_a) + (E_b - S_b) + (E_c - S_c) + \ldots}{(\text{number of sessions})} \right\}$$

```
  . . .
TotalTime     := 0;
SessionCount := 0;
read TimeRecord into NextRecord;
while NOT EndOfFile loop
    if type of NextRecord = StartRecord then
        SessionCount := SessionCount + 1;
        TotalTime     := TotalTime - NextRecord.Time
    else
        TotalTime     := TotalTime + NextRecord.Time
    endif;
    read TimeRecord into NextRecord;
endloop;
AverageSession := TotalTime / SessionCount;
  . . .
```

FIGURE 9.1   Tom's program for the Golden Hind Sailing Club.

which, because he understood algebra, he was able to transform into,

$$\left\{ \frac{(E_a + E_b + E_c + \ldots) - (S_a + S_b + S_c + \ldots)}{(number\ of\ sessions)} \right\}$$

Based on this, he was able to write a beautifully structured program with the algorithmic part shown in Figure 9.1, which, assuming that there was always at least one session during the day, would print the desired output.

The management was very pleased with Tom's program; they felt that they had indeed moved into the twentieth century and could now stand tall among their colleagues in the sailing boat rental industry. However, as always happens, their appetite for reports grew and they argued that they could make more profit if only they knew a little more about the habits of their clientele.

They spoke to Tom, told him how pleased they were with his work and asked him to modify his program to give them a histogram showing the frequency of sessions of different lengths. That is, they wanted a bar chart showing how many sessions lasted one hour, how many lasted two hours, and so on. Tom said that he would like to think about the problem. He looked at his program – and the reader should do so too before continuing.

After due time to show how carefully he had considered the problem and weighed the alternatives, Tom returned to the management and told them something like, 'I looked at what would be required and discovered that on the equipment that you have this would entail expanding the input buffer to accommodate 12.3 kilo baud in the 9725B disk drive using a communications vector with an enhanced blocking factor on the data bus connected to the output modem through the RTSI channel . . . with the result that we would need about $75,000 of new equipment.' The management said that they understood perfectly, and thanked him for his work, gave him a productivity bonus, and let him go back to managing the system.

For a while all was quiet. Then the Club's management called Tom again and told him that they had quite understood the difficulties with the last enhancement they had asked for but they now needed his help in obtaining information to help with staffing. They would like the program to print out the number of sessions that started and finished before noon, the number that started before noon and finished after, and the number that were entirely in the afternoon. This would allow them to schedule staff better. Again, Tom said that he needed to think about the problem and, again, the reader should look at Tom's program before continuing.

When he came back, his answer was essentially the same as before though the details of the computer gibberish were different. Again the management said they understood and Tom went back to the system.

Finally, the dénouement, the management called Tom and said that this time the program had to be modified no matter what. They had evidence that there were communication problems between Joe's input device and the computer and some of the timing records were being lost. It was essential that Tom modify the program to check that session start and session end records were matched so that losses of records could be properly recorded. Tom looked at his program and decided that the best thing to do was to get out his résumé and find a new niche for his talent.

Tom's program is essentially unmodifiable. The reason for this is that although it produces the required output for the original problem statement, it does not really model the real-world process because it does not have any representation of the session or of boats – the fundamental entities of the club's business. The program is thus not able to follow changes in the real world, quickly becomes useless, and must be replaced entirely. It would not have been difficult for Tom to model a session. Since there were a fixed number of boats, each with a number, and no boat can be involved in more than one session at a time, an array of start times indexed by boat number would have been sufficient to model sessions for the first problem. The size of the array depends upon the number of boats currently in use. Here, we assume that this does not change frequently and this number is built into the program, which is recompiled each time the number is changed. Actually, strictly speaking, this is not modeling sessions but boats and there is a correspondence between the two. The way in which Tom might have written the program, had he been wise as well as intelligent, is shown in Figure 9.2.

```
    .  .  .
TotalTime    := 0;
SessionCount := 0;
read TimeRecord into NextRecord;
while NOT EndOfFile loop
   if type of NextRecord = StartRecord then
      SessionCount := SessionCount + 1;
      Session[NextRecord.BoatNumber].StartTime := NextRecord.Time
   else
      TotalTime := TotalTime + NextRecord.Time -
                      Session[NextRecord.BoatNumber].StartTime
   endif;
   read TimeRecord into NextRecord;
endloop;
AverageSession := TotalTime / SessionCount;
    .  .  .
```

FIGURE 9.2 How a wiser Tom might have written the Sailing Club program.

The second version of the program is much easier to understand because a knowledge of Tom's algebraic sleight of hand is no longer required. Note that a simple array of CARDINALs would have been sufficient for the original problem; the use of an array of records, each with a single field, StartTime models the session more clearly with no extra cost in space or execution time. It also paves the way for later modifications when more details about the session may have to be added to the model in order to extend the process.

For all three of the requested enhancements, the session information is already available. In the case of the first two, representations of the histogram and the sessions counts need to be added together with a small amount of code to accumulate the totals and output the results. In the case of the third, the start time for a session must be cleared when a session is ended. With additional logic to check that a new session for a boat is not started while one is apparently continuing and that a session is not terminated without having been started, will provide the kind of checks the management required. Of course, this will not catch the loss of two successive records for a single boat, but that was beyond what the management requested.

9.3 DATA REPRESENTATION AND READABILITY

The problems with Tom's program in the previous section are not as artificial as the program. It is a general observation that a program that is hard to modify or understand is likely to have a data representation that is inappropriate for the problem being solved.

First of all, and this was clearly brought out by Tom's experience, the data representation has a strong effect on the modifiability of the program and hence its longevity. The user's view of the process, rooted as it is in the real world, will be enshrined in the program. Requests for enhancements are likely to be expressed in terms of the user's view and therefore easier to accommodate. The management of the Sailing Club made all its requests based on sessions because that was how they viewed their world. Tom's design fiasco was due to the fact that he conceived of the problem purely as performing a specified function rather than the modeling of something in the real world. While the real world is constantly changing, and that is the reason why programs require constant modification, it is more stable than a functional description of the problem. Tom found that the functions needed to solve the problem were changing even though management's view of the real world did not change.

The appropriate choice of data also has an important effect on the readability of the program. The data objects in a program are abstractions of the attributes of real-world objects, that is, they do not contain all the details associated with their counterparts. The reader of a program comes with a better understanding of the real world than of the sequence of mental steps that the author of the program went through in developing the data abstractions. While the reader's knowledge of the real world may not include detailed experience of the area being modeled, there will be a general pattern of what is reasonable. A visitor walking through a strange city for the first time will not know in

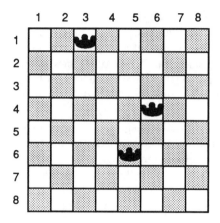

FIGURE 9.3 Three queens on a chessboard.

detail what to expect when turning the corner of a street, however there will be a general framework on which to construct the mental model when the corner is actually turned. Such is the stability of the real world. If the visitor were in a science-fiction world and turning the corner caused the visitor to be bodily transported to the surface of Mars, there would be little understanding of the new context because there would be no model on which to hang the visual impressions. If the correspondence between the abstract data objects of the program and the real world is obvious, the reader will be able to build on an already established corpus of knowledge and understand the program.

A second consideration when choosing the representation for data is the actual computation that has to be performed. A great deal of complexity in the program can often be avoided through a careful choice of data representation. Take, for example, the Eight Queens problem, which of course has nothing to do with the Running Example. We wish to write a program to determine an arrangement of eight mutually antagonistic queens on a standard chessboard so that peace is preserved and no queen can capture another. A chessboard can be viewed as an 8×8 array of squares. One queen can capture another if they are both in the same row, same column, or on the same diagonal.

For example, consider the arrangement shown in Figure 9.3. The queen in row 1, column 3 (board[1, 3]) can capture any other queen in row 1 or column 3. She can also capture the queen in board[4, 6] because they are on the same diagonal. The queen in board[6, 5] cannot be captured by either of the other queens. Our program is to find one of the possible configurations in which the eight queens can be placed.

The real-world object to be represented is an arrangement of queens, indexed by row and column number, on the board. The basic operations to be performed on the board are the setting and removal of queens at a given location, and testing whether it would be safe to set a queen at a given location. The data interface to these operations can be defined using the data types Board, RowIndex, and ColIndex whose representation is yet to be defined.

```
PROCEDURE SetQueen(Row: RowIndex; Col: ColIndex; VAR Configuration: Board);
PROCEDURE RemoveQueen(Row: RowIndex; Col: ColIndex; VAR Configuration: Board);
PROCEDURE IsSafe(Row: RowIndex; Col: ColIndex; Configuration: Board): BOOLEAN;
```

The obvious representation might be thought to be an 8×8 array of Booleans

```
TYPE
    RowIndex = [1..8];
    ColIndex = [1..8];
    Board    = ARRAY RowIndex OF ARRAY ColIndex OF BOOLEAN;
VAR
    Row:            RowIndex;
    Col:            ColIndex;
    Configuration:  Board;
```

The implementation of the operations SetQueen and RemoveQueen is obvious. The body of the function IsSafe consists of checking the following:

1. Row Row of Configuration does not already contain a queen.
2. Column Col of Configuration does not already contain a queen.
3. Neither of the diagonals through position [Row, Col] Configuration already contains a queen.

The program fragment shown in Figure 9.4 shows how the body of IsSafe might be coded using this representation. The first two tests are easy. The test of the diagonals is harder and consists of two parts differing in only small details of operations and tests. How easy is it to be sure that they are correct?

The brute force approach would be for the program to form every possible arrangement of eight queens on the board and test each of these as a solution. The difficulty with this approach is the large number of trials that must be made. There are about 4.4×10^9 ways of placing eight queens on the board, and if we even assume that we can generate and check a possible solution in $100 \, \mu s$, it will take about 122 hours to check every possibility. A solution based on Wirth (1971) first eliminates all configurations with more than one queen in any column by never generating them. We note that there are eight queens and eight columns so there must be one and only one queen on each column. The strategy is to start by placing a queen at board[1, 1]. Since this queen is the only one, she is safe. The next step is to find a safe position in column 2 where a second queen can be placed. Another queen is placed at board[1, 2]. Since this queen is on the same row as the first queen, she can be attacked. The row number is incremented by 1 and the queen is tested on that square. This process continues, successively advancing a queen until a safe position in a column is found. When this has been done for a column, the search is advanced to the next column. If a configuration arises in which no queen can be placed safely in a given column, the queen already positioned in the previous column is advanced to the next safe row. This is known as *backtracking* and may require retreating several columns before a new base for the search can be found. The entire process is continued until a complete configuration is found.

```
RowSafe := TRUE;
For TestCol := 1 TO 8 BY 1 DO;
    IF (Configuration[Row, TestCol]) THEN
        RowSafe := FALSE;
    END
END;
Safe := RowSafe;

IF Safe THEN
    ColSafe := TRUE;
    For TestRow := 1 TO 8 BY 1 DO;
        IF (Configuration[TestRow, Col]) THEN
            ColSafe := FALSE;
        END
    END;
    Safe := Safe AND ColSafe;
END;

IF Safe THEN
    SEtoNWdiagSafe := TRUE;
    TestRow        := 8;
    TestCol        := 8;
    WHILE((TestRow >= 1) AND (TestCol >= 1)) DO
        IF (Configuration[TestRow, TestCol]) THEN
            SEtoNWdiagSafe := FALSE;
        ELSE
            TestRow := TestRow - 1;
            TestCol := TestCol - 1;
        END
    END;
    Safe := Safe AND SEtoNWdiagSafe;
END;

IF Safe THEN
    NEtoSWdiagSafe := TRUE;
    TestRow        := 1;
    TestCol        := 8;
    WHILE((TestRow <= 8) AND (TestCol >= 1)) DO
        IF (Configuration[TestRow, TestCol]) THEN
            SEtoNWdiagSafe := FALSE;
        ELSE
            TestRow := TestRow + 1;
            TestCol := TestCol - 1;
        END
    END;
    Safe := Safe AND SEtoNWdiagSafe;
END;
```

FIGURE 9.4 Test for a safe diagonal.

The chosen representation of Configuration not only causes complexity in the implementation of the IsSafe operation but also in the program that uses it. When we discover that there is no safe square in the current column, we must move back to the previous column, remove the queen that has been placed there and advance her to the next safe square. Before we can remove her, we must find her. With the 8×8 array of Booleans representation, this means searching the column. A trivial task in itself but one requiring another loop, which adds complexity to the general impression of the process.

A difference in the representation, while still matching the real world, can make the test that a square is safe a good deal easier to understand. First of all, we note that not only is there one and only one queen to each column but there is also one queen to each row. The alternative representation of board as

```
TYPE
    Board = ARRAY ColIndex OF RowIndex;
```

where we now record for each column the queen's row number, makes the finding of the current position of a queen in any row trivial. (This representation allows another simplification of the main algorithm that searches for peaceful arrangements of the eight queens. The only possible configurations are the set of permutations of the set of eight distinct RowIndexs.)

Although this vector defines the board configuration entirely, some additional information that is maintained as the search proceeds can greatly simplify the implementation of the IsSafe operation.

```
TYPE
    RowIndex        = [1..8];
    ColIndex        = [1..8];
    NEtoSWdiagIndex = [2..16];
    SEtoNWdiagIndex = [-7..7];
    Board           = RECORD
                        OccupiedRow:       ARRAY ColIndex OF RowIndex;
                        RowIsSafe:         ARRAY RowIndex OF BOOLEAN;
                        NEtoSWdiagIsSafe:  ARRAY NEtoSWdiagIndex OF BOOLEAN;
                        SEtoNWdiagIsSafe:  ARRAY SEtoNWdiagIndex OF BOOLEAN;
                      END;
VAR
    Row:            RowIndex;
    Col:            ColIndex;
    Configuration:  Board;
```

The vector RowIsSafe records for each row whether it is safe to put a queen on it, if Configuration.RowIsSafe[Row] has the value TRUE then there is no queen in that row of the configuration. The vectors NEtoSWdiagIsSafe and SEtoNWdiagIsSafe record corresponding information for the diagonals. The somewhat strange ranges for the types NEtoSWdiagIndex and SEtoNWdiagIndex are due to the observation that for each square on one of the NE to SW diagonals, the sum of its row and column coordinates is constant. For each of the SE to NW diagonals, the difference between their row and column coordinates is also constant.

With this representation, the test whether the square [Row, Col] is safe becomes

```
IsSafeSquare :=  Configuration.NEtoSWdiagIsSafe[Row + Col] AND
                 Configuration.SEtoNWdiagIsSafe[Row - Col] AND
                 Configuration.RowIsSafe[Row];
```

which is much easier to understand.

Setting the value of Configuration in SetQueen is a little more involved with this representation,

```
Configuration.OccupiedRow[Col]            := Row;
Configuration.RowIsSafe[Row]              := FALSE;
Configuration.NEtoSWdiagIsSafe[Row + Col] := FALSE;
Configuration.SEtoNWdiagIsSafe[Row - Col] := FALSE;
```

however, this sequence is easy to understand since there are no loops in it and the static form exactly matches the dynamic form.

The difference between the two representations really amounts to keeping part of the representation in the execution structure of the program rather than keeping it in the data structure. It is easier to understand a representation that is maintained wholly in the data structure. Further examples of the effect of representation upon the clarity of programs are given in Kernighan and Plauger (1978) and Bentley (1986a, 1988).

It is also very important to note that this change was made *without changing* any of the statements that referred to the operations SetQueen, RemoveQueen, and IsSafe. The interface to these operations has remained constant while the representation of Board has changed.

9.4 THE DEFINITION OF ABSTRACT DATA TYPES

As we have seen, the development of the idea of type started with the early languages, which had a small number of primitive built-in types that could not be modified or augmented by the programmer to provide a more faithful model of the real world. This was followed by languages like Pascal where the programmer was able to define new data types by defining their representation structure and set of values. The data abstractions that support the building of understandable models of real-world processes require that data objects should be classified according to their expected behavior instead of their representation structure. Thus, the data objects must be defined in terms of the operations that can be performed on them.

This characterization corresponds to the idea, long known by writers, that verbs make for clearer writing than nouns. Goethe said, 'Immer Verben anwenden!' – 'Always use verbs!' Abstract data types help make programs easier to understand by providing the verbs and avoiding the program clutter of representational detail.

An *abstract data type* is a data type defined by the programmer. There are two views of this definition: the user's view and the implementer's view. The user's view is that the data type consists of a set of *abstract operations* that can manipulate these data objects and provide conversion to and from objects of other types. The implementer's view is that the data type consists of a set of *data objects*. This definition will specify the structure and representation of the objects. It also consists of a set of executable procedures that manipulate the objects in a manner that conforms to the operations defined to the user. The implementer must *encapsulate* the objects and operations so that the user of the

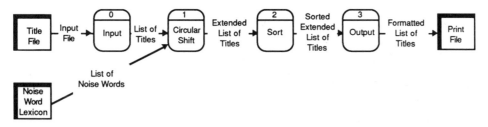

FIGURE 9.5 Dataflow design specification of BuildPrintfile program from Figure 5.2.

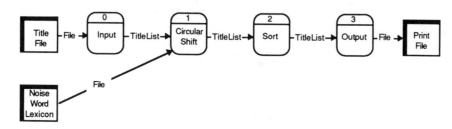

FIGURE 9.6 Flow of data types in BuildPrintfile program in Figure 9.5.

abstract type cannot manipulate the data objects of the type except through the use of the specified operations.

We will demonstrate the idea of encapsulation of an abstract data type through the Running Example. Although the design in Chapter 5 talked about a TitleStorage integrand, the approach presented here does not mention this integrand. This is because we are approaching the problem of designing the implementation from the point of view of abstract data types and this implicitly subsumes the idea of a TitleStorage integrand. Figure 9.5 repeats the data-flow diagram shown in Figure 5.2. At this level of abstraction, there are really two data types: File and TitleList. Input File, List of Noise Words, and Formatted List of Titles are all of type File and List of Titles, Extended List of Titles, and Sorted Extended List of Titles are of type TitleList. Figure 9.6 is derived from Figure 9.5 by replacing the data names by data types.

Since the details of input and output from a program depend so much on the particular system on which the language is implemented, they are handled through procedures that are provided by the implementation. Each implementation will supply its own library of procedures. Typically, it might do this through the implementation defined type File on which a set of operations can be performed. As an example of the set of operations that might be defined for the type File, Figure 9.7 shows a possible FileManager definition module showing the operations that can be performed on the type File. Note particularly that the implementation of the type File is not defined. Unless the source code for the implementation module is made available, the user has no way of finding out how objects of this type are represented.

```
DEFINITION MODULE FileManager;
   FROM SYSTEM IMPORT BYTE, WORD, ADDRESS;
   TYPE File;

   PROCEDURE Open      (VAR f: File; name: ARRAY OF CHAR): BOOLEAN;
   PROCEDURE Create    (VAR f: File; name: ARRAY OF CHAR);
   PROCEDURE Close     (VAR f: File);
   PROCEDURE Delete    (VAR f: File);
   PROCEDURE GetName   (f: File; name: ARRAY OF CHAR);
   PROCEDURE EOF       (f: File): BOOLEAN;
   PROCEDURE ReadByte  (f: File; VAR ch: BYTE);
   PROCEDURE ReadWord  (f: File; VAR w: WORD);
   PROCEDURE ReadRec   (f: File; VAR rec: ARRAY OF WORD);
   PROCEDURE ReadBytes (f: File; buf: ADDRESS; nbytes: CARDINAL): CARDINAL;
   PROCEDURE WriteByte (f: File; ch: BYTE);
   PROCEDURE WriteWord (f: File; w: WORD);
   PROCEDURE WriteRec  (f: File; VAR rec: ARRAY OF WORD);
   PROCEDURE WriteBytes(f: File; buf: ADDRESS; nbytes: CARDINAL);

END FileManager.
```

FIGURE 9.7 Definition module for the type File.

```
DEFINITION MODULE TitleListMngr;

   FROM Titles      IMPORT Title;

   TYPE TitleList;

   PROCEDURE CreateTitleList(): TitleList;
   PROCEDURE BeginTitleList(): TitleList;
   PROCEDURE GetNextTitle(TL: TitleList): Title;
   PROCEDURE AppendTitle (VAR TL: TitleList;  T: Title);
   PROCEDURE DumpTitleList(TL: TitleList);

END TitleListMngr.
```

FIGURE 9.8 Definition module for the type TitleList.

What are the operations that can be applied to objects of type TitleList? In many ways, a TitleList object has many of the characteristics of FILE objects. They are both sequential collections of objects. A FILE is a sequential collection of records, a TitleList is a sequential collection of Line objects. The operations that we will need to apply to TitleList objects are CreateTitleList, GetNextTitle, and AppendTitle. These correspond to the FILE operations Create, Open, ReadRec, and WriteRec respectively. In addition, there is the DumpTitleList operation, which is used in testing and debugging. These are implemented in the TitleListManager whose Definition Module is shown in Figure 9.8. The implementation of TitleListManager will contain the decision about the way in which Titles are stored. Two possible implementations that retain the interface definitions for the three operations would be the use of a file and a linked list.

Notice that there is no definition of the way in which objects of type TitleList are represented. All that is specified is that it is a type, which means that the user can import the type and use it in declarations. By importing from FileManager, a skeleton of the program BuildPrintFile can be written as shown in Figure 9.9.

The next step in this design process is to define the type Title in terms of the operations

```
MODULE BuildPrintfile;

    FROM TitleListMngr IMPORT TitleList;
    FROM Files        IMPORT File;

    VAR
        DataFile:                 File;
        PrintFile:                File;
        NoiseWordLexicon:         File;
        ListOfTitles:             TitleList;
        ExtendedListOfTitles:     TitleList;
        SortedExtendedListOfTitles: TitleList;

    PROCEDURE Input(InputFile: File; VAR ListOfTitles: TitleList);
    BEGIN
        (* Read the input data consisting of lines containing a Title-Part   *)
        (* followed by the reference marker [ and a Reference-Part terminated *)
        (* by ] and convert to internal format.                              *)
    END Input;

    PROCEDURE CircularShift(ListOfTitles: TitleList; ListOfNoiseWords: File;
                                    VAR ExtendedListOfTitles:TitleList);
    BEGIN
        (* From the Title-Part of each title in the list of titles, construct *)
        (* all possible titles consisting of circularly shifted Title-Parts   *)
        (* followed by copies of the Reference-Part from the original title.  *)
        (* Constructed titles, and possibly the original title, that start    *)
        (* a word contained in the Noise Word Lexicon are discarded.          *)
    END CircularShift;

    PROCEDURE Sort(ExtendedListOfTitles: TitleList;
                                    VAR SortedExtendedListOfTitles: TitleList);
    BEGIN
        (* Sort the extended list of titles produced by CircularShift into    *)
        (* alphabetical order.                                                *)
    END Sort;

    PROCEDURE Output(SortedExtendedListOfTitles: TitleList;
                                        FormattedKwicIndex: File);
    BEGIN
        (* Prepare the sorted data produced by Sort for printing.  The        *)
        (* Title-Part is shown in its original form and occupies TitlePartLen *)
        (* characters with the first word of its circularly shifted form      *)
        (* starting at KeywordPosition characters from the beginning of the   *)
        (* printed line. Where a TitlePart must be truncated at the beginning *)
        (* or end to fit into TitlePartLen after alignment, the truncation is *)
        (* shown by an ellipsis, (...). The Reference-Part is listed on the   *)
        (* same line as the TitlePart and starts TitlePartLen + TitleRefGap   *)
        (* characters from the beginning of the printed line.  If the         *)
        (* Reference-Part is too long to be printed on the line, it is trun-  *)
        (* cated and this is marked with an ellipsis.                         *)
    END Output;
BEGIN
    Input(DataFile, ListOfTitles);
    CircularShift(ListOfTitles, NoiseWordLexicon, ExtendedListOfTitles);
    Sort(ExtendedListOfTitles, SortedExtendedListOfTitles);
    Output(SortedExtendedListOfTitles, PrintFile);
END BuildPrintfile.
```

FIGURE 9.9 Skeleton of BuildPrintfile program version 3.

```
DEFINITION MODULE Titles;
    FROM TitlePartDef    IMPORT TitlePart;
    FROM RefPartDef      IMPORT RefPart;

    TYPE   Title;

    PROCEDURE MakeTitle(TP: TitlePart; RP: RefPart): Title;
    PROCEDURE GetTitlePart(T: Title): TitlePart;
    PROCEDURE GetRefPart(T: Title): RefPart;
    PROCEDURE TitleToChars(T: Title; VAR ch: ARRAY OF CHAR);
    PROCEDURE IsNullTitle(T: Title): BOOLEAN;

END Titles.
```

FIGURE 9.10 Definition modules for Titles.

that can be performed on objects of this type. Objects of this type consist of two objects, a TitlePart and a RefPart. There must be operations for the extraction of these two parts and for the construction of a Title object from its constituent parts. One further operation IsNullTitle. In certain circumstances, for example, if an attempt is made to apply the GetNextTitle operation to an empty TitleList, it is more convenient to return a null Title than to signal an error condition. IsNullTitle returns the value TRUE if it is applied to a null Title and FALSE otherwise. A more complete discussion of the handling of errors and exceptions is contained in Chapter 11. Thus the Definition Module for Titles is as shown in Figure 9.10.

There remain two more types to be defined: TitlePart and RefPart. The operations required are for the conversion between objects of these two types and character strings. These conversions are required since the input and output files are files of character strings. Since we are required to sort a TitleList, it might be argued that there should be an operation for comparing two TitlePart objects. However, since the ultimate form in which the Titles are presented to the human reader is as character strings, it would probably be better to perform the comparison between two TitleParts by converting them to character strings for comparison. This has the advantage of giving the control of the sorting rules to the writer of the Sort integrand. In other words, *all* details of the sorting process can be hidden in the Sort integrand. Operations that are analogous to IsNullTitle are also required to test for null TitlePart and null RefPart objects. The Definition Modules for TitlePartDef and RefPartDef are shown in Figure 9.11.

This hierarchy of abstract types has been defined without commitment to any particular implementation. Indeed there are many possible implementations of objects of type TitlePart. For example:

1. As a character string containing a marker showing how the title part has been circularly shifted.
2. As a record with two fields: the first containing a pointer to a character string and the second having a count of the number of characters that the pointed-to character string must be circularly shifted to obtain the actual title.

Of these, the second is likely to save storage space but will take longer to execute. The crucial point about abstract data types is that the actual representation of the values of

```
DEFINITION MODULE TitlePartDef;

    TYPE TitlePart;

    PROCEDURE CharsToTitlePart(ch: ARRAY OF CHAR; VAR TP: TitlePart);
    PROCEDURE TitlePartToChars(TP: TitlePart; VAR ch: ARRAY OF CHAR);
    PROCEDURE IsNullTitlePart(TP: TitlePart): BOOLEAN;

END TitlePartDef.

DEFINITION MODULE RefPartDef;

    TYPE RefPart;

    PROCEDURE CharsToRefPart(ch: ARRAY OF CHAR; VAR RP: RefPart);
    PROCEDURE RefPartToChars(RP: RefPart; VAR ch: ARRAY OF CHAR);
    PROCEDURE IsNullRefPart(RP: RefPart): BOOLEAN;

END RefPartDef.
```

FIGURE 9.11 Definition modules for TitlePartDef and RefPartDef.

that type is hidden from the user and thus can be changed without requiring the application program to be changed.

9.5 PASSING DATA ACROSS THE INTERFACE

In Chapter 5, we discussed the complexity of interfaces between integrands. In particular, in Section 5.5 we discussed the three ways in which data can be passed across the interface between integrands at execution time. These are listed below, in increasing order of desirability:

1. Through global variables.
2. Through control blocks referenced by a pointer.
3. Through the argument-parameter correspondence.

In addition to the method of passing, there are two other attributes that need to be considered when designing the interface between integrands: the direction of passage – input or output – and what is passed.

The two categories, input and output, define the procedure's interface. Provided the relationship between input and output remain unchanged, the algorithm can be modified without any consequential changes required in the users' programs. The definitions of input and output must be both precise and complete. Under input, not only must the information passed through parameters be specified but also any information that is obtained from global variables or from files that are read during execution of the procedure. The output specification should include values returned as a value by the procedure, values that are obtained as a consequence of executing the procedure, terminal responses, error messages, and reports.

Sometimes, there is some disagreement about exactly what is meant by input and output. In order to resolve this question, we will now consider a sequence of increasingly complex examples, none of which has any direct relation to the Running Example.

9.5.1 Simple returned value

The simplest case is the function procedure that returns a value through the use of a return statement.

```
PROCEDURE Example1(Parm: INTEGER): INTEGER;
BEGIN
    RETURN Parm + 2
END Example1;
```

The input to Example1 is the integer Parm and the output is the value returned by the function. This would be defined in the header as:

```
(*   CALL SEQUENCE: ReturnedInteger := Example1(Parm);     *)
(*                                                          *)
(*   INPUT:   Values: Parm  INTEGER                         *)
(*                                                          *)
(*   OUTPUT:  The integer value returned by the function    *)
(*                                                          *)
```

If we follow the discipline that a function does not change the value its parameters, and the function does not reference any global variables, it will not have any side effects. Were the function to have side effects, these too would have to be documented as outputs. Functions with side effects are inherently more difficult to understand than pure functions and should therefore be avoided.

9.5.2 Simple parameter

Procedures operate entirely by side effects, which makes the definition of output more difficult. For the rest of this section, we will limit the discussion to procedures. The principles that we derive will apply, with only minor modifications, to functions. The procedure Example2 is extremely simple:

```
PROCEDURE Example2(VAR Parm: INTEGER);
BEGIN
    Parm := Parm + 2;
    RETURN
END Example2;
```

It seems clear that, since the procedure itself uses the formal parameter as input and then sets it to a new value, this must be documented as being the input and output of the procedure.

```
(*   CALL SEQUENCE: Example2(Parm);                *)
(*                                                 *)
(*   INPUT:   VAR  Parm: INTEGER                   *)
(*                                                 *)
(*   OUTPUT:  VAR  Parm: INTEGER                   *)
(*                                                 *)
```

9.5.3 Indirect use of parameters

In Example3,

```
PROCEDURE Example3(VAR Parm: INTEGER);

    PROCEDURE Sub3(VAR Subparm: INTEGER);

    BEGIN
        Subparm := Subparm + 2;
        RETURN
    END Sub3;

BEGIN
    Sub3(Parm);
    RETURN
END Example3;
```

the situation is still fairly clear. Even though Example3 uses Sub3 to do the work for it, it is obviously passing output through its parameter. The function of Example3, from its user's point of view, is the same as Example2, to produce this output; how it achieves this is its own private business.

9.5.4 Global variables

Example4 is essentially similar to Example2. It differs in using a global variable as its interface instead of a parameter. To see this, we must provide a little of the context of the containing block.

```
   . . . .
VAR
   Glob: INTEGER;
 . . . .
   PROCEDURE Example4;

   BEGIN
       Glob := Glob + 2;
       RETURN
   END Example4;
     . . . .
BEGIN
   . . . .
   Example4;
   . . . .
```

Again, from the user's point of view, the function of Example4 is to use the value contained in the variable Glob to calculate its output. The fact that the input and output are passed through a global variable merely betrays a lack of programming aesthetics, and does not change the fact that Glob should be documented as the input and output of the procedure.

```
(*    CALL SEQUENCE: Example4;                          *)
(*                                                       *)
(*    INPUT:    Global variable: Glob: INTEGER           *)
(*                                                       *)
(*    OUTPUT:   Global variable: Glob: INTEGER           *)
(*                                                       *)
```

9.5.5 Indirect use of global variables

The same argument applies to Example5, which is the analogous form to Example3.

```
  . . . .
    VAR
        Glob: INTEGER;
    . . . .
    PROCEDURE Example5;

        PROCEDURE Sub5;

        BEGIN
            Glob := Glob + 2
            RETURN
        END Sub5;

    BEGIN
        Sub5;
        RETURN
    END Example5;
    . . . .
BEGIN
    . . . .
    Example5;
    . . . .
```

Although Example5 uses Sub5 to do the actual setting of Glob, the user's perspective of Example5 still has the same purpose. It takes the current value of Glob, calculates a new value from it and sets Glob to the new value. Thus, the interface is still Glob and should be documented as both the input and output of the procedure. This is true despite the fact that Glob is not referenced in Example5 but only in Sub5. It would also be true even if Sub5 were not nested in Example5.

Again, the test should be to use the one-sentence description of the precise function of the procedure from the point of view of the abstraction level of the user. Although this is only a sketched example, one must assume that some procedure higher up the calling chain will be accessing the value that has been inserted in Glob, otherwise why would it have had a value assigned?

One possibility is that the assignment to Glob was done purely for access by Sub5 during some future invocation. That is to say, as a way of preserving the value between invocations. As a result of the design of Modula-2, the only way of preserving values between invocations is through the use of a variable that is declared in some containing procedure that will remain active, or through the use of a variable that is in the outermost scope of the integrand. Such variables are a rather peculiar part of the procedure's interface. Although they are intended to be private to the procedure, it is as if they were renting space from a containing procedure. In order that the reader can understand the purpose of these variables, it is important that they be mentioned as part of the interface, with the proper commentary. This peculiarity is a consequence of there being no equivalent of PL/I's **STATIC INTERNAL** or Algol 60's *own* in Modula-2.

Although this whole discussion has involved the use of global variables, it must be remembered that *their use should be avoided*. Much of this discussion should be viewed in the light of further arguments against their use.

9.5.6 Aggregate data

Before we consider the interface documentation problem in the context of a database, we will consider a slightly more complicated instance of one of the early examples. Example6 is a minor variation on Example2:

```
  . . . .
    TYPE Complex = RECORD
                      RealPart: REAL;
                      ImagPart: REAL;
                   END;

    VAR
       Z: Complex;
    . . . .
    PROCEDURE Example6(VAR Parm: Complex);

    BEGIN
       . . . .
       Parm.ImagPart := Parm.ImagPart + 5.73E5
       . . . .
    END Example6;

  BEGIN
     . . . .
     Example6(Z)
     . . . .
```

The question to be resolved here is whether the description of **Example6** should define its interface as **Parm** or as the imaginary part of **Parm**. This will depend on the way in which the user of **Example6** views its function. If **Example6** were invoked to produce a complex value then the fact that it is only the imaginary part that is changed is incidental. For example, had the assignment statement of **Example6** been

```
Parm.ImagPart := - Parm.ImagPart;
```

then a functional description of the procedure is probably that it produces the complex conjugate of its argument. In such a case, its input and output should be listed as being **Parm**. However, if the function of the procedure were viewed as being one of changing the imaginary part of a complex number, then it is the imaginary part of **Parm** that should be documented as the input and output.

In this latter case, the interface between the user and the subroutine has been poorly designed. The subroutine should really have been written as **Example7**:

```
PROCEDURE Example7(VAR Parm: REAL);

BEGIN
    Parm := Parm + 5.73E5
    RETURN
END Example7;
```

and it should have been invoked with the call

```
Example7(Z.ImagPart)
```

where Z is declared as it was in **Example6**. The input and output of the subroutine should be documented as being the real quantity **Parm**. The context of its invocation is not part of the interface; it could, just as well have been operating on a real number that was not the imaginary part of a complex number. At the level of abstraction of the invocation of the procedure, the focus of the programmer is on the imaginary part of the complex number rather than the complex number as a whole. The decision on the proper way to document the interface depends on the level of abstraction that has been used in the design. In the case of **Example6**, it is the whole record that is being worked with, whereas, in **Example7**, it is only a part of the record. The difference in the two levels of abstraction must be shown by the difference in the interface specifications. The important element here is the view that the user has of the abstraction represented by the procedure, not the mechanics performed by the code that implements the abstraction. In other words, is **Example7** an operator on an object of type **Complex** or an operator on an object of type **REAL**?

9.5.7 Use of pointers

Example8 shows a simple case of passing a value indirectly through a pointer or reference value.

```
PROCEDURE Example8(Parm: POINTER TO INTEGER);

BEGIN
    Parm^ := Parm^ + 2;
    RETURN
END Example8;
```

Here, the value of Parm is not itself changed, in fact, it is passed by value so that it cannot be changed, but the anonymous integer value that it references is. The interface to Example8 is this nameless integer value; the procedure was invoked in order to cause a change in it, therefore this effect is the one that should be documented as the procedure's interface.

```
(*    CALL SEQUENCE: Example8(Parm);                                    *)
(*                                                                      *)
(*    INPUT:    VAR INTEGER referenced by Parm: POINTER TO INTEGER      *)
(*                                                                      *)
(*    OUTPUT:   VAR INTEGER referenced by Parm: POINTER TO INTEGER      *)
(*                                                                      *)
```

Example8 showed a value being changed through a single level of indirection. We next consider a more complex situation shown in Figure 9.12.

The pointer ListStart is a pointer to a list and used by Example9 as the head of a trail leading to a particular instance of a ListElement. Although, in this case, we are dealing with a simple list, the particular field that is changed could have been buried deeply in a very complex data structure or database. The value of none of the parameters to Example9 is changed, however the fact that Example9 changes one of the fields in an element of the list must certainly be documented. What is less clear is the level of detail to which the change should be documented.

As we have seen in some of the previous examples, the amount of detail contained in the documentation should reflect the way in which the procedure is viewed by its user. In the case of Example9, there are two extreme positions with a range of levels of detail between them. At the most detailed level, the user may invoke Example9 to set a value in a specific instance of ListElement in the database referenced by ListStart. In this case, the documentation should specify that the database with the modified ListElement is the output. At the other end of the scale, the documentation should describe the fact that the

```
. . . .
TYPE
   ListPointer = POINTER TO ListElement;
   ListElement = RECORD
                       NodeID: INTEGER;
                       Value:  INTEGER;
                       Next:   ListPointer;
                 END;

VAR
   ListHead:  ListPointer;
   Number:    INTEGER;
   NewNumber: INTEGER;
. . . .
PROCEDURE Example9(ListStart: ListPointer; Key: INTEGER; NewValue: INTEGER);

   VAR
      NodePointer: ListPointer;
      ItemChanged: BOOLEAN;

BEGIN
   (* Code to search a linked list, starting with the node pointed to by ListHead, for   *)
   (* the ListElement whose Value matches Key. Set the Value field of the ListElement to *)
   (* NewVAlue.   If no ListElement with matching Key found invoke TakeErrorAction.       *)

   NodePointer := ListStart;
   ItemChanged := FALSE;
   WHILE NOT ItemChanged AND (NodePointer <> NIL) DO
      IF NodePointer^.NodeID = Key THEN
         NodePointer^.Value := NewValue;
         ItemChanged        := TRUE;
      ELSE
         NodePointer := NodePointer^.Next;
      END;
   END;
   IF NOT ItemChanged THEN
      TakeErrorAction;
   END;
   RETURN;
END Example9;

BEGIN
. . . .
Example9(ListHead, Number, NewNumber);
```

FIGURE 9.12 Modification of element in list structure.

database is modified, however this should be done at a level of detail that is consistent with the way that the user thinks of the operation. For example, 'The database pointed to by ListStart is modified to include the widget count'.

In the example given here, the fact that the user has access to the structure of ListElement implies that the operation is being thought of in a rather detailed manner. A better approach would be to hide the detail of the list structure through the use of an abstract data type.

To summarize the last few paragraphs and examples, the documentation of input, output, and purpose of a procedure define the interface with the user. The detail with which the output is described should match the level of abstraction at the point at which the procedure is invoked. In simple cases, it is possible to define the way in which the output is to be defined. However, when the interface is more complex, the documentation level will depend on the nature of the function performed by a procedure and the way in which it is thought of by its users.

9.6 THE RUNNING EXAMPLE CONTINUED

In Section 9.4, we developed a data flow model and corresponding data type flow that would serve as a basis for an implementation of the Running Example. To refresh your memory, the data type flow diagram is repeated in Figure 9.13.

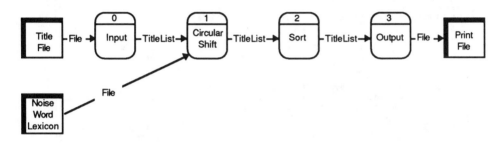

FIGURE 9.13 Flow of data types in BuildPrintfile program in Figure 9.6.

Based on this model, we produced an outline for implementation that was based on abstract data types. Nevertheless, there are still some design issues that need to be elaborated, in particular the way in which information is to flow between the procedures. Input reads the data, separates the Title-Part and Ref-Part and puts them into a TitleList, which is implemented by TitleListManager. Thus the information about the storage of a Title is hidden entirely in TitleListManager. CircularShift gets the Titles from the TitleList and generates all the interesting circularly shifted titles and puts them into another TitleList, which is passed to Sort and thence to Output. From the point of view of information hiding, it would be a good plan to put Input, CircularShift, Sort, and Output into separate integrands.

Let us now consider CircularShift. It obtains its data from the TitleList and generates the interesting versions of the titles. These need to be passed to Sort. There are now two versions of a Title-Part, the original and the circularly shifted one. Both are needed. Sort needs the circularly shifted version for sorting and Output needs the circularly shifted forms but separated into buckets as called for in the specifications. Output must also be possible to obtain the alignment point from a circularly shifted title so that it can be arranged on the printed line.. A solution to this problem would be to introduce some new data types and a specific process to convert from one kind of Title-Part to another. The

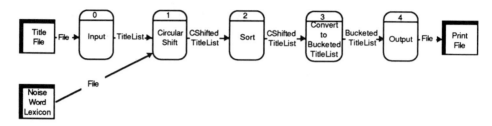

FIGURE 9.14 Revised flow of data types in BuildPrintfile program in Figure 9.13.

```
MODULE BuildPrintfile;

(* FUNCTION NAME:  BuildPrintfile                                            *)
(*                                                                            *)
(* AUTHOR:  Michael Marcotty      DATE CREATED: 1990 May 02                   *)
(*                                                                            *)
(* PURPOSE: Build Printfile from the data contained in Titlestore and Lexicon.*)
(*          Each Title-Part of Titlestore contains keywords, that is words that*)
(*          are not contained in Lexicon. For each keyword in the Title-Parts *)
(*          there will be an element in Printfile with a designation of the   *)
(*          keyword.  The elements of Printfile are ordered alphabetically by  *)
(*          designated keyword, the complete file being split into 26 parts   *)
(*          according to the initial letter of the designated keyword, there being*)
(*          one part for each letter of the alphabet.                         *)
(*                                                                            *)
(*   INPUT:  Titlestore: an ordered set of character strings consisting of words*)
(*           separated by blanks.  Each string consists of two parts, a Title-Part*)
(*           and a Reference-Part.  The Reference-Part is enclosed in brackets.*)
(*                                                                            *)
(*           Lexicon: an ordered set of character strings, each string consists of*)
(*           a single word.                                                   *)
(*                                                                            *)
(*   OUTPUT: Printfile: an ordered set of representations of the elements of  *)
(*           of Titlestore, separated into 26 parts, see PURPOSE above.       *)
        FROM InputMod          IMPORT Input;
        FROM CSmod             IMPORT CircularShift;
        FROM Sortmod           IMPORT Sort;
        FROM CvtMod            IMPORT CvtToAlignedTitleList;
        FROM OutputMod         IMPORT Output;
        FROM TitleListManager  IMPORT TitleList;
        FROM CSTListManager    IMPORT CShiftedTitleList;
        FROM BTListManager     IMPORT BucketedTitleList;
        FROM FileInterface     IMPORT File;

        VAR
           DataFile:                   File;
           PrintFile:                  File;
           NoiseWordLexicon:           File;
           ListOfTitles:               TitleList;
           ExtendedListOfTitles:       CShiftedTitleList;
           SortedExtendedListOfTitles: CShiftedTitleList;
           AlignedListOfTitles:        BucketedTitleList;
BEGIN
    Input(DataFile, ListOfTitles);
    CircularShift(ListOfTitles, NoiseWordLexicon, ExtendedListOfTitles);
    Sort(ExtendedListOfTitles, SortedExtendedListOfTitles);
    CvtToBudketedTitleList(SortedExtendedListOfTitles, AlignedListOfTitles);
    Output(AlignedListOfTitles, PrintFile);
    RETURN
END BuildPrintfile.
```

FIGURE 9.15 Outline of BuildPrintfile program version 4.

data type CircularlyShiftedTitle must allow the operation to find the alignment point. Figure 9.14 shows a data type flow diagram that represents this change.

This organization has the advantage there is better localization of the use of the different types. We can now define the top level integrand as shown in Figure 9.15. The data types CShiftedTitleList and BucketedTitleList are defined in a similar manner to TitleList as described earlier. Note that the procedures Input, CircularShift, Sort, CvtToBucketedTitleList, and Output have been made into separately compiled integrands.

The next step will be the actual implementation of the integrands. This subject will be addressed in the next chapter.

CHAPTER TEN

THE LOGICAL ORGANIZATION
OF AN INTEGRAND

The executable body of an integrand is made up of segments of code that correspond to paragraphs in expository writing. The external interface specification for the integrand provides a context in which the executable statements are to be understood; this specification must therefore be contained in the integrand's introductory comments, which provide a synopsis of the actions performed by the executable statements of the integrand. The intelligibility of an integrand depends greatly upon its logical organization. For the executable statements to be easily understandable, they must be organized so that the structure of the process is obvious. As an illustration of the need for this organization, a sort procedure is discussed. Paragraphs, like their text counterparts, require unity and simplicity of flow, which is achieved by employing a flow of control based on single-entry, single-exit structures. These are the sequence, conditional, and iterative schemas used in structured programming. The proof that these constructs are sufficient for all sequential programming is demonstrated. Other control structures are described together with a summary of the arguments against the GOTO statement and a discussion of the efficiency question. Other principles of expository programming are covered including proper usage of the language, careful choice of identifiers, and presentation of the program to enhance its readability. Part of the organization of a program must be plans and support for validating and debugging it. The requirements for such support are discussed. Finally, some of the points discussed in the chapter are illustrated through the Running Example.

10.1 INTRODUCTION

Clear exposition requires logical organization. The logical organization of an integrand and its associated documentation are essential to the clarity that we hold to be mandatory in programming. For it is this clarity that makes possible the testing, improvement and – ultimately – correction of the program that follow its implementation. In this chapter, we start from the context in which a procedure operates, i.e., its external interface. This is described with some introductory comments. In the light of this, we consider the way in which the executable body of a procedure is constructed from segments of code in the same way that a section of a technical report is constructed from paragraphs. A paragraph in a program consists of one or more executable statements that constitute a major step in the algorithm.

At the beginning of a chapter in a nineteenth-century novel, it was common to provide the reader with a synopsis of the events of the chapter. For example, Chapter XXXV of an 1881 edition of Mark Twain's *A Tramp Abroad* has the heading:

> A New Interest – Magnificent Views – A Mule's Preferences – Turning Mountain Corners – Terror of a Horse – Lady Tourists – Death of a Young Countess – A Search for a Hat – What we did find – Harris's Opinion of Chamois – A Disappointed Man – A Giantess – Model for an Empress – Baths at Leuk – Sport in the Winter – The Gemmi Precipices – A Palace for an Emperor – The Famous Ladders – Considerably mixed up – Sad Plight of a Minister.

This synopsis served two purposes; it gave the new reader an inkling of what was to follow in the chapter and, by reading the chapter headings separately, someone who had read the book before would be able easily to locate a chapter that contained a favorite passage.

In programming, the situation is similar. An integrand should have a block of introductory comments that both define the purpose of the integrand and also abstract and present in a convenient form the details contained in the executable code. This information is intended for two different classes of readers: programmers who want to use the routine without knowing anything about its internal working and programmers who must modify the procedure in some way, the *maintenance programmers*. This dual readership must be borne in mind in writing the introductory comments. In programming languages that have definition modules as well as implementation modules, for example, Modula-2, the comments defining the purpose of the integrand should appear in the definition module, where they are accessible to the user. The synopsis of the executable code forming the actual implementation should appear in the implementation module. Figures 10.1 and 10.2 show examples of such introductory comments.

It is a good plan to adopt a standard format for the introductory comments to an integrand. Figures 10.1 and 10.2, based on the Running Example, show a possible layout for the heading of a separately compiled integrand. The sequence of characters *n* where n is some upper case letter, at the beginning of each line serve as patterns so that lines may be extracted from the header for use in external documentation. This provides a simple scheme for the automatic construction and maintenance of external documentation that matches the source code. If a source code management system is used, the inclusion of modification records may be performed automatically. This is a great advantage since programmers often, in the heat of the battle to fix something, are likely to forget to include the modification record.

There are a number of reasons for maintaining a modification log:

• If something goes wrong with an integrand, a good place to look is the last place that it was modified.

```
DEFINITION MODULE TitleListMngr;
(* *N*  FUNCTION NAME:  TitleListMngr                                        *)
(* *N*  AUTHOR: Michael Marcotty      DATE CREATED: 1990 May 03              *)
(* *P*  PURPOSE: To implement the storage and manipulation of the TitleList data type *)

    FROM Titles     IMPORT Title;

    TYPE TitleList;

    PROCEDURE CreateTitleList(): TitleList;
(* *N*  FUNCTION: NAME: CreateTitleList                                       *)
(* *P*  PURPOSE:  Create an empty TitleList.                                  *)
(* *O*  OUTPUT:   VAR:  TL - An empty TitleList                               *)

    PROCEDURE BeginTitleList(): TitleList;
(* *N*  FUNCTION: NAME: BeginTitleList                                        *)
(* *P*  PURPOSE:  Reset TitleList so that GetNextTitle will get the first     *)
(* *P*            title in the list.                                          *)
(* *I*  INPUT:    VAR   TL - TitleList to be reset                            *)
(* *O*  OUTPUT:   TL - TitleList reset so that next Title is its first Title  *)
(* *E*  ERROR ACTION: If the TitleList referenced by TL has not been created an error *)
(* *E*               is reported.                                             *)

    PROCEDURE GetNextTitle(TL: TitleList): Title;
(* *N*  FUNCTION: NAME: GetNextTitle                                          *)
(* *P*  PURPOSE:  Get the title following the one obtained by the previous application*)
(* *P*            of this operation.  If this is the first application since  *)
(* *P*            BeginTitleList was applied, the first title in the TitleList is *)
(* *P*            obtained.  If the previous Title obtained was the last one in the *)
(* *P*            TitleList or if the TitleList is empty or has not been created, a *)
(* *P*            null Title is obtained.                                     *)
(* *I*  INPUT:    Value: TL-the TitleList from which the next title is to be obtained.*)
(* *O*  OUTPUT:   VAR:   The next title in the list or a null title.          *)

    PROCEDURE AppendTitle (VAR TL: TitleList;  T: Title);
(* *N*  FUNCTION: NAME: AppendTitle                                           *)
(* *P*  PURPOSE:  Append the Title to the given TitleList.                    *)
(* *I*  INPUT:    Value: Title to be appended to the TitleList.               *)
(* *I*            VAR:   TitleList to which Title is to be appended           *)
(* *O*  OUTPUT:   VAR:   ListOfTitles to which the Title has been appended.   *)
(* *E*  ERROR ACTION:  An error is reported if the TitleList referenced by TL has not *)
(* *E*                been created or if the Title cannot be appended.        *)

    PROCEDURE DumpTitleList(TL: TitleList);
(* *N*  FUNCTION: NAME: DumpTitleList                                         *)
(* *P*  PURPOSE:  Produce a formatted dump of the Titles in the given TitleList. *)
(* *I*  INPUT:    Value: The TitleList to be dumped.                          *)
(* *O*  OUTPUT:   Character string representation of the titles in the TitleList *)
(* *O*            appended to the debugging file.                             *)

END TitleListMngr.
```

FIGURE 10.1 Definition module for TitleListManager.

- Since the name of the modifier is recorded, there is an indication of where questions about the integrand might be asked.
- If an integrand starts to amass a large number of modification records, it is often an indication that there is something fundamentally wrong with the way in which it is written. Jones (1986) reports that IBM discovered that there were *error-prone* integrands in virtually all large systems and these modules were responsible for a large percentage of the maintenance costs of the system. As a consequence, a program of redesigning and reimplementing error-prone integrands was instituted and this

```
DEFINITION MODULE Titles;
    FROM TitlePartDef   IMPORT TitlePart;
    FROM RefPartDef     IMPORT RefPart;
    FROM MacSystemTypes IMPORT Str255;
    EXPORT QUALIFIED Title,                          (* Type      *)
                     MakeTitle, GetTitlePart, GetRefPart, (* Procedures *)
                     TitleToChars, IsNullTitle;
    TYPE    Title;

    PROCEDURE MakeTitle(TP: TitlePart; RP: RefPart): Title;
(* *N*    FUNCTION: NAME: ConstructTitle                              *)
(* *P*    PURPOSE: Construct a Title from a RefPart and a TitlePart.  If either part *)
(* *P*             is null, a null Title is constructed.              *)
(* *I*    INPUT:   Value: TP-the TitlePart and RP-the RefPart, the TitlePart and *)
(* *I*             RefPart from which the Title is to be built.       *)
(* *O*    OUTPUT:  VAR:   The constructed Title or null Title.        *)

    PROCEDURE GetTitlePart(T: Title): TitlePart;
(* *N*    FUNCTION: NAME: GetTitlePart                                *)
(* *P*    PURPOSE: Get the TitlePart of the given Title.  If the Title is a null Title*)
(* *P*             the TitlePart will be a null TitlePart.            *)
(* *I*    INPUT:   Value: The Title from which the Title-Part is required. *)
(* *O*    OUTPUT:  VAR:   The Title-Part of the Title or a null Title-Part. *)

    PROCEDURE GetRefPart(T: Title): RefPart;
(* *N*    FUNCTION: NAME: GetRefPart                                  *)
(* *P*    PURPOSE: Get the RefPart of the given Title.  If the Title is a null Title, *)
(* *P*             the RefPart will be a null RefPart.                *)
(* *I*    INPUT:   Value: The Title from which the Reference-part is required *)
(* *O*    OUTPUT:  VAR:   The Reference-Part of the Title or a null Reference-Part. *)

    PROCEDURE TitleToChars(T: Title; VAR ch: Str255);
(* *N*    FUNCTION: NAME: TitleToChars                                *)
(* *P*    PURPOSE: Convert a Title to printable character string form. *)
(* *I*    INPUT:   Value: The Title to be converted.                  *)
(* *O*    OUTPUT:  The character-string version of the Title.         *)

    PROCEDURE IsNullTitle(T: Title): BOOLEAN;
(* *N*    FUNCTION: NAME: IsNullTitle                                 *)
(* *P*    PURPOSE: If the Title is a null Title, return the value TRUE otherwise *)
(* *P*             return FALSE.                                      *)
(* *I*    INPUT:   Value: The Title being tested.                     *)
(* *O*    OUTPUT:  The value of the function.                         *)

END Titles.
```

FIGURE 10.2 Definition module for Titles.

ultimately led to a reduction of about 45 per cent in maintenance costs and a reduction of an order of magnitude in errors reported from the field.

Figures 10.1 and 10.2 show the Definition Modules for TitleListManager and Titles with the interfaces to the operations documented in accordance with the conventions described in Sections 9.6 and 9.7. In particular we have examples of the following:

1. Two procedures CreateTitleList and BeginTitleList whose effects are not directly accessible to the user.
2. Procedures, IsNullTitle, IsNullTitlePart, and IsNullRefPart that have input and a return value.
3. A procedure, AppendTitle, that has input and output. This could have been specified as a function that returned a value but since it also changes its input parameter by

appending a Title, it would then be a function with a side effect, which makes for difficult understanding. In addition, Modula-2 does not allow functions to return non-scalar values and this would have limited possible implementations. This procedure can also have the side-effect of producing an error message.

4. A procedure, BeginTitleList whose single parameter serves as both input and output.

5. A procedure, DumpStore, with a value parameter that is itself not changed although the file referenced by it has data added.

10.2 LOGICAL ORGANIZATION

Logical organization of an integrand means the arrangement of the programming language statements used to express the integrand's design. Expository writing depends upon clear organization for comprehensibility. The same is true of programs. The overall design and organization of the program must be carefully thought out before embarking on the actual detailed writing of the executable statements. As Halmos (1970) puts it:

> The main contribution that an expository writer can make is to organize and arrange the material so as to minimize the resistance and maximize the insight of the reader and keep him on the track with no unintended distractions.

Organization of the complete integrand can be approached from several different points of view:

- Organization to make integrands more easily readable.
- Organization to make subsequent modifications easier.
- Organization to make testing and debugging easier.

Generally, these objectives all lead to the same result. In this chapter, we concentrate on the organization of an integrand so that it is more easily understandable. At the same time, we will indicate how the other objectives are satisfied by this approach.

By *organization*, I mean the orderly arrangement of the subject matter. This allows the reader to obtain a mental image of what an integrand does and how this is accomplished. This mental image of the way in which the program works serves as an abstraction. This means that it is possible to obtain an abstraction of the program easily and see the structure without being mired in details.

As an example of the essential part that organization plays in understanding a program consider the problem of translating one of the Collected Algorithms from the Association for Computing Machinery (ACM 1980), which first appeared in Boothroyd (1963b), into Modula-2. Although this algorithm is expressed in only a few lines, it is sufficiently complex to illustrate the problem. The algorithm, reproduced in Figure 10.3 is written in Algol 60. However, it is not the fact that Algol 60 may be unfamiliar to you that will make it difficult to translate it. The purpose of Algol 60 was 'to describe computational processes' and most practicing software engineers should be able to read it based on their intuition for programming and programming languages that they have built up. Those

procedure *stringsort (a, n)*; **comment** elements $a[1]\cdots a[n]$ of $a[1:2n]$ are sorted into ascending sequence using $a[n+1]\cdots a[2n]$ as auxiliary storage. Von Neumann extended string logic is employed to merge input strings which are sent alternately to either end of a receiving area. The procedure takes advantage of naturally occurring ascending or descending order in the original data.
value *n*;   **integer** *n*;   **array** *a*;
begin integer *d, i, j, m, u, v, z*;   **integer array** $c[-1:1]$;
       switch $p := jz1$, *str i;* **switch** $q := $ merge, *jz2;*
oddpass: $i := 1$; $j := n$; $c[-1] := n + 1$; $c[1] := 2 \times n$;
allpass: $d := 1$;   **go to** firststring;
merge: **if** $a[i] \geq a[z]$
                then begin go to $p[v]$;
                 jz1: **if** $a[j] \geq a[z]$
                      then *ij*: **begin if** $a[i] \geq a[j]$
                                then *str j*: **begin** $a[m] := a[j]$
                                  $j := j - 1$ **end**
                              else *str i*: **begin** $a[m] := a[i]$;
                                $i := i + 1$ **end**
                        end
                     else begin $v := 2$;   **go to** *str i* **end**
                end
                else begin $u := 2$;
                   jz2: **if** $a[j] \geq a[z]$
                     then go to *str j*
                     else begin $d := -d$; $c[d] := m$;
                           firststring: $m := c[-d]$;
                                $v := u := 1$;
                              go to *ij*
                     end
                end;
$z := m$; $m := m + d$;   **if** $j \geq i$ **then go to** $q[u]$;
if $m > n + 1$ **then begin comment** evenpass; $i := n + 1$;
               $j := 2 \times n$; $c[-1] := 1$; $c[1] := n$;   **go to** allpass **end**
              else if $m < n + 1$ **then go to** oddpass
end stringsort;

FIGURE 10.3 Original Algol 60 version of Algorithm 207. Copyright 1963, Association for Computing Machinery, Inc., reprinted with permission.

who really need a written description of the language should refer to Dijkstra (1962), Higman (1963), or Naur (1963). Although the Running Example does contain a sort process and the algorithm treated here could have been used for this process, this example should be considered to be outside the Running Example.

    The problem is that it is impossible to make a direct transliteration of the algorithm into Modula-2. The author of the algorithm has relied heavily on the goto statement, which does not exist in Modula-2. In order to be able to translate the program, you must first create a mental image or abstraction of the process and then, having understood the algorithm, recreate it in Modula-2. I am sure that the author of the algorithm used the goto statement in a search for efficiency. At the time this algorithm was written, the apparent efficiency was the touchstone by which algorithms were judged. It should also be remembered that this algorithm was written before the term *structured programming* was generally understood.

From the point of view of expository programming, it would be argued that the primary purpose of an algorithm such as this one, published as part of the Collected Algorithms from the ACM, is to communicate the way in which the process works. Questions of efficiency, other than the intrinsic efficiency of the algorithm, whether it is an n^2 or $n\log n$ process, are secondary. Today, there are few Algol 60 compilers available so that, if we are to make use of this algorithm, we must translate it into some other language before we can use it.

It is easy to write a Modula-2 definition module for the sort routine. (You will remember that the 'Definition Module' is the Modula-2 name for an integrand that defines the external data interface of a procedure.) This is shown in Figure 10.4.

The body of the algorithm as presented in Figure 10.3 shows nothing of the structure of the process. Any sorting method involves iteration or recursion. The list is repeatedly reordered until it is in the proper sequence. This is true whether we are rearranging a set of index cards by hand or sorting the elements of an array by program. The major barrier to understanding the StringSort algorithm is that its iterative structure is hidden so that it can only be found by painstaking tracing. The only way of getting a mental image of the process used in a tangled structure like that shown in this algorithm is to take a small sample of data and work through the process on paper, using lists, diagrams, or any other convenient notation. Once the process has been understood, it is possible to translate it into a better logical structure. Before you read any further, study the original version of the algorithm carefully until you understand how it works.

```
DEFINITION MODULE SSort
(* *N*  FUNCTION NAME:  StringSort                                        *)
(* *N*  AUTHOR:  Michael Marcotty      DATE CREATED: 1989 January 12      *)
(* *P*  PURPOSE: To sort the elements of the A[1]...A[DataCount] of the array *)
(* *P*           A[1]...A[2*DataCount] into ascending sequence using      *)
(* *P*           A[DataCount+1]...A[2*DataCount] as auxiliary storage.  The  *)
(* *P*           procedure takes advantage of naturally occurring ascending  *)
(* *P*           or descending order in the original data.                *)
(* *S*  CALL SEQUENCE: StringSort(DataCount, A)                           *)
(* *I*  INPUT:   Value: DataCount defining the number of elements of data. *)
(* *I*           VAR:  A       an array of at least 2*DataCount elements  *)
(* *I*                         whose first DataCount elements contain the *)
(* *I*                         data to be sorted.                         *)
(* *O*  OUTPUT: VAR:  A        The sorted data is contained in the first  *)
(* *O*                         DataCount elements.                        *)

    PROCEDURE StringSort(DataCount: CARDINAL; VAR A: ARRAY OF CARDINAL);

END SSort.
```

FIGURE 10.4 Top level of Modula-2 version of Stringsort.

As the preamble to StringSort says, the process makes use of the half of the input data array as auxiliary storage. During each major iteration, the data is copied from one half of the storage, the 'source', to the other, the 'target', the direction of copy reversing between iterations. We can imagine the data array to be laid out as a row of cells from left to right with element 1 at the left and element $2n$ at the right. For the first iteration, the data are in the left half and the target area is the right half. In the source area, the data is treated as two ascending sequences, one starting at the left and going to the right and the other starting at the right and going to the left. The following diagram represents the state at the beginning of an example sort of ten digits:

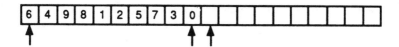

The two arrows in the source area mark the beginnings of the data sequences to be merged and the arrow in the target area marks the cell into which the first element will be copied. Merging continues until the two next available data elements in the source are both less than the last copied element in the target. At this point, the next available elements are treated as the beginnings of new sequences and merging continues, forming a sequence at the opposite end of the target area. The next four diagrams show successive steps in the merging process up to the end of the first sequence. Although the data is really copied, for clarity, the diagrams show it as being moved. In the last diagram, the arrow in the target area has been moved to show where the next sequence will be put.

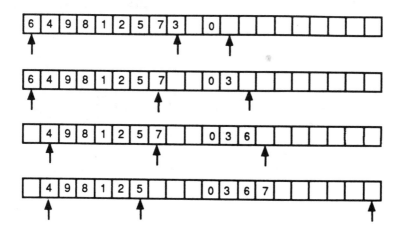

The merging continues until the end of the next sequence is reached, as shown in the next three diagrams.

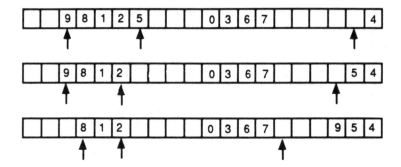

Sequences are formed in the target area in this way until all the data has been copied at which point the source and target designations are interchanged. This is shown in the next three diagrams.

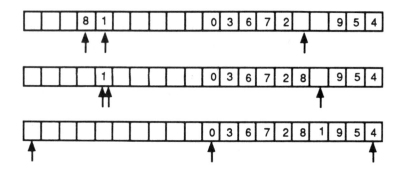

In the example, four sequences, $(0, 3, 9, 7)$, $(4, 5, 9)$, $(2, 8)$, and (1) were constructed in the target area. The process continues by merging these four sequences to form two sequences in the newly designated target area. The situation at the end of the second iteration is

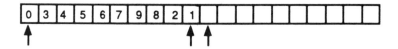

with two sequences $(0, 3, 4, 5, 6, 7, 9)$, and $(1, 2, 8)$. These are merged in the third iteration to produce

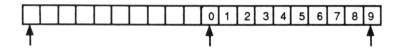

Since there is only one sequence, the sort is complete. However, since it is in the right half of the data array, it must be copied back into the left half to give

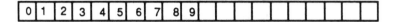

The sorting process thus consists of three nested iterations. The outermost copies the data from the source area to the target area and continues until only one sequence was formed in the target and therefore the data are sorted. At the next level, each iteration constructs a single sequence in the target area and looping continues until the end of the data is reached. In the innermost loop, each iteration copies a data element and the loop terminates at the end of the sequence. Finally, the data are copied back into the leftmost half of the array if necessary. Thus, we can sketch the algorithm as:

```
REPEAT
    REPEAT
        WHILE sequence being copied LOOP
            copy element from source to target
        END;
        count sequences
    UNTIL data all copied from source to target
UNTIL only one sequence copied
IF sorted data is in right half THEN
    copy data into left half
END
```

Even though the sorting process is understood, it is difficult to relate it back to the Algol program shown in Figure 10.3. Figure 10.5 contains a Modula-2 program modeled on the above outline. In this, the iterative nature of the sort is evident and identifiers that are representative of the quantities that they represent are used. This version is intended to be an exposition of the sorting process.

10.3 PARAGRAPHS

Paragraphs are not just groups of statements separated from other groups by blank lines; they are the basic units of thought out of which the process is described. They are building stones, parts of a larger whole. Though we shall necessarily in this chapter discuss paragraphs without reference to their context, they are in fact inseparable from that context. That is to say, the problem of programming is not so much to write an effective paragraph of code, as to write paragraphs in such a way as to make an effective – and integrated – algorithm.

The context of a paragraph is its interface – paragraphs have interfaces just as procedures and integrands do. A paragraph does not have arguments and parameters; all

```
IMPLEMENTATION MODULE SSort;

    PROCEDURE StringSort(DataCount: CARDINAL; VAR A: ARRAY OF CARDINAL);
(* *N*  FUNCTION NAME:  StringSort                                      *)
(* *N*  AUTHOR:  Michael Marcotty      DATE CREATED: 1989 January 12    *)
(* *P*  PURPOSE: To sort the elements of the A[1]...A[DataCount] of the array *)
(* *P*           A[1]...A[2*DataCount] into ascending sequence using    *)
(* *P*           A[DataCount+1]...A[2*DataCount] as auxiliary storage.  The   *)
(* *P*           procedure takes advantage of naturally occurring ascending *)
(* *P*           or descending order in the original data.              *)
(* *A*  METHOD:  The array A[1]...A[2*DataCount] as two separate areas of *)
(* *A*           storage: A[1]...A[DataCount] and A[DataCount+1]...      *)
(* *A*           A[2*DataCount].  At the beginning of the process, the area *)
(* *A*           A[1]...A[DataCount] is designated as a source and the area *)
(* *A*           A[DataCount+1]...A[2*DataCount] as a target.  At the end of *)
(* *A*           each iteration the designations are interchanged.  During *)
(* *A*           each iteration, data is copied from the source to the target.*)
(* *A*           The array A is treated as a row of cells going from A[1] on *)
(* *A*           the left and A[2*DataCount] on the right.  The left and right*)
(* *A*           ends of the source area are taken as the start of sequences. *)
(* *A*           The left sequence going to the right and the right sequence *)
(* *A*           going to the left.  The process consists of merging the two *)
(* *A*           sequences into an ascending sequence in the target.  The   *)
(* *A*           merging continues as long as possible, i.e. until the last *)
(* *A*           element of the merged sequence has a higher value than the *)
(* *A*           next elements of the source sequence.  At that point, a new *)
(* *A*           sequence is begun.  The merged sequences are put alternately *)
(* *A*           at the left and right ends of the target area.  The iter- *)
(* *A*           ations are continued until only one sequence of merged data *)
(* *A*           has been copied.  Before the process is terminated, the *)
(* *A*           sequence is, if necessary, copied into A[1]...A[DataCount]. *)

    CONST
        Left  = -1;
        Right =  1;
    VAR
        TargetSide:            (Left..Right);
        LSourceIndex:         CARDINAL;
        RSourceIndex:         CARDINAL;
        LSourceBegin:         CARDINAL;
        RSourceBegin:         CARDINAL;
        LTargetBegin:         CARDINAL;
        RTargetBegin:         CARDINAL;
        SequenceCount:        CARDINAL;
        TargetIndex:          CARDINAL;
        NextTarget:           CARDINAL;
        PrevTarget:           CARDINAL;
        PrevTargetIndex:      CARDINAL;
        TempForSwapping:      CARDINAL;
        EndOfSequence:        BOOLEAN;

    BEGIN
        LSourceBegin  := 1;
        RSourceBegin  := DataCount;
        LTargetBegin  := DataCount + 1;
        RTargetBegin  := DataCount + DataCount;
        SequenceCount := 0;
```

FIGURE 10.5 Implementation of Stringsort in Modula-2.

```
      REPEAT
         TargetSide     := Right;
         LSourceIndex   := LSourceBegin;
         RSourceIndex   := RSourceBegin;
         TargetIndex    := LTargetBegin;
         NextTarget     := RTargetBegin;
         SequenceCount := 0;
         WHILE LSourceIndex <= RSourceIndex DO
            IF A[LSourceIndex] < A[RSourceIndex] THEN
               A[TargetIndex] := A[LSourceIndex];
               LSourceIndex   := LSourceIndex + 1
            ELSE
               A[TargetIndex] := A[RSourceIndex];
               RSourceIndex   := RSourceIndex - 1
            END;
            PrevTargetIndex := TargetIndex;
            TargetIndex      := TargetIndex + TargetSide;
            EndOfSequence    := FALSE;
            WHILE NOT EndOfSequence DO
               IF (LSourceIndex <= RSourceIndex) THEN
                  IF A[LSourceIndex] >= A[PrevTargetIndex] THEN
                     IF A[RSourceIndex] >= A[PrevTargetIndex] THEN
                        IF (A[LSourceIndex] < A[RSourceIndex]) THEN
                           A[TargetIndex] := A[LSourceIndex];
                           LSourceIndex   := LSourceIndex + 1
                        ELSE
                           A[TargetIndex] := A[RSourceIndex];
                           RSourceIndex   := RSourceIndex - 1
                        END
                     ELSE
                        A[TargetIndex] := A[LSourceIndex];
                        LSourceIndex   := LSourceIndex + 1
                     END
                  ELSIF (A[LSourceIndex] < A[RSourceIndex]) THEN
                     A[TargetIndex] := A[RSourceIndex];
                     RSourceIndex   := RSourceIndex - 1
                  END;
                  ELSE
                     EndOfSequence = TRUE
                  END
               ELSE
                  EndOfSequence = TRUE
               END;
               IF NOT EndOfSequence THEN
                  PrevTargetIndex := TargetIndex;
                  TargetIndex      := TargetIndex + TargetSide;
               END
            END
            TempForSwapping := NextTarget;
            NextTarget      := TargetIndex;
            TargetIndex     := TempForSwapping;
            SequenceCount   := SequenceCount + 1;
            TargetSide      := TargetSide;
         END;
         TempForSwapping := LSourceBegin;
         LSourceBegin    := LTargetBegin;
         LTargetBegin    := TempForSwapping;
         TempForSwapping := RSourceBegin;
         RSourceBegin    := RTargetBegin;
         RTargetBegin    := TempForSwapping;
      UNTIL SequenceCount = 1;
      IF LSourceBegin <> 1 THEN
         LTargetIndex := 1;
         FOR LSourceIndex := LSourceBegin TO LSourceBegin + DataCount DO
            A[LTargetIndex] := A[LSourceIndex];
            LTargetIndex    := LTargetIndex + 1
         END
      END;
      RETURN
   END StringSort;
END SSort.
```

FIGURE 10.5(CONTINUED)   Implementation of Stringsort in Modula-2.

data are passed through its data context in the program unit where it occurs. Nevertheless, it does have inputs and outputs and these are an important part of the design of a paragraph, just as they are in the design of a procedure or integrand.

Program paragraphs are analogous to textual paragraphs, which consist of a group of sentences – occasionally, just a single sentence – that develop one main point or controlling idea. The reader expects these sentences to have:

- *Unity of purpose:* that is, they are all relevant to the main point of the paragraph. We have already discussed this in relation to integrands in the programming context.
- *Continuity:* which means that the sentences follow a definite plan with one leading to the next in an orderly progression that the reader finds easy to follow.

For a group of statements to constitute a well-designed paragraph in a program, it must satisfy the same criteria required of a procedure – unity of purpose and continuity.

10.3.1 Unity of purpose

Everything in the paragraph should be concerned with performing a single basic algorithm step. This is the thesis or the goal of the paragraph.

The unity of a paragraph is achieved by ensuring that all the statements in the paragraph are directed towards the goal. Conversely, there should be no statements elsewhere in the procedure that are directed towards this goal. A consequence of this is that, contrary to usual practice, any initialization of variables that is required for the paragraph's purpose should be done in the paragraph itself rather than in a separate initialization paragraph.

Within the complete algorithm, we define the *span of reference* of a variable as being from the point at which the variable first gets a value to the point where it is last referenced. At all points within its span of reference, a variable is carrying some data value that is important to the algorithm and can be said to be *active*. The reader of a paragraph must keep the state of all active variables in mind in order to understand the algorithm that is being described. Of course, there is nothing explicit in the text of the program that shows which variables are active; the reader must infer this. The fewer the active variables, the easier will be the paragraph to understand. Initializing variables at the beginning of the procedure renders them all active. Keeping the initializing assignment close to the point of reference limits the reader's textual attention span to a smaller segment of text and, should the paragraph need modifying later, there is less chance that a corresponding change in the initialization will be forgotten.

10.3.2 Continuity

The statements in the paragraph must not only satisfy the criterion of unity, but their sequence must be such that the reader can easily follow their flow.

This is achieved by having for each group of statements a single entry and single exit for the flow of control and a downward control flow within the paragraph. This allows the reader's attention to concentrate on the action in the paragraph without having to worry about comings and goings of control flow. Typically, a paragraph consists of a short sequence of statements, a decision involving differing actions depending on some condition, or a loop. The concept of *structured programming*, as it applies to control flow, consists of restricting the flow of control constructs to the three single-entry, single-exit forms of sequence, conditional, loop. Thus, structured programming is a natural consequence of paragraph organization for clarity and continuity.

10.4 STRUCTURED PROGRAMMING

The term *structured programming* was introduced by Edsger Dijkstra in his paper 'Structured Programming' (Dijkstra 1969). He introduces the subject with:

> The leading question was if it was conceivable to increase our programming ability by an order of magnitude and what techniques (mental, organizational or mechanical) could be applied in the process of program composition to produce this increase.

In this paper, Dijkstra investigates how an assertion of a program's correctness could be justified. Since testing can never show the absence of errors, the assertion should depend only upon the program text. The process of proving the correctness of a program, as we have seen in Chapter 7, is a long process. He continues:

> Therefore, I have not focused my attention on the question 'how do we prove the correctness of a given program?' but on the questions 'for what program structures can we give correctness proofs without undue labour, even if the programs get large?' and, as a sequel, 'how do we make, for a given task, such a well-structured program?' My willingness to confine my attention to such 'well-structured programs' (as a subset of the set of all possible programs) is based on my belief that we can find such a well-structured subset satisfying our programming needs, i.e. that for each programmable task this subset contains enough realistic programs.

In an earlier paper, Dijkstra (1968a) already sets the groundwork for restricting the control flow constructs to a small number because:

> . . . our intellectual powers are rather geared to master static relations and . . . our powers to visualize processes evolving in time are relatively poorly developed. For this reason we should do (as wise programmers aware of our limitations) our utmost to shorten the conceptual gap between the static program and the dynamic process, to make the correspondence between the program (spread out in text space) and the process (spread out in time) as trivial as possible.

There is, unfortunately, an idea that structured programming is no different from ordinary programming except that the programmer is not allowed to use the GOTO statement. Dijkstra's quotations show that this is not true. It is programming that only uses a restricted number of control structures *so as to make the static and dynamic forms of the program as close to each other as possible*. When this is done, the idea of flow of control almost disappears. The program becomes a sequence of control abstractions. Conditional statements become viewed as stating that, under certain conditions, certain actions take place. A loop becomes a sequence of actions that are repeated as long as a particular condition is true.

Before we continue with discussion of the practice of structured programming, we will look at the theoretical underpinnings. The following discussion is based on the presentation in Marcotty and Ledgard (1986).

10.4.1 Basic control structures and flowgraphs

In the study of flow of control, it is useful to represent a program as a *flowgraph*. This is a set of nodes, representing actions in the program, connected by directed lines that represent the sequence in which the actions occur during program execution, the *flow of control*. There are three kinds of node:

- *Basic actions*. These are represented by rectangles and denote actions that can change the values of variables but cannot alter the flow of control. Thus, a basic action node has only one flow line entering it and one leaving it.
- *Conditions*. These are represented by diamonds and denote actions that can change the flow of control but cannot alter the values of variables. A condition node has two flow lines leaving it, implying that a binary choice of flow sequence is made.
- *Junctions*. These are represented by a simple junction of two flow lines. Junctions do not denote any action and thus cannot change the values of variables and have only a single flow line leaving them.

Following Bruno and Steiglitz (1972), we define a class of simple control structures called *D-structures*, D for *D*ijkstra. A D-structure is either a

- *Basic action:* for example, an assignment, procedure call, or input-output statement. Each of these has a single entry and single exit and can change the values of variables. The assumption we have made is that there is no mechanism by which control can return from a called procedure to a statement other than the one immediately following the call statement. This is represented as a basic action node.

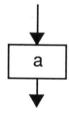

or it is constructed from D-structures through one of the following constructs:

- *Sequence:* $s_1 s_2 \ldots s_n$ of two or more D-structures s_1 to s_n. This is represented as a sequence of basic actions stacked vertically with the flow of control going downwards.

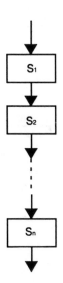

- *Conditional:* represented as:

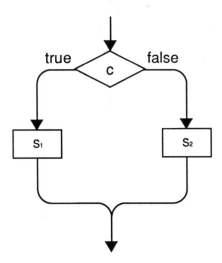

where c is a condition and s_1 and s_2 are D-structures. We will use the convention that in all flowgraphs, the true branch is always shown on the left side of the condition node.

- *Iteration:* represented as:

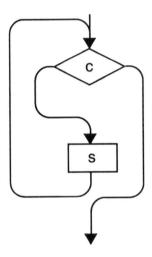

where c is a condition and s is a D-structure.

D-structures built from single-entry, single-exit actions are themselves single-entry, single-exit structures. A program that is constructed entirely from D-structures is itself a D-structure. Consequently, it will have only one entry and one exit.

The flow of control of any program, whether D-structure or not, can be depicted as a flowgraph. A flowgraph that is a D-structure can be readily diagrammed without any flow lines crossing, that is, it is planar.

10.4.2 The fundamental control structure theorem

We now show that D-structures are sufficient for the construction of any program. The proof given here is long – some might say too long – but is included here because it presents its elegant result in a more intelligible form than some shorter versions. This theorem was initially demonstrated by Böhm and Jacopini (1966) and was almost unnoticed at first, perhaps partially because the title of the paper 'Flow Diagrams, Turing Machines, and Languages with only Two Formation Rules' gave little inkling of its range of application. Later, it had a far-reaching effect on programming and started much controversy about the proper use of control structures. Here we give an informal version of the Mills (1972) proof of the theorem.

The theorem states:

> For any proper program there exists an equivalent program that is a D-structure.

Where a *proper program* is any computer program, irrespective of its control structures, such that the following rules apply:

1. There is precisely one entry and one exit to the program.
2. For every node in the flowgraph representation of the program, there is at least one path from the entry point, through that node, to the exit point.

The first criterion does not reduce the theorem's generality since a program P with two entry points can be represented by a program with a single entry point that leads immediately to a condition node that connects to the Ps two entry points. Similarly, a program with two exit points can be represented by a program with a single exit point connected to the original two exit points through a junction node. The second criterion rules out programs containing infinite loops (except those caused by a loop condition that can never be satisfied) and statements that cannot be reached by the flow of control from the program's entry point.

By *equivalent program* we mean a program that will always give the same result as the original one for the same input data. Two equivalent programs may have very different flowgraphs. For example, we can compare two programs that calculate the square root of their input. One obtains the result by successive approximation, while the other uses a table look-up method. These two programs will be equivalent if their results are exactly equal for all possible input values.

The proof of the existence of an equivalent D-structure program consists of a step-by-step method of deriving a D-structured flowgraph that is equivalent to the flowgraph for the original program. This derived flowgraph corresponds to a D-structure program that is equivalent to the original one.

To convert a program to an equivalent one that is a D-structure, we first construct a flowgraph G corresponding to the original program. We then make a sequence of changes to G, working from the entry point step-by-step until the whole flowgraph is a D-structure. At each stage, the change to be made is determined by the first node of the unexamined part of the flowgraph.

There are three cases to consider:

- *Case 1. The first node of G is a basic action,* a.
  In this case, G is of the form:

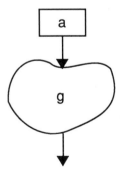

where g is an as yet unexamined part of G. This case is simple: we already have a sequence of two structures and we apply our step-by-step process to g. After g has been converted to a D-structure, we will have a sequence of the action a and a D-structure. This sequence is itself a D-structure. The flowgraph g has fewer nodes than the original G and therefore we have made progress in the conversion process.

- *Case 2. The first node of G is a conditional c.*
  In this case, G is of the form:

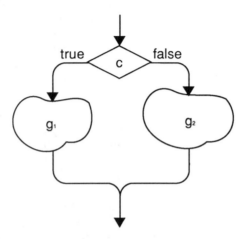

We convert by constructing two flowgraphs g_1 and g_2 from G. The flowgraph g_1 is derived from G by making a copy of those parts of G that can be reached from the true branch of c. Similarly, the flowgraph g_2 is constructed by copying those nodes of G that are reached by the false branch of c. Both must end at the same exit since there is only one exit from G.

Although both g_1 and g_2 may contain copies of identical parts of G, neither g_1 nor g_2 can contain more nodes than G. The process is next applied to g_1 and g_2 separately. When the conversion is completed, we will have a conditional structure where each branch is a D-structure, which is itself a D-structure.

- *Case 3. The first node of G is a junction.*
  The flowgraph G is thus of the form:

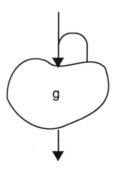

In this case, our action depends upon the next node in G, that is, the first node of G. Again, there are three cases to consider.

- *Case 3.1. The first node of G is an action* a.
In this case, the flowgraph G has the form:

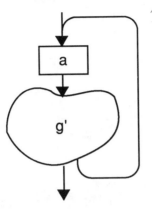

Here, we transform G by moving the junction to the other side of the action a and inserting a copy of the action into the flowpath from g' to the junction. This gives the flowgraph:

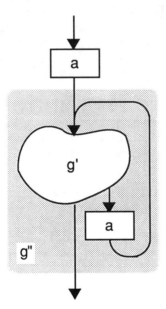

This is a sequence of the action a and a new flowgraph g" shown inside the shaded area. We next apply the transformation process to g".

- *Case 3.2. The first node of G is a conditional c.*
  Here the flowgraph G has the form:

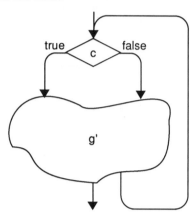

This case is more complicated. As we did in Case 2, we construct two flowgraphs, g_1' and g_2', that consist of all the nodes of g' that can be reached from the true and false branches of c. Both g_1' and g_2' may have two exits, one for the return to c and one that is linked directly to the exit from g'.

In order to make the transformation in this case, we must add a new variable, say V, that can take the values 0 and 1. We insert a new action node before the junction that assigns the value 1 to V. In each of the flowgraphs g_1' and g_2', we insert action nodes on each of their exit lines. On the exit line that leads back to c, the new action assigns the value 1 to V and on the exit line that goes directly to the exit of G, the action assigns the value 0 to V. Finally, we join the exit lines from both g_1' and g_2' back to c and insert a new conditional node that tests the value of V between the junction and c. The result of this is shown in Figure 10.6.

Effectively, what we have done is to put G inside an iteration construct that will continue to loop until the value of V has been set to 0. This will happen when control passes along the exit line of g_1' or g_2', which were directly connected to the exit of G. The transformation process is then applied separately to the new flowgraphs g_1'' and g_2'' shown in the figure.

- *Case 3.3. The first node of G is also a junction.*
  The flowgraph in this case has the form:

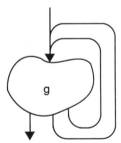

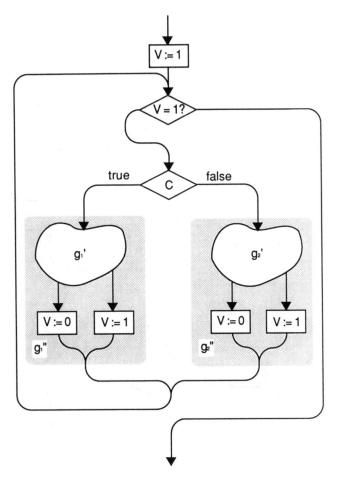

FIGURE 10.6 Derived flowgraph in Case 3.2.

The conversion here is simple. We transform G into:

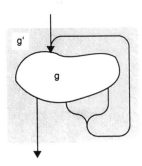

and then apply the transformation process to g'.

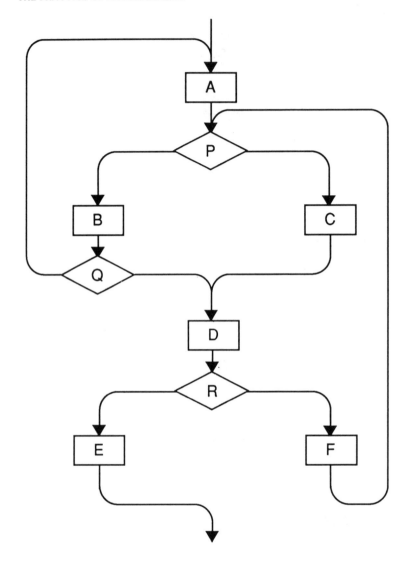

FIGURE 10.7 Example flowgraph for transformation.

This completes our informal proof. As an illustration of the three transformations of Case 3, which are the most complicated to understand, consider the flowgraph shown in Figure 10.7.

The three figures, Figures 10.8, 10.9 and 10.10, show the three transformations that lead to a flowchart that is a D-structure equivalent of the original flowchart.

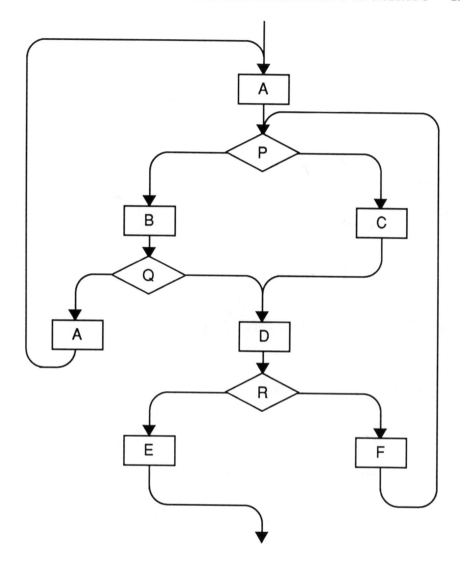

FIGURE 10.8 First tranformation: application of Case 3.1.

10.4.3 Consequences of the theorem

The major consequence of the theorem is that it is possible to write *any* proper sequential program as a D-structure. The definition of proper program excludes only those that contain infinite loops or unreachable instructions. The theorem *guarantees* that any process that can be programmed as a proper program can be programmed using only

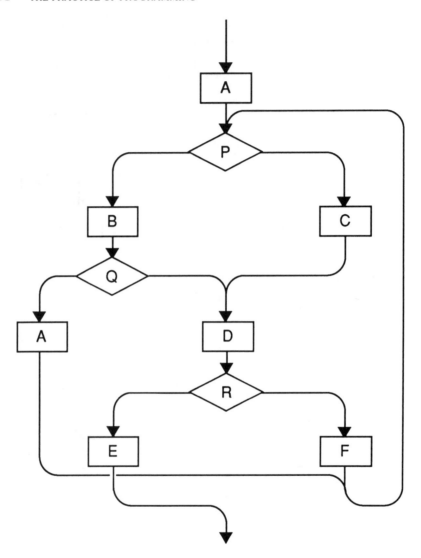

FIGURE 10.9 Second transformation: application of Case 3.3.

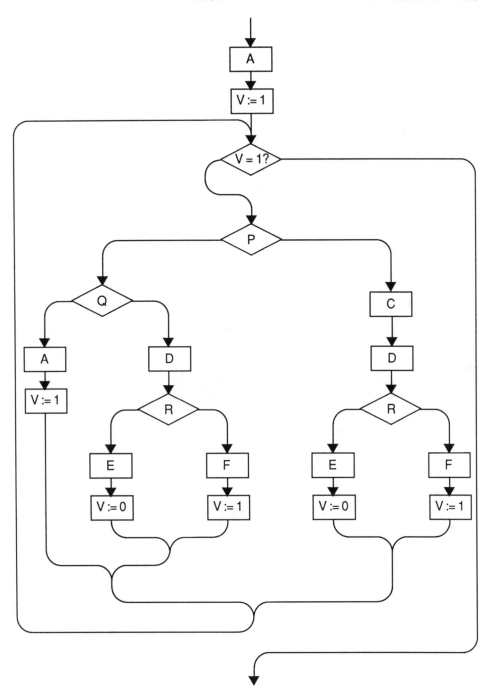

FIGURE 10.10 Third transformation: application of Case 3.1

D-structures. If you stick to using only D-structures from the very start, you are sure to have enough ammunition to write your program. In particular, if your programming language includes only the following control statements:

1. Sequences of one or more statements.

2. Conditional statements of the form

```
IF condition THEN
    statement...
ELSE
    statement...
END
```
or
```
IF condition THEN
    statement...
END
```

3. Loops of the form
```
WHILE condition DO
    statement...
END
```

or their equivalent, then this is all that you need, at least theoretically. We will discuss other possible control flow statements in the next section.

Of lesser importance is the method by which the theorem is proved. It is a proof by construction. We take an arbitrary flowgraph and transform it into a sequence of equivalent flowgraphs according to the rules until we reach an equivalent D-structure. From the example demonstrated at the end of the previous sub-section, it should be clear that converting a program using the method used in the proof of the theorem does not always result in a clearer or more efficient program. In *many* instances, the program converted in this way will be less efficient and far less clear. The important point is that restructuring a poorly designed algorithm in a mechanical way will probably not improve it. As Dijkstra (1968a) puts it:

> The exercise to translate an arbitrary flow diagram more or less mechanically into a jumpless one, however, is not to be recommended. Then the resulting flow diagram cannot be expected to be more transparent than the original one.

Applying the technique to the StringSort program introduced in Chapter 9 does not yield a program that describes the process any more clearly than the original. The only way to restructure a poorly written program is to build a mental image of the process and write a completely new version of the program with clarity of expression in mind. *There is no substitute for understanding!* A discussion of practical techniques for restructuring an unreadable program is contained in Chapter 14.

10.5 DISCUSSION OF OTHER CONTROL STRUCTURES

The D-structures form only three basic control structures. Even though the Böhm and Jacopini theorem shows them to be theoretically sufficient, there are many other structures offered in various languages. In this section some of these are discussed.

10.5.1 Other single-entry, single-exit structures

A single-entry, single-exit control structure is such that if control reaches the entry point, it is bound to reach the exit. For example, in a structure of the form

```
IF condition THEN
    statement-1
    statement-2
    statement-3
END
```

our definition excludes the use of any statement, say statement-2, that causes an explicit branch out of the if–then statement. In this section we discuss some other single-entry, single-exit statements and also other control constructs.

Beyond the if–then–else, while–do, and repeat–until, there are other single-entry, single-exit control structures that help in the clear expression of some algorithms. These structures are available in some programming languages. An important single-entry, single-exit structure found in many languages is the case or select statement. It is a form of conditional statement where the actions to be carried out depend upon the value of an expression given at the head of the statement. In a simple form, it has a structure of the form

```
CASE expression OF
    WHEN value-1 => statement...
    WHEN value-2 => statement...
    WHEN value-3 => statement...
        . . .
    WHEN value-n => statement...
END
```

Here, the expression following CASE is evaluated and its value is compared with the values that follow the WHEN clauses. When a match is found, the corresponding sequence of statements is executed. Following that, control is transferred to the statement immediately after the END.

There are many variants of this kind of statement. One of the most useful contains an OTHERWISE option to cover any values not explicitly given in WHEN clauses. Another variant has no expression after the CASE but has a Boolean expression after each WHEN. These expressions are then evaluated and the first to evaluate to TRUE leads to the execution of the corresponding sequence of statements and transfer to the statement after the END.

For iteration structures, there are numerous useful forms. One of them is a variant of the *while loop* where, instead of testing the termination condition before each iteration, it is tested after the body of the loop has been executed. Thus, at least one iteration of the loop is guaranteed. This iteration structure is generally called an *until loop*. Another useful form is the *for loop*, where a number of iterations of a loop is specified before starting iteration and, at each iteration, a variable, called the *control variable*, is assigned one of a sequence of values.

All these structures illustrate a general point. Even within the basic framework of single-entry, single-exit forms it is possible to provide considerable expressive power.

10.5.2 Exit and goto statements

It is often stated that, while the single-entry, single-exit constructs are theoretically adequate for writing programs, in practice they are not sufficient. The typical case cited in support of this statement arises when it is 'necessary' to exit from the middle of a loop.

Loops with exits in the middle can be easily coded with a GOTO statement, which unconditionally transfers control to a specified labeled statement. Often there are few restrictions on the placement of the labeled target statement. The Algol 60 version of StringSort gives ample examples of the use of this statement. Because the unrestricted use of GOTO statements can lead to badly structured programs and their restricted use for exit from a loop is thought necessary, several languages, for example, Modula-2 and Ada, provide an EXIT statement for this purpose. The EXIT provides a restricted form of the GOTO that can be used only to terminate loops. Execution of the EXIT statement transfers control unconditionally to the statement following the loop.

Some years ago, Henry Ledgard and I performed an experiment (Marcotty and Ledgard 1986). We took a problem that seemed to require exits from the middle of loops and investigated the clarity that an EXIT statement would bring to the solution of the problem. In order to avoid the bias that converting one form to another would introduce, I wrote a solution using only single-entry, single-exit constructs and Ledgard wrote a solution that made use of the EXIT. When we compared the clarity of the results, we found that the EXIT provided no improvement in clarity. Since then, I have found no problems that might be helped with the use of an EXIT statement.

A different kind of exit from a loop can be obtained with a RETURN statement, which is used to return to the point of invocation of a procedure or function. This too complicates the understandability of the code and gives procedures with multiple exits.

10.5.3 Why the GOTO statement causes trouble

In recent years, there has been a great deal of discussion of the GOTO statement. Although not the first to speak against its use, Dijkstra (1968a) provided the first recognized argument against it. He said:

For a number of years I have been familiar with the observation that the quality of programmers is a decreasing function of the density of **go to** statements in the programs they produce . . . The **go to** statement as it stands is just too primitive; it is too much an invitation to make a mess of one's program.

Reaction was strong. Many people appeared to have misunderstood what Dijkstra was saying. He was not arguing for a general restriction on transfers of control but rather against the use of undisciplined transfers of control. For a considerable period following Dijkstra's letter, debate in the journals was more notable for heat than light.

One tongue-in-cheek suggestion in Clark (1973) was that the GOTO statement could be eliminated in favor of a COME FROM statement! Although intended as whimsy, such a statement might be useful with some help from a compiler, just as a subroutine call statement helps. If the programmer writes CALL Fred the compiler should check that the subroutine Fred has been defined. Similarly, a compiler that matches GOTO and COME FROM statements could check that they match properly. Thus, programmers would eventually get used to writing

```
        .  .  .
Joe:   GOTO Fred
        .  .  .
Fred:  COME FROM Joe
        .  .  .
```

Indeed, the compiler, given the GOTO Fred, could insert the COME FROM Joe thus making the program slightly clearer than the programmer had made it. However, the program would still be a rat's nest, albeit a slightly better decorated one. No matter how much the nest aspires to *Home and Garden* standards, it is forever a rat's nest and no compiler can make it intelligible.

After a while, the public clamor died down and it seemed that the consensus agreed with Dijkstra. However, debate about the GOTO statement seems interminable. Almost twenty years after Dijkstra (1968a) there appeared a very strongly worded article (Rubin 1987) in favour of the GOTO, which raised the whole matter again.

At any point in a computation, there is a particular value associated with each of the program's variables. The set of these values constitutes the *computation state* at that point in the program. In a program that contains GOTO statements like:

```
       .  .  .
L1:  GOTO LA
       .  .  .
L2:  GOTO LA
       .  .  .
LA:  .  .  .
       .  .  .
L3:  GOTO LA
       .  .  .
```

when control is transferred to the statement labeled LA, the computation state will depend upon whether control came from the textually preceding statement or one of the statements labeled L1, L2, or L3. To understand the program, the programmer must be aware of all the possible states and therefore must be able to keep in mind the state at each GOTO statement. Thus, it is not so much a GOTO problem as a COME FROM problem and Clark (1973) was right!

Understanding a program involves the mental conversion from the static form of the text to the dynamic form of execution. The greater the difference between the two forms, the harder it is to make this mental leap. Programs that contain GOTO statements are likely to have dynamic forms that are very different from their static forms. This is the real problem with GOTO statements.

This problem of mental conversion from static to dynamic forms is much simpler with the D-structures because they are closer together. Of these restricted structures, the loop is the most difficult to understand. This is why we make more errors with loops than with the other constructs. The problem is that we do not always know how many times the loop will be traversed. The idea of the *loop invariant* introduced in Chapter 7 helps with this. However, it is always important to know the conditions under which the loop will terminate. The trouble with the EXIT statement is that the condition for termination is not always clear. With a construct of the form

```
LOOP
    . . .
    IF condition THEN
        EXIT;
    END;
    . . .
END;
```

the reader has to examine the entrails of the loop to find the actual termination condition, which might be buried much more deeply than is shown here. This turns program reading into a form of divination by the study of entrails, as was common in Roman times. The problem is compounded if the actual loop is also controlled by a WHILE condition DO so that arrival at the statement following the loop can be either due to the condition on the WHILE or the condition controlling the buried EXIT. As we saw in Chapter 7, exits from the middle of loops can considerably complicate the assertions that can be made about the program.

An iterative construct is a control abstraction. If the body of the loop has to be examined closely to find the conditions for termination, the reader is having to cross levels of abstraction. The use of the EXIT statement increases the difficulty in understanding a program and therefore should be avoided.

10.5.4 The question of efficiency

The most common reason given for writing programs in an unclear fashion is that 'it was done for efficiency'. Knuth (1974) said that 'Sometimes it is necessary to exit from several levels . . . and the most graceful way to do this is a direct approach via the goto or its equivalent.' I am sure that the author of StringSort felt that his use of the GOTO was in the interests of efficiency. When I reprogrammed StringSort as a structured program, I measured the change in execution time. I made the comparison by transliterating the original Algol 60 program into PL/I and writing the structured version also in PL/I. I wrote the structured version as a single procedure, to match the Algol 60 version. The first comparison showed that the structured version was 25 per cent faster and took slightly more storage, 4 bytes in 1000! I also made the comparison on a completely different computer and compiler; this time the structured version ran three times faster than the unstructured version. While this is a specific case and no generalizations can be made, the efficiency question is not decided. Only when it can be shown that a loop is executed millions of times is there any justification for sacrificing clarity for efficiency. For such a demonstration, a 'profiling tool' is required. This will count the number of times each statement is executed.

There is a need for efficiency but, in a large program, efficiency obtained by the clever use of control structures is a tiny fraction of the overall cost. In some circumstances, certain levels of performance must be achieved for the program to attain compliance to the requirements. However, it is rare that the only way of achieving the required level of performance *requires* lack of clarity.

No optimizing compiler can be expected to perform *macro-efficient* optimizations, such as converting a linear search into a binary one. Redundant tests and repeated actions are typical of the *micro-efficient* conditions that can be eliminated by good optimizing compilers. It is this type of optimization that is the province of the compiler and not that of the programmer, who should be primarily interested in developing *clear* macro-efficient programs. Indeed, general optimization can often be done automatically with greater effect when the program is built from D-structures. This is because the analysis that must be performed by the compiler is much easier for programs built of D-structures.

The code improvement phase (generally called *optimization*, though there is no idea that optimality of code is achievable) makes a careful analysis of the flow of data between the statements of the program. Such analysis is based entirely on the *possible* flow of control as specified by the program. There is no access to the programmer's knowledge about the interactions of the values of the data, for example, if A is positive then B must also be positive. Thus anything in the program that makes the analysis more difficult and opens more possibilities is likely to make the code improvement less effective. While a programmer may be able to achieve some local small improvements through the use of unstructured forms, it is unlikely that consistently good code can be written that will match that of a good compiler. To summarize, we should follow Jackson's (1975) rules on optimization, the first of which was based on *Punch*'s (1845) advice to persons about to marry:

Rule 1. Don't do it.
Rule 2. (For experts only.) Don't do it yet – that is, not until you have a perfectly clear and unoptimized solution.

Once the program has been written and validated, then is the time to investigate the questions of efficiency. Then, any changes made should only be made on the basis of actual measurement. Our intuition can often be very much at variance with the results obtained. For example Kernighan and Plauger (1978) cite the example of a sort routine that was written so as to take advantage of many conditions that would allow saving of time. They compared this with a simple no-frills interchange sort and discovered that up to 2000 data items, the largest number of items tested, the simple sort ran faster. However, Shell sort, Boothroyd (1963a) at 2000 elements is a factor of nine faster. Time spent in selecting a good algorithm is likely to pay much larger dividends than that spent polishing the implementation of a poor method. Moreover, as pointed out in Stevens (1981), if the development time saved by implementing the simplest solution is applied to optimizing that running solution, the result will always be a faster running program than one where optimization efforts are applied to all parts of the program.

The real problem in improving the efficiency of a large program is finding out where the time is being spent. Don Knuth is of the opinion that in non-I/O-bound programs, less than 4 per cent of a program usually accounts for more than half the running time. In order to find the 4 per cent, it is impossible to rely on guesswork and special software tools must be used.

Three important rules are given by Kernighan and Plauger (1978):

- Make it right before you make it faster.
- Make it clear before you make it faster.
- Keep it simple to make it faster.

10.6 PROPER USE OF PROGRAMMING LANGUAGE

Although there are many ways in which to express an algorithm, only a few will be clear to the reader. A first step in programming clearly is to have a thorough mastery of the language so that the proper choice of statement can be made for each purpose. However, mastery of the language should not be confused with the use of arcane expressions. It is much more important to use the language to make the algorithm clear than it is to display virtuosity.

There is another aspect of proper use of the programming language; this one does not stem from vanity but from sloppy thinking. Do not allow the language to mislead the reader. Consider the following, abstracted from a much larger program:

```
  . . .
FOR II := 1 TO 999999 BY 1 DO
     . . .
END;
  . . .
```

When I saw this, I immediately thought that 999999 might be the programmer's synonym for infinity and that the loop had an exit buried inside it. Sure enough, the loop really looked like

```
. . .
FOR II := 1 TO 999999 BY 1 DO
   . . .
   IF EOF THEN
       EXIT;
   END;
   READLN(InFile, NextLine);
   . . .
END;
. . .
```

Worse than that, the variable II was not referenced anywhere inside the loop and the statement following the loop shown, to which the EXIT transferred control, was

```
FOR II := 1 TO 20 BY 1 DO
```

In other words, the use of the variable in the FOR statement was completely misleading and was part of the programmer's device for writing an infinite loop. This shows a lack of knowledge of the programming language on the part of the author.

I know that the reader would not do anything so flagrantly stupid as this example shows, but there are programmers out there who do perpetrate horrors like this.

If the programmer really wanted to express this operation through an infinite loop terminated by an EXIT in the middle, then it should have been written

```
. . .
LOOP
   . . .
   IF EOF THEN
       EXIT;
   END;
   READLN(InFile, NextLine);
   . . .
END;
. . .
```

It is then clear to the reader that this is an infinite loop that will be terminated at some interior point by an EXIT statement. The reader can then search for it instead of going off on a wild-goose chase searching for the II counter mare's nest, if the reader will pardon the metaphor type mismatch.

The reason for the loop's termination should be clear from its header statement and should not have to be searched for. A better construct would have been

```
. . .
WHILE(NOT EOF) DO
   READLN(InFile, NextLine);
   . . .
END;
. . .
```

It is then clear to the reader that this loop will terminate when the end of file has been reached.

An infinite loop should only be used in circumstances where it will make the program clearer. When I see an infinite loop in a program, I read it as exactly that, a loop that will never terminate. Some interactive programs are designed in this way, after having processed their last input, they go into an infinite loop waiting for the next input to cause an interrupt that will take them out of the loop. This is a loop with an even more mysterious termination than the one just described. There is nothing explicit inside the loop to show that an interrupt will come along to stop its apparently interminable thumb twiddling. Far easier to understand is a loop whose termination condition announces clearly that the loop will continue until the next input arrives. The asynchronous interrupt routine that receives the next input item should put it on a queue and then terminate. The loop that is waiting for the next input takes it off the queue, terminates and continues with the program.

10.7 CLARITY OF EXPOSITION

Unity, continuity, and proper use of the programming language do not guarantee a clear readable program though they help. Attention must be paid to details. Expository programming requires attention down to the detailed construction of the statements. In this section, some of these details are discussed.

10.7.1 The use of comments

In Section 10.1, we discussed the need for header comments. These are only one of two types of comments that should appear in programs, the others are inline comments – comments that are included with the actual source code to assist the reader in understanding the program. Inline comments are almost in the nature of footnotes to the actual text. In this sub-section, we discuss inline comments.

The management of one organization decided that comments were essential to program readability and decreed that some specified proportion of every program was to consist of comments. Since they did not have the time and, in that organization, it was beneath the status of a manager to read code, they obtained a program that automatically analyzed programs for comments. This program rejected those programs that did not have the proper comment content. Needless to say, it was not long before the programmers constructed a program that would insert the requisite amount of comment-like text into their programs. The net effect was a total reduction in the readability of the programs produced by that department.

It is very difficult to describe what the proper amount of comments should be. In Chapter 9 there is discussion of the introductory comments for a procedure. These serve to set the context for the reader to understand the executable part of the text. It is quite proper for these comments to be extensive if they will help the reader make the transition from the problem to the solution described by the program. Since they are placed at the beginning of the procedure, they do not get in the way of reading the executable statements. How much commentary should be included in this part of the program? As little as possible! The art of writing clear programs is to produce code that speaks for itself. Ideally, there should be no need for additional explanation. In fact, every time the programmer feels the need to add a comment, the question 'How could the code be made clearer so that the comment would be unnecessary?' should be asked.

Comments that merely repeat the information contained in the programming language statements are worse than useless as in the trite example:

```
Temp      := Array[I];   (* Copy Array[I] into Temp     *)
Array[I] := Array[J];   (* Copy Array[J] into Array[I] *)
Array[J] := Temp;       (* Copy Temp into Array[J]      *)
```

and provide no useful information. The programmer should not insult the reader by implying ignorance of the programming language. In addition to annoying the reader, they obscure by adding needless complexity.

Sometimes it is useful to have a single line comment at the beginning of a paragraph. This is in the nature of a high-level comment describing what the paragraph does. If it were thought necessary to provide a comment for the above code fragment then

```
(* Interchange contents of Array[I] and Array[J] *)
Temp      := Array[I];
Array[I] := Array[J];
Array[J] := Temp;
```

would be better. If the interface to the paragraph is suitable, it might be a good plan to convert the whole paragraph into a procedure and give it a name that is a compression of the comment that was planned. The restructured version of StringSort shown in Chapter 9 used this technique. Procedure names like SetTargetLimits, SetIndexes, and BuildSequencesInTargetArea were derived using this recommendation.

Where comments are included in the body of the paragraph itself, there is a danger of having too many comments – 'danger' for the following reasons:

- They get in the way of reading the program text, which is the important part of the program.
- By the time the maintenance programmer has understood enough of the program in order to modify it, the comments will have become superfluous and essentially invisible. There is thus a great danger that they will not be changed to match the modifications to the program and will become misleading, which adds negative information. Sometimes, the function of an integrand is changed so that its name no longer represents it correctly. If the function is changed, then it is really a *different* integrand, and should be given a new name, added to the libraries according to local procedures, and generally treated as a different integrand from the original.

• If the programmer concentrates too much on producing comments, there is a possibility that the comments might be correct and the program incorrect. It is more important to work on the correctness of the integrand.

Sometimes it is useful to add comments in the form of assertions. For example, in Section 7.3 we showed the example code fragment

```
{(Numerator ≥ 0) ∧ (Divisor > 0)}
    Remainder := Numerator;
    Quotient  := 0;
    WHILE (Remainder >= Divisor) DO
        Remainder := Remainder - Divisor;
        Quotient  := Quotient + 1
    END;
{(Remainder ≥ 0) ∧ (Remainder < Divisor) ∧
        (Numerator = Divisor × Quotient + Remainder)}
```

Comments of this type can be very useful to the reader as they give indications of tests that might be made during verification after a modification. However, there is still the danger that the assertions will not be changed as the program is changed and, unless one has access to a compiler that will generate verification code from such assertions, they too can be misleading.

10.7.2 Choice of identifiers

A program is an allegory. That is to say, a figurative representation conveying a meaning *other* than the literal. The meaning conveyed by the program is the real-world process that it is modeling. Its literal meaning is the electronic manipulation of bits. The reader of an allegory must understand the correspondence between the participants in the literal story and those in the non-literal meaning. John Bunyan's (1678) *Pilgrim's Progress* provides one of the best known examples of the allegory. The names in *Pilgrim's Progress* make it easy for the reader to make the inference. With names like Christian, Giant Despair, Mr Malice, Mr Enmity, Doubting Castle, and the Slough of Despond, it is easy to infer the non-literal meaning. The identifiers used for data items in a program should make it just as easy for the reader.

> It is more important for the reader to be able to infer the correspondence from the identifier to the real world equivalent than from the real world object or process to the identifier.

As a coarse example, compare the understandability of

```
X1 := X2 * X3  +  X4 * X5;
X6 := X7 * X1;
X8 := X9 * X1;
X  := X1 - X6 - X8;
```

with

```
GrossPay             := Wage * Hours  +  OvertimeWage * ExtraHours;
Tax                  := TaxRate * GrossPay;
PensionContribution  := ContributionRate * GrossPay;
NetPay               := GrossPay - Tax - PensionContribution;
```

Electronically, the two are exactly equivalent. Even if the first example had declarations like

```
VAR
    X1: INTEGER; (* Gross pay                                            *)
    X2: INTEGER; (* Wage per hour worked                                 *)
    X3: INTEGER; (* Number of hours worked during week                  *)
    X4: INTEGER; (* Wage per hour of overtime                           *)
    X5: INTEGER; (* Number of hours of overtime worked during week      *)
    X6: INTEGER; (* Income tax to be withheld                           *)
    X7: INTEGER; (* Income tax rate * 100 to make integer               *)
    X8: INTEGER; (* Employee's contribution to pension                  *)
    X9: INTEGER; (* Pension contribution rate * 100 to make integer     *)
    X:  INTEGER; (* Employee's net pay after tax and pension deductions *)
```

which actually define the values represented by the identifiers more fully than the mnemonic names, it still would not have been an easy program to read.

Choosing names is a serious business. It is so important that it was the first task given to Adam in the Garden of Eden. The conscientious expository programmer will give careful thought to the choice of each identifier. It is helpful to choose an appropriate part of speech for identifiers so that the program statements will read naturally. Identifiers for data objects will naturally be nouns, those for procedures verbs, and conditions will often be adjectives or participles.

```
IF TableNotFull THEN
    AddNewEntry(NextItem);
ELSE
    Terminating := TRUE;
END;
```

A good test to apply when checking for readability is to read the program aloud. If it sounds reasonable, there is a good chance that a reader will be able to understand and correct it easily. This test will also help to ensure that the identifiers evoke the proper real-world object in the reader's mind. Table 10.1, based on one contained in Ledgard (1987), shows some examples of the association from identifier to real-world object. Keller (1990) also provides some useful guidelines.

Often, the proper choice of an identifier can obviate the need for an introductory comment on a paragraph. The choice of better names in the value interchanging code sequence can make its meaning clear without the use of a comment.

TABLE 10.1 Whose name is it?

Temp	This is an anonymous variable. The only thing that its name implies is that its useful life is likely to be short. Surely, whatever value is to be stored in it will have some relevance in the real world. Names like TempTaxID or TempXCoord would have given the reader an indication of what kind of value would be stored. To use the general-purpose name Temp is to invite its use for several different kinds of values and to risk overwriting one value prematurely with another. Of course, the inference that the name refers to a temporary value may be wrong and it really refers to a temperature in which case, it requires additional qualification to show what kind of temperature it represents, for example, BodyTemp or OilTemp.
Flag	The reader might infer that a BOOLEAN value was represented but would be able to deduce nothing about the meaning of that value. The variable is, so to speak, a flag without a country. The setting of the flag must signify something and this should be implied by its name, for instance, EndOfData, NameFound, Overflow, or FileOpen. Note that a name such as FileStatus is less helpful since the reader must remember whether the value TRUE means that the file is open or closed.
A, B, C, U, T	These are all satisfactory names in a context where their meaning can be assumed to be part of formulae that are *well known* by *all* readers, for example, in a program that is evaluating the roots of a quadratic equation using the formula $(-b \pm \sqrt{b^2 - 4ac})/2a$ or the distance travelled from the formula $ut + \frac{1}{2}at^2$. Outside contexts like these, names must be much more evocative of their meaning.
I, J	These are often used as the names for general-purpose counters or array indexes. The problem is that they are *general purpose* and add to the reader's mental burden in remembering their current use.

```
TempForSwapping       := Array[HighValueIndex];
Array[HighValueIndex] := Array[LowValueIndex];
Array[LowValueIndex ] := TempForSwapping;
```

Figure 10.11 shows an example, outside the Running Example, of a small non-trivial procedure based on an example treated in Gries (1976). The aim has been to choose identifiers that will help in understanding the procedure and convincing the reader that it is correct. Gries' version of the example is shown in Figure 10.12 and shows how he annotates his procedure with assertions that show its correctness. While these serve his purpose of demonstrating the derivation of correctness proofs in most languages, they do not form part of the executable program and therefore may or may not match. Of course, there is no guarantee that the names chosen by the programmer match the meaning of the variables either!

It is important that names should be psychologically 'distant', that is, it should not be easy to confuse two names. For example, the names BKRPNT and BRKPNT are so close as to be indistinguishable. The eye sees what it wants or expects to see. Identifiers must not be confused with each other and must be easily distinguished. The identifiers Epsilon and Upsilon are too close for safety, while Root and Discriminant are unlikely to be confused.

When I was writing Chapter 9, I spent some time choosing the two identifiers to represent the two diagonals in the Eight Queens problem. I eventually decided on

```
NEtoSWdiagIsSafe: ARRAY[2..16] OF BOOLEAN;
SEtoNWdiagIsSafe: ARRAY[-7..7] OF BOOLEAN;
```

```
PROCEDURE Justify(LineNumber, NumberOfWords, NumberOfBlanks: INTEGER;
                  VAR WordStartCols: ARRAY[1 : NumberOfWords] OF INTEGER);
(* This procedure inserts extra blanks between words on a line so that the last character  *)
(* of the last word appears in the last column of the line. The number of blanks between   *)
(* different pairs of words on a line differs by no more than 1. In order to lessen the     *)
(* impact of extra blanks on the reader, more blanks are inserted toward the right if       *)
(* LineNumber is odd and on the left if LineNumber is even.                                 *)
(*                                                                                          *)
(* Using W[i] to represent word i and B[b] to represent b blanks, the line before           *)
(* justification has the form                                                               *)
(*     W[1] B[1] W[2] B[1] ... B[1] W[NumberOfWords] B[NumberOfBlanks]                       *)
(* where the array element WordStartCols[i] defines the starting column of word i in the    *)
(* line. This procedure adjusts the values of WordStartCols so as to define a line of the   *)
(* form                                                                                     *)
(*     W[1] B[LeftPad+1] W[2] B[LeftPad+1] ...                                              *)
(*             B[LeftPad+1]  W[LeftRightBoundary] B[RightPad+1] ...          *)
(*                                             B[RightPad+1] Word[NumberOfWords]   *)

    VAR SmallerPad:        INTEGER;
        NumberOfGaps:      INTEGER;
        RemainingBlanks:   INTEGER;
        LeftRightBoundary: INTEGER;
        LeftPad:           INTEGER;
        RightPad:          INTEGER;
        TotalPad:          INTEGER;
        WordIndex:         INTEGER;
BEGIN
    IF NumberOfWords > 1 THEN
        BEGIN
            NumberOfGaps     := NumberOfWords - 1;
            SmallerPad       := NumberOfBlanks DIV NumberOfGaps;
            RemainingBlanks  := NumberOfBlanks - NumberOfGaps * SmallerPad;
            IF Odd(LineNumber) THEN
                BEGIN
                    LeftPad           := SmallerPad;
                    RightPad          := SmallerPad + 1;
                    LeftRightBoundary := NumberOfGaps - RemainingBlanks + 1;
                END
            ELSE
                BEGIN
                    RightPad          := SmallerPad;
                    LeftPad           := SmallerPad + 1;
                    LeftRightBoundary := RemainingBlanks + 1;
                END;
            TotalPad  := LeftPad;
            WordIndex := 2;
            WHILE WordIndex < LeftRightBoundary DO
                BEGIN
                    WordStartCols[WordIndex] := WordStartCols[WordIndex] + TotalPad;
                    TotalPad                 := TotalPad + LeftPad;
                    WordIndex                := WordIndex + 1;
                END;
            WHILE WordIndex < NumberOfWords DO
                BEGIN
                    WordStartCols[WordIndex] := WordStartCols[WordIndex] + TotalPad;
                    TotalPad                 := TotalPad + RightPad;
                    WordIndex                := WordIndex + 1;
                END;
        END;
END;
```

FIGURE 10.11 Example based on Gries (1976).

procedure justify (z, n, s: integer; var b: array [*] of integer);
{input:

> z: a line number;
> n: the number of words on the line;
> $s \geq 0$: the number of blanks at the end of the line;
> $b[i] = Bi$: the column number where word i begins on line, $1 \leq i \leq n$.
> Using Wi to represent word i and $[e]$ to represent e blanks, the
> line has the form
> > $W1$ [1] $W2$ [1] $\cdots$ [1] Wn [s]

output: if $n \leq 1$, no change is made—$b[il = Bi$ for $1 \leq i \leq n$.

> if $n > 1$, the column numbers $b[i]$ are changed to right-justify the
> line. This means that the line will look like
> > $W1$ [p +1] $W2[p+1]$ $\cdots$ [p+1] Wt [q+1] $\cdots$ [q +1] Wn
>
> where p, q and t are defined by
> > A1: $p \geq 0, q \geq 0, 1 \leq t \leq n, s = p \cdot (t - 1) + q \cdot (n - t)$,
> > > (odd(z) and $q = p + 1$) or (even(z) and $p = q + 1$))

Hence, upon exit we have

> A2: $b[i] = Bi + p \cdot (i - 1)$ for $1 \leq i \leq t$,
> > $b[i] = Bi + p \cdot (t - 1) + q \cdot (i - t)$ for $t < i \leq n$.}

var p, q, t, k, incr, ptl: integer;
begin {Loop 1 and 2 below use the invariants $P1$ and $P2$, resp.:

> P1: $1 \leq k \leq t$, incr $= p \cdot (k - 1)$, $ptl = p \cdot (t - 1)$,
> > $b[i] = Bi + p \cdot (i - 1)$ for $1 \leq i \leq k$,
> > $b[i] = Bi$ for $k < i \leq n$.
> P2: $t \leq k \leq n$, incr $= p \cdot (t - 1) + q \cdot (t - 1)$,
> > $b[i] = Bi + p \cdot (i - 1)$ for $1 \leq i \leq k$,
> > $b[i] = Bi + p \cdot (t - 1) + q \cdot (i - t)$ for $t \leq i \leq k$,
> > $b[i] = Bi$ for $k < i \leq n$.}.

> if $n > 1$ then
> > begin {Determine p, q, t, thus establishing $A1$}
> > > if odd(z)
> > > > then begin $p := s$ div $(n - 1)$; $q := p + 1$;
> > > > > $t := n + p (n - 1) - s$ end
> > > > else begin $q := s$ div $(n - 1)$; $p := q + 1$;
> > > > > $t := s - q(n - 1) + 1$ end;
> > > {Determine new $b[1 : t]$, establishing first line of A2.
> > > The loop invariant is $A1$ and $P1$.}
> > > > $k := 1$; incr $:= 0$; $ptl := p*(t - 1)$;
> > > > while incr $\neq ptl$ do
> > > > > begin $k := k + 1$; incr $:=$ incr $+ p$;
> > > > > > $b[k] := b[k] +$ incr   end;
> > > {Determine new $b[t + 1 : n]$, establishing A2.
> > > The loop invariant is $A1$ and $P2$.}
> > > > $k := t$; {Note: last loop establishes incr $= p \cdot (t - 1)$}
> > > > while $k \neq n$ do
> > > > > begin $k := k + 1$; incr $:=$ incr $+ q$;
> > > > > > $b[k] := b[k] +$ incr   end

> > end

end

FIGURE 10.12 Example as given in Gries (1976). © 1976. I.E.E.E., reprinted with permission.

though I was not entirely satisfied with the distance between the two. The other alternatives that I tried such as DownLeftDiagIsSafe and UpLeftDiagIsSafe did not seem much better.

Occasionally, usually due to the strange requirements of operating systems and languages, identifiers are severely restricted in length and must be abbreviated. If this is necessary, the following rules, based in part on Schneiderman (1986), are suggested:

1. Abbreviate every significant word in a name, up to a maximum of three or four words.
2. The initial letters of the words must be present. If the first letter is a vowel it may or may not be retained.
3. As the Semitic languages discovered, consonants are more important than vowels. H, Y, and W may or may not be considered as vowels.
4. The beginning of a word is more important than its end.

with these principles in mind, an algorithm for abbreviating is:

1. Within a word, delete vowels successively from the right end of the word, until all vowels except an initial vowel have been deleted or the word has been reduced to the required size.
2. If all vowels have been deleted and the word is still too long, the process is repeated, deleting consonants until the required length is obtained.

The following are some examples, assuming a length limit of six, of this process:

```
ReadTable   becomes RedTbl
WriteTable  becomes WrtTbl
MaxValues   becomes MaxVls
Direction   becomes Dirctn
```

Sometimes it is helpful to use standard abbreviations from other contexts: familiar abbreviations such as Qty for Quantity, No for Number, or Ptr for Pointer. Schneider (1984) finds that truncation is the most effective mechanism overall, but when conflicting abbreviations occur, vowel dropping makes decoding easier than truncation. These rules should not be followed blindly; the programmer must always keep in mind that it is meaning that is being communicated. Therefore, use other tricks as they come to mind. I would abbreviate SEtoNWdiagIsSafe by SEupOK. This has reasonable distance from its partner NEdnOK.

10.7.3 Magic numbers

Constants are required at various places in a program. If they are written with their literal denotation it makes the program more difficult to understand. One number looks very much like another and it is impossible to make the inference back to the real world equivalent. Consider

```
IF CursorPosition <= 119 THEN
```

What is this mysterious 119? The statement

```
IF CursorPosition <= (LineLength - 1) THEN
```

makes it a lot clearer. If the statement had been written

```
IF CursorPosition <= (120 - 1) THEN
```

it might have been clearer. The reader might have remembered a comment about the line length being 120 characters. But then, what programmer can resist doing the arithmetic (120 − 1) for the compiler? The use of the declaration

```
CONST
    LineLength = 120;
```

avoids this temptation and improves the clarity of the program. Even more importantly, it has the advantage of making the program more easily modified. The values of constants like LineLength in programs are very likely to change as the program evolves. While it would be possible to go through the program mechanically and change all occurrences of 120 to a new value, though making sure that there are no clashes with other uses of 120 is difficult, there is no way of finding the 119 and changing that appropriately.

As a further improvement, it is helpful to adopt a convention like prefixing all names of constants with Const so that it is clear that ConstLineLength is not the name of a variable.

10.7.4 Arithmetic expressions

Arithmetic expressions should be simple and should not assume that the reader has perfect knowledge of the language's rules of operator precedence. The operator precedence rules for Modula-2 are:

1st priority:	(Highest)	NOT
2nd priority:		*, /, DIV, MOD, AND
3rd priority:		+, −, OR
4th priority:	(Lowest)	=, #, <, >, >=, <=, <>

Operations of highest precedence are evaluated first; operations of equal precedence are evaluated from left to right. Operations within parentheses are of the highest priority and are evaluated first.

Even given this information, it is not easy to understand

```
IF B1 = B2 OR B3 # B4 THEN
```

It will be a lot more difficult to understand if the precedence rules are not handy. In fact, my experience is that most programmers would intuitively expect the branch to take place if either B1 = B2 or B3 # B4. In fact, since OR has greater precedence than either = or #, first B2 and B3 are ORed together then the result of that is compared for equality with B1 and the result of that is compared for inequality with B4. Parentheses should be added to improve the clarity and to avoid any potential ambiguity. I suspect that the programmer probably meant

```
IF (B1 = B2) OR (B3 # B4) THEN
```

Now, with the added parentheses, there is no doubt what was meant. If what the precedence rules took the expression to mean was actually intended, then it should have been parenthesized accordingly to show the reader that this strange sequence of operations was no accident.

```
IF (B1 = (B2 OR B3)) # B4 THEN
```

The temptation to put everything in one big expression should be avoided. The penalty of declaring and using temporary storage for partial results is not large; in fact, with many modern compilers it may be nothing because of the sophisticated data-flow analysis that is performed during code generation. This is really a question of writing with the comfort of the reader rather than the comfort of the writer in mind. The cleverness of compressing everything into one line soon palls.

10.7.5 Aphorisms to live by

In Section 1.7, I quoted some aphorisms taken from Strunk and White's (1979) manual on the writing of clear prose and showed that there are similar versions that applied to expository programming. The following is a complete list of Strunk and White's rules, in alphabetical order, compared with their 'equivalent' in programming, most of which are taken from Kernighan and Plauger (1978):

A participle phrase at the beginning of a sentence must refer to the grammatical subject	Initialize all variables near their first use
Avoid a succession of loose sentences	Use the fundamental control flow constructs
Avoid fancy words	Choose variable names that will not be confused
Avoid foreign languages	Avoid implementation dependent constructs
Avoid the use of qualifiers	Avoid long chains of pointers in a single reference
Be clear	Write clearly; do not be too clever
Choose a suitable design and hold to it	Make your programs read from top to bottom
Do not affect a breezy manner	Program defensively
Do not break sentences in two	Do not diddle code to make it faster – find a better algorithm

Do not construct awkward adverbs	Avoid expressions with side effects
Do not explain too much	Let the compiler do the simple optimizations
Do not inject opinion	Let the machine do the work
Do not join independent clauses by a comma	Each integrand should do one thing well
Do not overstate	Do not overcomment
Do not overwrite	Do not comment bad code – rewrite it
Do not take shortcuts at the cost of clarity	Write clearly – do not sacrifice clarity for 'efficiency'
Do not use dialect unless your ear is good	Make sure comments and code agree
Enclose parenthetic expressions between commas	Parenthesize to avoid ambiguity
Express coordinate ideas in similar form	Avoid unnecessary branches
Form the possessive singular of nouns by adding 's	Make sure special cases are truly special
In summaries, keep to one tense	Document your data layouts
Keep related words together	Follow each decision as closely as possible with its associated action
Make sure the reader knows who is speaking	Make the line easy to read aloud
Make the paragraph the unit of composition	Modularize – use subroutines
Omit needless words	Avoid temporary variables with names like Temp1, . . . etc.
Place a comma before a conjunction introducing an independent clause	Indent to show the logical structure of a program
Place the emphatic words of a sentence at the end	Exit carefully
Place yourself in the background	Build in debugging techniques
Prefer the standard to the offbeat	Use the good features of language; avoid the bad ones
Put statements in positive form	Avoid negative Boolean expressions
Revise and rewrite	Do not stop with your first draft
The number of the subject determines the number of the verb	Watch out for off-by-one errors

Use a colon after an independent clause to introduce a list of particulars, an appositive, an amplification, or an illustrative quotation	Make the program structure match the data structure
Use a dash to set off an abrupt break or interruption and to announce a long appositive or summary	Make the coupling between integrands visible
Use definite specific concrete language	Match names of variables to the quantity they represent
Use figures of speech sparingly	Say what you mean, simply and directly
Use orthodox spelling	Avoid tricks
Use the active voice	Leave loop variables alone
Use the proper case of pronoun	Use intermediate variables to clarify expressions
Work from a suitable design	Make sure every module hides something
Write in a way that comes naturally	Choose a data representation that makes the program simple
Write with nouns and verbs	Use abstract data types

10.8 PRESENTATION

At one stage in the development of writing in ancient Greece, a style of writing where alternate lines went in opposite directions was adopted. While, in theory, this made more efficient use of the reader's eye movements during reading, in fact, this kind of text was very difficult to understand. Since those days, we have come a long way in developing conventions for presenting text in a readable manner, for example, indenting the first line of a paragraph. One of the early operations in the design of a book is the construction of a style sheet. This style sheet specifies how the text in the book will be laid out so that the reader will find it easy to read and pleasant to the eye. Similar considerations are required in the design of program layout conventions, particularly when there is a group of programmers involved in a single project.

The object of careful layout is much more than pure aesthetics, it is to assist the reader's task by supporting the meaning of the text by its visible display. The term *prettyprinting* is often used but I prefer the term *formatting*. For a thorough discussion of this subject the reader is referred to Baecker and Marcus (1990) and Oman and Cook (1990). The authors describe experiments using a special compiler that takes advantage of the many fonts and styles that are available on moderately priced laser printers to present programs written in the programming language C in the most readable manner.

10.8.1 Formatting conventions

Formatting consists of using blank lines, blank spaces, page breaks, and alignment to enhance readability. Most modern programming languages are *free format*, that is, the programs can be written in almost any format. Several statements can be put on a single line or a single statement can be broken at almost any point and continued on another line. Generally, the first rule is to put each statement on a separate line. However, even this rule is not followed universally. In a book that aims to teach programming, I found the following excerpt amid several pages of similarly packed programs:

```
PROCEDURE Record(t: Table; VAR
                 x: ARRAY OF CHAR;
                 n: INTEGER);
 VAR p: TreePtr; q: ListPtr; i: CARDINAL;
BEGIN i := 0;
 REPEAT id[i] := x[i];i:=i+1
 UNTIL(id[i-1] = " ")OR(i=WordLength);
 p:=Search(t);
 IF p = NIL THEN overflow:=2 ELSE NEW(q);
  IF q = NIL THEN overflow:=3 ELSE
   q^.num:=n;q^.next:=p^.first;p^.first:= q
  END
 END
END Record;
```

I assume that the publisher typeset the program and the author did not have time to check the formatting very carefully. I think the program would have been easier to read if it had been written

```
PROCEDURE Record(    t: Table;
                 VAR x: ARRAY OF CHAR;
                     n: INTEGER);
    VAR
        p: TreePtr;
        q: ListPtr;
        i: CARDINAL;
    BEGIN
        i := 0;
        REPEAT
            id[i] := x[i];
            i     := i + 1
        UNTIL (id[i-1] = " ") OR (i = WordLength);
```

```
   p := Search(t);
   IF p = NIL THEN
      overflow:=2
   ELSE
      NEW(q);
      IF q = NIL THEN
         overflow:=3
      ELSE
         q^.num   := n;
         q^.next  := p^.first;
         p^.first := q
      END
   END
END Record;
```

The difference between the two forms is just white space. Better choice of identifiers would have further improved the program's clarity. The rules of indenting are to some degree subjective. Much time can be spent by a team in debating the fine points of indentation. It is better to choose a set of rules set by somebody outside the team, even though they satisfy no member completely. Complaints will subside in a short time and during the grumbling period, it is always easier to blame somebody who is not connected with the team.

I prefer to indent for each level by three columns. Some argue that this means that, since the line length gets shorter by three characters each time, the line rapidly becomes too short. I think that, rather than this being a disadvantage, this is an *advantage*. If the line becomes short, it very quickly brings to mind the fact that the program's nesting is becoming deep and therefore the logic is becoming too complicated for easy under-standing. It would therefore greatly help the readability if, when the line becomes short, a new procedure were established, thus constructing a new lower level of abstraction as befits the depth of nesting.

I find it helps to line similar items in columns. The eye moves over columns and can spot anomalies more easily. Compare the following two different forms of test data for a program. The first has been written without any consistent layout and the second is put into columns. Both sets have errors in them, the same number and kind of error in each set. The specific errors are different in the two forms.

```
ClientNumber=1 OldBalance=12.00 Deposit=5.00 Payment=9.00; ClientNumber=2
OldBalance=5.00 Depoist=8.00 Payment=4.00 ClientNumber=3 OldBalance=13.21
Deposit=24.91 Payment=27.82; ClientNumbe=4 OldBalance=568,72 Deposit=163.71
Payment=147.51; ClientNumber=4 OldBalance=62.87 Deposit=27.82 Payment=16.17;
ClientNumber=6 OldBalance=2.13 Deposit=4.17 Payment:1.15; ClientNumber=7
OldBalance=121.34 Deposit=51.72 Payment=5.23; ClientNumber=99;
```

```
ClientNumber = 1  OldBalance =  12.00  Deposi  =   5.00  Payment =   9.00;
ClientNumber = 3  OldBalance =   5.00  Deposit =   8.00  Payment =   4.00;
ClientNumber = 3  OldBalance =  13.21  Deposit =  24.19  Payment =  27.82;
ClientNumber = 4  OldBalance = 568.72  Deposit = 163.71  Payment = 147.51
ClientNumber = 5  OldBalance =  62,87  Deposit =  27.82  Payment =  16.17;
ClientNumber : 6  OldBalnace =   2.13  Deposit =   4.17  Payment =   1.15;
ClientNumber = 7  OldBalance = 121.34  Deposit =  51.72  Payment =   5.23;
ClientNumber = 99;
```

While this is rather an extreme example and it does not help in finding errors in the data values, this type of layout is very helpful in spotting simple errors. This kind of arrangement is useful in sequences of similar statements in a program. I usually arrange assignment statements so that the assignment operator is aligned.

10.8.2 Use of white space

The use of blanks to separate operators and operands and of blank lines to make the individual paragraphs easily distinguished is important. We have already discussed the use of blanks to arrange items in columns, but blanks are also useful in other contexts to let some fresh air and daylight into the statements.

It is common to see programs with lists of items separated by commas. The rules of style for text insist that we put a blank after a comma and this rule should be followed in programs. However, many programmers, and some authors, when they write programs, write lists of items without any blanks at all. For example, from the same author as above:

```
TYPE color = (red,orange,yellow,green,blue,violet);
weekday = (Monday,Tuesday,Wednesday,Thursday,Friday,Saturday,Sunday);
month = (Jan,Feb,Mar,Apr,May,Jun,Jul,Aug,Sep,Oct,Nov,Dec);

IF id[i] <= key[m,i] THEN

Record(T,id,lno)
```

instead of

```
TYPE color   = (red, range, ellow, green, blue, violet);
     weekday = (Monday, Tuesday, Wednesday, Thursday, Friday,
                Saturday, Sunday);
     month   = (Jan, Feb, Mar, Apr, May, Jun, Jul, Aug, Sep, Oct,
                Nov, Dec);

IF id[i] <= key[m, i] THEN

Record(T, id, lno)
```

The author would not think of writing lists without separating blanks between the items in the text of the book, so why do it in programs? The best general rule about spacing is to follow as closely as possible the rules of style used for expository text because, after all, that is what a program is.

Very occasionally, it is possible to have too much space. The programmer should be aware of the physical restrictions of page and screen boundaries. However, if it appears that the segment of program, after adding a proper amount of white space, will exceed the page or screen boundaries, consideration should be given to splitting the program or providing another layer of abstraction.

10.8.3 Splitting statements between lines

Sometimes statements will not fit on a single line; they must be split. Just as we cannot split words arbitrarily, the splitting of statements requires careful thought. Care should be taken to keep phrases together. A line should be split at a carefully chosen point, so that it is clear that it will be continued on the next line. The continuation should be indented additionally so as to indicate that it is a continuation. If it is an expression that must be split, I find that breaking the line at an infix operator provides a link to the next part and shows clearly that the line is to be continued. This is particularly important in a language like Modula-2 where not all statements are terminated by a semi-colon so that it is not obvious when the end of the statement is reached. If it is a procedure invocation that must be split, the obvious place is between arguments.

As a general rule of paragraph layout, keep a paragraph to such a size that it can be contained on a single page or screen of the listing. This is a kindness to the reader – and the reader needs all the kindness available – so that it is not necessary to keep turning over the page or switching to the next screen to see the part of the paragraph that is not visible.

10.8.4 Making details easy to find

A book without an index is very hard to use as a work of reference. While we do not suggest that programs should be written with an index, it is nevertheless important to make the details of a program easy to find. (Some compilers provide a cross-reference listing, which is a kind of index. However, readers often look at the actual source code on a screen rather than the listing provided by the compiler.) An example of this is the ordering of the declarations. The designs of Pascal, Modula-2, and Ada stipulate that the declarations of identifiers shall come at the beginning of the procedure; however, within the confines of this rule, the programmer has considerable choice. Ordering the names of the variables alphabetically, rather than according to data type or arbitrarily, allows the reader to find easily the declaration and thus the type and perhaps some commentary on the variable.

10.9 HOW ARE YOU GOING TO DEBUG THE PROGRAM?

The time to make preparations for debugging the program is right at the beginning of the implementation, while designing the logical organization. If these preparations are left too late, it will be difficult to add the necessary facilities.

A common answer to this question is 'We will use the interactive debugger provided by the operating system.' I believe that this is the wrong decision, it is one that suggests the belief that there will be no real need for debugging. There are several good reasons why this is not an adequate solution:

1. System debuggers tend to provide too localized a view of the execution environment. The temptation is for the programmer to set a breakpoint and when that is reached, metaphorically to pop the head up, look around and, on the basis of the values of a few variables, make a decision on what the problem is. Sometimes, having made the decision, the values of a few variables are 'fixed' and execution is resumed. Decisions made in this atmosphere tend to be superficial and the remedies palliative rather than curative – attacking the symptoms instead of the disease. Gerry Weinberg gave as a motto *Never debug standing up!* His reasoning was that this put too much urgency into the diagnostic process, leading to patches instead of corrections. Perhaps the modern equivalent of this is *Never debug sitting at a shared terminal.*

2. It is very important to be able to have a permanent record of the execution for later examination. System debuggers do not provide this as a general rule. A machine-readable execution trace has the advantage that it can be searched by program, which avoids the programmer getting into a state of data overload by the amount of debugging information presented at the screen of a terminal.

3. When the program goes into production, there is still a need for a facility so that errors detected by the program can be recorded. If the system debugger has been used, it is no longer there when the program becomes productive and there is no mechanism for recording these errors. Usually, what the programmer is left with is a meaningless set of hexadecimal digits from which to infer the cause of the program's death.

10.9.1 Error reporting

Right at the beginning of the implementation, a standard error-reporting system, which can be used both for debugging and for error reporting during production running should be designed. This error reporting system needs at least the following capabilities:

1. Access to a file reserved for error trace and execution log information. Inclusion of a time stamp, giving the time and date of the log entry, is worth while. While such information is only used occasionally, when it is needed it is essential. As a matter of precaution, access to the file should be arranged so that information is not left in a buffer if the program terminates abnormally. This is a vital point since it is the last error report that is the most important. To do this may, depending upon the supporting operating system, mean that the file has to be opened explicitly before an entry is made and closed after writing the trace information. By passing all information for debugging through this one error-reporting procedure, control over its destination is maintained in one place – another example of information hiding.

2. To be able to obtain the name of its caller so that this can be included in the error trace information. The crudest way in which this can be done is to establish the rule that the caller must provide its name as one of the arguments. Far better is to interrogate the

host operating system for this information. Typically, when a program aborts due to some execution error, for example an access violation, the operating system will provide, by way of epitaph, a stack dump showing the invocation chain. However, there are many cases where this information is useful to record during the life of a program. The problem is to obtain it. Systems do not usually provide services that provide a listing of the invocation chain complete with line numbers during execution. In one system, I took the time to go through the microfiche listings of the system code to find out how the invocation chain was obtained during system processing following abnormal termination by a program. I then recreated that process as a subroutine that could be called by the error-reporting system. It took time, but it was well invested time. Of course, it is tied to a non-standard feature of the operating system and may need modification when a new version of the operating system is installed. In the system just mentioned, this happened twice in five years and took two hours to repair on each occasion, a very modest investment for the return obtained. However, I had been more than usually careful when writing the program to make the process clear and give references to the microfiche from which I derived the technique.

3. To have access to formatted dump routines provided as part of the abstract data type implementations. As a part of the implementation discipline, there should be a rule that each abstract data type provide a dump procedure that will convert a value of that type into readable format. This is not only of assistance in debugging the entire application program, it is essential for verification of the correct implementation of the abstract data type.

10.9.2 Provision of test data

In addition to building an error-reporting mechanism into a new program from the beginning, the logical organization must also consider another area of debugging – the use of test data. At this stage, we are not concerned with the design of test data but how it will be made available to a program. In the case of programs that read their input data from a file and then put the results into another file, the solution is easy. The mechanism is already there in the problem specification. In the case of an interactive program, a different answer is needed. To have users typing from 'scripts' is not satisfactory because of potential inaccuracies.

Instead, during execution, a journal should be maintained that records all keystrokes and mouse movements as they are read by the program. The details of such a journaling system must be tailored for each particular application. Points to consider include the following:

1. Is the journal always maintained? In some applications, the recording of a journal may introduce interactive delays that are unacceptable.
2. When 'playing back' a journal, should it be possible to provide additional input from the terminal?
3. How is the retention of journal files to be managed?

4. Should it be possible to edit a journal file? This will require either that the journal be recorded in a form readable by humans or that translation programs be provided.
5. What happens if, for some reason, a journal entry cannot be created during program execution?
6. How can multiple interactive users of a single application be handled?
7. Should such a journaling system be provided as a central service by the operating system rather than have each application create its own journaling system?

Such a journal file also provides the user with a means of recovery for interactive applications, such as editors, should a power failure occur during use.

10.10 THE RUNNING EXAMPLE CONTINUED

When we left the Running Example in Section 9.6, we had a top level integrand for the BuildPrintFile program, shown in Figure 9.15. In light of the previous section, before continuing with the implementation of the integrands Input, CircularShift, etc, we shall need a means of recording debugging and error messages. Thus, the first detailed integrand to be implemented and used is Reporter. Its external interface, specified in its Modula-2 Definition Module is shown in Figure 10.13.

In order to make use of this, the body of BuildPrintFile becomes as shown in Figure 10.14. At this stage, each of the integrands Input, CircularShift, etc. consists of a 'stub' – a skeleton of code whose sole action is to report that it has been executed. For example, the body of CircularShift is:

```
IMPLEMENTATION MODULE CSmod;

    FROM Reporter        IMPORT Report;
    FROM TitleListMngr   IMPORT TitleList;
    FROM CSTListManager  IMPORT CShiftedTitleList;
    FROM FileInterface   IMPORT File;

    PROCEDURE CircularShift(ListOfTitles: TitleList;
            VAR ExtendedListOfTitles: CShiftedTitleList);
        CONST
            MyName = "CircularShift";
    BEGIN
        Report(MyName, "Arrived");
    END CircularShift;

END CSmod.
```

and the file recorded by Recorder during the first actual execution of BuildPrintFile is shown in Figure 10.15. From this, we can determine that control actually passed through

```
DEFINITION MODULE Reporter;

(* *N*   FUNCTION NAME:  Reporter                                              *)
(* *N*                                                                         *)
(* *N*   AUTHOR:  Michael Marcotty      DATE CREATED: 1990 May 02              *)
(* *N*                                                                         *)
(* *P*   PURPOSE: To maintain an execution trace file that permits the application to   *)
(* *P*            write messages to this file during execution.  These messages are used*)
(* *P*            for logging or debugging purposes.  At the beginning of execution, the*)
(* *P*            Reporter subsystem must be initialized by executing InitializeReporter*)
(* *P*            and terminated through TerminateReporter.  Messages are logged through*)
(* *P*            the Report procedure.                                         *)
(* *P*            If an attempt is made to invoke Report without initializing Reporter  *)
(* *P*            the message is displayed on the screen and the program is aborted.    *)
(* *P*            If an attempt is made to invoke Report recursively, i.e. while it is  *)
(* *P*            already invoked, which could happen if an error is discovered by one  *)
(* *P*            of the FileInterface procedures, the message is displayed on the     *)
(* *P*            screen.                                                        *)
(* *P*            If the message is too long, it is split into segments at blanks.      *)

        PROCEDURE InitializeReporter(CallerName: ARRAY OF CHAR);
(* *N*   FUNCTION NAME:  InitializeReporter                                     *)
(* *N*                                                                         *)
(* *P*   PURPOSE: The procedure initializes the Reporter subsystem. The name of the file*)
(* *P*            used for logging messages is obtained by Reporter from the FileNames  *)
(* *P*            module.  The trace file is initialized with a date stamp, the screen  *)
(* *P*            is cleared and a message showing that execution has started displayed.*)

        PROCEDURE Report(CallerName: ARRAY OF CHAR; Message: ARRAY OF CHAR);
(* *N*   FUNCTION NAME:  Report                                                 *)
(* *N*                                                                         *)
(* *P*   PURPOSE: The procedure records the given message has having been written by the*)
(* *P*            named caller. If the message is longer than 80 characters, it is split*)
(* *P*            onto several lines.                                           *)

        PROCEDURE TerminateReporter();
(* *N*   FUNCTION NAME:  TerminateReporter                                      *)
(* *N*                                                                         *)
(* *P*   PURPOSE: To insert an ending time stamp into the trace file and to close it.   *)

END Reporter.
```

FIGURE 10.13   Interface specification for Reporter integrand.

all of the expected procedures and the next step is to implement them, one by one, demonstrating correct performance as we go.

As an example of how some of the points discussed in this chapter are applied in the detailed implementation of an integrand, the definition and implementation modules for TitleListMngr are shown in Figures 10.16 and 10.17.

The procedure DumpTitleList, which produces, through Reporter, a list of what is stored in a TitleList is used to verify during early testing that the list has been built correctly. It is possible that it will be useful also during later stages of debugging. The log file produced by DumpTitleList after reading and storing the first set of test data is shown in Figure 10.18.

```
MODULE BuildPrintfile;

(* *N*  FUNCTION NAME:  BuildPrintfile                                    *)
(* *N*                                                                    *)
(* *N*  AUTHOR: Michael Marcotty      DATE CREATED: 1990 May 03           *)
(* *N*                                                                    *)
(* *P*  PURPOSE: Build Printfile from the data contained in Titlestore and Lexicon.  *)
(* *P*           Each Title-Part of Titlestore contains keywords, that is words that  *)
(* *P*           are not contained in Lexicon. For each keyword in the Title-Parts  *)
(* *P*           there will be an element in Printfile with a designation of the    *)
(* *P*           keyword.  The elements of Printfile are ordered alphabetically by   *)
(* *P*           designated keyword, the complete file being split into 26 parts    *)
(* *P*           according to the initial letter of the designated keyword, there being*)
(* *P*           one part for each letter of the alphabet.  The interface with these *)
(* *P*           data are handled by the Input, CircularShift, and Output procedures *)
(* *P*           respectively                                              *)
(* *P*                                                                    *)
(* *I*  INPUT:  Titlestore: an ordered set of character strings consisting of words *)
(* *I*          separated by blanks.  Each string consists of two parts, a Title-Part *)
(* *I*          and a Reference-Part.  The Reference-Part is enclosed in brackets.  *)
(* *I*                                                                    *)
(* *I*          Lexicon: an ordered set of character strings, each string consists of *)
(* *I*          a single word.                                            *)
(* *I*                                                                    *)
(* *O*  OUTPUT: Printfile: an ordered set of representations of the elements of  *)
(* *O*          of Titlestore, separated into 26 parts, see PURPOSE above. *)

    FROM InputMod        IMPORT Input;
    FROM CSmod           IMPORT CircularShift;
    FROM Sortmod         IMPORT Sort;
    FROM CvtMod          IMPORT CvtToBucketedTitleList;
    FROM OutputMod       IMPORT Output;
    FROM Reporter        IMPORT InitializeReporter, TerminateReporter, Report;
    FROM TitleListMngr   IMPORT TitleList;
    FROM CSTListManager  IMPORT CShiftedTitleList;
    FROM BTListManager   IMPORT BucketedCSTitleList;

    CONST
        MyName = "BuildPrintfile";
    VAR
        ListOfTitles:             TitleList;
        ExtendedListOfTitles:     CShiftedTitleList;
        SortedExtendedListOfTitles: CShiftedTitleList;
        BucketedListOfTitles:     BucketedCSTitleList;

BEGIN
    InitializeReporter(MyName);
    Report(MyName, "Started");

    Input(ListOfTitles);
    CircularShift(ListOfTitles, ExtendedListOfTitles);
    Sort(ExtendedListOfTitles, SortedExtendedListOfTitles);
    CvtToBucketedTitleList(SortedExtendedListOfTitles, BucketedListOfTitles);
    Output(BucketedListOfTitles);

    Report(MyName, "Completed");
    TerminateReporter;

    RETURN
END BuildPrintfile.
```

FIGURE 10.14 BuildPrintfile modified to make use of Reporter.

```
Trace of execution of BuildPrintfile begun at 1990MAY18 14:24:34
================================================================================
BuildPrintfile=>
   Started
Input=>
   Arrived
CircularShift=>
   Arrived
Sort=>
   Arrived
CvtToBucketedTitleList=>
   Arrived
Output=>
   Arrived
BuildPrintfile=>
   Completed
================================================================================
End of execution of BuildPrintfile at 1990MAY18 14:24:35
```

FIGURE 10.15 Log file recorded by Reporter during first execution of BuildPrintfile.

```
DEFINITION MODULE TitleListMngr;
(* *N*  FUNCTION NAME:  TitleListMngr                                         *)
(* *N*  AUTHOR: Michael Marcotty     DATE CREATED: 1990 May 03               *)
(* *P*  PURPOSE: To implement the storage and manipulation of the TitleList data type *)

   FROM Titles    IMPORT Title;

   TYPE TitleList;

   PROCEDURE CreateTitleList(): TitleList;
(* *N*   FUNCTION: NAME: CreateTitleList                                      *)
(* *P*   PURPOSE:  Create an empty TitleList.                                 *)
(* *O*   OUTPUT:   VAR:  TL - An empty TitleList                              *)

   PROCEDURE BeginTitleList(VAR TL: TitleList);
(* *N*   FUNCTION: NAME: BeginTitleList                                       *)
(* *P*   PURPOSE:  Reset TitleList so that GetNextTitle will get the first    *)
(* *P*             title in the list.                                         *)
(* *I*   INPUT:    VAR   TL - TitleList to be reset                           *)
(* *O*   OUTPUT:   TL - TitleList reset so that next Title is its first Title *)
(* *E*   ERROR ACTION: If the TitleList referenced by TL has not been created an error *)
(* *E*                 is reported.                                           *)

   PROCEDURE GetNextTitle(TL: TitleList): Title;
(* *N*   FUNCTION: NAME: GetNextTitle                                         *)
(* *P*   PURPOSE:  Get the title following the one obtained by the previous application*)
(* *P*             of this operation.  If this is the first application since *)
(* *P*             BeginTitleList was applied, the first title in the TitleList is *)
(* *P*             obtained.  If the previous Title obtained was the last one in the *)
(* *P*             TitleList or if the TitleList is empty or has not been created, a *)
(* *P*             null Title is obtained.                                    *)
(* *I*   INPUT:    Value: TL-the TitleList from which the next title is to be obtained.*)
(* *O*   OUTPUT:   VAR:  The next title in the list or a null title.          *)

   PROCEDURE AppendTitle (VAR TL: TitleList; T: Title);
(* *N*   FUNCTION: NAME: AppendTitle                                          *)
(* *P*   PURPOSE:  Append the Title to the given TitleList.                   *)
(* *I*   INPUT:    Value: Title to be appended to the TitleList.              *)
(* *I*             VAR:   TitleList to which Title is to be appended          *)
(* *O*   OUTPUT:   VAR:   ListOfTitles to which the Title has been appended.  *)
(* *E*   ERROR ACTION:  An error is reported if the TitleList referenced by TL has not *)
(* *E*                  been created or if the Title cannot be appended.      *)

   PROCEDURE DumpTitleList(TL: TitleList);
(* *N*   FUNCTION: NAME: DumpTitleList                                        *)
(* *P*   PURPOSE:  Produce a formatted dump of the Titles in the given TitleList. *)
(* *I*   INPUT:    Value: The TitleList to be dumped.                         *)
(* *O*   OUTPUT:   Character string representation of the titles in the TitleList *)
(* *O*             appended to the debugging file.                            *)

END TitleListMngr.
```

FIGURE 10.16 Definition Module for TitleListMngr.

```
IMPLEMENTATION MODULE TitleListMngr;

FROM Titles       IMPORT Title, NullTitle, TitleToChars;
FROM Storage      IMPORT ALLOCATE, DEALLOCATE;
FROM TitlePartDef IMPORT MaxTitleLength;
FROM RefPartDef   IMPORT MaxRefLength;
FROM Reporter     IMPORT Report;

TYPE
   ListElemPtr      = POINTER TO TitleListElement;
   TitleListElement = RECORD
                          Next:  ListElemPtr;
                          Value: Title;
                      END;
   TitleListHead    = RECORD
                          ListStart:      ListElemPtr;
                          CurrentElement: ListElemPtr;
                      END;
   TitleList        = POINTER TO TitleListHead;

PROCEDURE CreateTitleList(): TitleList;
   VAR
      NewList: TitleList;
BEGIN
   ALLOCATE(NewList, SIZE(TitleListHead));
   NewList^.ListStart      := NIL;
   NewList^.CurrentElement := NIL;
   RETURN NewList;
END CreateTitleList;

PROCEDURE BeginTitleList(VAR TL: TitleList);
BEGIN
   TL^.CurrentElement := NIL;
   RETURN;
END BeginTitleList;

PROCEDURE GetNextTitle(TL: TitleList): Title;
   VAR OutTitle:    Title;
BEGIN
   IF TL = NIL THEN
      OutTitle := NullTitle();
   ELSE
      IF TL^.CurrentElement = NIL THEN
         TL^.CurrentElement := TL^.ListStart;
      ELSE
         TL^.CurrentElement := TL^.CurrentElement^.Next;
      END;
      IF TL^.CurrentElement = NIL THEN
         OutTitle := NullTitle();
      ELSE
         OutTitle := TL^.CurrentElement^.Value;
      END;
   END;
   RETURN OutTitle;
END GetNextTitle;
```

FIGURE 10.17 Implementation module for TitleListMngr.

```
PROCEDURE AppendTitle (VAR TL: TitleList;  T: Title);
   VAR
      CurrentElementList:  TitleList;
      TitleText:               ARRAY[0..(MaxTitleLength + MaxRefLength)] OF CHAR;
      NewTitleListElement: ListElemPtr;
BEGIN
   ALLOCATE(NewTitleListElement, SIZE(TitleListElement));
   NewTitleListElement^.Next  := NIL;
   NewTitleListElement^.Value := T;

   IF TL = NIL THEN
      TL := CreateTitleList();
   END;
   IF TL^.ListStart = NIL THEN
      TL^.ListStart := NewTitleListElement;
   ELSE
      TL^.CurrentElement^.Next := NewTitleListElement;
   END;
   TL^.CurrentElement := NewTitleListElement;

   RETURN;
END AppendTitle;

PROCEDURE DumpTitleList(TL: TitleList);
   CONST
      MyName              = "DumpTitleList";
   VAR
      TitleText:               ARRAY[0..(MaxTitleLength + MaxRefLength)] OF CHAR;
      CurrentListElement: ListElemPtr;
BEGIN
   IF TL = NIL THEN
      Report(MyName, "Title list is null");
   ELSIF TL^.ListStart = NIL THEN
      Report(MyName, "Title list is empty");
   ELSE
      Report(MyName, "Dump of Title list follows");
      CurrentListElement := TL^.ListStart;
      WHILE CurrentListElement <> NIL DO
         TitleToChars(CurrentListElement^.Value, TitleText);
         Report(MyName, TitleText);
         CurrentListElement := CurrentListElement^.Next;
      END;
   END;
   RETURN;
END DumpTitleList;

END TitleListMngr.
```

FIGURE 10.17(CONTINUED) Implementation module for TitleListMngr.

```
Trace of execution of BuildPrintfile begun at 1990MAY24 16:32:15
===================================================================================
BuildPrintfile=>
  Started
DumpTitleList=>
  Dump of Title list follows
DumpTitleList=>
  Watership Down[Adams 1972]
DumpTitleList=>
  Notes on the synthesis of form[Alexander 1964]
DumpTitleList=>
  Concepts and Notations for Concurrent Programming[Andrews and Schneider 1983]
DumpTitleList=>
  Fortran[Backus and Heising 1964]
DumpTitleList=>
  Principles of concurrent programming[Ben-Ari 1982]
DumpTitleList=>
  An introduction to the study of programming languages[Barron 1977]
DumpTitleList=>
  Hardware requirements for the fourth generation[Blaauw 1970]
DumpTitleList=>
  The High Cost of Software[Boehm 1973]
DumpTitleList=>
  Software Engineering: R&D Trends and Defense Needs[Boehm 1979]
DumpTitleList=>
  Software Engineering Economics[Boehm 1981]
DumpTitleList=>
  Software Engineering with Ada[Brooch 1983]
DumpTitleList=>
  The Mythical Man Month[Brooks 1975]
Input=>
  Completed
CircularShift=>
  Arrived
Sort=>
  Arrived
CvtToAligned=>
  Arrived
Output=>
  Arrived
BuildPrintfile=>
  Completed
===================================================================================
End of execution of BuildPrintfile at 1990MAY24 16:32:16
```

FIGURE 10.18 Logfile containing output from DumpTitleList.

CHAPTER ELEVEN

HANDLING EXCEPTION CONDITIONS

An exception condition is one that prevents an operation from completing normally, even in the presence of invalid data or other anomalous events. Programs must be able to handle exception conditions so as to avoid terminating abnormally in the face of invalid input, which is always a possibility when real-world data is being processed. Exception conditions are not always errors, it depends upon the context in which they occur. The contextual information required for the proper handling of them is generally not available to the operation that detects them and therefore there must be some means by which the conditions can be passed to the proper place for handling. The programming considerations required in the design of an exception-handling technique are discussed. Some programming languages provide support for the handling of exception conditions and this is described. Finally, a useful programming method that can simplify the handling of exception conditions is described.

11.1 INTRODUCTION

There are 'exception' conditions that can arise in every program. Input data may contain values that are out of range, a hardware unit may fail, a table may become full, or the wrong reel of tape may be mounted. Well-designed programs protect themselves against improper input data, for example, a square-root function should check that it has not received a negative value. The degree of paranoia that we give a routine is a matter of choice. To follow this precept, a binary search routine should check that the list being searched is properly sorted before making the search. However, their programmers generally handle the problem by putting sentences such as 'Searches a sorted list' or 'The list is assumed to be sorted into ascending sequence' in the specifications. Much program complexity, and thus unreliability, stems from the need to handle exceptions.

To think of all exception conditions as errors is too limiting. Some exception conditions, though occurring rarely, are required for the proper termination of the program. For example, the end of the input file may mark the end of the input phase of a program and the beginning of its computation phase. While every file has its end, coming to the end of file may not be 'normal', for some definition of normal, if, for example, the end is reached after five elements of what is supposed to be a ten-element list. It is not possible to make a general distinction between exception conditions that signal an error and those that are a normal part of the program's execution. What is normal in one context may be an error in another.

A compiler builds a symbol table to handle the identifiers in the program being compiled. The two operations needed for the management of the symbol table are a procedure that inserts an identifier and associated attributes into the table and a function SearchTable that takes an identifier and returns a pointer to the table entry for the identifier. What should happen if there is no entry for the identifier? Is this exception condition an error? If Search is invoked during the translation of the executable statements, then it is an error because it means that a reference to an undeclared identifier has been encountered.

However, if Search is invoked during the parsing of the declarations, to have found an entry might be an error since, depending upon the language being compiled, it might mean that the identifier was being declared twice. Thus:

> It is the context that determines whether an exception condition is an error.

11.2 SOME DEFINITIONS

We will define an *exception condition* as: a condition that prevents the completion of the operation that detects it, that cannot be resolved within the local context of the operation, and that must be brought to the attention of the invoker of the operation.

The operation that detects the condition can be one of the following:

1. *A hardware operation:* for example, the division operation will detect an exception condition if the divisor is zero.
2. *A built-in support library function:* for example, the function that reads a file will detect an exception condition if an attempt is made to read beyond the end of the file.
3. *A procedure written by an application programmer:* for example, the symbol table Search function already mentioned detects an exception condition if no entry corresponding to the given identifier can be found.

The action of bringing the condition to the invoker's attention is called *raising* the condition. Once the condition has been raised, the invoker must determine what action has to be taken, this is called *handling* the condition. If the invoker does not handle the exception condition, the program is in error.

There are two broad classes of exceptions:

1. *Domain failure.* The input data to the operation do not satisfy the requirements of the operation. For example, the subscripting operation, when applied to an array, has a domain failure when any of the subscripts lie outside the bounds of the corresponding dimension of the array.

2. *Range failure.* The operation is unable to produce a result that is in its range. For example, an input statement can encounter an end-of-file mark instead of data. As we have seen, this is not necessarily an error; it depends on the context of the operation.

The classification of exceptions into one of these two classes can be a matter of opinion. For example, is the reading of an end-of-file mark by an input statement really a range failure or should it be classed as a domain failure because the file passed to the operation was at the end-of-file mark? Nevertheless, these two classes help to show the basic causes of exception conditions.

Since exception conditions are linked to particular operations, they are *synchronous* in the sense that they can only occur at specific points in the program. For example, a subscript range error can only occur during array manipulation and the end of file will only be detected during the reading of the file. *Asynchronous* events, such as an interrupt caused by a user pressing the break key on a terminal, can occur at any point during the execution of a program. In this chapter, only synchronous conditions, apart from one example, will be discussed. The handling of asynchronous conditions belongs to the area of concurrent programming, which is such a large subject as to be beyond the scope of this book.

There are some circumstances where asynchronous conditions can be easily processed synchronously with great simplification and improvement in reliability. Although keyboard input actually occurs asynchronously, a simple process can be written that is invoked asynchronously by the operating system and records the keystroke on an input queue.

The main process, to which the keystrokes are destined, can then remove the keystrokes from the queue as and when required in a synchronous manner. This concentrates the handling of asynchronous events into the small area of the program that handles the input queue. This technique is in keeping with the ideas expressed in Wirth (1969) where he writes:

> It has become well known that, for the sake of reliability and clarity of programs, use of instructions which modify other instructions should be avoided . . . An even more dangerous source of pitfalls is the concept of the *interrupt*. Its danger stems from the same cause as that of self-modifying programs: *The program which is actually being executed is not directly visible on the coding sheet.* The high degree of difficulty with interrupts is because an interrupt effectively consists of the insertion of one or several instructions at points of the program which can be neither foreseen nor reconstructed . . . it seems that any notation amenable to a technique of program verification must be based on the premise that the program executed is precisely that which is written on the paper.

Does the programmer need to worry about exception conditions? If the program is to make any pretense at *robustness*, then the handling of exception conditions is essential. As programs grow in size, special cases and unusual circumstances proliferate. Even the performance of a seemingly simple task like a tape-to-tape copy procedure abounds with possibilities for exception conditions. The end-of-input condition will generally be handled properly since it probably marks the end of the process. However, what can be done about tape label checking, and the multitude of possible hardware malfunctions? Exceptions exist in even the simplest task and the complexity that they induce in a program is large. It is common to find that the actual code that performs the ostensible purpose of the program is small compared with the code that is required to handle all the possible exception conditions.

It is clear that, for a program to be robust, any exception condition that can arise must be handled or at least prepared for. The challenge to the implementor is to design a *simple* mechanism of sufficient generality to handle all possibilities.

One common method is to make an explicit test for each exception at all possible points of occurrence. Some argue that this is the best solution since it has the great advantage that no special mechanism is required. However, that side-steps the issue since it does not address the basic point of what is to be done. Further, the inclusion of appropriate tests at every possible place where it would make a difference in a program can complicate the structure of the program and hide the algorithm behind a multitude of special cases. In designing the technique, the implementor must choose a stratagem that is sufficiently general, has manageable complexity, and yet remains clear enough so that the normal is not obscured by the handling of the exception.

In designing a method, there are a number of issues that need to be addressed:

- The way in which the action that handles the exception condition is to be specified.
- While it is expected that most integrands will handle the exceptions detected by operations that they invoke, what kind of default handling can be provided for the cases that they miss? While it is agreed that if the integrand does not handle the condition, it is in error, there needs to be some kind of safety net that can catch those that are missed. The attempt here is to avoid the program dying under mysterious circumstances. The default handler should preserve sufficient information so that the cause of death can be properly established and the error in the integrand repaired.
- Under some circumstances, the integrand that invokes the operation that detects the exception may not have enough contextual information to handle the condition properly. There should be some method of passing the condition on up the chain of invoking integrands until the proper contextual level is reached.
- It may be possible that the input data to the operation that detected the exception can be corrected and the correct action following this is for the operation to be reinvoked. There should be some means of doing this.
- Finally, there are situations where an anomalous event occurs that is not really an exception condition in the sense that we are using in this chapter. This is what occurs when there is what might be termed a 'massive insult to the system' such as a power or hardware failure. The problem is that there is not time to raise a condition, let alone handle it before all processing is terminated. Strictly speaking, this is an asynchronous event. However it needs some discussion here because all programs are liable to these events even though they are not explicitly in a concurrent processing application.

If the program is easy to rerun then the right response to this condition might be to do nothing. However, if it is a program like an interactive editor where the user stands the potential of losing hours of precious work, there should be some means of recovering without great loss. To do this could involve keeping a file that records each keystroke as it is used. The recovery from the failure then consists of replaying the keystroke file. Similarly, a computation that runs for many hours should have provision for recording information at intervals to mark restart points. Restarting involves using the restart information to reset the computation process to the condition at the last restart point and continuing. One of the first major programming tasks I did was to write a restart mechanism for a multi-tape sort. I well remember the feeling of triumph and the client's gratitude when I saw the mechanism applied following a power failure after four hours of tape processing.

The remainder of this chapter discusses these issues and suggests some techniques. The current state of programming language design does not provide an adequate mechanism for implementing a general, simple method. Some of the support offered by languages will be discussed.

11.3 A REVIEW OF DIFFERENT APPROACHES

Hill (1971) and Goodenough (1975) have reviewed programming techniques for handling exceptions. These are reviewed in this section.

11.3.1 Immediate termination

This is the 'Doomsday' approach. The operation that detects the exception causes immediate program termination, generally with an explanatory message. This rather drastic step allows the user no possibility for error recovery or orderly termination. It is a method beloved of operating systems and is often accompanied by hysterical outpourings in hexadecimal. The unformatted hexadecimal or octal dump is a terrible admission of defeat and of lack of proper control. It is possible to imagine situations where all the system information is so corrupted that it is impossible to make any sense of it, but these situations do not occur as often as the number of such dumps would lead one to believe. It is completely unreasonable for an application program to terminate with a storage dump in hexadecimal.

Termination of the program by the operation that detects the exception is only rarely a proper response. This is not to say that the program can always continue, but there must be some way in which the termination takes place in an orderly manner with information that will allow the programmers to make the diagnosis easily.

11.3.2 Error parameter

This is the simplest method of reporting back to the invoker that something has gone awry. The operation is provided with an extra parameter that is set as a side-effect of the operation. In the simplest case this is an error flag that reports whether the operation was successful or failed. In more sophisticated implementations, a numeric or text value is used to pass back information about any exception detected.

The conventional use of error parameters can only complicate the control flow of the invoking procedure since its value must be tested upon return from the operation. The chief claim for some of the 'higher level' control flow constructs such as an EXIT statement is that they provide a mechanism for escaping from a loop when an error is discovered. In Chapter 10 we maintained that there was no demonstrated need for such constructs and that they added unneeded complexity to the language. Their proponents counter that they in fact enhance simplicity by allowing control to leave the structure without the deep nesting that occurs with the use of error flags and that this outweighs any additional complexity. The argument is still weak in this situation since an error indication can only add complexity to a program since it is a parameter that is passing control information. The passing of control information increases complexity by forcing a decision to be made twice, once when it is created and once when it is tested. As we saw in Chapter 9, the building of data representation into control flow increases the complexity of the program and makes the program harder to understand by increasing the distance between its static and dynamic forms.

11.3.3 The error return

This is a mechanism that involves a non-standard control structure and embodies the same principle as the escape from the middle of a loop. The invocation statement passes one or more label parameters designating error returns. These label values mark the beginnings of code to handle various exception conditions in the invoking procedure. This mechanism is only available in languages that permit a GOTO statement to effect an inter-procedure transfer of control. Pascal, Modula-2, and Ada do not permit this, however. Fortran, Basic, and PL/I do. For example, consider

```
Interpolate(Table, Argument, Result, OutOfRange, Overflow);
.   .   .
OutOfRange: . . .
Overflow:. . .
```

The idea is that, if the invoked operation detects an exception condition, it executes a GOTO statement to the label value specified by the appropriate parameter. The use of parameters allows the operation to be used in a number of contexts since it is not tied to specific sections of code to handle the exceptions. This technique imposes little overhead and requires no checking after each return. However, it does raise serious program structuring issues since the invocation of the operation does not always return to the statement following the invocation. In addition, the programmer may have difficulty in knowing where the program is to be resumed after the exception has been handled.

In some block structured languages, where the operation is a block that is internal to the block that invokes it, the label of the handler does not have to be passed as an argument. This makes the control flow even more difficult to understand since this is using global information and all the arguments against global variables apply to this situation.

11.3.4 Error routines

In this case, the operation is invoked with a parameter that specifies a procedure that is to be invoked by the operation if an exception is detected. For example

```
Interpolate(Table, Argument, Result, ExceptionHandler);
```

where ExceptionHandler is the name of a procedure that handles exceptions. This procedure is to be invoked by Interpolate if it wishes to raise a condition. ExceptionHandler is a procedure and thus returns to its invoker on completion. The control flow structure in the invoking procedure and in Interpolate is therefore preserved and it is able to respond to any recovery action taken by ExceptionHandler. Thus the issue of resuming the operation after corrective action has been taken is properly addressed. The fact that ExceptionHandler is a procedure also has the advantage that the invoking operation is able to pass parameters to assist in the recovery process.

The exception-handling procedure does not need to be specified explicitly by the invoker, it could be implicitly associated with the object Table for example. This kind of structure is common in object-oriented programming languages.

11.3.5 Implicit exception handlers

The implicit association of an exception handler with an object, as mentioned in the previous sub-section, is a recent development of an older idea. In Cobol, as part of the specification of a file, it is possible to specify a paragraph to be executed when the end of that file is detected.

The dynamic association of a handler with a condition is typified by the PL/I on-unit mechanism. This was perhaps the first attempt to provide an explicit exception mechanism in a high-level language. It has the disadvantage that, although the handler has many of the attributes of a procedure, there is no parameter-passing mechanism. All communication between the operation and the handler must be passed through global variables. This reduces both flexibility and clarity.

11.3.6 The impossible value

In another technique described by Hill (1971), a function returns an 'impossible' result, one that is outside the function's range. For example, a function whose value represents the height of a person, and thus must be positive, might be specified to return the value of -1 to indicate an error. Hill argues that this technique has the disadvantage that the programmer must always be aware that this 'impossible' value might be returned; otherwise, it may be used in subsequent arithmetic operations with unpredictable results.

Problems like this arise in languages where the programmer is not able to define types that match the problem data more closely than the primitive built-in types of the language. In this case, the programmer must use the language's arithmetic data type to represent the height. The range of the arithmetic data type is much larger than the range of the problem's height data type and the arithmetic operations on the primitive data type make no check that values are within the range permitted for a man's height. Had an abstract data type been used for the height data type, the mapping into the concrete internal representation would have been handled by the compiler and the appropriate range check could have been made and suitable action taken. However, since this was handled by the compiler, which has no access to the information about the program's data that assist in deciding what 'appropriate' action would be, the likely solution will be the catch-all doomsday approach of Section 11.3.1, which is seldom really appropriate.

The idea of an 'impossible value' provides a very useful method for handling exception conditions and we will return to it later in this chapter.

11.4 WHAT LANGUAGES PROVIDE TO HANDLE EXCEPTION CONDITIONS

Most programming languages offer no special help to the programmer to handle exception conditions. The only traditional language that provides any support for exception condition handling is PL/I. Among the more modern languages that offer support, Ada is the chief example. Although the mechanisms offered by these two adopted this view and provided what is a very powerful and flexible mechanism, despite the question of where execution is resumed after the exception has been handled.

The basic language design choice is whether, after execution of the appropriate handler, control can return to the point where the exception was raised. If so, the handler can make some repairs and terminate so that normal processing can be resumed. PL/I adopted this view and provided what is a very powerful and flexible mechanism despite the shortcomings of its reliance on global variables for communication between operator and handler. However, it has been argued that there is a danger that its use can lead to the unsafe programming practice of fixing a symptom without dealing with the cause. For example, if a division by zero condition were raised, it would be possible to fix it by arbitrarily setting the value of the divisor to 1.

We will now review briefly the support offered by PL/I and Ada for the handling of exception conditions.

11.4.1 Exception handling in PL/I

PL/I divides exception conditions, referred to as 'conditions', into six categories:

1. *Computational conditions.* These are conditions that arise during numeric computation, for example, ZERODIVIDE, OVERFLOW, SIZE, and CONVERSION. The SIZE

condition is raised if a target variable is too small to accommodate a numeric value without loss of significant digits. The CONVERSION condition is raised during conversion of a character string to a numeric value if the character string does not denote a valid number, for example, '13G5'.

2. *Input–output conditions.* These conditions can arise during input or output operations, for example ENDFILE and TRANSMIT, which is raised if there is a data transmission error.

3. *Program checkout conditions.* These conditions are associated in the minds of the designers with program validation. Since detecting them tends to slow program execution, they are only detected if the programmer specifically requests it. An example of this condition is SUBSCRIPTRANGE, which is raised if there is an attempt to reference an array outside its bound.

4. *Storage management conditions.* These are concerned with the allocation of storage during execution and are raised if there is insufficient storage for a requested allocation.

5. *System action conditions.* These conditions are general conditions that are raised as a last resort, for example, ERROR, which is raised if some other condition is raised and the programmer did not handle it.

6. *Programmer-defined conditions.* These are conditions that are defined by the programmer to meet the needs of the application, for example, a symbol table manager might raise CONDITION (TABLE_ENTRY_NOT_FOUND).

It is possible to arrange for these conditions to be monitored so that an occurrence will raise an exception. Such a condition is said to be *enabled*. As explained above, conditions can also be disabled to avoid generating the code to detect their occurrence. Enabling and disabling are performed statically and controlled by constructs in the language.

If an enabled condition is detected, it is raised. The programmer can define the handling of a condition that has been raised through the special on-statement, for example:

```
ON ZERODIVIDE
   BEGIN;
      Quotient    = 0.0e0;
      Error_Count = Error_Count + 1;
   END;
```

The on-unit, which constitutes the handler, can consist of either a single statement or a block of statements. Executing an on-statement specifies that if the named condition is raised, then the on-unit is to be invoked. The on-unit is treated as a simple parameterless procedure that is invoked by the block that detected the condition when the condition is raised. When the on-unit completes execution, control is returned either to the statement in which the condition was raised or to the next statement. This depends upon the particular condition.

The STORAGE condition is an example of a condition where control is returned to the statement that raised the condition for re-execution of the statement. The assumption is that the on-unit will have performed some recovery action to make more storage available, for example, some programmer-implemented garbage collection.

Once the execution of an on-statement associates an on-unit with a particular condition, this association holds until it is overridden by the execution of another on-statement for the same condition in the same block or until the block containing the on-statement terminates. The association between on-unit and condition may be pushed down by the execution of another on-statement for the same condition in a descendant block. The pushed-down association will be re-established when the descendant block terminates. The SIGNAL statement is used to raise programmer-defined conditions. This statement can also be used to simulate the occurrence of the predefined language conditions for program testing.

11.4.2 Exception handling in Ada

Ada has fewer predefined exception conditions, referred to as 'exceptions', than PL/I; it recognizes:

1. CONSTRAINT_ERROR. This exception is raised if a range, index, or other constraint of the language has been violated. For example, the exception will be raised if the bounds of an array are violated, or an attempt is made to reference an object through a pointer whose value is currently null.
2. NUMERIC_ERROR. This exception is associated with a numeric operation that yields a result outside the bounds of the implemented range, for example, if the computation leads to overflow.
3. PROGRAM_ERROR. This exception can be raised when none of the alternatives of a select statement is true and there is no else part to the statement. This exception is also raised in response to a number of other erroneous exceptions.
4. STORAGE_ERROR. This exception is raised when the storage allocator cannot obtain the needed space.
5. TASKING_ERROR. This is raised when exceptions are detected during intertask communication in concurrent processes.

As with PL/I, the programmer is also able to define additional special exceptions that can be used in a raise statement. Also as in PL/I, the detection of exceptions can be suppressed through special directives.

Handlers can be defined at the end of a block following the keyword exception:

```
begin
   . . .
exception
   when CONSTRAINT_ERROR =>  . . .
   when TABLE_FULL        =>  . . .
end;
```

If the unit that raises the exception provides a handler for the exception, control is transferred immediately to that handler, the handler is executed, and then the unit is terminated. If there is no handler in the unit that raises the exception, the unit is terminated and the exception is raised in the invoking unit. Upon execution of the handler, the unit that contains the handler is terminated.

11.4.3 Comparison of the Ada and PL/I mechanisms

The view adopted by Ada is like the ancient Greek custom of killing the bearer of bad news – execution of the operation that raised the condition is terminated and control is transferred to the exception handler. This means that execution of the operation that raised the condition cannot be continued, in fact, in most implementations, all its local storage will have been deleted before control is passed to the handler. The Ada designers possibly used the argument 'if the same condition can be handled sensibly without using the exception mechanism, it should be done that way and then it is reasonable to treat all remaining exceptions as errors' to support their view. In contrast, implementations of the PL/I mechanism treat handlers as unnamed procedures that are invoked as parameterless subroutines of the operation that raised the condition.

I believe that the difference between these two language designs stems from their difference in view of the role of an exception condition in a program. The Ada view is that an exception is really an irremediable error and therefore there can be no possibility of continuing with the operation that raised it. The PL/I position is that there are some circumstances in which the operation can be continued. This aligns it with the view that not all exception conditions are errors, in some circumstances more information from a higher context is needed. This is modeled by invoking the handler, which is at a higher contextual level in the program, as a subroutine of the operation that detects the condition. By 'higher contextual level' is meant that while the operation that raised the condition knows more about the details of the condition, the handler is in a broader context and can assess whether this condition is an error or is part of the normal running of the program. To repeat, the view that an exception condition is always an error is too restrictive.

One major criticism of the handler definitions in both Ada and PL/I is that they are too limited in the actions that they can perform, making it very difficult to use the mechanisms provided. In both languages, handlers are essentially parameterless subroutines. They are supposed to *complete* the work of the operation that raised the condition. While the handler can have access to the complete environment of the operation, there is no easy way to determine which one of several operations that have the potential for raising the exception condition actually raised it. For example, in a numeric computation, a handler that is supposed to handle overflow has no way in which to find out which of the numeric operations invoked in the defining block actually caused the overflow. Thus, the operands are unknown and there is little that can be done in the way of repair. In the case of the PL/I CONVERSION condition, which is raised during conversion of a character string to a numeric value if the string contains an illegal character, there are built-in functions that allow the handler to interrogate and set the string that caused the exception condition to be raised.

Unfortunately, this is the best that is available with the current languages. However, in the next section, we will discuss a technique, particularly applicable to abstract data types, that can be used to ease the situation.

11.5 THE USE OF 'UNDEFINED' VALUES

In the CDC 6000 series of computers (CDC 1965), the architecture allows for a special floating-point data value, called the *indefinite* value. An error condition, such as overflow during addition, produces the *indefinite* result. The use of an *indefinite* value as an operand for a floating-point operation also results in the *indefinite* value. More recently, the IEEE standard for binary floating-point arithmetic (IEEE 1981, 1985), requires the special representation of the values that are obtained from floating-point arithmetic operations that lead to error conditions. These special values are known as 'NaNs' (*Not a Number*). It is defined that 'every operation involving one or two input NaNs . . . shall raise no exception but deliver as a result either the same NaN (if operating upon just one) or one or the other of the input NaNs'. Thus a program can continue execution in the presence of errors until a test for the *indefinite* value is made and the appropriate error action is taken.

This principle can also be implemented in software as a technique for the orderly handling of exception conditions. This is done by defining a particular data value, referred to as UNDEFINED, for each data type. Thus, each data type has a distinguished value UNDEFINED that is specific to the type and has the meaning UNDEFINED to those operations that manipulate data of that type. These operations then treat UNDEFINED in the same way that the IEEE standard floating-point operations treat NaNs. When an operation detects an exception condition, the condition is raised in two steps:

1. A unique description of the error is recorded. This recording operation may include inserting a message into a trace file for debugging.
2. All the results of the operation are set to UNDEFINED.

By testing the results of the operation for the UNDEFINED value, the invoker can check whether an error condition has been raised. When an UNDEFINED value is found, the invoker can obtain the description of the exception condition, recorded at the time the error was detected through a special access function.

Operations that operate on data types that have UNDEFINED values are specified so that any UNDEFINED input value will produce UNDEFINED results without recording a new error message. In this way, the results of an operation that detected an error condition may be used as input to succeeding operations without raising spurious error conditions. Processing can continue without damage to the environment and the original error message remains unobscured. Operations that obey these conventions can therefore be used in expressions.

```
DEFINITION MODULE LineStorage;

    TYPE Line;
         Key;
    . . .
    PROCEDURE StoreLine(VAR NewLine: Line): Key
    PROCEDURE FetchLine(LineKey: Key): Line;
    PROCEDURE IsUndefinedLine(TestLine: Line): BOOLEAN;
    PROCEDURE IsUndefinedKey(TestKey: Key): BOOLEAN;

    . . .
END LineStorage.
```

FIGURE 11.1 Part of a definition module for LineStorage.

```
IMPLEMENTATION MODULE LineStorage;
    . . .
    TYPE LineRecord = RECORD
                        Undefined: BOOLEAN;
                        Text:      ARRAY[0..MaxLineLength] OF CHAR;
                      END;
         KeyRecord  = RECORD
                        Undefined: BOOLEAN;
                        Value:     CARDINAL;
                      END;
         Line       = POINTER TO LineRecord;
         Key        = POINTER TO KeyRecord;
    . . .
    PROCEDURE FetchLine(LineKey: Key): Line;
       VAR
          RetrievedLine:    Line;
          LineNotFound:     BOOLEAN;
    BEGIN
       ALLOCATE(RetrievedLine, SIZE(LineRecord));
       IF IsUndefinedKey(LineKey) THEN
          RetrievedLine^.Undefined := TRUE;
       ELSE
          Code to find line with given LineKey
          IF (LineNotFound) THEN
             Record error message describing error
             RetrievedLine^.Undefined := TRUE;
          ELSE
             Build Line object for return
             RetrievedLine^.Undefined := FALSE;
          END;
       END;
       RETURN RetrievedLine;
    END FetchLine;
    . . .
END LineStorage.
```

FIGURE 11.2 Sketch of part of Implementation module for LineStorage.

As an example, consider a LineStorage integrand whose function is to provide storage for lines of text so that they can be retrieved through the use of a key. This Key is returned by the procedure StoreLine in return for putting the Line into storage, rather like the way in which a cloakroom attendant gives a token in exchange for putting a coat into storage. A sketch of part of a version of a Definition Module that makes use of the idea of UNDEFINED is shown in Figure 11.1.

The first thing to note in this Definition Module is that Line and Key are private types – *opaque types* in Modula-2 vocabulary – that is, the representation of values of the type is hidden in the implementation module and is not accessible to the user. This allows both Line and Key to have their own UNDEFINED values. There are also two additional operations, IsUndefinedLine and IsUndefinedKey, which allow the user to test Line and Key objects for the UNDEFINED value. Operations of this type are exceptions to the rule that if the value of an argument to an operation is UNDEFINED then its output value is also UNDEFINED. An equivalent approach would be to have an Exists operator for every data type, which returns TRUE if the object passed to it exists. How its existence is determined is hidden from the user. Thus Exists is an overloaded operator whereas UNDEFINED is an overloaded value identifier. Part of the Implementation Module corresponding to this Definition Module is sketched in Figure 11.2.

The Implementation Module shows the representation of the Line and Key objects as having a BOOLEAN field to mark the object as being UNDEFINED. The sketch shows the outline of a single operation FetchLine. It first constructs a new Line object for return. If the value of the LineKey parameter is UNDEFINED then the Line object is marked as being UNDEFINED and no other action is performed. Otherwise, storage is searched for the Line corresponding to the given Key. If it cannot be found, an error message is logged and the Line object is marked as UNDEFINED. Although the UNDEFINED field in each of the objects is just a simple BOOLEAN it could be more complicated to allow the recording of the cause of UNDEFINED value. The user would then be able to use this value to obtain information to recover from the exception condition.

11.5.1 UNDEFINED values as a programming aid

The use of UNDEFINED values is helpful with many aspects of reliability including testing, validation, and the fault tolerance of programs. For example, UNDEFINED values provide a standardized error processing mechanism that can be applied to most types of errors. When all operations deal with errors in this uniform manner, there are fewer details for the programmer to remember.

UNDEFINED values are particularly effective when used with top-down development techniques. We have already described the use of *program stubs*, which are dummy integrands that stand-in for as yet unwritten integrands and permit the higher-level integrands that reference them to be executed at an early stage of their development. Generally, the purpose of a stub is to record the fact that it has been called and to return a result in the range of the operation that the stub replaces. Stub integrands that return UNDEFINED values are easily generated and the error-reporting facility associated with the use of UNDEFINED values can record the stub's execution. As the stub integrand is expanded towards its full functional capability, the error-recording capability is always available to replace that portion of the function that is still incomplete.

Because all stub integrands initially return UNDEFINED values, and all operations that receive an UNDEFINED input return UNDEFINED values, basic control flow for the program can be checked early. Additional paths can then be opened by implementing error-handling paths in the invoking modules or by implementing the function of a stub more completely. This use of UNDEFINED values allows the following:

1. The programmer can choose the order of implementing operations.

2. Parallel debugging between co-workers on a team can become the normal way of working.
3. The correct meaning of the program can be retained throughout development.

These advantages are particularly significant when several programmers are working together on a single program consisting of many integrands. Execution of the program does not terminate with the first bug; furthermore, a bug does not propagate through the program producing wild symptoms that lead to misinterpretation of the actual cause. In actual experience with a large application program with more than 100 000 lines of source code and several programmers working in parallel, the use of UNDEFINED values greatly reduced the total debugging time and resources required for testing. The number of bugs whose cause was not obvious within a few minutes could be counted on the fingers of one hand.

I believe that with a mechanism of this form, the exception handling facilities in Ada and PL/I are probably not needed.

CHAPTER TWELVE

PROGRAM REVIEW AND REVISION

Nobody can write clear readable programs without reviewing and revising the early versions. Each paragraph should be reviewed immediately after it is written. Then, when the complete procedure has been written, there should be a thorough review by the author. The gap in time between the act of writing and the review will help the author to view the work through the eyes of the future readers. This will allow, for example, the association path between the names used and their corresponding real objects to be checked. The thrust of the review should be the clarity of expression. The correctness of the statements will follow as a by-product. In addition to review by the author, review of programs by the author's peers is essential for assuring correctness and clarity. The organization of a peer review is discussed. In addition to review, actual testing of programs is required, in fact the two processes are complementary and reveal different kinds of errors. The proper mental attitude to testing and the choice of appropriate test data are essential to effective testing. The techniques for choosing test data are reviewed. Finally, the art of debugging is described.

12.1 INTRODUCTION

The real work of expository programming takes place once the program has been written for the first time. Poor programmers are inclined to scorn review and revision and to assume that *real programmers* produce correct programs first time. Until programmers are disabused of this belief, they are at best half-hearted about reviewing and revising their work and at worst unwilling to change a line of what they have written unless faced by a blatant error discovered by the compiler or during execution.

Stubborn refusal to change what has been written is a major block to program improvement; almost as frequent is management's refusal to permit rewriting of 'working code'. Just following the rules and recommendations of the previous chapters will not lead automatically to clear and correct programs. There are two other major requirements, the discipline of review and revision, and a proper frame of mind that continues to strive for good style and correctness. To learn expository programming requires learning the principles of review and revision.

12.2 AUTHOR'S REVIEW AND REWRITING

The key to all good writing, be it in English or in Modula-2, is rewriting. Nobody but a genius is capable of writing perfect prose or programs at the first attempt. Ernest Hemingway when asked how much he re-wrote, replied 'It depends. I rewrote the ending to *Farewell to Arms*, the last page of it, thirty-nine times before I was satisfied' (Dick 1963, p. 222). Aldous Huxley answered a similar question, 'I write everything many times over. All my thoughts are second thoughts. And I correct each page a great deal, or rewrite it several times as I go along' (Dick 1963, p. 197). In a sense, the programmer's first draft is already the product of a review and revision process in which some constructs and name choices have been rejected in the mind and when they first appeared on the editing screen. Once a paragraph of a procedure has been written, it should be reread by the programmer. This is not particularly a check that the grammatical rules of the programming language have been obeyed; the compiler will do that with reasonable thoroughness. Of course, syntax errors should be corrected if found, but it is not worth spending a great deal of time searching for them since there is only minor loss of time if the compiler discovers a syntax error. There should be no more embarrassment in the detection of a syntax error by the compiler than occasioned by the discovery of a grammatical or spelling error in one's prose writing. Unless, of course, and this applies to both programming and prose, the error betokens ignorance of the language used. Without proper internalized knowledge of the language of exposition, there is little hope for clarity of exposition. The primary focus of this running review during the writing of the procedure is for clarity. The programmer must look at the paragraph through the reader's eyes and mental database. It is very easy to assume that the reader will have access to the same mental database as oneself and thus make implicit assumptions about the reader's understanding.

Once the first version of a procedure has been written, it should be reviewed in its entirety. This requires checking that the procedure's introductory comments are accurate and complete and that the unity or purpose, organization, and coherence of each paragraph do not depend upon some knowledge that exists only in the programmer's mind. Another important check to make at this time is that the names chosen will evoke the corresponding real-world object in the reader's mind. Already, some time will have elapsed since the name was chosen and some of the initial flush of enthusiasm may have worn off. When choosing a name, one generally builds an association starting with the object being represented. In other words, the object itself brought the name to the programmer's mind. The reader will be working in the opposite direction. What is needed is a name that will bring the object to the reader's mind. Although this was mentioned in Chapter 10, when we discussed the choice of names, the association must be retested during the first review of the procedure, after the choice has lain fallow during the writing. Objectivity grows in the period between brainwave and review.

A good technique is to read the program aloud. Adopt some convention for pronouncing the symbols used. The assignment symbol := is perhaps the only difficult one. I find 'becomes', 'is set to', or 'gets' are reasonable choices. The statement

```
LineIndex := LineIndex + 3;
```

can then be read as 'LineIndex becomes LineIndex plus 3'. In languages like Fortran, PL/I, and C, which use = to denote assignment, I still use 'becomes'. This is particularly important in PL/I, where there is no distinction between the uses of = to denote assignment and equality.

This first review is not the final one; the procedure will have to be able to stand the test of some independent reader before it can be accepted as satisfactory. However, a test reading made immediately after writing is an important one if the reviewer's time is not to be wasted. It is no sign of weakness when you find that your program is in need of major surgery to make it understandable. It is only weakness when you do not perform the surgery.

12.3 ACHIEVING STYLE

The whole purpose of a readable style is aimed at achieving communication with the reader. In his essay *The Philosophy of Style*, Herbert Spencer (1852) provides one of the best introductions to the subject of readability even though he never uses the word. He notes that the standard handbooks on composition and rhetoric of his time presuppose a common principle:

> the importance of economizing the reader's or hearer's attention. To so present ideas that they may be apprehended with the least possible mental effort, is the desideratum towards which most of the rules point . . . A reader or listener has at each moment but a limited amount of mental power available. To recognize and interpret the symbols presented to him requires part of this power: to arrange and combine the images suggested a further part; and only that part which remains can be used for the realization of the thought conveyed. Hence the more time and attention it takes to receive and understand each sentence, the less time and attention can be given to the contained idea; and the less vividly will that idea be conceived . . . Hence, carrying out the metaphor that language is the vehicle of thought, there seems reason to think that in all cases the friction and inertia of the vehicle deduct from its efficiency; and that in composition the chief if not the sole thing to be done, is to reduce this friction and inertia to the smallest possible amount.

Behind Spencer's principle of least effort on the part of the reader lay the idea that language was a means rather than an end in itself. Although Spencer wrote well over a hundred years ago, his characterization of readability applies well to expository programming. There, the goal is to describe a process, the algorithm, so that it can be understood by the reader with the least amount of effort.

Students have often complained to me that although their program still did not work, they had spent many hours working on it and therefore should get more credit for their work. My invariable reply was that the computer did not care how long one spent writing the program, if it was not correct, it was not correct and there was no argument. From the point of view of the computer, the only moment of truth is the execution, everything else is incidental. As the students gain more experience they learn that there is more than this single moment of truth to programming. There is also crafting the program so that it can easily be transformed into other programs so that its life consists of a long sequence of such moments of truth. They also learn that the computer is not the only audience for the program; there is also the reader. Again, there is a similar principle at work. For the reader there is a similar moment of truth, the moment when the program is read for the first time. How much revision went into the program is immaterial. What counts is how well the final version of the program communicates the working of the process it describes.

The review of the program after it has been written is aimed primarily at the clarity of its exposition. Each paragraph in turn must be reread carefully to look for statements that are not easily read and understood. Many would argue that the main purpose of the review is to check the program for its correctness and that the question of clarity can be addressed later. There is a danger with this approach that neither correctness nor clarity will be achieved. If the program is not easily understandable, it will be difficult to validate its correctness. Conversely, if the primary target of the review is readability and clarity the validation of the program's correctness will follow as a natural by-product. For, in revising for clarity, the author will be forced to read the program for understanding and will constantly compare this understanding with the known process that it is describing. Thus, revisions to attain clarity will naturally expose errors in the program, which will be corrected as part of the revision step.

Up to this point, we have been concerned with general guide lines and rules for good style in programming. Will following these rules blindly necessarily lead to clear readable programs? This is no more true than obeying slavishly the rules given in Strunk and White's *The Elements of Style* will lead to beautiful clear prose. These principles only lay the groundwork. Within these rules, there are myriad modes of expression of different clarity. The purpose of the review and revision for clarity is to choose the mode that best expresses the working of the algorithm. This can no more be dictated by rule than can the production of a beautiful picture be mandated within the rules of artistic composition. This is one of the many places where the skill of the programmer comes into play.

12.4 PEER REVIEW

As long as programs were viewed as private communications between programmers and machines, it was assumed that the only way to test a program was by executing it with suitable test data, for some definition of 'suitable'. As we have seen, testing is a very unreliable way of validating a program. In the early 1970s, largely as a result of the appearance of Weinberg (1971), this view began to change. The reading and review of programs by the author's peers was seen as an effective way of finding errors. It was noticed that, if the author knew that the program would be subject to peer review, it was better organized and more readable.

As the idea of peer reviews developed, they became more formalized. In the literature, they are referred to as *code reviews*, *code inspections*, or *walkthroughs*. The term 'walkthroughs' sometimes has the fashionable adjective *structured* prefixed.

Where peer reviews have been introduced as a formalized part of the implementation process, they have been found to be highly successful in producing clear error-free programs. A typical experience for installations without peer review is for 3–5 errors to be discovered per *hundred* lines of code over the lifetime of the program. Where peer review has been followed diligently, 3–5 errors per *ten thousand* lines is not uncommon. Myers (1978) reports that in a controlled experiment, peer reviews detected an average of 38% of the total errors in the program studied. The human review process is probably more effective than testing in finding certain types of errors only. For other types of errors, testing is better. Thus peer review and testing are complementary processes that should be used together.

12.4.1 Organization of a peer review

Although the subject of peer review under various names is discussed in many papers in the journals the most complete discussion of formalized peer reviews is in Yourdon (1977). A discussion of more informal *work reading* is in Ledgard (1987).

Essentially, the review should have the following aims:

- It should be carried out with an explicit purpose of *error detection not error correction*.
- It should be carried out with as small a group as is practicable, ideally just one very knowledgeable and insightful reviewer. If others are to be invited, they should include a representative of the group that will eventually be charged with maintaining the program.
- Since it has the explicit purpose of error detection, it is an essential part of the quality control schedule and its occurrence should be reported.

The primary question to be answered by the review is whether the program will work as written. The question of whether the program is written the way the reviewers would have written it is not worth asking because the answer is always 'No!'. The reviewers' responsibility is to make constructive criticism, comments, and suggestions. Needless to say, these should be directed to the product and not to the producer. Such a review is potentially bruising to sensitive egos, and the author must resist the temptation to defend the product, otherwise the discussion can degenerate into a 'Yes, it is!', 'No, it isn't!', 'So's your mother!' . . . discussion.

There are three possible conclusions of the review:

1. To accept the program in its present form.
2. To accept the program subject to certain revisions.
3. Another review is required after certain errors or clarifications to the exposition have been made.

The recommendation is recorded. The review is terminated. The presenter acts according to the recommendation. Management are informed that the review has taken place, if they want to know. In most projects, the process should follow Einstein's dictum, 'Keep it as simple as possible, but no simpler.' For large projects with large bureaucracies, the 'cast of thousands' approach may be needed and for this the reader is referred to the references cited above.

Sometimes there is a problem convincing management that time spent in peer reviews is actually time well spent. With most managers schooled in the conventional wisdom of short-term return on investment, the view may be that the long-term maintenance of the product is another manager's budget and headache. It is well acknowledged that it takes three times the effort to find and fix bugs during system test than when done during development. It takes ten times the effort to find and fix bugs in the field than when done during system test. Finding about twelve errors in an hour's review with four people involved is common. The discovery of three errors per person-hour is time very well spent. Thus, it makes economic sense to discover errors during a peer review. The other problem is that the manager may feel a loss of power in that the peer review is not directly under management control. However, that should be a minor penalty compared with the gains of being invisible (and inaudible) at the reviews.

12.4.2 Questions to be asked during peer review

The following is a set of questions to be applied to each block (procedure or function) in the program being reviewed. Even though the answer to some questions may be 'no', this does not mean that the block should be rejected as unclear; there may be well-documented reasons for departures from good programming style. However, these questions should trigger an examination of the reasons.

BLOCK INTERFACE
1. Does the block perform a single functional purpose?
2. Is the name of the block adequately descriptive of its function?
3. Does the block have only a single entry and exit?
4. If the block is a function, does it change the value of any of its parameters?

INTRODUCTORY COMMENTS
1. Does the block have a set of introductory comments in the correct format?
2. Do the block's introductory comments adequately define the purpose of the block?
3. Do the block's introductory comments completely define the sources of the block's input, including parameters, global variables, and files?
4. Do the block's introductory comments adequately define the block's output, including parameters, global variables, files, and error messages?
5. Do the block's introductory comments adequately describe the algorithm with any limitations of accuracy and proper references to external material if needed?
6. Do the block's introductory comments contain modification records that are linked to the corresponding changed lines?

7. Do the block's introductory comments adequately describe the exceptional conditions handled by the block?

8. Do the block's introductory comments give the name of the author and date of writing?

9. Are there short comments that introduce and describe each paragraph?

USE OF DATA

1. Are functionally related data elements organized into logical data structures that contain all the elements needed for the adequate representation of the corresponding real-world objects?

2. Are the identifiers descriptive of their functional use?

3. Do the identifiers have adequate psychological distance?

4. Is each variable used for only one purpose?

5. Is a variable referenced whose value is uninitialized?

6. Are all subscript references within the bounds of the corresponding array declaration?

7. Are all subscript references integer values?

8. For all references through pointer or reference variables, is the referenced storage currently allocated?

9. When indexing into a string, is there any possibility of exceeding the limits of the string?

10. Are there any 'off by one' errors in indexing into a string or array?

ORGANIZATION OF THE BLOCK

1. Are the flow of control structures used in the block restricted to sequence, if, case, while, repeat or until, and for statements?

2. Are all uses of variant records for overlaying of storage with different data structures adequately justified?

3. Is the use of global variables restricted to cases that require them to have a lifetime between invocations of the block and are they only referenced by the block, that is, are they really a substitute for Algol **own** or PL/I STATIC variables?

4. Is the block split into separate paragraphs, each of which performs a single step in the algorithm?

5. In conditional statements, are all possible cases covered?

6. In loop statements, are the termination conditions clear and related to the completion of the algorithm?

7. Will every loop terminate?

8. Is it possible that some loop will never execute? If so, is this an oversight?

9. Is the number of executable statements in the block reasonable? As many as can be put on one page is generally thought to be about right.

10. Will it be possible to make most foreseeable modifications to the block without completely rewriting it?

PRESENTATION
1. Does each source line contain at most one executable statement?
2. Where statements are too long for a single line, does the split occur at a suitable point so that it is clear that the line will be continued?
3. Are all Boolean expressions used in conditional statements simple?
4. Are there any Boolean expressions involving negative logic that could be rephrased to be positive?
5. Are all expressions properly parenthesized to avoid ambiguity either in the compiler or in the mind of the reader?
6. Are the executable statements properly indented in accordance with the accepted convention?
7. Are there any 'clever' programming tricks?
8. Has adequate white space been used to make the presentation of the algorithm clear?

12.4.3 Purpose and outcome

Peer group review is undertaken by both the author and author team members, and by this latter group replaced by peers from an independent, quality assurance group. In the first case, jointly undertaken code reading is a part of quality control and follows on from a design review, where an author and a benevolent 'adversary' review the former's creation. When the adversary is not so benevolent, not being part of the author-team, then the peer review is aimed at quality inspection as part of quality assurance. In both cases, the fundamentals of review, as described above, apply.

Code review of this sort should have a definite and traceable outcome. It is not enough, for either quality control or quality assurance, to assume that all that is required is for the author to make the change. Whatever changes are required are likely to have repercussions in design. To be sure that this possibility is never overlooked, code reading reviews – whether for quality assurance or quality control – *must be documented*. The case for this in quality assurance is obvious; the independent quality assurance group must *require* the corrective change on pain of failing the system on these grounds. In the case of quality control, the normal bonhomie of non-adversarial peer groups, where boat-rocking and whistle blowing are considered social gaffes, may feel that documentation of errors is 'bad for team spirit!' On the contrary. It is the best thing for team spirit to document reviews, with a copy to the project archive for the Chief Programmer's perusal, so long as it is the original ethos of the team.

12.5 TESTING

As a boy traveling in Europe, I remember noting the difference among the approach of customs officials of various countries. Some would ask 'Anything to declare?' while others would say 'Nothing to declare?' Clearly, the second kind were expecting the answer 'No, nothing', or however it is that one should answer a negative interrogative.

er 'Yes, I have something to declare,' was not expected and would be a bother to ways did what was expected and was treated gratefully and politely.

ogrammers approach program testing in the same way. They regard testing as of showing that a program 'does what it is supposed to do'. There is the world ui uifference between this attitude and the more appropriate one of 'executing a program *with the intent of finding errors*'. Since testing can only show the presence of errors in a program, never their absence, to approach testing with the intent of demonstrating the program's correctness is to embark on an impossible task. The alternative is much more gratifying. One can attain success and rejoice even if it is one's own program. How much greater is the pleasure if it is another's!

12.5.1 Principles of testing

Myers (1978) is probably the best book available on the subject of program testing and much of the material in this section is based on it. There are two fundamentally different approaches to program testing:

- *Black-box testing*. This is also called *specification based*, *data-driven*, or *input/output-driven* testing and is for compliance demonstration. The program is viewed as a black box whose internal mechanism is completely invisible. The tests are limited to searching for circumstances in which the program does not behave according to its specifications. Since exhaustive testing is in general impossible, a repertoire of test cases must be chosen so as to have the highest probability of detecting errors. In addition, test cases that cover invalid input are included to ensure that the program recognizes erroneous inputs and produces appropriate outputs.
- *White-box testing*. This is also known as *program-based*, or *logic-driven* testing and is more for modifiability and defensiveness. Here, the internal structure of the program is known to the tester. The analog of the black-box exhaustive testing is the execution of every possible path in the program. It is an equally impossible goal in most programs. Even apparently trivial logic can have a combinatorial explosion of possibilities. Again, the strategy is to select a repertoire of test cases that will cover as many paths and conditions as possible.

In the extreme case, black-box testing can be characterized as exhaustive input testing while-white box testing is exhaustive path testing. While the first might be said to be the superior of the two, neither prove to be useful techniques since they are both infeasible. However, they both have important uses in deriving test cases, as will be discussed later in this chapter. Both black- and white-box testing are required if the quality of the final program is to be assured.

It is important to distinguish between various attributes that can be ascribed to the testing process:

- *Benevolent vs. Adversary*. Benevolent testing is performed by the author of the software whereas adversary testing is performed by an independent tester, see Section 2.4.8, who has no personal attachment to the program.

- *Static vs. Dynamic.* Static testing consists of searching for errors by reading the program and performing a mental simulation of its execution. This is in contrast to dynamic testing where the program is actually executed using test cases derived from both the black-box and white-box views.
- *Part vs. Composite.* Part testing consists of exercising one particular integrand with test cases especially derived to detect errors in it. Composite testing consists of exercising a linked group of integrands with the goal of finding errors in the way in which they work in concert.

In this section we are dealing with benevolent testing of programs, both static and dynamic. Although this testing is 'benevolent' testing since the really aggressive component of human nature is missing when one tests one's own product, it is, nevertheless, an essential part of the overall quality control process and must not be skimped.

A proper mental attitude is essential to testing and the following principles form a good basis for this:

1. The intent is to find errors.
2. It is expected that errors will be found.
3. A test case is successful if it finds a previously unknown error.
4. The more errors that are found, the more likely it is that there are more.
5. No test should be conducted without specifying the correct output from the program.
6. There is no point in testing if the output is not examined.
7. In addition to producing the correct output, the program must not produce any incorrect output.
8. Never throw away a test case, it will be needed after each modification to revalidate the program.
9. The test of a program by its author is not reliable.
10. The test of a program by the group that developed it is not reliable.

Even so, with the best possible mental equipment, benevolent testing remains . . . benevolent. The inner urge will be to prove that the rubbish really works, and in this, author-testing of programs is like all other forms of self-policing. Errors of commission and omission in code are often complemented by corresponding errors of commission and omission in testing.

12.5.2 Test case design

A test is no better than its test data. The choice of test cases is a complex subject that can only be summarized here. For a proper treatment, the reader is referred to Myers (1978). The two major classes of testing, black-box, and white-box, each have their own methods for identifying test cases.

1. *Equivalence partitioning for black-box testing.* A good test case, in addition to detecting a previously undiscovered error should also reduce by more than one, the

number of remaining test cases required to achieve the goal of reasonable testing. This means that the test should exercise as many different input conditions as possible. It should also act as a representative of other possible test cases. The method consists of partitioning the sets of input data into a finite number of *equivalence classes* such that, as far as one can tell without examining the internal structure of the program, a test using a representative value of a class is equivalent to a test using any other value of that class. That is, if a test case from one class demonstrates an error, any other test case from the same class would demonstrate the same error. Some of the equivalence classes for the Running Example would be:

- Titles consisting of both keywords and noise words, starting with a keyword.
- Titles consisting of both keywords and noise words, starting with a noise word.
- Titles consisting of keywords only.
- Titles consisting of noise words only, for example "Is it 'To be or not to be'?"

2. *Boundary-value analysis for black-box testing.* Experience has shown that the handling of input data values on, or immediately above or below the boundary values of equivalence classes is frequently incorrectly programmed. Thus test data that cover these cases are often valuable. One boundary condition that needs testing in the Running Example is a title with only one word. In addition to examining the input data equivalence classes for boundary value test cases, the output data equivalence classes should also be examined. The selection of test cases for boundaries is an area where the tester's creativeness is important.

3. *Error guessing for black-box testing.* Beyond the test cases generated from input equivalence classes and boundary value analysis, there are likely to be a number of special cases that also need testing. For example, the Running Example program should be tested with an empty input file and also with duplicate titles in the input file. The generation of these special cases depends largely on the intuition and imagination of the tester who should muse, 'I wonder what happens if . . .' and generate a test case to find out. Myers (1978) aptly refers to this technique as *error guessing*.

4. *Statement coverage for white-box testing.* This is the basic requirement that there should be test cases so that every statement in the program is executed at least once. This is a weak criterion and is not sufficient to warrant much confidence in the program.

5. *Decision coverage for white-box testing.* This requires that there should be a test case such that each decision in the program has a TRUE and FALSE outcome at least once. As for case statements, each possible case must be executed at least once including any otherwise clause present.

6. *Condition coverage for white-box testing.* This is a further refinement of the previous criterion. It requires that there be test cases so that each condition in a decision takes on all possible outcomes at least once. Thus, if there is more than one possible condition that can end a loop, each of those conditions must be exercised separately. In addition, all exception handlers must be executed. Since some handlers can be entered from many different places in a procedure, for example, a handler that deals with overflow, it may be very difficult to cause all these potential paths to be executed. Generation of these test cases will require a great deal of careful analysis.

7. *Multiple condition coverage for white-box testing.* Here, the requirement is further strengthened by requiring that each condition in a decision take on all possible outcomes at least once. In addition, when more than one condition is combined logically in a decision, there should be test cases devised so that all possible combinations of these conditions are exercised at least once.

White-box testing, like black-box testing, is also a technique used in beta-testing the complete composite program by adversaries as part of quality assurance. Above all, the seven techniques listed here, plus those about to be described, are instrumental in making a *judgmental* assessment of that Cinderella of software attributes – modifiability. Macro (1990) quotes Einstein from another context when he describes white-box testing as 'opening the watch'. As Gogol said of watches: 'You have to admit, it's chaos in there.' Sadly this is true for many software systems that otherwise seem to be of passable quality – that is, they have passed the black-box tests at alpha- and beta-levels, and have not yet broken down in operation since last Thursday. We need to remember Belady and Lehman's (1979) Law of Increasing Unstructuredness, quoted in Section 2.3.6, which tells us that work must be done to preserve – or improve – the structure of software during its inevitable changes for either correction or enhancement. It is a happy circumstance, rarely found in practice, when software structure and documentation are so good that changes can be made without a quite high risk.

White-box testing can and should be done by a tester within the Chief Programmer team, as part of quality control during development up to and including alpha-tests; white-box testing must be done by the independent quality assurance group, as part of beta-tests, lest a system go into operation that is unmaintainable.

Additional techniques in white-box testing, specifically aimed at the quality of modifiability are:

- *Static code inspection.* Just looking at a code listing can often tell enough about it. If the 'peer' reviewer blanches visibly, one may reliably infer the worst. The sins on view may comprise violations of any or all of the issues of good programming practice discussed in this book.
- *Error-seeding.* This is a crude form of disturbance, rather like prodding a strange shape on the beach. Will it lie there, revealed as a lump of harmless jetsam? Will it scuttle away, leaving a phosphorescent track and a smell like burnt almonds? Will you disappear in a puff of blue smoke? Error seeding *may* demonstrate the instability and lack of defensiveness of a software system. However, it is a very blunt instrument for the purpose compared with controlled change.
- *Controlled change.* Here, a competent software engineer will attempt to add, or replace one or more integrands for some well-planned and specific purpose. To do so, the software engineer will need to understand the system, which will beta-test the documentation when the controlled change is made during quality assurance. When the change is attempted, the software may stand up well to the modification, or it may go into spasm with strange 'errors' appearing, and bugs apparently propagating through the system in baffling and seemingly random fashion.

There is no scale of values for modifiability. In one case the white-box tester will have enough confidence to proclaim the system 'modifiable with suitable care'; in another, they will not. There is no rational way to argue with the tester's judgement.

12.6 DEBUGGING

It is frequently said that most programmers find debugging is the part of software production that they like the least (e.g. Myers 1979, p. 130). It may be that this is because it brings them face to face with the reality that they, too, are fallible and make mistakes. I have the contrary view of debugging, it is my favorite part of programming. In fact, I sometimes wonder if my subconscious does not cause me to make errors so that I can have the pleasure of finding them. Finding the error and tracking down its cause is like reading a murder story by Agatha Christie, or any of the other great mystery writers who play fair with the reader by providing all the clues. The ease with which a bug can be tracked down depends upon the following:

- The design of the program. A program that has well-designed interfaces between the integrands will in general be easier to debug. The principles of unity of purpose, minimization of interconnections, and information hiding all contribute to localizing the area in which to look for the error. Other aspects of the total design such as the intelligibility of the program through documentation, or the data dictionary are important in reducing the search space.
- The degree to which the programmer planned for debugging. Building debugging tools into the program as an integral part of the design means that the tools fit the environment and do not have to be adapted.
- The mental attitude of the debugger. If the problem is approached as an exercise in deduction and as a challenge to the intellect, there is a much better chance of solving the problem than if it is seen as a burden that must be overcome somehow.

12.6.1 The first step

First, it must be possible to repeat the error reliably. Until that is achieved, the chances of finding the problem are small. This is true whether the debugging is in the context of initial testing before release or as part of ongoing maintenance following release. Inability to repeat the error at will generally means that the correct set of input data and conditions have not yet been found. In the maintenance context, this may mean that the full conditions for failure were not properly recorded. However, the very fact that the program does not always fail in the same way when apparently presented with the same input data is a clue. Where there are no concurrent processes and real-time interrupts involved, the basic premise is that the hardware and software together form a deterministic system. That is, given the same starting conditions and the same input data, the outcome must be the same. Differing outcomes with constant input data implies that the starting conditions must be different. Typically, this indicates that there is an uninitialized variable and that a proper initial setting of storage must be found so that the error can be repeated. Doing this generally does *not* find the error, it merely establishes the context in which the search for the error can be conducted. However, performing the experiments to discover the proper initial setting of storage for repetition often affords valuable clues to the actual error.

There is little point in continuing until the proper conditions for recreating the failure have been discovered and recorded. Unless this is done, there will be no means of being sure that the problem has been solved. If there is no sure way of repeating the error, the fact that it does not occur in some number of trials does not mean that it has been eliminated, it may mean that the right starting conditions have not been recreated in the trials.

12.6.2 Find the scene of the crime

Often the nature of the error will point straight at the procedure that is the cause of the trouble. However, there are many cases where it is completely unclear where the program is going wrong. It may just be that the answers are incorrect or that the program terminates with some system message reporting an access violation – which often means that a pointer value has become corrupted or there is an out-of-bounds array reference. These system messages are often accompanied by a mass of hexadecimal gibberish that is of no help.

I find that a methodical search for the point of termination is the best method. This is where the effort spent during the implementation design in preparation for debugging is repaid. This preparation should include the trace of executions referred to previously and the ability to write messages, perhaps containing values, to a trace file during execution. It is important that these messages be put into a file rather than flashed on the screen. Often these traces need more study than can be seen in the transitory screen message. Using this technique, message commands are put into the program, which is then recompiled, linked and re-executed. The aim is to insert message-producing statements that bracket the point of termination, that is, some messages are produced and some are not. This brackets the problem. Once the problem is bracketed, the aim is to narrow down the point of termination until it is properly located. However, this may only be a first step, the program may have blundered on for a long way in its death throes following the fatal error, obliterating and obfuscating clues as it went. If the point of termination does not yield the answer then the values of variables need to be examined and the program's path traced back to the error. Again, the trace facility is helpful in this backtracking.

Many programmers make use of interactive debuggers; I feel that these tools are dangerous. As Mills (1986) puts it:

> An interactive debugger is an outstanding example of what is not needed – it encourages trial-and-error hacking rather than systematic design, and also hides marginal people barely qualified for precision programming.

The use of a more static system forces the programmer to think seriously about the most likely solution to the problem and to prepare carefully for the next test. Interactive debugging always puts a subtle, almost subliminal, pressure on the sleuth. This can lead to looking at the current value of a variable, making a wild guess at what it should be, changing it and continuing execution on the chance that it might fix the problem. This treats the symptoms instead of making a carefully reasoned hypothesis about the cause and then constructing a proper test. Debugging must be a thoughtful process.

12.6.3 Use the little gray cells

Agatha Christie's famous Belgian detective M. Hercule Poirot often remarked that difficult crimes were solved through the use of the little gray cells of the brain rather than bloodhounds and car chases. The finding of the programming error is more often solved by careful sifting of the available clues than by taking massive hexadecimal storage dumps. Of course, the programmer surrounded by piles of paper is a much more impressive sight than the programmer who sits gazing into space concentrating on the organization of the information that has been obtained. Car chases make better TV scenes than the detective sitting and thinking.

It is dangerous to jump to conclusions without making sure that all the available clues have been considered. Sometimes it is what a program does *not* do that is the important clue to the problem. In *Silver Blaze*, Sherlock Holmes, who was a master at solving the kind of puzzle presented by the debugging task, is asked:

> "Is there any point to which you would wish to draw my attention?"
> "To the curious incident of the dog in the night-time."
> "The dog did nothing in the night-time."
> "That was the curious incident," remarked Sherlock Holmes.

The fact that a dog did not bark at the time of the crime showed that the culprit must have been well known to the dog. If there is a need for more information, there is no disgrace in making another run of the program to obtain it. In *A Study in Scarlet*, Mr Holmes said, 'It is a capital mistake to theorize before we have all the evidence. It biases the judgement.' Similarly, no clue should be neglected, all the facts must be accounted for. No anomaly should be discounted just because it does not fit in with the current theory.

I have found that if the problem seems impossible, it is very helpful to do something completely different. Many times, I have found that on a drive home the solution has become absolutely clear. Another technique is to describe the problem to a colleague. Frequently, halfway through my description, I have said, 'Never mind, I know what the problem is.' My co-worker, without really understanding the problem was instrumental in solving it, by forcing me to organize the facts for presentation. If, by chance, we found some other error during the presentation, we always fixed that before we went any further. This often changed the effect of the error we were searching for and thus gave us additional clues.

12.6.4 Fix the problem

Once the problem has been located, it must be corrected. Care should be taken to actually repair the error, not just eliminate the symptoms. This means that one should not jump to conclusions. The diagnosed error must explain *all* the symptoms. Probably, the most common example of eliminating symptoms rather than correcting an error is the 'fix' by insertion of an if-statement that handles a particular case. For instance, if it is discovered that a value is negative when it should be positive, a fix that negates the value if it is negative is not usually a proper repair. The extra work to discover exactly *how* the value came to be negative must be done. Of course, it may be discovered that the negative value is 'correct' and that the original programmer did not understand the problem fully. In such a case, it is possible that the 'fix' is the proper repair. Generally, there is a deeper-seated error that needs correction.

A correction must preserve the structure of the code. This will probably require additional work, but if it is not done the program will become even more incomprehensible. Once the program has been corrected, it must be tested and the output verified as correct. Once this has been done, there remain four more steps:

1. Record the change that has been made. It is important to maintain a log of all changes to an integrand. When an error is localized to a particular procedure, it is often profitable to examine the last change that was made to it. This may often contain the seed of the latest error.
2. Preserve the input data used to demonstrate the error just fixed as test data for validating future modifications to the program. This prevents regression, where a program that once worked correctly on certain data ceases to do so after some 'improvement'.
3. Consider whether the defect was a design error. If so, the design must be corrected – this change may necessitate additional changes in other parts of the program in order to maintain its integrity.
4. If the error is a coding error, search for other occurrences of the same error that have yet to be exposed by testing.

12.7 TESTING STRATEGIES

To begin testing a program that is larger than about 500 statements by treating it as a single entity will usually cause problems. The possible interactions between its various parts make for a complexity that is too great for us to handle without loss of attention to the actual testing. Instead, the program must be tested integrand by integrand. This reduces the area of search for test data and for culprits when an error is detected. Each integrand must be tested against its defined function, using its specified interface.

We have already discussed the selection of test cases, however the way in which the test cases are applied to the integrands can have a considerable effect on the cost of the total testing process. There are two different approaches to the testing of individual integrands:

1. *Test each integrand in complete isolation.* This requires a special *test harness* or *driver* that invokes the integrand being tested and passes it the appropriate arguments for the test case. In addition, *stub integrands*, which simulate the integrands invoked by the integrand under test, must be provided. Following this testing strategy, after all the integrands have been tested separately, they are combined together to form the complete system and undergo a final *system test*.
2. *Test each integrand by combining it with other previously tested integrands.* This is known as *incremental* or *accretive testing*. There are two ways of performing incremental testing: *top-down* and *bottom-up*. In top-down testing, the process starts with the top or initial integrand and tests it using stub integrands to stand in for all integrands that it invokes. When this is complete, *one* of the stubs is replaced by the actual integrand that it represented and any new required stubs are added. This process is repeated, step by step, until the complete program has been tested. The converse, bottom-up testing, starts with the terminal integrands, those that do not call any integrands other than standard library integrands, which are assumed to be already validated. These are tested through a driver. When this test is complete, a new terminal integrand is tested in the same way. When all the terminal integrands have been tested then an integrand that invokes only already tested integrands can be tested. Again, a step-by-step process is followed.

Incremental testing has the following advantages:

- Incremental testing requires less work because either only stubs or only drivers need to be written.
- Programming errors due to interface incompatibilities that are not detected by the programming language are detected earlier. This is because the integrands are combined earlier whereas with non-incremental testing, the actual interfaces between the integrands are not exercised until the final system test.

The alternative to incremental testing, big-bang testing see Section 2.2.4, makes the complete program the field of search for errors so that it is extremely difficult to narrow it down to manageable proportions and find the problem.

CHAPTER THIRTEEN
DOCUMENTATION

The purpose of documentation is, like that of a map, to answer questions. Various kinds of documentation are required by the different groups who have an interest in the program. Users require documentation that will tell them what the program does, how it does it, how they can use it, and how to install it on their computer. They require both introductory material for training and reference manuals that define the detailed usage of the program. Programmers, both development and maintenance, require information about the interfaces between the individual integrands, and the way in which files are laid out. Documentation is useless unless it is up to date, therefore strict procedures, preferably automatic, have to be established in order to ensure that the modifications to the program are reflected in the documentation.

13.1 INTRODUCTION

Documentation is the information about a program that is made available in prose and other forms of written communication such as mathematical notation, extended Backus–Naur Form notation, data flow diagrams, structure diagrams, finite state diagrams, etc., as opposed to the specification of the executable part of the program, which is written in a formalized programming language. Some documentation is made available on paper while some may be available electronically, for example through a 'Help' facility in an interactive system. There is a need for documentation in all phases of a project and each phase makes its own particular demands. A program's documentation includes the following:

1. User's manual.
2. Operator's manual.
3. Maintenance manual:
   - Functional specifications extracts.
   - Design – all stages down to integrand documentation.
   - Code listings.
   - Test data and results from *all* levels of testing.

There must be a definition of what information is required in the documentation and how it is to be presented. Such specifications are essential to check the completeness of the documentation and to make sure that all relevant aspects are covered.

Since programs evolve with time and undergo frequent modification, so must the documentation. Documentation that is out of date is of as little use as last month's weather forecast. Guaranteeing the continued validity of documentation is no easy task, especially if there are many people working on a project. The best way to achieve this, *after management commitment to its existence and quality*, is through the use of an automated system.

Since documentation is an essential part of the complete software – the program is essentially unusable without documentation – the quality of the documentation is a factor in the quality of the complete software. To this end, it is subject to beta-testing as part of quality assurance and therefore must be subjectively tested during alpha-testing quality control.

13.2 PURPOSE OF DOCUMENTATION

The purpose of documentation is to answer questions. Documentation is directed towards two main groups, the users and the programmers who are developing or maintaining the product. The latter are generally strangers to the specific software that they must correct or improve; therefore, the documentation must allow them to gain an understanding of the software without having been exposed to all the oral folklore of the development team. For this group of readers, the quality of the documentation is paramount. In addition, documentation is used to train new employees and to provide a history of the project. The latter use has the potential of saving a great deal of time that would otherwise be wasted. In a large project employing many people and extending over several years, the reasoning behind many of the decisions will be lost. Some of these decisions are of the form 'We decided not to do X for the following reasons . . .' Unless decisions of this sort are captured, there is a danger that time will be lost later reinvestigating some apparently attractive avenue that has already been explored and found fruitless.

The typical user consults documentation to answer such questions as:

- What does the program do?
- How do I use this program?
- What is the meaning of this error message?
- How do I install the product on my computer?

In theory, the error message should be so clear that documentation is not needed to understand it. Nevertheless, in practice, it is a typical user's question. Programmer's questions are different:

- What is the interface to the XYZ integrand?

- How is the data laid out in the ABC table?
- Where does this error message come from?

Over and above accuracy, which is an implicit necessary condition, there are two major requirements of the documentation:

- It must provide answers to whatever level of detail the reader requires with the minimum amount of access difficulty. There could be a tree-like organization that allows tracing from the root at the most abstract level to the details found at the ends of the tree's branches. The documentation should provide much more overview information than is generally given. Very often the reader needs a quick grasp of some area in order to decide whether more information is needed. All too frequently, readers are plunged in at the deep end and are told more than they wanted or needed to know about some topic without ever getting a view from the mountain top.
- Not only must the answers be complete, but they must cross-reference related areas that the reader may not have known existed or may have forgotten about.

Many projects fail because these conditions are not met. Users find that they are unable to use the product. Many times, I have found out some apparently undocumented facility in a program quite by accident. Programmers have similar needs. Programming is a creative task; nobody can perform it efficiently if it takes too long to find out about the basis of the work. If programmers cannot get a clear understanding of how their work relates to the work of others, they make wrong decisions and become frustrated.

13.3 USER DOCUMENTATION

The documentation required by the user consists of the following:

- The introductory manual.
- The reference manual.
- The installation guide and operator's manual.

An excellent book that describes how to write user's manuals is McGehee (1984).

13.3.1 The introductory manual

This document gives an informal introduction and overview of the problems to which the program can be applied and what its limitations are. Ideally, this part of the documentation should be drafted before the design of the program starts because it specifies the objectives of the program in a form that the users can understand and comment on. Writing the documentation early avoids many documentation problems. Once the program has been completed, the introductory manual should be reviewed and possibly modified to ensure that it reflects what *has* been accomplished and not the designer's original aspirations for the project.

The introductory manual also describes the 'standard use' of the program. That is the simplest possible application of it without going into any of the advanced facilities. This part of the manual should contain sufficient details so that the user can repeat the example application to get the feel of the program. If it is an interactive program, a step-by-step narrative of a complete session showing illustrations of the screen at each stage is very helpful. This allows the reader to obtain painlessly an idea of the special terms that are used in other parts of the manual. These terms should be introduced informally, without any attempt at proper definition, so that the reader picks them up much as we learn a language at our mother's knee.

The major part of the introductory manual describes the possible applications of the program. This description is informal and presented in simple language that can be understood by all users. That is to say, the language should require no special knowledge of programming, mathematics, or other specialized training unless the use of the program absolutely requires it. The level of language and detail distinguish the introductory manual from the reference manual. The reference manual assumes that the reader has some knowledge in the area of the program. The informal description provides the reader with some background information to motivate the best usage of the program.

13.3.2 The reference manual

The reference manual supplies complete information on how to use the product. The level of description must be clear and complete. For example, the reference manual for a compiler will contain a formal definition of the syntax of the programming language, preferably in extended Backus–Naur Form. The reference manual will also define all the options available in the program, the format of the input, the format of the output, and a reference list of all error messages together with probable cause and corrective action. The reference manual too should be drafted before the code is written.

The reference manual must be organized so that the reader can find a question's answer quickly. One effective arrangement is the *Encyclopaedic Reference*, which consists of topical entries arranged in alphabetical sequence with extensive cross-references. If this is not possible, the index must be bountiful. There must be no need to give the reader the instruction contained in the 1897 catalogue of the American mail-order firm, Sears, Roebuck and Company, 'If you don't find it in the index, look very carefully through the entire catalog.'

For interactive systems, the reference manual can also be made available at the terminal. By associating a particular key, the Help key, with this function, the user is able to have access to this information very rapidly. It can be organized so that the entry point into the reference information is keyed to the current state of the program. For example, if an error message has just been displayed, pressing the Help key will cause a description of the error message and related information to be displayed. Then other keys become available so that the reader is able to move through the electronic reference manual to obtain either an overview of the environment of the message or more details. It must be recognized that such interactive access to a reference manual requires a different organization of the information to that required for a printed reference manual.

13.3.3 The installation guide and operator's manual

This manual describes the following:

- The system requirements: minimal hardware configuration, and operating system version.
- How to install the program: what permanent files are required, what resources need exclusive access, how the program is read from the distributed medium, and how to determine the proper values for any execution parameters.
- Performance guidelines: what steps can be taken in system organization in order to improve any performance difficulties.
- Time and space estimates as a function of input data.
- Instructions for the operator if operator intervention is required by the program either for mounting devices or for reacting at the console. These instructions must include action to be taken for handling abnormal conditions.
- Procedure for reporting errors and obtaining advice on running the program.

13.4 PROGRAMMER DOCUMENTATION

Programmers are rightly suspicious of documentation. They know from their own experience that there is nothing so easy to postpone as writing and updating documentation. Consequently, the programmer relies almost entirely on the actual source programs and takes everything else with a generous pinch of salt. Nevertheless, there is some documentation at a higher level than the executable program statements that development and maintenance programmers need on a day-by-day basis for their work. As with user documentation, overviews are essential but often hard to obtain. It is almost as if the documentors feel it is demeaning to produce such documents. They feel that there is safety in detail, just as during the design process there is always a tendency to slip into a lower level of abstraction than is desirable. Since such overview material is at a more abstract level, it is more immune to the frequent detailed changes that the actual integrands undergo. There must be a commitment on the part of management to ensure the production of the overview documentation.

13.4.1 General design documentation

Before a new development programmer can become fully effective or a maintenance programmer start to take over a program, they must understand the general design of the program. This requires a clear, sharp overview of the internal structure. The components of such an overview are:

1. A program structure graph showing how the major components of the complete program are connected by control flow and the data transmission paths between them. This should be depicted in a hierarchy of diagrams, each no larger than a single page so

that it can be understood. If the reader has to turn over the page to follow a path, the 'out of sight, out of mind' phenomenon disrupts comprehension. There is no need for an elaborate set of conventions in the graph, the simplest boxes and lines are sufficient to give the overview required. Such a diagram should be a by-product of the implementation design process and be preserved as part of the documentation.

2. An overview of the pass structure – the sequence in which major units of data and programs are brought into play – and what is accomplished on each pass. The information presented in this overview should be at a very generalized level with few details. As with the previous item, a diagram is probably the best way in which this can be represented.

3. An explanation of the layout of all files. This is at a more detailed level than the previous two items but is required as a constant source of reference.

13.4.2 Integrand interface definitions

The integrand interface definitions are required on a daily basis by the development and maintenance programmers. These definitions specify the function of the integrand's procedures and the meaning of their parameters. Essentially, this information is the same as is contained in the header comments in the integrands. Because this information is at a lower level of abstraction than that discussed in the previous section, it is more susceptible to change and pains must be taken to see that it is kept up to date. One way of doing this is to use a tool that will generate it automatically from the source code. In the integrand header

```
(* *N*  AUTHOR:  Michael Marcotty     DATE CREATED: 1989 January 12          *)
(* *N*                                                                        *)
(* *P*  PURPOSE: To sort the elements of the A[1]...A[DataCount] of the array *)
(* *P*           A[1]...A[2*DataCount] into ascending sequence using          *)
(* *P*           A[DataCount+1]...A[2*DataCount] as auxiliary storage.  The    *)
(* *P*           procedure takes advantage of naturally occurring ascending   *)
(* *P*           or descending order in the original data.                    *)
(* *P*                                                                        *)
(* *S*  CALL SEQUENCE: StringSort (DataCount, A)                              *)
(* *S*                                                                        *)
(* *I*  INPUT:   Value: DataCount defining the number of elements of data.    *)
(* *I*           VAR:   A          an array of at least 2*DataCount elements   *)
(* *I*                             whose first DataCount elements contain the  *)
(* *I*                             data to be sorted.                          *)
(* *I*                                                                        *)
(* *O*  OUTPUT:  VAR:   A          The sorted data is contained in the first   *)
(* *O*                             DataCount elements.                         *)
(* *O*                                                                        *)
```

the markers *P*, *I*, *O*, etc., are used as markers for such a tool to select the correct lines.

13.5 PRODUCTION OF DOCUMENTATION

Documentation is like the weather – everybody talks about it but nobody does anything about it. In preparation for writing this chapter, I consulted as many books on software engineering as I could find, and discovered that most of them, with the notable exception of Macro and Buxton (1987) and Macro (1990), give only minor lip service to the need for documentation. Much of what they prescribe seems to be designed to cushion the manager's tender parts against attack in the event of fortune not looking kindly upon the project. Very little is said about the documents that would be needed during the active lifetime of the program – the materials required by the users and the maintenance programmers. Still less is said about how the documents should be produced. Part of this is a reflection of the way in which programmers tend to look down on the documentation group. Weinberg (1971) recounts:

> The manager was telling some visitors about the training program they had, in order to demonstrate that he understood the concept of stability through change. He showed the visitors a list of the new trainees arranged by their final evaluations scores, and called their attention to the fine scores they 'all' had achieved.
> 'But,' asked one of the visitors, 'what about these three at the bottom? Their scores seem to be way below the others.'
> 'Oh, that,' shrugged the manager. 'That's nothing. They're going into the documentation group, so it's nothing to worry about.'

We are clearly left with the impression that documentation, despite protestations to the contrary, is not regarded with any great seriousness. It requires a commitment by management to high-quality documentation for it to be produced.

13.5.1 Flowcharts

Conventional wisdom still tells us that the indispensable part of program documentation is the flowchart. Like much conventional wisdom, this is more convention than wisdom. Many procedures do not need flowcharts. If a procedure is so complicated that it needs a flowchart, it probably should be split into a hierarchy of procedures, each of which is so simple that it does not need a flowchart.

However, that is not the major problem. Flowcharts require painstaking drafting efforts if they are to be sufficiently aesthetic as to be understood. It takes planning to draw a communicative flowchart and in these days of life at a mile a minute, nobody has the time to think about the proper layout. But the flowchart does show the decision structure of the program and the incompetent programmer soon realizes that the flowchart clearly displays the terrible complexity of the program. The program that needs a flowchart in order to be understood has something dreadfully wrong with it. The good programmer writes programs so that the flowchart only restates the obvious.

Since flowcharts are arduous to produce, they are also arduous to maintain as the procedures they describe change. Because of the agony of producing them, there are numerous flowcharting tools that take a program and generate a flowchart from them. Unfortunately, these tools are unable to perform the abstraction and clustering needed to provide good comprehension and instead become a welter of space-hogging boxes connected by lines and arrows. The level of detail of the automatically produced flowchart is just too low to be of help to the programmer. A hand-produced flowchart, containing the proper abstractions is better but it remains a hand-produced flowchart – costly to produce and almost always done after the fact. If it is costly to produce, it is also costly to maintain. Since management is invariably appalled by the cost of modifying a program, the truth of the flowcharts tends to be one of the first casualties in the budget war. Maintaining a program on the basis of an inaccurate flowchart is like trying to find your way through a city using an obsolete map. The very cost of maintaining flowcharts dooms them to be nothing more than a sop that is thrown to organization standards that, in their infinite bureaucratic stupidity, require flowcharts as a part of any program product. In short, flowcharts are rarely worth the paper to print them, let alone the effort to produce them.

13.5.2 Use of word processors and text formatters

To repeat, documentation can always be postponed and, unless someone with authority insists on it, nothing will ever be produced. A major part of the problem is that the very mechanics of producing it is generally burdensome. If the method involves the usual writing of a draft to be passed through a secretarial department followed by proof reading, review by management, and publication, then it would be better for all if the idea were forgotten. The frustrations of battling through a system like that will only engender ill will and a poor product that will waste more time than it will save.

If documentation is to be produced, then the task of producing it must be made easy. Word processors and text formatters are tools that help. Using these, the initial production can be eased and tolerable documents produced. This is particularly true of the overview documents, those with a description of high-level abstractions of the program. These descriptions do not become obsolete quickly. However, documentation tools like these do not solve the entire problem. There is no automatic connection between the process of modifying a program and of updating the documentation. There is an automatic check that the program modification has been done – execution on the computer with the proper set of test data – but there is no equivalent test to ensure that the documentation has been changed accordingly. All sorts of automatic checks can be made: a big message flashed on the programmer's screen when the modification is integrated, a check that the documentation has been changed within some specified period, and so on. However, none of this attacks the basic problem of documentation:

> Do the program and documentation mean the same thing?

Until this artificial intelligence problem is solved, we will have to rely on the programmer and management to ensure the match between the two. Better yet, write the program as an exposition that is its own documentation.

13.5.3 Automatic generation of documentation

Small inroads on this problem can be made. Tools can be developed on a very *ad hoc* basis. As an example, the project I have been working on for the last few years consists of over 1500 integrands, each of which consists of a single procedure, about 200 000 lines of high-level language code. Our interface documentation consists of a document for each of these procedures describing its purpose and parameter requirements. These documents are produced through a word-processing system and printed on a laser printer. We have developed tools that take the header comments from the integrands and convert them to the format required by the word processor so that they require only minor editing. This helps in the initial production of the documentation – establishing what is sometimes called the *documentation baseline*. An alternative is to work in the opposite direction – produce integrand specifications on the word processor and use a tool that converts them into the required skeleton code and comments in the desired programming language.

We do not have a solution that forces the maintenance programmer to change the documentation when a change is made to an integrand. However, we do have an audit tool that checks the correctness of the interface description contained in the documents against the definition contained in the actual procedure statements written in the programming language. This audit is run on a regular basis and is used as a basis of reminding the programmers that there is documentation work that remains to be done.

13.5.4 Conclusion

The conclusion of this discussion was well stated by Brooks (1975):

> Our practice in programming documentation violates our own teaching. We typically attempt to maintain a machine-readable form of a program and an independent set of human-readable documentation consisting of prose and flow charts.
>
> The results in fact confirm our teachings about the folly of separate files. Program documentation is notoriously poor, and its maintenance is worse. Changes made in the program do not promptly, accurately, and invariably appear in the paper.
>
> The solution, I think, is to merge the files, to incorporate the documentation in the source program. This is at once a powerful incentive toward proper maintenance, and an insurance that the documentation will always be handy to the program user. Such programs are called *self-documenting*.

That is, as I understand Fred Brooks, the only reliable documentation is the program itself. However, it is important to realize that the program listing only documents the *static* properties of the program. There is no such thing as documentation that defines the dynamic form of the software except at the grossest level of abstraction. The program is the 100 per cent accurate representation of the static program, all else is at best a distorted image of what is executed by the computer. The only real solution to marrying documentation and program is to make them identical. The documentation is expository text. Expository programs are the only possible accurate documentation. Even then there is no guarantee that the names used for variables will be any more representative of the objects that they represent than our family names are representative of us.

The current trend is towards better specification and design. To modify a program, the maintainer should first turn to the design documents, change them if necessary, then change the code. The design documents are at a different level of detail from the code. Keeping two versions of documentation at different levels of detail is necessary; keeping two versions at the same level of detail leads to errors.

CHAPTER FOURTEEN

WHAT DO YOU DO WITH AN UNREADABLE PROGRAM?

It is all very well to describe how to write clear understandable programs but there are a large number of unreadable programs in the world and these have to be modified. It is often important to salvage the programs so as to prolong their life. Improving the readability of a program is presented as an iterative process where transformations and improvements are made as more and more of the program becomes understandable. The process and the transformations are described.

14.1 INTRODUCTION

The facile answer to the question of what to do with an unreadable program is, of course: 'Throw it away!' However, this is not always an option. There are many examples where the investment in the program is too large or too recent for it to be written off. In the long run, it is often cheaper to transform the program into a readable one than to start the whole software implementation over again from scratch.

The modification of computer programs is a costly job that never ends during the life of the program. Elshoff (1976) reports on the results of an informal study of 120 commercial PL/I programs and concludes that about 75 per cent of all programmers' time in a commercial programming installation is spent on program modification. This conclusion agrees with independent assessments in Liu (1976), Boehm (1976), and Lientz and Swanson (1980). Because of the ever-changing real world, the need for program modification will not disappear. As new software is developed, the inventory of programs to be maintained grows. Program maintenance is a growth industry.

14.2 THE MODIFICATION CYCLE

The generally described sequence of steps in the modification cycle is typically as follows:

1. The user requests a change to the program.

2. The specifications for the change are written and the cost of the change estimated.
3. It is decided that the changes are worth the expense.
4. The program is changed in accordance with the change specifications.

This is, of course, largely fiction. An analogous fiction is the textbook description of a scientific discovery, which would have us believe that the scientist slavishly follows the scientific method of making a theoretical hypothesis based on strict logical deduction and then performs an experiment to test the hypothesis. What actually happens is that the scientist makes a mental leap into theory space, invents a hypothesis, tests it and then builds the logical bridge to connect the new discovery to previous knowledge. Similarly, the maintenance programmer often misses many of the steps and may write the specifications and justification after all is done.

The common denominator of all variants of the modification process is that it starts with an existing program and its documentation. In most cases, the only reliable documentation is the program itself. Hence the question: what do you do with an unreadable program?

Despite the progress that has been made in engineering over the last twenty years, most computer and data processing installations still have large inventories of programs that are nearly impossible to read. The program Big Bertha, mentioned in Chapter 1, is not an isolated example. Programs from this inventory must regularly be modified or replaced. Before the program can be modified, it is necessary to understand exactly what the program currently does. In fact, the decision whether to modify or completely replace a program may well hinge on how well the program is understood. The thesis of this chapter is that it is possible to perform a sequence of transformations on a program as a means towards understanding it and that this is generally a worthwhile effort. It is an investment that will considerably reduce the cost of future maintenance.

14.3 READABILITY TRANSFORMATIONS

The Mills' proof of the Böhm and Jacopini theorem shown in Chapter 10 is really an algorithm for the transformation of a program into an equivalent form. Ashcroft and Manna (1971) also present a transformation algorithm. Both of these, as well as a number of others, have been implemented in computer programs. However, experience has shown that the automatic restructuring, as opposed to reformatting, of programs does not yield any improvement in clarity. However, there are some transformations, discussed in the next section, that when performed manually can help make a program more readable. The actual manipulation of the text while making these transformations gives the programmer an increased understanding of the program and insights for further modifications.

The transformations described in Section 14.4 are based on Elshoff and Marcotty (1982) and aim to simplify the program by modifying the executable statements and rearranging the sequence in which they are executed. As a result of these changes, the program may need to be reformatted and additional comments added. These operations are really program transformations that enhance readability without altering the program's execution and are discussed in this section. Reformatting and commenting should be done for each pass over the source text. As understanding increases, the programmer will be able to add more meaningful comments.

14.3.1 Add comments

Programmers consistently state that few programs have documentation outside the source text. Moreover, when there is external documentation, it is most frequently out of step with the program text. Since the source text represents reality, the final authority on what is executed, it should be self-documenting, which means it must be self-explanatory. However, even the most self-explanatory program must be understood within the context of the user and functional specifications, to both of which the maintenance programmer will need to refer.

When the program is not readable, comments should be used to make the source text more understandable. As was described in Section 10.7.1, comments are of two kinds, introductory and inline. Introductory comments should be placed at the beginning of a program to describe the program's purpose, external interface, and how it works. The body of the program should be divided into paragraphs, separated by blank lines or page boundaries. Inline comments should be placed at the beginning of each paragraph to describe its function.

During the program transformation process, the addition of inline comments can be the most important contribution that a programmer can make. The programmer modifying a program must be able to read and understand it, even though it is difficult, before any reliable changes can be made. This difficulty can be reduced for all future modifications by adding appropriate comments *as discoveries about the program are made*. Adding comments is often one of the later tasks that can be done; the programmer cannot understand the program text well enough to add comments early on. However, it is sometimes worthwhile to add comments even though they are tentative and incomplete. As the transformation process continues and greater understanding is gained, the comments should be augmented and modified as required.

The names of variables are really a form of comment. The choice of name does not affect the execution of the program and a consistent change of name throughout a program will leave its execution unaltered. The readability of the program can be greatly improved by replacing meaningless or misleading names with names that correspond more closely to the real-world objects as the correspondences are discovered. Unfortunately, one finds all too frequently that a single name has been used to represent multiple-world objects in different parts of the program. It might be that in one part of the program, the variable N is used to represent the number of hours worked by an employee while in other parts of the same program, the same N is used to represent the number of days of sickness to which the employee is entitled. If the program is well enough understood that the different usages of the name can be separated reliably, then the single variable should be replaced by several, one for each usage, for example HoursWorked and SickDays, and the appropriate changes made in the program text. If too little of the program is understood to be able to do this, a composite name that reflects the multiple usage, for example, HoursWorkedOrSickDays, must be chosen and replaced consistently. Later, as the programmer's understanding of the program increases, it will be possible to determine the separation between the different uses of the name and use distinguishable names for them as appropriate.

Clearly, not all comments are equal. As was discussed in Section 10.6.1, comments that merely repeat in words what is evident from reading the code, merely add to the visual clutter of the page without adding useful information. Properly done, the semi-essay comments in the introductory header, described in Section 9.6, are more useful than inline comments. Sometimes, it is useful to insert temporary comments as an *aide-mémoire* during the restructuring process. Once this process has been completed, the temporary comments are likely to be redundant, having been subsumed into the header and names of variables, and should be deleted.

14.3.2 Reformat

A program is much easier to read if a consistent format is maintained. Just as paragraphing and sectioning can help with written text, so can indentation, keyword positioning, and logical grouping aid the readability of a program. By maintaining a consistent format, the eye becomes accustomed to the visual patterns and the reader is able to make use of these to obtain a high-level control flow abstraction of the program.

Although a reformatting program provides the advantage of automatic consistency, doing the same job 'by hand' forces the programmer to study the program carefully and thus gain further insights into its meaning. Let me re-emphasize that consistency of style is more important than the details of the style itself. The few extra minutes the programmer spends keeping a program consistently formatted will pay dividends the next time the program is read.

14.4 PROGRAM TRANSFORMATIONS

This section describes a set of simple changes that can be made to a program to improve its readability. A programmer using a good editor can quickly apply these transformations. Where sample program text is provided as an illustration, the Modula-2 language is generally used. However, while Modula-2 has managed to throw away the GOTO crutch, there are still many languages that use it. Since this is a major culprit in making code unreadable, transformations that involve the elimination of the GOTO are illustrated with simple PL/I. Most of the transformations described have direct analogies in other programming languages that should be obvious to the reader.

The transformations are presented in approximately the order that they can be applied as the programmer's understanding of the program grows. Moving labeled blocks is an easy transformation to apply and should be done early. Frequently, the application of one transformation will change the pattern of the program text so that additional transformations may be applied. The recommended approach is to read the source code, apply a set of straightforward and obvious transformations, add comments, and readjust the indentation.

Since the programmer may make a mistake while applying a transformation, a practice of testing the program after each pass is recommended. The first simple check is recompilation. The compiler will validate the syntactic correctness of the program and produce a symbol table that can easily be compared with the symbol table produced for the preceding pass. A second test is to execute the program against a set of test data. The idea behind this testing is not to check all possible paths but to simply check the repeatability of results. An execution test can prevent an error in an early pass from being compounded in succeeding passes.

The modified program should then be reread to find the next set of transformations to apply. The process is thus an iterative one with the program's readability and the programmer's understanding increasing simultaneously. Depending on the size of the program and its degree of unreadability, the number of passes will vary, but sooner or later the control flow of the program will begin to become obvious and the program will be understood by the programmer.

14.4.1 Move single-entry labeled blocks

A structure frequently found in an unreadable program is a sequence of statements, the first of which is labeled, that may only be entered at the first statement and, when executed, will be executed to the last statement without any other possible exit, for example, a GOTO. This is a *single-entry labeled block*. If this block cannot be reached by normal sequential execution, and its label is only referenced once, the block can be moved to its proper location. That is, code of the form

```
   . . .
   GOTO Label1;
   . . .
Label1:
   code-block
Label2:
   . . .
```

is transformed into

```
   . . .
   code-block
   GOTO Label2;
   . . .
Label2:
   . . .
```

There are many minor variations on this change. It may be necessary to embed the code-block in some delimiting markers, such as BEGIN, END, to preserve the syntactic correctness of the program. The code-block may end with a GOTO statement and the additional GOTO Label2 is unnecessary. In any case, this modification removes a label and relocates a code-block textually closer to the decisions governing its invocation.

14.4.2 Duplicate labeled blocks

The next transformation is directly analogous to the previous one except there is more than one path into the code-block. This either means that execution can enter the code-block sequentially as well as through a GOTO to the label at the head of the block or that there is more than one reference to the label. In this case, provided that the code-block is small (say, less than ten statements), the code-block is simply replicated at each of the locations where a GOTO Label1 occurs. If the code-block is large or invoked many times, consideration might be given into making it into a separate procedure, as described in Section 14.4.11. However, at this stage in the transformation process, we are expanding text in order to gain understanding. The fact that a sequence of code is repeated several times does not necessarily mean that it would be wise to make it into a procedure; the function that it performs must be considered carefully. The two related criteria of unity of function and cohesion must still apply. This kind of decision cannot be made until understanding is reached.

It might seem strange that in the process of simplifying the program we are actually expanding it. I well remember making a wry smile in my school algebra classes at the exercise command 'simplify the following expressions'. The process of arriving at the answer in the back of the book seemed invariably to require an initial process of complication, after which, if the gods of algebra smiled on one, there would be a frenzy of term-cancelling and the simplified form would emerge. That is the hope here but since the program was not constructed to demonstrate to the student the wonders of simplification, there is no guaranteed feast of factoring – proceduring – at the end.

14.4.3 Add ELSE clauses

The structure

```
    .  .  .
    IF test THEN
        GOTO Label1;
    code-block-a
    GOTO Label2;
Label1:
    code-block-b
Label2:
    .  .  .
```

is not uncommon. Its readability can be improved by making the relationship of the code-blocks to the IF test explicit in terms of the THEN and ELSE clauses.

```
 .   .   .
IF test THEN
    BEGIN;
        code-block-a
    END
ELSE
    BEGIN;
        code-block-b
    END;
 .   .   .
```

Some languages, such as PL/I and Pascal, have an IF statement construct with an optional ELSE clause and no separate terminator for the construct. As a consequence, when IF statements are nested, the matching of ELSE clauses with IF statements is not always easily seen. In such cases, the addition of an ELSE clause to every IF statement that does not already have one clarifies the program immensely. In the simplest case, the programmer works through the program finding each IF statement that has no ELSE clause and adds one with a null statement. The null ELSE clause is a construct that many programmers view as a waste of time but it takes a second to write and has no effect on a program's compilation or execution, and can save a reader hours of effort by making a program more explicit and thus easier to read. The presence of the ELSE clause on all IF statements resolves ambiguities that might otherwise be present in the reader's mind because of the optional nature of the ELSE clause.

14.4.4 Renest IF statements

After null ELSE clauses have been inserted as suggested in the previous sub-section, it will become obvious in many instances that the ELSE clause is not really null. The pattern

```
 .   .   .
IF test THEN
    BEGIN;
        code-block-a
        GOTO Label1;
    END;
ELSE
    ;
code-block-b
 .   .   .
```

is found in the program such that code-block-b is really the ELSE clause but is not packaged in that way. Eliminating the null statement and encasing code-block-b in a

BEGIN-END make the structure more obvious. This change has the additional benefit of increasing the likelihood that the GOTO Label1 can be easily removed.

14.4.5 Make loops obvious

Using a GOTO statement to implement a loop greatly obscures a program. The program segment

```
.  .  .
   Label1:
      code-block
      GOTO Label1;
.  .  .
```

in which the code-block may be from one to several hundred statements long is not unusual. The problem is that the programmer reads the source text from top to bottom and does not realize the code-block is a loop body until the GOTO Label1 is reached. Simply replacing the label and the GOTO Label1 with a LOOP as in

```
.  .  .
   LOOP
      code-block
   END;
.  .  .
```

establishes the fact that the program contains a loop structure at this point. The modification also alerts the reader to the existence of a loop whose termination condition is not yet understood, as will be described in the next sub-section.

Experience has shown that making more than one of these modifications during a pass can sometimes result in intersecting loops. When this occurs, either the modification of one of the GOTO loops will have to be delayed until a subsequent pass or some sub-code-blocks will have to be interchanged.

14.4.6 Make loop termination explicit

As has been explained before, one of the hardest programming constructs to understand is the loop. This difficulty is increased considerably when the conditions for terminating the loop are not explicit, which can arise when the loop itself is hidden, as discussed in the previous sub-section. Another method is to use an EXIT or GOTO statement to branch out of the loop, as will be discussed in the next sub-section. The basic problem is that the reader cannot determine from the statement at the head of the loop the exact conditions that will cause termination of the loop and thus it is harder to understand the purpose of the loop.

Another fault is the use of an iterative FOR loop when the use of a regularly increased or decreased control variable is not an intrinsic part of the process being performed, as in

```
 .   .
   FOR I := 1 TO 9999 BY 1 DO
      .  .  .
      IF test THEN
          I := 10000;
      ENDIF;
      .  .  .
   END;
 .   .   .
```

This is an example of a misleading loop termination. The programmer probably used the wrong form of the FOR statement, did not understand the programming language well, or perhaps learnt programming in a language with no WHILE loop. If the index I is not used anywhere else in the body of the loop, a simple WHILE loop should have been used as in the example

```
   VAR
      ContinueLoop: BOOLEAN;
 .   .   .
      ContinueLoop := TRUE;
      WHILE ContinueLoop DO
         .  .  .
         IF test THEN
             ContinueLoop := FALSE;
         ENDIF;
         .  .  .
      END;
 .   .   .
```

to clarify the loop termination condition. The selection of the name for the loop control variable, ContinueLoop in the above example, can greatly improve the program's readability. A name that makes the WHILE ... DO read in a straightforward manner, such as

```
   WHILE NotEndOfFileA DO
   WHILE OutsideErrorBounds DO
   WHILE MoreCharactersInString DO
```

also helps make the program easier to understand. When the programmer really understands the loop, the termination condition will be obvious – understanding a loop requires understanding the termination condition – and the selection of a variable name follows naturally. In the interim, a name such as ContinueLoop, which shows that there is some as yet unclarified condition that controls the termination of the loop, should be used.

If the statement at the head of the loop is of the form FOR I := . . . and the index I is modified within the loop, the variable I should be explicitly controlled by initializing it before entering the loop and incrementing it within the loop with an assignment statement

```
I := I + 1;
```

and replacing the FOR I := . . . with a WHILE . . . DO. Whether the WHILE . . . DO statement at the head of the loop explicitly mentions the maximum value of I will depend whether there is a possibility that the loop will terminate on that condition. In such a case, the WHILE . . . DO might read

```
WHILE (I <= MaxI) AND ItemNotFound DO
```

This is a form of multiple loop termination that is examined more closely in the next sub-section.

14.4.7 Remove multiple exits from loops

It is not unusual to find a loop with more than one exit. In addition to the normal loop termination specified in the loop's heading statement, the loop may be terminated from within the body. This may be through EXIT or GOTO statements that branch out of it or through exception conditions that are trapped by handlers. In order to change the multiple exit loop

```
   ·  ·  ·
   FOR I := 1 TO 9999 BY 1 DO
      ·  ·  ·
      IF test-1 THEN
         GOTO Label1
      ENDIF;
      ·  ·  ·
      IF test-2 THEN
         GOTO Label2
      ENDIF;
      ·  ·  ·
   END;
·  ·  ·
```

to a single exit loop, a WHILE . . . DO with a compound conditional as described in the preceding sub-section. Sometimes clarity of loop termination is improved by the introduction of variables with suitably mnemonic names so that the WHILE . . . DO can be read naturally as in

```
WHILE NotEndOfFileA AND NoErrorEncountered DO
```

In some more difficult cases, the introduction of a state variable may be required. A

CASE statement or a nest of IF statements can then be used to maintain the proper logical flow. For example an enumeration type State and a variable of that type could be introduced to modify the code shown above to

```
TYPE
    State = (Normal, Label1State, Label2State);
VAR
    LoopState: State;
. . .

LoopState := Normal;
WHILE LoopState = Normal DO
    . . .
    IF test-1 THEN
        LoopState := Label1State;
    ELSE
        . . .
        IF test-2 THEN
            LoopState := Label2State;
        ELSE
            . . .
        END;
    END;
END;
CASE LoopState OF
    Label1State: GOTO Label1;
    Label2State: GOTO Label2;
ELSE
    Error;
END
. . .
```

A proper choice of names for the values assigned to LoopState can further increase the readability of the program. Some experience with this tougher case has shown that changing loops with many exits into single-exit loops greatly clarifies the program text even though a multiple-exit CASE construct is introduced. Generally, the subsequent passes over the program quite easily transform this multiple-exit structure into a single-exit one.

14.4.8 Remove label variables

Some languages allow label variables. These are occasionally used to simulate internal, nonparameterized procedures – generally through a mistaken idea that this is more efficient. For example, the code sequence

```
   LabelVariable := Label1;
   GOTO SubRoutine;
Label1:
. . .
SubRoutine:
   code-block
   GOTO LabelVariable;
   . . .
```

sends control to the code-block at SubRoutine and then returns control to the next sequential statement following Label1. Either the code-block should be made into a procedure that is invoked, or copies of the code-block should be replicated throughout the program. Generally, the first alternative is to be preferred but care should be taken to avoid constructing procedures with low unity of purpose. In either case, the GOTOs and the label variable with its multi-way branch are removed and the program becomes more readable in a top-to-bottom fashion.

Another common use for label variables is to remember a particular decision or path in a program by assigning a label to a label variable. In the code sequence

```
   . . .
   LabelVariable := Label1;
   . . .
   LabelVariable := Label2;
   . . .
   LabelVariable := Label3;
   . . .
   GOTO LabelVariable;
   . . .
```

for example, LabelVariable is used to remember which of three different paths was last executed in order to determine which path of the multiway branch is taken. The modification suggested in this case is the same as that recommended for the more difficult multiple-exit loops. Use a state variable as the memory device instead of a label variable. The resulting code

```
TYPE
   State = (Label1State, Label2State, Label3State);
VAR
   FlowState: State;
   . . .
   FlowState := Label1State;
   . . .
   FlowState := Label2State;
   . . .
   FlowState := Label3State;
   . . .
```

```
CASE FlowState OF
    Label1State:
        GOTO Label1;
  | Label2State:
        GOTO Label2;
  | Label3State:
        GOTO Label3;
ELSE
    Error;    (* Should not occur *)
END;
    . . .
```

may appear slightly more complex initially. However, as with multiple-exit loops, experience has shown that removing label variables is necessary to clarify the program text so that the multiple-exit CASE structure can, in turn, be changed into a single-exit structure by applying other simple transformations within each of the actual cases. Although we appear to be swapping one kind of memory for another, this form makes the program easier to read. An alternative to the use of a special type State is to use a string variable with actual text values. This has the advantage that its value can be printed for debugging purposes.

14.4.9 Use state variables to track execution

A frequently used programming form that contributes to unreadability is the use of long branches to a label that does standard error processing. Whether long branches are for error handling or other purposes, the introduction of a state variable is recommended to eliminate the branches and the resulting multiple-exit, multiple-entry code. As with the examples for multiple-exit loops and label variables, a state type is introduced along with a variable of that type. The variable is set to the value Normal and in the event of an error being uncovered, it is set to a value indicating the nature of the error. The variable can then be tested at the beginning of each major functional block within the program to determine whether that function should be performed or bypassed. The program text has a form like

```
    . . .
IF ErrorState = Normal THEN
    major-function-1
END;
IF ErrorState = Normal THEN
    major-function-2
END;
    . . .
```

and execution proceeds through the functions as long as everything is normal.

The judicious selection of the names for the state values assigned to ErrorState can also make the program clearer by making it more self-documenting.

14.4.10 Localize references

This transformation consists of moving statements around so that the references to a single variable or name are closer together. The use of a FILE variable in the source text

```
VAR
    InFile: FILE;
. . .
IF Open(InFile, InName) THEN
    . . .
    many-statements
    WHILE NOT EOF(InFile) DO;
        ReadRec(InFile, InRecord);
        . . .
    END;
    . . .
    many-statements
    . . .
    Close(InFile);
    . . .
END;
. . .
```

is not uncommon. However, there is no rule that opening a file must come at the beginning of a program and closing at the end. Putting these close together

```
VAR
    InFile: FILE;
. . .
IF Open(InFile, InName) THEN
    WHILE NOT EOF(InFile) DO;
        ReadRec(InFile, InRecord);
        . . .
    END;
    Close(InFile);
END;
. . .
```

means that the reader does not have to keep details of that file in mind while reading other parts of the program. Similarly, initializing a variable just before its first use and arranging the program so that all uses of a variable are grouped together helps with the readability.

14.4.11 Extract common code sequences

The final area to be discussed is the extraction of common code sequences into procedures. Common sequences may be labeled blocks that are either too large or too frequently referenced to be distributed throughout the program, in the way described earlier. They may be labeled blocks that are terminated by GOTO label variables, as discussed earlier. They may just be duplicate blocks of code that the programmer discovers in the code. Finally, a common code sequence may simply be a single-entry, single-exit, functional block of code, in which case the extraction of the code block will make the main program easier to comprehend merely by making it smaller.

Just because a large block of code happens to appear many times is not sufficient reason for making it into a procedure. In order to be of help in the readability and subsequent modifiability of the program, procedures should be constructed so that they have proper unity of purpose and be given clear simple names that indicate their purpose to the reader. The fact that an identical sequence of instructions happens to occur repeatedly does not imply that those instructions have sufficient unity of purpose to be separated into a separate procedure. Guidelines for recognizing and organizing code into functional procedures have already been discussed in earlier chapters and are also given in Stevens (1981).

Once a sequence of instructions has been identified as suitable for transformation into a procedure, a simple method can be followed:

1. Remove the common code sequence from the main program and wrap the appropriate PROCEDURE . . . BEGIN . . . END around it, and give it a name that is indicative of its function.
2. Replace each occurrence of the common code sequence in the main program by an invocation of the procedure.
3. Determine the parameters by finding names that are common to the main program and the procedure.
4. Determine the local variables of the new procedure by finding the symbols that are no longer referenced in the main program.
5. Add the appropriate set of declarations to the new procedure and arguments to all invocations of it.
6. Add a header comment to the new procedure defining its interface.
7. Recompile the main program and the new procedure and test.

14.4.12 The final step

Whatever transformations are made on the program, after they are completed, a most thorough set of quality control and quality assurance test procedures must be performed, not one whit less rigorous than those used in the original creation of the program.

14.5 CONCLUSION

Rehabilitating an unreadable program is not an easy or quick task, however it is generally much quicker and more cost effective than throwing the old one away and starting from scratch. To throw the old one away without having understood its function makes the construction of a replacement an almost impossible task if there are no proper specifications. If the program is unreadable, it is unlikely that its written specifications, if they ever existed, reflect what it does. Once the program has been rehabilitated and its function and structure understood, the information required for writing the specification and design document is available and should not be allowed to evaporate without being recorded.

PART FOUR

THE ENVIRONMENT
FOR PROGRAMMING

CHAPTER FIFTEEN
THE PROGRAM AS DATABASE

There are many forms to a software product, and these forms may exist in many versions. The source code, the compiled code, and the documentation are just three of them. Each of these forms consists of a number of components that must be consistent with each other. In addition, the forms themselves must be consistent with each other for each version. The compiled code must be derived from the current version of the source code and the documentation must describe the behavior of the compiled code. The biggest problem of maintaining a software product is to preserve these consistencies as modifications are made. To do this, the program must be treated as a database with management tools that ensure the preservation of the consistency.

15.1 INTRODUCTION

Instead of a program, let us start by considering another familiar example of expository writing – a business letter. When we compose a letter on a wordprocessor, the letter passes through many forms. The letter starts as an idea in our brain. Since we are able to think about it while we drive to the office and recall it more or less perfectly when we get there, it must exist in some form in our brain. We then transcribe it from its cerebral form into an electronic form through the keyboard, where it exists in a physical form spaced over time. The electronic form is stored as a set of magnetic domains on a hard or floppy disk. We look at a representation of the stored form on the screen of our terminal where we modify either the mental or electronic form until the two match. We print the letter and it appears in another form as a printed image on paper. Finally, we send a copy of the letter to our manager through electronic mail for comments and a copy of the electronic form is transferred to a separate computer dataset. There are therefore four 'copies' of the letter:

- The mental form in the brain of the author.
- The electronic form in the author's wordprocessor file.
- The printed form on paper.
- The electronic form in the manager's wordprocessor file.

Of course, our manager comments. After all, that was why the copy was sent! It takes more than human restraint to refrain from comment on a subordinate's work, especially when invited! And, of course, the higher salary must be shown to be earned. When a modification to the letter is required, the author's mental version, wordprocessor file version, and the printed version must all be revised. A copy of the revised letter should be sent to the manager to confirm that the suggested revision has been made. The problem is to make sure that the letter in all its forms is consistent. (The author could keep a copy of the original version so as to be able to demonstrate in the future why the manager's amendments caused a problem. That version is retained only for historical reasons and its whole purpose is its inconsistency with the 'official' version.) The first printed form must be destroyed and replaced by the new one. This is an analogous problem to that of keeping the various forms of a program consistent.

Like a business letter, a program can exist in one or more forms; in practice usually more than one. Furthermore, the system of which it is a part may be one of several versions, and there may be a variety of versions of the program itself within this scheme, perhaps identical in function but different in detail. The forms that a program can take are, in hierarchical order of abstractness of form:

- Textual documentation, including graphical notations and standard text such as pseudocode.
- Properly commented source code.
- Object code.
- Formatted bit patterns.

The versions of a program that can exist in these forms are:

- Corrective maintenance (M-) versions.
- Improved versions for evolved requirements, including versions for different hardware configurations, (E-) versions.

As a software system goes into service, the number of M-versions increases fairly rapidly, depending on the release policy of its supplier; less rapidly, E-version releases appear as minor and major improvements are incorporated. In both cases, the danger is that changes will be effected at the level of code (which one – source, object, or bit pattern is a concern of a different sort), but with no corresponding and collateral changes to other forms in which the program may exist.

Coordinating changes, as required for such purposes, is known as *configuration management*, and is discussed in Macro (1990). Clearly, in the course of performing configuration management, all programs in a system, in all forms and all versions, can be seen as a database, and the totality of databases of these sorts is the basis for configuration management. Here, since configuration management is not really our subject, we will consider the problems of controlled change as it applies to a single program, and the reader is left to imagine the complexity of the task when it concerns the whole product-set of a major software supplier, say.

15.2 THE CONSTITUENTS OF A COMPLETE PROGRAM

Although the programmer may view the program as the current version of the source code – 'the only thing one can trust' – there are many versions and components of the program, just as there are for the letter just described. These are stored in several related datasets organized into separate groups.

- *The source code for the individual integrands.* These datasets, in a sense, constitute the heart of the program in that they define what the program does. In some cases, a software system may have integrands written in different programming languages, for example, there may be some integrands in Pascal and others in Fortran or Assembler. Generally, the source programs in the different languages will be kept in separate sets of files.
- *Fragments of source code that are common to several integrands.* Some languages like Cobol, PL/I and C, for example, provide a dataset inclusion facility to handle collections of declarations and definitions. In C, any line that has the form

    # include *"datasetname"*

    is replaced by the contents of the dataset. This is the preferred way to tie the declarations together for a large program and to ensure some consistency between the individual integrands. It guarantees that all the source programs will be supplied with the same definitions and thus eliminates a particular kind of bug. Of course, when an included dataset is changed, all integrands that depend on it must be recompiled. These fragments of source code are stored in a group of datasets. The equivalents of these fragments in Modula-2 are the definition modules.
- *The object code for the integrands.* The result of compiling an integrand is to produce the *object code* for that integrand. The group of datasets containing these object codes is often called an *object library*.
- *Executable programs.* These consist of the object code for several, possibly all, integrands linked together to establish their mutual references possibly with additional object integrands from support libraries, for example, the run-time support library supplied as part of the programming language compiler. There are likely to be several of these executable programs, corresponding to different versions of the program or perhaps separate parts of the complete program.
- *The standard command language procedures used by the software system.* In any project there will be command language procedures that perform such functions as executing the program, managing the libraries, selecting sets of object integrands to be linked together to form an executable program, or making back-up copies of all the datasets belonging to the project. These command procedures are just as much part of the project as are the source programs.
- *The documentation text.* This includes the text for all the manuals, for both the users and the programmers, that are produced to support the project.
- *The test data.* The construction of good test data is a difficult task and once it has been produced should not be thrown away. The test data and corresponding 'correct' results

are resources of the project that are used to ensure that the modifications made to the program to produce future versions of the programs do not introduce new errors into the program.

The members of these groups of datasets are not independent from each other and must be consistent. For example, the arguments in a procedure invocation must match in number, type, order, and significance with the corresponding parameters in the procedure being invoked. Similarly, the descriptions of the program contained in the *User's Manual* and the *Reference Manual* must match each other and the executable program.

Not only must the members of a group of datasets be consistent among themselves but also there are consistency requirements between the groups. The following are some of the consistency requirements:

1. Each object integrand must have been derived by compiling the current version of the source code for the corresponding integrand.
2. The object integrands must have been compiled using the current version of code fragments and definition modules.
3. The executable integrands must have been produced by linking the object integrands that are currently in the program's database.
4. The documentation text must describe the behaviour of the executable integrands.
5. The test data that is supposed to represent correct input data must conform to the requirements of the executable integrands.

The challenge is to maintain this consistency.

15.2.1 Programming in the small

The term 'programming-in-the-small', introduced by DeRemer and Kron (1976) refers to a program that can be completely handled by one programmer. Such programs still consist of several parts contained in a database and the same requirements for consistency apply. However, because of the small number of integrands and thus consistency connections, the programmer is under the impression that the management of the database can be handled by careful bookkeeping using 'back-of-envelope' technology. In other words, the programmer responsible can maintain the consistency accurately enough without the need of support tools beyond those provided by most operating systems, such as recording the date of the last modification to a dataset. On the occasions where an error is made it is hoped that the error will be discovered quickly before any great damage has been done and the recovery, even if it requires some serious debugging, will not be too painful. There are many programs where this has been achieved with good success.

The danger is that the scope and size of the program grow unnoticed like children and weeds until one is suddenly astonished and wonders where the little program one used to know so well has gone. By this time the program is too big to be managed informally and it is very difficult to install the proper automatic program database management system after a large amount of the program is already written and in place. Consequently, it is better to use formal program database management right from the beginning even if the program is not expected to grow large enough to need it.

15.2.2 Programming in the large

The difference between the implementation of a small program and a large one does not lie in the techniques that are used to write the integrands. In both cases, the goals of writing readable integrands that can be easily modified are the same. The production of large software systems requires the coordination of the activities of many people. Very large programs may consist of up to a million lines of code, written by hundreds of programmers over a period of several years. They consist of thousands of integrands that must remain consistent with each other in the face of modifications performed by the programmers working concurrently. The real difference lies in the management. As Aron (1974) puts it:

> As in all things, increasing size leads to disproportionately increasing complexity; therefore, much programming activity is now directed toward the management of complexity instead of toward designing efficient instruction sequences. The emphasis on management rather than technology represents a major change in the nature of programming since the 1950s.

15.2.3 The audit trail

In the days before computers, the company auditor was a senior accountant who knew as much about the mechanics of accounting as any of the divisional accountants in the company. The auditor would go round to the division and inspect the books, run cross-checks to ensure that everything was being done correctly, and generally make sure that nobody was cheating. This was reasonably easy to do since everything was open and could be seen on paper. That was before computers.

Nowadays, it is considerably different. The accounting data goes in at one end of the computer and the checks and statements come out at the other. What goes on in between is not visible. The best that the auditor can do is to run spot checks and ask for listings of the programs that are executed. How can the auditor be assured that the listings produced actually match the programs that are executed?

Consider another example. A supersonic military plane suddenly crashes while on a training exercise. A careful examination of the wreckage shows that one of the critical engine parts was incorrect for supersonic speeds, it was only designed for lower speeds. How did it get there? Further investigation showed that it had been specified by the parts explosion program that generates a list of the parts required to build the plane by amalgamating the lists of parts for each of the components. How could it have specified the wrong part? It turned out that the program operated by building totals for all the parts in a large data structure that stored part number and number required. The total required for one of the parts exceeded the capacity allotted for it and it overflowed, corrupting the data in the next field, which was a part number. This caused the part number to change from one that specified a part suitable for supersonic speeds to one that was only designed for subsonic speeds. When programs corrupt data, they sometimes do so in bizarre ways. That error in the program had been found, though its potential consequences not appreciated, after the late lamented plane had been built. Question: what are the serial numbers of the planes whose part lists had been generated by that version of the program?

This example demonstrates that it is not enough to be able to maintain consistency between all the components of the program database. It must be possible to maintain a proper history of the development of the succeeding versions of the program. Each new version of the program must be identified so that it can be traced to the actual source code from which it was created.

15.3 MANAGEMENT OF THE PROGRAM DATABASE

A software system is a collection of data with relationships linking the basic entities together. It has the characteristics of a database; however, the basic information entities are not stored for easy access and it has seldom been treated as a proper database with the relations verified. The treatment of a program as a database is known as *Software Configuration Management*, which is defined in Bersoff *et al.* (1980) as:

> the discipline of identifying the configuration of a system at discrete points in time for purposes of systematically controlling changes to this configuration and maintaining the integrity and traceability of this configuration throughout the system life cycle.

In this volume, we are primarily concerned with keeping this control through the implementation and maintenance part of the cycle.

15.3.1 Management of change

The basis of managing the program database is to control the modifications to the source code automatically. A system such as SCCS (*Source Code Control System*), described by Rochkind (1975), can provide such control. Change control systems offer the ability to maintain multiple versions of text datasets such as source programs, documentation, or test data. When a programmer wishes to modify one of the datasets that is being controlled, the dataset must be reserved under the name of the programmer. This prevents more than one programmer from modifying the same dataset concurrently.

When the modification has been completed, the dataset is replaced. When the command to replace the dataset is given, the programmer is required to provide a description of the change and the reason for it. While it is recognized that there can be no way of checking the description and reason for accuracy, the fact that the change description is required and the change is logged with the programmer's name goes a long way to ensuring proper change documentation.

Change management systems usually store the original version of the dataset as it was created and then retain the modifications as incremental changes. The programmer can obtain any version of the dataset, ask to see the differences between two versions of the dataset, or to see a history of the changes to the dataset. This information is of critical importance during maintenance. For example, knowing what was the last change to an integrand is often a good lead to the error when debugging. All too often it turns out that it was the last change that is the cause of the latest bug.

15.3.2 Integration of changes

Once a change has been made to one of the datasets in the database, the change must be *integrated* into the database as a whole. This means making other consequential changes and checking for inconsistencies caused by the change. When the source code for an integrand is changed, the corresponding object code must be changed. After the text of one of the fragments of code that is included in some integrands during compilation is changed, then all the integrands that make use of it must be recompiled and the new object codes inserted into the database. When the interface of an integrand is changed then all the integrands that invoke it must be modified to make them consistent. This is not something that can be done automatically, however it is possible to search the database for all those integrands that need to be modified and have not been. This is an example of checking for possible inconsistencies.

An effective means for accomplishing this is to arrange for an integration procedure to be run during the hours when the programmers are not using the computer. In some systems this procedure is started every night at midnight. It performs the operations I have just described and by the time the programmers start work in the morning, all the automatic changes have been made and there is a report available on inconsistencies that have been discovered.

Checking for the consistency of the documentation during the integration process is much more difficult to automate. However, some of this can be accomplished by analyzing the source code for the integrands and generating parts of the documentation from that analysis directly. This works for programmer documentation that describes the interface specifications for the integrands but it will not work for documents like user manuals and reference manuals. For human readability, the format of these documents generally needs to be too informal for automatic analysis to be performed.

Finally, the integration process must keep proper records so that it is possible to determine exactly what happened during the integration. This is particularly important should there be some kind of hardware failure or electricity interruption. At such times, it is very important to be able to examine the records and determine exactly what was and was not done.

15.3.3 Maintenance of integrity

In this context, *integrity* concerns the preservation of programs and data against loss or corruption. By the time information has passed all the checks and is, as far as is known, correct and has been entered into the program database, a great deal of work has usually been spent in creating it and it represents a considerable investment. As with all valuable property, it must be safeguarded against the ravages of entropy, which represent loss of information. Sub-section 15.3.1 discusses methods for the management of the changes that must take place in the ordinary development process of the program. One danger is malicious change by unauthorized agents – hackers, disgruntled employees, terrorists, and other kindred spirits. The protection of the computer system against such invasions is a subject outside the scope of this book. Even if the computer system is perfectly secure – which it can never be – against attack, there is still the possibility of loss or corruption of data in the program database due to hardware malfunction and it is important to take steps to minimize the potential damage due to this. Such action will also serve to reduce the effects of damage to the database from outside attack.

A common way to protect against loss of data is to perform regular copying of the program database to tape or removable disk, which is then stored in some safe place away from the computer. There is a danger of being lulled into a false sense of security with this system. Typically, only a limited number of back-up copies of the database are stored. That is, after they have been kept for a year, the recording media are reused to prevent the storage facility from becoming overfilled. Some items in the database may only be referenced very infrequently. They may lie dormant for more than a year even though they are important to the system. For example, the source code for an integrand is generally not touched unless a change has to be made. This means that one of the datasets could be lost and the loss go undetected until a particular change requires access to it. If it disappeared more than a year earlier, the back-up storage will have been purged of all copies of it and it will have to be recreated. This may be the equivalent of re-implementing it.

On any particular day, the datasets that should be members of the database consist of those that were there the day before less any that have been deleted plus those that have been created in the intervening period. Since the creation and deletion of datasets must leave a record in the audit trail, it is possible to create the list of all datasets that should be present. Thus, any variances between this list and the list of actual members can be reported as anomalies and the loss of a dataset detected while there are still copies available from the back-up storage.

CHAPTER SIXTEEN
THE PROGRAMMING SUPPORT ENVIRONMENT

A programming support environment is a set of software tools designed to assist the programmer in the production of a program. The earliest software tool was the compiler. The assistance that a compiler offers, in addition to translating the source program, varies considerably between compilers and depends largely on the error diagnosis during both compilation and execution of the translated program. The next most common tool is an editor. Language-sensitive editors, which have some aspects of the programming language's structure built into them are discussed and some of their capabilities are described. Other tools that are of use to the programmer are summarized and finally, an outline of an integrated programming support environment is presented.

16.1 INTRODUCTION

As generally conceived, the purpose of a *programming support environment*, generally referred to as 'PSE', is to *support the programmer* in software development or maintenance. Some environments place restrictions on the user, for example, permitting only syntactically correct source code to be produced or requiring things to be done in a particular order. Others are simply collections of tools and data management facilities that are intended to be helpful in the general area of software development and maintenance.

The idea of a programming support environment goes back a long way before it was given such an impressive title. Examples of three early environments are APL, described in Falkoff and Iverson (1978), Basic (see Kurtz 1978), and Lisp, described in McCarthy (1978). These three systems provided a self-contained environment in which the programmer was able to develop programs without having to interact directly with the host operating system provided by the hardware manufacturer. The system thus catered to the user who wanted to solve a problem on the computer and did not want to learn to use the hostile user interface provided by the system's indigenous operating system. The user was thus able to work in an inner operating system that was consistent with the programming language in which the problem was being solved. In the case of Basic, the design of the language and the operating system were in sympathy. Kurtz (1963), in an early memorandum of this project, states:

> The Time Sharing System should be externally simple and easy to use for the casual programmer . . .

The fact that APL, Basic, and Lisp have enjoyed such continued success attests well to the appeal of a single environment in which a programmer can work without having to use the host operating system. I don't think it can be argued that the success of these three languages is due to their wonderfully clear language structure!

The need for a complete environment to support the development of Ada programs was realized by the US Department of Defense while the language was still being designed, although this need was not seen in time to include it in the original requirements for the language. After much debate, the requirements for an Ada programming support environment (Apse) were published as the 'Stoneman' document (Buxton 1980). (In the mid 1970s after the Department of Defense had identified the need for a single programming language for all of its applications, it issued a sequence of specifications, each *harder* in the sense of more specific that its predecessor, as suggested by the sequence of names: Strawman, Woodenman, Tinman, Ironman, and Steelman. A similar, though shorter, sequence culminating in Stoneman was used for the Apse requirements.) Since then, there have been many projects aimed at developing so-called 'integrated' environments. There are now several of these environments in use. Some are limited to the tools required by the programmers during the implementation phase; some attempt the support of other activities in the life-cycle such as specification, design and verification. All are known as 'PSEs'. In addition, the integration of management and technical support has been attempted in what is known as an 'Integrated *project* support environment', Ipse. These and the more extended PSEs are beyond our scope here – an account being available in Macro (1990) – except to explain that the term 'integrated' means that the individual tools that constitute the environment can communicate with each other, allowing accesses to common data and interaction. The elements of such a compendium are known as its 'tool-kit' and 'infrastructure'. The whole subject of tool-kit integration is discussed in Section 16.5.

Most current PSEs follow the tool-kit model, providing a separate but interconnecting tool for each of the tasks in program development. We will first present an overview of a number of these tools required for implementation and found in good PSEs at that level. We then discuss the integration of these tools into a single system where all parts cooperate.

16.2 COMPILERS

These are the most obvious and most assumed of the tools in a programming support environment. A compiler is language specific in that it can only translate its source language. There are a number of differences in the services that a compiler provides its users.

16.2.1 Error diagnostics

Compilers would be very much simpler if they only had to translate syntactically correct programs. Some of the very early compilers would find the first error in the source program, print a helpful diagnostic and terminate. This generally meant that the programmer was only able to discover and correct one error every run and since almost all computers used at that time were in batch mode with a turn-around time that could last several hours, productivity was very slow.

The problem with the detection of several errors at a time is that, once the first error has been encountered, the analysis has to find a new starting point that can be assumed to be correct. Thus it is possible for one error to mask other errors or to make it appear that there are errors where there are none. The usual approach is for the compiler to attempt to recover from an error by proceeding on the basis of an assumed correction to the program to give the 'nearest' syntactically correct version and to attempt to continue with the analysis. The 'correction' is not intended to make a correct program out of an erroneous one but to establish the firm base for the fresh start. Without this new base the effect of a single error causing a cascade of error messages is often seen.

As the technology improved, it was possible to produce diagnostic messages that were more accurate and tailored more to the specific error so as to help the programmer find and correct it. The production of diagnostics became quite a large part of the compiler. In the very early days of the IBM PL/I compiler, there would be an occasional appearance of the mysterious message

```
WHERE IS IT SAM HAWKINS?
```

It turned out that all the error messages for the compiler had been put into a single message library integrand and were accessed through a message number. The name of the man in charge of the message library was Sam Hawkins. The integrand that was responsible for the printing of the message would be given the message number and all the information that applied to a specific error and would invoke the message library to obtain the message template. As an excellent example of defensive programming, if no template was returned, either because the message number was wrong or the template had not yet been put into the library, the strange message was produced.

Despite the best efforts, it was never possible to be absolutely sure that the first error would not mask other errors or give rise to spurious error messages. With the advent of better and better interactive access to computers, the turn-around on a compilation became a matter of less than a minute, especially if the size of the integrand being compiled were kept to a very few hundred lines. In addition, when it became possible to invoke the compiler from within the editor, many programmers adopted the principle of fixing the first error and running the compiler again. This has led to the production of fast compilers that diagnose only the first error and then stop. This makes for a smaller compiler that can probably run faster than one with an elaborate error recovery mechanism. What we have seen is a roundabout effect; the error detection process is very like that of the first compilers. The effect of syntax-directed editors is to combine the functions of editing and syntax analysis and provide the programmer with error messages interactively.

16.2.2 Runtime support

The function of the compiler is not over when the source program has been translated. In that the function of the compiler is to produce a version of the program that can be executed, part of the compiler must provide a library of routines that make execution possible. These are subroutines that are invoked from the translated program to manage storage, provide input and output, calculate mathematical functions, and handle errors. As with the detection of errors during compilation, the assistance that is provided during execution varies with the compiler and the language.

In a previous chapter we have already described the handling of exception conditions from within a program. Here we are discussing the detection of errors during execution. The handling of these varies with the type of error; three representative examples are:

1. *Division by zero.* This is usually detected by the hardware and signaled to the support library through the operating system interrupt handlers.
2. *Attempt to access non-existent dataset.* This is generally detected by an operating system routine and signaled to the support library through the operating system's protocol.
3. *Attempt to access an array beyond its bounds.* Short of an indexing error that causes an access violation that is detected by the hardware or operating system, this type of error can, on most systems, only be detected reliably by special code generated by the compiler to evaluate the index expression and compare its value against the declared bounds of the array. Some computers provide detection of bound errors as part of the microcode that is executed every time an indexed reference is made.

The real way that runtime support differs from one programming environment to another is in the amount of help that is provided to the programmer when a runtime error is detected. Sometimes there are two versions of the compiler, one for 'checkout' and the other for 'production'. The difference usually lies in the amount of checking that is done during execution and the amount of diagnostic information that is stored. It is implied that the overhead of performing the checking is tolerable during program checking but during actual production running of the program, such checking is an unaffordable luxury. Hoare (1973) writes:

> it is absurd to make elaborate security checks on debugging runs, when no trust is put in the results, and then remove them in production runs, when an erroneous result could be expensive or erroneous. What would we think of a sailing enthusiast who wears his lifejacket when training on dry land, but takes it off as soon as he goes to sea?

Another difficulty with two different versions of the compiler is to be sure that, apart from the checking, both versions are identical. The differences may be very subtle yet none-the-less devastating. Part of the problem is that a compiler is a very complex program and the only known way of validating it is with a large suite of test cases. The United States Department of Defense has assembled such a collection for the validation of Ada compilers; however, this would still leave some margin for discrepancy between two supposedly identical compilers.

16.2.3 Optimization

Some compilers attempt to achieve increased execution performance by rearranging and changing the program being compiled. There are two different kinds of optimization:

1. *Modification of the original source program.* This class of transformations is independent of the target machine on which the program will be executed. Generally, the modifications are such that they could have been performed by the programmer on the source program.
2. *Modification of the generated code.* Here, the transformations are aimed at improving the efficiency of the program when it is run on a particular processor. This type of modification is beyond the power of the programmer to perform.

In all cases, the transformations must preserve the meaning of the program. The analysis performed by the compiler must be very thorough to make sure of this and, if there is the slightest doubt, the form of the program must be left unchanged.

In general, it would be better if the compiler were to report suggested modifications of the first sort to the programmer so that the actual source program could be modified to achieve the improved performance. This has two advantages:

- The behavior of the machine properly reflects the written form of the program. This can be of considerable advantage when searching for an error.
- The compiler can suggest many modifications that require additional information that is not contained in the program but would be obvious to the programmer because of a wider knowledge of the characteristics of the data.

16.3 LANGUAGE-SENSITIVE EDITORS

A PSE is aimed at assisting the programmer in the production of programs written in some programming language. Thus, the first step must be to have *language-based tools*, that is, tools that have aspects of the programming language's structure built into them. The degree to which the language's structure is used to assist the programmer varies considerably between products.

Conventional text editors are designed to create and modify objects of many different classes, including programs, documents, and data. Some of these editors are extensible, for example Emacs (Stallman 1981), and Z (Wood 1981). The authors of these editors argue that the most natural representation of programs is text and that the editor should impose no more structure on the text than is required to implement the program-editing functions. This simplifies the design of the editor and presents the user with a simple but powerful model of program structure. Examples of the assistance that can be offered through the extensibility provisions of an extensible editor are:

- *Automatic indentation.* It is possible to define an indentation pattern based on the language structure tokens such as BEGIN and END.
- *Balanced expressions.* A balanced expression is a sequence of tokens bracketed by a pair of unique balance tokens such as parentheses or BEGIN, END. As an extension modeled on the specific tokens of the language, it is possible to instruct the editor to close off the most recent opening token and to move the cursor over balanced expressions as a single unit.
- *Structure commands.* Assuming that the programmer maintains a consistent indentation convention, provided by the editor, it is possible to select complete syntactic units with a single keystroke and to display the program with lower levels of detail suppressed. Thus an IF statement could be displayed as:

```
IF LineCount > 13 THEN
      . . .
ELSE
      . . .
END;
```

where the . . . are actually displayed. This allows the programmer to inspect the program at various levels of detail.

- *Program compilation.* A frequent complaint with many text editors used for program composition is the large amount of time spent in moving back and forth between the editor and the compiler while debugging the syntax errors in a program. By tying the compilation command to a single key and giving the ability to invoke the compiler, it is possible to launch the compilation and, when it is complete and there are errors, split the screen to show the first error diagnostic in the second half. Wood (1981) argues that the time spent in watching the compiler is unproductive, however forcing the programmer to wait for the compiler does encourage the construction of short integrands.

As can be seen, extensible editors offer little more than typographical assistance to the programmer.

The next level of sophistication is a *syntax-directed editor* where entry and modification of program text are guided by a grammar for the host programming language. The incorporation of the grammar into the editor guarantees syntactically correct programs, there is no need for the programmer to repair syntax errors detected by the compiler. By the time the program reaches the compiler, it will be syntactically correct. In one such editor, described by Teitelbaum and Reps (1981), the grammar of the programming language is represented by a collection of language templates. Programs are created in top-down sequence by inserting new statements and expressions at a cursor position within the skeleton of previously entered templates. The movement of the cursor differs from that of a conventional text editor where it moves from line to line. In general the cursor can only be moved from one template to another and from one template to its constituents. Templates reinforce the view that a program is much more than a sequence of characters, it is a hierarchical composition of syntactic objects.

Templates consist of keywords and placeholders. The keywords are part of the language structure and cannot be modified. The placeholders identify the locations where insertions are permitted and designate the syntactic class of permissible insertions. For example, the template for an IF statement might be

```
IF condition THEN
    list-of-statements
ELSE
    list-of-statements
END;
```

where *condition* and *list-of-statements* are placeholders. The placeholders are replaced by the programmer by typing a phrase that is a member of the syntactic class denoted by the placeholder. The syntax of the typed phrase is checked as soon as the cursor is moved away from it. If an error is discovered, a message is displayed and the cursor is positioned as close to the site of the error as possible. A placeholder can be replaced by another template, for example, another IF template could be inserted into a *list-of-statements* placeholder. Since this placeholder represents possibly many statements, after a statement has been inserted into it, it is still possible to put further statements both before and after the inserted statement.

Reps (1984) describes the implementation of an editor that makes use of the semantic structure of the programming language to provide early feedback of errors to the programmer. This editor is able to detect context-sensitive program errors such as type violations immediately while the program is still being written. For example Modula-2 requires that any variable name used must be declared in the current or an enclosing block. To detect violations of such constraints, it is necessary for the editor to analyze the context given by the rest of the program. In addition, the editor performs global data-flow analysis and is able to provide feedback about errors in the program's possible execution. Such errors include the following:

- Use of uninitialized variables.
- Computation of a value that is never used.
- Conditions that are always true or always false.
- Modification of an input parameter.
- Array subscript out of bounds.
- Division by zero.
- Code that is unreachable and hence never executed.

Anomalies like these often reflect logical errors, lack of knowledge of the programming language, or poor understanding of the algorithm being described. The important thing about detecting these errors is that they are brought to the attention of the programmer immediately while the construct is still fresh in the mind.

16.4 GENERAL TOOLS

In this section we list and describe some of the general tools needed for software development. These are general in that they can be used for many different styles of development:

TEXT EDITOR

This is used to enter programs and other types of documents. Analogous to the language-sensitive editors discussed in the previous section are the word processors, which are really editors designed specifically for manipulating text; however word processors do not provide the same sort of encouragement to correct writing as language-sensitive editors. Nevertheless, word processors take a great deal of the drudgery out of writing documentation and should be available.

MACROPROCESSOR

This is a simple translator that can replace specified strings in a source document with newly constructed strings. More sophisticated processors allow for parameterization of the source string so that generalized patterns can be described. They can be used to overcome deficiencies in the language as is done in Ratfor, described in Kernighan and Plauger (1976) and can be used for considerable 'extensions' to a language. Beckermeyer *et al*. (1974) describe using macros to extend a simple language so that it handled asynchronous interrupts. More modern examples are Sed and Awk in Unix; Bentley (1988) contains several examples of their use.

LINKER

A linker takes several independently compiled integrands and produces a single executable program that includes subroutines selected from standard libraries.

DATASET ADMINISTRATION TOOLS

A compatible set of tools that supports back-up, archiving, computer to computer transfers, and management.

DATASET MANIPULATION TOOLS

A set of tools that can perform a range of operations on datasets such as finding the differences between two datasets, searching for all occurrences of a given pattern, and sorting.

PROGRAM ANALYZERS

These tools analyze a program during its execution. Typical measurements are the number of times each statement or each subroutine is executed or the amount of time that is spent in various parts of the program. If the efficiency of a program is to be improved, it can only be done on the basis of measurements made by tools like these. Any other basis, such as theoretical calculation, is pure guesswork that may or may not have some correlation with reality, depending on the validity of the data on which it is based.

16.5 INTEGRATED PROGRAMMING ENVIRONMENTS

In the previous section, a selection of general software tools was described. For such a kit to be truly useful, they need to be *integrated*; we can define this as follows:

- *Connectivity*. The programmer is able to move from one tool to another in a simple and convenient manner. Elements of the program database can be created with one tool and then worked on further with another tool as part of a single process by the programmer.
- *Consistency*. The interface between the tool and the user is consistent across all tools in the set. This manifests itself mainly in the syntax of the interactions – equivalent commands should have the same syntax and keyboard assignments should be identical. If key F15 means 'Provide online help' in one tool, it should mean that in all. Ideally, this would mean that the tool command syntax and the programming language syntax should be identical.
- *Protectivity*. There should be an adequate trail so that it is possible for the user to backtrack to the starting-point and begin again once it has been discovered that the wrong path has been followed.

A kit of integrated software tools constitutes a programming environment.

There are two types of environment. They can be closed, that is, they contain a fixed set of tools that cannot be altered or extended. Alternatively, they can be open, where the toolset can be modified or extended at any time to support the user's style of working. A good example is shown in those environments developed for supporting programming in Ada.

The Ada Programming Support Environment described in Buxton (1980) is an example of an open environment. This description defines three separate layers in the environment built around the operating system of the host computer as shown in Figure 16.1. The program database exists at the operating system level.

The innermost layer of the programming environment, called the *Kernel Ada Programming Support Environment* (Kapse), defines the requirements for the minimal support for the rest of the environment. This layer provides the interface between the Apse and the underlying machine and the low-level services for querying and manipulating the database. It is the Kapse that allows the program to be moved from one host machine to another by creating a new implementation-dependent Kapse on the new

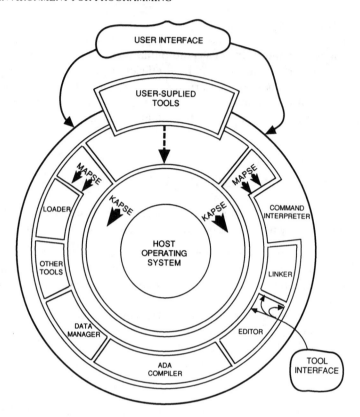

FIGURE 16.1 The Ada Programming Support Environment, from Buxton (1980).

host. Outside the Kapse, everything is machine-independent. This level is essentially hidden from the user by the tools, which are all built using the services provided by the Kapse.

The next layer out is the *Minimal Ada Programming Support Environment* (Mapse). This layer provides the minimal set of tools sufficient for software development. As can be seen from the diagram, these consist of a command interpreter, linker, editor, compiler, data manager, loader, and other tools such as were described in the previous section. Additional tools can be created by the user either by writing them in Ada or in the command language.

The outermost layer provides for the most abstract and generalized tools that are designed to help in all phases of the lifecycle. These tools are specified least and offer the greatest scope for the construction of tools to support specific ways of working that might be adopted by a team. It might include tools for the automatic generation of programs, program stubs, or test data.

The command language serves as an important way of unifying the programmer's interface with the tools. So as to minimize the amount of learning that the programmer must do, the language should be as close to the style of Ada as possible.

This outline of the construction of an example of an integrated programming support environment shows, albeit sketchily, the direction in which programming development support is going and will continue to go in the future. An environment of this type provides the computer to perform the drudge bookkeeping involved with developing the program and allows the programmer to be free for the more creative task of designing and specifying the program.

The Apse described above is an example of a large programming support environment that requires a great deal of computer hardware, communication support and is very expensive. Apart from systems like this, there is little available. One notable exception is the software available on the Apple® Macintosh™* series of computers. The design of the hardware and the operating system have set a paradigm for the interface between applications and their users. There is a large repertoire of applications available for these computers and their authors have in general, though not always in particular, followed this paradigm. The programmer is able to build a more or less integrated tool kit by choosing particular items from the many software catalogs that are available and buying them from their individual software companies – a compiler from here, an editor from there, and a debugger from a third place – and installing them. This is much like building a conventional workshop from tools obtained from a variety of manufacturers. Even though they come from a disparate set of authors, a well chosen set will function in concert as an excellent programming environment, largely due to the adherence to the original interface paradigm. Because of the great variety of software tools available in this way, a programming team can build an environment for many specialized purposes such as generating programs for execution on some other machine. It is thus possible to obtain the advantages of a good programming environment in situations where it would be uneconomic to build a special-purpose one for a particular project. However, it does require two key ingredients:

- The availability of a wide range of software tools that match a common user interface, and
- The recognition on the part of the programming team and its management of the great advantages that can be obtained from a good programming environment.

16.6 CURRENT STATE-OF-THE-ART AND THE FUTURE

Simple tools are inexpensive, more elaborate ones are less so. Extensive tool kits can be costly, whilst the 'all singing, all dancing extravaganza', if it exists, is likely to jolt the financial controller right into an intensive care unit. Such systems involve a very great

*Apple and Macintosh are registered trademarks of Apple Computer, Inc.

deal of software – which accounts for part of the cost – they also require extensive 'host' hardware and ancillaries – and that can be the dominant cost.

Most large-scale software implementation is carried out today with a properly furnished tool kit that is itself integrated and may, or may not, have wider features. The equipment in use is either 'host' – program preparation on hardware other than the target – or 'self-host' – preparation and execution on the same hardware. Programmers for such systems are thus reasonably well provided with implementation tools for their trade. On the other hand, many medium and small systems – particularly involving microprocessors to be 'embedded' as components in electronic assemblies, for example, household appliances – are very underprovided at the PSE level. In these circumstances, development is likely to be of the old-fashioned sort, with all the old problems of an unmaintainable result. The only antidote to this would seem to be the development of host-based PSEs, for multipurpose use, within the economic range of companies in this sector of software development.

However generally satisfactory the PSE might be for implementation-level work, after all, the notion grew 'bottom up' out of rudimentary operating system features, many implementors find the general facilities in need of amplification or enhancement. The development of software tools is an essential, though often neglected, part of the programmer's task. Many of the tools that are needed for the efficient production of programs are too specialized to be available through commercially available programming environments. A programming team must therefore expect to produce tools that are of general use within the project. This chapter reviews some of the tools that are likely to be useful in program production. Such tools include code auditors, error-reporting systems, automatic back-up, documentation verification, and integration tracking. The last is an example of a tool that makes use of many other tools, some of them generally available and some constructed specifically for the project. This is not intended as a chapter of recipes but as a compendium of ideas and examples that might be adapted to a particular project.

16.7 SPECIAL SOFTWARE TOOLS

In their introduction to *Software Tools*, Kernighan and Plauger (1976) broach the subject of tools by suggesting the problem of finding all the FORMAT statements in a large Fortran program so that they can be modified. One solution is to go through the listing, about 500 pages, and mark each FORMAT statement with a red pencil. This is a process fraught with possible error. Even if there are no interruptions from co-workers or the telephone, the job is so boring that our attention span may not be up to it. An alternative is to make use of the computer for this mindless work: not to write a program to find FORMAT statements but a general-purpose pattern finder, Find.

> Find is a *tool*: it uses the machine; it solves a general problem, not a special case; and it's so easy to use that people will use it instead of building their own.
>
> Far too many programmers are red pencillers. Some are literal red pencillers who

do things by hand that should be done by machine. Others are figurative red pencillers whose use of the machine is so clumsy and awkward that it might as well be manual. (Kernighan and Plauger, 1976)

In the last chapter we discussed a number of general tools that are useful in the production and development of programs. However, these only provide the bare necessities of a tool kit. Commercial programming support environments can only be expected to provide tools that are of use to a wide spectrum of programmers.

Every programming team develops its own style of working, which will be slightly different from the way in which other teams work. This style will evolve with time as the members become more experienced and new members join bringing fresh ideas. Consequently, there is a need for tools that are special to the team's way of working and will not necessarily be exactly what is required by other teams. These tools are so important to reducing the drudgery of programming that every team must be prepared to invest 10 per cent of its time constructing tools for the general use of the project. This does not mean that each member spends that amount of time or that for every ten programmers that are assigned to the team, one of them should be engaged in full-time development and support of tools. This figure of 10 per cent sounds excessive but I have found through experience that this is a good estimate. The difficulty is that, while programmers can be persuaded that this is a good investment, management will be much harder to convince. However, that too is worth the effort.

The tools described in this chapter are examples of special-purpose tools that have been found to be very useful in the projects that I have worked on. Versions of some of these tools might well be found in many integrated programming environments but we are not yet at the stage where such an environment can be assumed. In fact, looking at some of the editors that are being used regularly, very little can be assumed about the fitness of the tools available to the majority of the world's programmers. I am sometimes astonished at the temerity of the suppliers of these editors to use the term 'editor'.

This is not intended as a chapter of recipes but one of ideas. In some cases a brief outline of how the tool could be constructed is given to provide some concrete foundation for the discussion. Most of these tools are not built from scratch but are constructed from the tools supplied by the host operating system linked together with command procedures written in the command language. Sometimes, a small program will be required as a part of a tool but generally these small programs require no more than half a day to produce.

Efficiency is not always of great importance; it is the service rendered by the tool that is important. In many installations it has been found that switching the computers off at night is expensive because of the hardware failure problems that it causes. Some of these tools can be run during 'dead time' in the middle of the night when the machine is just twiddling its disks and not doing anything useful. Cycles are cheap then.

16.7.1 Code auditors

Code auditors check that the standard formats adopted by the team as the programming style have been adhered to and that other verifiable programming formats are maintained. This is not a question of checking that specific indentation rules have been observed but more of checking that the header comments have the appropriate fields and, where it is possible to check, the contents of these fields match the information contained in the actual code. A language-sensitive editor, especially one that allows the user some ability to tailor structures to suit individual requirements, can render the use of a code auditor superfluous.

The use of these fixed formats for comments and other key ingredients to the integrand is an important style decision that must be made at the early stages of the project. It is on these parts that other consistency checks, described later in this chapter, depend. They can also lighten the burden of constructing integrand documentation since they allow some of it to be done automatically. While there is no method of checking the information content of the comments against the source code, the use of these formats is also of great help to the programmers in reminding them of the information that needs to be included.

16.7.2 Defect reporting systems

A defect reporting system keeps track of failures detected during the product testing and maintenance stages of the project. The idea is that when a user or programmer finds a defect, the reporting system is invoked. This will prompt the person reporting the defect for information that the maintenance programmers will need to track down the problem. Without this information, it is often difficult to make the first step in debugging; reliable and repeatable recreation of the failure. Typical information that will be needed is listed below:

1. A description of the symptoms of the problem from the point of view of the user together with an outline of what was being attempted.
2. A copy of the input data that was used at the time of the failure. This will include copies of any files that were being used.
3. A copy of any output that the program produced including any error trace file that it generates.
4. Identification of the precise version of the program that was being used. This is a situation where the maintenance of proper version control through a configuration management system is important since this will allow the maintenance programmers to determine exactly what versions of all the source integrands were used in the construction of the executable program. Rerunning the input data with the latest version of the program and demonstrating that the same error no longer exists is not sufficient to show that the problem has been fixed. There may be other effects that mask the error, which is still there.

Much of this information can be gathered automatically. Once the information has been assembled it must be transmitted to the maintainers. This can be done either through an electronic network transmission or by recording the information on tape or floppy disks.

Another part of the defect reporting system resides on the system used by the maintainers. This part logs the failure and makes sure that the information is made available to the maintainers. It also tracks the repair of the problem and provides proper response to the person who reported the error. This may consist of electronic mail messages or letters that are generated automatically. Such a Defect Reporting System exists in some Ipses currently in use.

16.7.3 Automatic back-up

In the world of literature one has heard the story of a writer who leaves the manuscript that has taken thousands of hours of creation in a taxicab. Sometimes these are recovered, often they are not. Generally, the writer does not have the fortitude to recover from such a loss and recreate the work. The labor investment, almost always the major cost item, in a large program is chiefly represented by the program database stored in the computer system. Hardware failures are still sufficiently common that it is quite possible for such information to become unreadable or corrupted. This is the electronic version of the taxi driving off with the manuscript and becoming lost in the traffic.

Automatic back-up of files is an important tool for any system, so much so that it should be a standard part of the system's procedures. Although it may sometimes be thought of as a standard part of any operating system, this is not always the case. Even if it is thought that it is handled by the operations staff, it is worthwhile checking that this does in fact happen. In some cases, when datasets are lost and the backed-up versions called for, after the foot shuffling and finger pointing has died down, it becomes apparent that, due to some communication failure, nothing has been backed-up for several months. The discovery that the files are lost is a warning of what might happen if there were a serious hardware failure. This is of little comfort to the programmer who has accidentally deleted the datasets and has to recreate them.

One system that I used had no operators and the programmers were responsible for everything. We set up a program that copied all the project's files to tape. This program was executed every night except at weekends, when the system was not used. Every day one of the programmers would visit the machine and change the tape. We used a set of eight tapes. Tape 1 was used every second day. Tape 2 was used every four days. In general, Tape n was used every 2^n days except where its place was taken by a higher-numbered tape. Since we could not trust the tape-changing programmer to work out which was the next tape to use, there was a program that had to be executed to set the next back-up to take place during the following night. This program printed instructions on the console specifying which tape had to be mounted and then verified that the correct tape had been used. It also sent a mail message to all programmers to inform them that the new tape had been mounted. This indicated that somebody had already done the job that day, and the other programmers did not need to go down to the basement to do it, only to find that it had already been done. This was arranged without any form of roster on a purely voluntary basis and it turned out that the task was very evenly divided among the programmers and was rarely missed. Of course, a log was kept so that we could check which tape was used on any particular date.

A related tool that is very useful is what might be termed a 'bed-check'. In some athletic training camps it is common to check that all members of the team are in their dormitories and not carousing. This is a bed-check. When applied to datasets, a bed-check consists of making sure that all datasets that are supposed to be in the database are there. In the simplest form, this program compares today's list with yesterday's and reports any changes. This process can be made more sophisticated by taking account of the day's activities of creating and deleting integrands. The importance of this tool is that a dataset that is not referenced can go AWOL without being noticed and if the reference interval is longer than the longest back-up retention cycle it will be lost and have to be recreated.

16.7.4 Documentation verifier

In the development of programs and their subsequent maintenance, the days just before the release of a new version are hectic – there are always myriad small details to be taken care of. The maintenance of strict synchrony between the source programs and the documentation is often a casualty of the final rush. In the heat of the moment, modifications to the source are forgotten and the documentation is not changed. This is even true with the best will in the world and programmers rarely bear the best will towards documentation.

A documentation verifier is a software tool that ensures the following:

1. Every integrand has its associated documentation.
2. There are no documents that describe integrands that have been superseded and deleted from the program database.
3. That the documents, as far as is mechanically verifiable, are in the correct format and accurately describe the program and individual integrands.

Items 1 and 2 are the converse of each other and are performed in the same way. The technique is to construct two lists, a list of the integrands and a list of the documents describing integrands. The first list can generally be obtained directly from the file management system. If the documents are produced on a word processor, it may be possible to obtain the second list in a dataset prepared by the word processor itself. While this can often be done interactively, many word processors do not have the ability to be invoked in 'batch' mode. In most word-processing applications, this is satisfactory. However, for the toolmaker, this is a problem that illustrates an important point about the design of this kind of tool. A documentation verifier is an 'audit' tool and the user needs to be sure that its results are trustworthy. This means that its analysis must be complete. To interpose manual intervention in the form of performing interactive processes always runs the risk that the user will be distracted at a critical moment and the sequence of actions not completed properly. Thus, for a reliable audit, some way of obtaining the document directory during batch execution must be found. This probably means finding the structure of the directory and writing a simple program to extract the required information. Often the word processor documentation will not contain the detailed layout of the directory dataset and some experiments have to be run. Generally, it is easy to build such a tool. When I implemented this tool, it took me less than two hours to find the directory layout by experiment and construct the program to produce the document list.

Once the two lists, IntegrandList and DocumentList, have been constructed, two new lists IntegrandAndNotDocumentList and DocumentAndNotIntegrandList can be built. There are generally tools in the system that can be used to produce these two lists. The first of these derived lists gives the documents that need to be produced and the second gives the documents that are candidates for deletion from the system or integrands that need to be produced. I use the word 'candidates' advisedly because it is dangerous for the tool to actually perform the deletions without considered approval from the programmer. Essentially, the second list is a list of anomalies that need to be investigated. The list of documents yet to be prepared can be improved by using it as input to a program that interrogates the history records maintained by the code management system for the integrands to find out the name of the integrand's author. This indicates the proper source for the documentation.

Item 3 requires careful planning at the beginning of the project. The format of the integrand specifications must be rigidly defined so that they can be analyzed mechanically without great difficulty. One way of achieving a fixed format for the specification documents and also reducing some of the pain associated with producing the documents is to define a fixed format for the introductory comments at the beginning of the integrand. Since the information to be included in the documentation is partially derived from these comments and partially from parts of the actual code, defining this fixed format for the comments makes it possible to write a tool that will extract much of the information required for the documentation from the actual code and put it into a form that can be accepted by the word processor. Again, this may require some experimentation since the specification of the word processor files may not be available. If this is done, the audit program checks that the code and the documentation match and reports anomalies.

16.7.5 Integration tracking tools

These tools augment the work of the source code management system and ensure that program changes are properly integrated into the program's database. They can also serve as the vehicle for running some of the tools described in the previous sections. One such tool runs every night, starting at midnight, maintaining a log of its activities as it goes. The following list of major tasks performed by this program gives some idea of the range of book keeping jobs that must be performed to keep proper track of a modest sized project.

1. *Integrate new documents*. All new documents produced during the day are properly catalogued and logged. If these documents were under the control of the source code management system, this would be done automatically but, because of the word processor that was chosen to handle the documentation, this was found to be impractical. However, this illustrates that tools can be constructed to handle such

situations and a project is not necessarily locked in by the choice of a particular programming environment support tool. (Although developed for code management, systems such as Unix's SCCS and VMS's CMS, actually manage text; whether the text is source code is immaterial. A more opposite name might be 'document management system'.)

2. *Integrate new help text.* As part of the documentation for an interactive system being developed, the user is able, through a special keyboard button, to display documentation text tailored to the user's current activity. The text for this documentation is stored in a special library and new or changed text is added to the program database and recorded.

3. *Integrate new tools.* The production of software tools is a continuing task and new tools need to be added to the database as they are produced. Even though there are many days where no new tools are developed, this step is performed each time. A report of no activity is sometimes important.

4. *Integrate new include datasets.* Include files are the source code fragments that contain text that is common to many integrands and is included in their source text automatically by the compiler. The integration of new or modified versions of these datasets into the system requires searching all the integrands that reference these included datasets and adding them to the list of integrands that need to be compiled.

5. *Integrate new source code.* The source code management system will have handled the inclusion of these new and modified versions of the integrands into the database. However, they must be added to the list of integrands that need to be compiled to bring the set of object integrands up to date to reflect the day's activity.

6. *Compile the integrands that have been marked for compilation.* The two previous steps have built a list of integrands that need to be compiled in order to make the set of object integrands consistent with the rest of the database. This is also an important step to check that the integrands compile without any error messages. Occasionally, in the rush of completing a modification, a programmer may accidentally integrate the wrong version of a source code dataset, one that contains syntax errors. Any error messages are put into the log.

7. *Produce new executable version.* Once the object integrands have been produced, a new version of the executable program must be constructed. This is done by linking all the object integrands using the linker.

8. *Check that the interfaces are correct.* Depending upon the language chosen, the correctness of the interface may or may not be enforced by the compiler. In those languages where this is not so, a tool that checks that the declarations of the arguments in the calling integrands match the declarations of the parameters in the called integrands is important to run. Any anomalies are reported.

9. *Run bed-check.* Check that all the datasets that are expected to be in the database are there. This includes verifying that for each object integrand there is a source integrand dataset.

10. *List the outstanding source code reservations.* With a source code management system, programmers reserve an integrand before they start modifying it so as to avoid the problem of having more than one programmer working on the same

integrand at the same time. Preparing a list of integrands that are reserved is a good way of making sure that a programmer does not reserve an integrand and then forget about it.

11. *Process the error reports – received and closed.* All error reports that have been received and closed are logged.

12. *Produce microfiche of log.* Throughout the running of this program, a log is maintained of everything that is done so that if there are any questions, there is a reference document that records what actually was done. Paper listings of such logs are difficult to file, and we found that we could make use of the microfiche system available on a connected computer system to build a record of the integration procedure.

13. *Report any anomalies.* The complete log is examined for any inconsistencies detected during the whole process. If any are found, they are reported by electronic mail to the project management and the programmers concerned.

This set of activities and sequence in which they are performed was particular to the project that the tool was supporting. However, this description gives some idea of the range of processes that can be performed in order to maintain proper book-keeping for such a project.

This tool was built largely from procedures specified in the operating system's command language with relatively few programs written in an actual programming language. The procedure was started every night at midnight and generally continued execution for about four hours. On the night following modifications to a large number of integrands or to included code fragments that require the recompilation of a large number of integrands, the process could last much longer.

Although this may seem to be a very large tool for the use of a single project, it was constructed by the programmers working on the project in about 10 per cent of their time, the appropriate fraction for tool-building.

ENVOI

This brings the book proper to its end by revisiting its main themes. Not least of its purposes is to reveal the fate of our 'Running Example', which was left in a state of suspended animation earlier in the book.

This book is a polemic against amateur *programming*. It has nothing to say against amateur *programmers* because that is where we all start. It is a beginning which is not peculiar to programming but true of any of the skills that we pretend to in life – we all have been or still are amateur gardeners, drivers, . . . human beings if we come down to it. What kind of programming the amateur programmer does in private is not our concern, the object of our attack is amateur programming in a context where professional standards of programming are required, i.e., in any context where programs are to be shared with others, either as programs *per se* or by the effects of their execution. The dangers of amateur driving make a striking analogy. The object is improvement, and this text is motivated by that on every page, whether that is clear or not. Any failures in clarity are due to me being too much an 'amateur writer', and I shall take the reader's 'physician heal thyself' as a given.

OLD PROGRAMS NEVER DIE, THEY JUST BECOME MORIBUND

Programming is an expository act between (it is hoped) consenting peers. The aim of the programmer must thus be directed to the imperatives of this exposition to all 'heirs and assigns' – for programs never live out their appropriate life span and then die in a dignified way. It is time that we realized that we are drowning in ancient – and modern but decrepit – software, much of it hovering on both sides of the brink of maintainability. Whilst I write, a few hundred thousand or more programmers with amateur skills are compounding the felony, hacking away in some lamentable dialect of an inappropriate programming language to produce software whose requirements specification was never

354

written down and whose design was pure happenstance. Exaggeration? – probably. Gross exaggeration? – I hope so but wouldn't wager much on it.

In many cases, the sheer investment in software development militates against a clear judgement of its worth. Take the fictitious case of a major clearing bank that, in 1975 say, invested in a very large main frame system, which filled a room the size of a gymnasium. Two hundred person-years of effort went into coding their off-line applications, and another seventy five for an on-line terminal-based transaction system. Linking it all to *Swift*, the inter-bank network, cost another fifty person-years . . . the staff are exhausted, the programming group has trebled in size, there is an uncounted number of unresolved complaints about software malfunctions, abnormal terminations, lost or spurious transactions . . . Can you imagine that bank going through this pain barrier again before all the present management have retired?

While the bank is fictitious, the scenario is not and, furthermore, exists in myriad replications and variations throughout at least Europe and North America. This is one side of the problem that has been ramifying as I write. The other side concerns the maintenance of this software mess. It has been estimated by Boehm (1973), Putnam (1982), and others, that between 50 per cent and 60 per cent of all software engineering work goes into its maintenance and the generation of new versions without an entire rewrite. The total amount of software work being performed is an exponentially increasing function of time that carries its own concerns for resources. In my view, three factors are driving the rate of increase upwards:

1. The present skills shortage among software engineers (as distinct from amateur programmers) tends to keep software systems in service far longer than they should be. How can we rewrite our system when we are so understaffed? – this was exactly the state that the company with the program Big Bertha (see Section 1.2.2) found itself. This is compounded by the fact that three-fifths of the staff are already doing maintenance work that must be continued during a new development.
2. The tendency, due to the same skills shortage, to use amateur programmers in too large a proportion on new developments. All programmers must learn by doing, but when the only form of education is by trial and mainly error it is very costly – either in failed developments, or the subsequent maintenance costs.
3. The investment problem, acting as a braking force on top of the skills shortage, that keeps old systems in use when they have been modified many, many times, and whatever 'work to maintain, or improve structure' (see Section 2.2.6) has or has not been attempted.

These three will do for now. Our concern here is the implementation stage of a life-cycle that can have problematical features at any or all steps. If I were pressed to provide a list of desiderata, if not imperatives, for this implementation phase, I would offer the following items without any ranking:

1. All precursor life-cycle activities competently managed and carried out – see other volumes in this series.
2. Education in good software engineering (and in this case implementation) practices

for *all* exponents. My ideas on good implementation practice, and why it works, are stated in this book.

3. Not too many amateur programmers on a development, in proportion to experienced (and educated) software engineers; a ratio of 1:3 is about as far as one can safely go.

4. *Clarity is next to godliness*, rather than 'correctness' is the aphorism that should be writ large on the wall of every programmer's office. Then make sure that there is adequate Quality Assurance to guarantee that the correctness is there before the system is put into service.

5. Provision of the proper tools of the trade and adequate training in their use.

6. Enough time is allowed; there is no such thing as 'half a program'.

7. Remember constantly that the only thing in software that will not change is the need for change and program accordingly.

The magic number seems a good place to stop this list. The reader may like to rephrase these dicta as self-examination questions. Do you undertake software implementation in such an environment and frame of mind? Of course you do! So do I – naturally! It's all the others that create the software problems. It always is 'the others' isn't it?

THE RUNNING EXAMPLE . . . WHERE DID IT RUN TO?

In fact, our Running Example seemed to emulate Hazel in *Watership Down* (Adams 1972), who 'stopped running' when he met the angel of death, the feared and fearsome 'black rabbit of Inlé'. In our case, the Kwic Index program that we began in Chapter 3 was used, thereafter to illustrate points in the text and is currently 'running on the spot' in Chapter 10. But it is only dormant, not dead.

If one pieces together the bits spread over text between Chapters 3 and 10, one will not get a coherent example in the sense that a specification and design decomposition will be seen to be revealed by an implementation on page such-and-such. That was not my purpose in creating the Running Example. However, it seems unfair to leave the poor thing in Section 10.9 to its fate, and the reader will surely feel cheated if having thundered about good expository practices, I shrink out of the book without even a backward wave at it. Ah, the loneliness of the long-distance running example (apologies to Sillitoe).

This is the end of the book proper. What follows includes as a first offering a complete implementation of the specifications and derived designs first met in Chapter 3.

PART FIVE

APPENDICES

APPENDIX A
OVERVIEW OF MODULA-2

This appendix contains a brief overview of a sub-set of the programming language Modula-2 sufficient for the reader who is new to the language to understand the excerpts contained in the book.

This appendix describes a sub-set of Modula-2 rather than the full language so as to provide the reader unfamiliar with Modular-2 with sufficient information to understand the Running Example while minimizing the mental investment required. For each of the constructs discussed, its syntax is defined by a simple formalized rule sometimes amplified by a short commentary on its semantics. Readers who would like to see a complete description of the full language, are referred to texts such as Kelly-Bootle (1987).

The rules define the correct sequence of elements in the various constructs of the language. The form of rules is modeled on a syntax definition technique known as Backus–Naur Form, which was introduced in 1959 by John Backus as a method for the definition of the syntax of Algol 60 and described in Naur (1963).

Each rule has the form:

Thing-being-defined　　　⇨ *Definition*

Thus, the symbol → can be taken to mean 'is defined as'. The *Thing-being-defined* is a class of syntactic constructs, for example a *Pointer-Type*. The *Definition* part consists of a combination of actual characters that must appear and other syntactic categories. The rule for *Pointer-Type* is

Pointer-Type　　　　　⇨ POINTER TO *Type*

This rule specifies that a member of the class *Pointer-Type* in a Modula-2 program consists of the actual characters 'POINTER TO' followed by member of the class *Type*, which is defined by another rule in this appendix.

Some classes are defined as being one of a number of alternatives, which are separated by a '|', thus the rule

Multiplication-Operator   ⇨   `*`
                                | `/`
                                | `DIV`
                                | `MOD`
                                | `&`

specifies that a *Multiplication-Operator* is an occurrence of one of `*`, `/`, DIV, MOD, or `&`.

Another situation that can be shown in the syntactic rules is that of optional parts, that is, sequences that may or may not occur in a construct. This is shown by enclosing the optional parts in the brackets [and]. For example, the rule

Expression   ⇨   *Simple-Expression* [*Relation Simple-Expression*]

shows that an *Expression* is a *Simple-Expression* optionally followed by a *Relation* and a *Simple-Expression*.

Finally, the rules can show that a construct can contain zero or more occurrences of some elements. This is done through the use of braces, { , }. Thus, a *Term* is defined with the rule

Term   ⇨   *Factor* { *Multiplication-Operator Factor* }

which shows that a *Term* is a *Factor* possibly followed by one or more occurrences of the sequence *Multiplication-Operator Factor*.

Modula-2 specifies the following reserved words, not all of which are defined in this appendix, which may not be used as identifiers in a program:

AND	ELSIF	LOOP	REPEAT
ARRAY	END	MOD	RETURN
BEGIN	EXIT	MODULE	SET
BY	EXPORT	NOT	THEN
CASE	FOR	OF	TO
CODE	FORWARD	OR	TYPE
CONST	FROM	POINTER	UNTIL
DEFINITION	IF	PROCEDURE	VAR
DIV	IMPLEMENTATION	QUALIFIED	WHILE
DO	IMPORT	RECORD	WITH
ELSE	IN	REM	

Contrary to the normal bottom-up way of presenting programming languages, even by those who espouse the top-down view, the subset of Modula-2 described here is presented strictly top-down. That is to say, we start with the largest element, a compilation unit, and define that in terms of other elements that are defined later in this

appendix. As an assistance in locating the rule that defines a construct, the rule number is
appended to the construct name in the rule. Thus the rule for *Term* is actually given as:

Term   ⇨ *Factor:33* { *Multiplication-Operator:41 Factor:33* }

showing that the rule for *Factor* is given in Section 34 and the rule for *Multiplication-Operator* is given in Section 42.

A.1 COMPILATION-UNIT

A *compilation-unit* represents a set of source code that can be submitted to the compiler.
The syntax of a compilation unit is

Compilation-Unit   ⇨ *Definition-Module:02*
                          | [IMPLEMENTATION] *Program-Module:03*

The basic unit of compilation in Modula-2 is the 'module' and, as is shown here, there are
three kinds of module:

A.1   A *Program-Module*, which is a main module in that although it may use other
      modules, it is not used by any other module.
A.2   A *Definition-Module*, which defines a set of objects that can be accessed by other
      modules.
A.3   An *Implementation-Module*, which has the same syntax as a program module but
      is preceded with the word IMPLEMENTATION. Definition and implementation
      modules go together in pairs and the implementation modules specifies the
      implementation of the objects defined by the corresponding definition module.

A.2 DEFINITION-MODULE

The Definition-Module specifies the objects – procedures, types, and constants – that are
accessible to users of the module. This module defines the user interface with the objects
that are implemented in the corresponding implementation module. The syntax of a
Definition-Module is:

DefinitionModule   ⇨ DEFINITION MODULE *Identifier:46* ;
                            {*Import:-List:04* }
                            {*Definition:05* }
                            END *Identifier:46* .

The identifier following END must match the identifier following DEFINITION
MODULE. The function of any Import-Lists is to provide access to objects – usually types
– that are defined in other Definition-Implementation-Module pairs and are required for
the interface definitions in the current module.

A.3 PROGRAM-MODULE

Each standalone Modula-2 program has one and only one *Program-Module*. The syntax of the *Program-Module* is:

Program-Module   ⇨   MODULE *Identifier:46* ;
       { *Import-List:04* }
       { *Data-Declaration:06* }
       { *Procedure-Declaration:15* }
      BEGIN
       Statement-Sequence:19
      END *Identifier:46* .

The syntax of an *Implementation-Module* is the same as for a *Program-Module* with the addition of the keyword **IMPLEMENTATION** before the keyword **MODULE**, as shown in A.1. The *Import-List* provides access to objects defined in other Definition-Implementation-Module pairs. The data elements defined in the *Data-Declaration* can be accessed from the *Statement-Sequence* and also from the procedures defined in the *Procedure-Declarations*. The part of the program where an object can be referenced by name is the *scope* of that identifier.

In the case of a *Program-Module*, execution of the *Statement-Sequence* begins as soon as the program is loaded. In the case of an *Implementation-Module*, execution of the *Statement-Sequence* begins as soon as the *Implementation-Module* is imported. In both *Program-Modules* and *Implementation-Modules*, the life of the data objects defined in the *Data-Declarations* is the life of the program. Thus, for *Implementation-Modules*, the *Statement-Sequence* is often used to initialize variables that will be shared by the procedures since there is no automatic initialization of values defined in the language . . .

A.4 IMPORT-LIST

An *Import-List* specifies identifiers of all objects that are declared outside the module but are used within the module. The syntax of an *Import-List* is:

Import-List: ⇨   [FROM *Identifier:46*] IMPORT *Identifier:46* { , *Identifier:46* } ;

Since Modula-2 modules, are separately compilable, it is necessary to be able to indicate in a module what resources are needed from other modules. This is achieved through *Import-Lists*. Only objects that are exported by other modules by being declared in *Definition-Module:2* can be imported. The FROM clause indicates the module from which the import is to be made and the list of identifiers names all the objects that are to be imported from that module. If the FROM clause is omitted, then the identifiers are module names. Every exportable identifier in the named modules are imported. However, to use them, it is necessary to qualify each reference to them by prefixing the name of the containing module followed by a period, for example, Math. Sqrt.

A.5 DEFINITION

A *Definition* in a *Definition-Module:2* lists the objects that can be exported from the module and thus can be imported into another module through an *Import-List:4*.

> *Definition*   ⇨ *Constant-Declaration:07*
> | TYPE {*Identifier:46* [= *Type:10* ;] }
> | *Variable-Declaration:09*
> | *Procedure-Heading:16* ;

Type definitions may specify the type in full, in which case its representation is available to users. If only the type name occurs, the representation of the type is hidden in the corresponding implementation module. Such types are said to be *opaque* and are implemented as pointers. Where procedure names are exported, only the procedure heading is given in order to provide the user interface to the procedure while keeping the actual details of the procedure out of the user's sight in the implementation module.

A.6 DATA-DECLARATION

A *Data-Declaration* can either appear in a *Program-Module:03* or in a *Procedure-Declaration:15*. It defines constants, types and variables to be referenced in the corresponding program or procedure.

> *Data-Declaration*   ⇨ *Constant-Declaration:07*
> | *Type-Declaration:08*
> | *Variable-Declaration:09*

A.7 CONSTANT-DECLARATION

A *Constant-Declaration* associates a constant value with an identifier. This value cannot be changed during execution.

> *Constant-Declaration*   ⇨ CONST { *Identifier:46* = *Constant-Expression:35* ; }

A.8 TYPE-DECLARATION

A *Type-Declaration* associates an identifier with a data type.

> *Type-Declaration*   ⇨ TYPE { *Identifier:46* = *Type:10* ; }

A data type specifies a set of values that variables of that type can take and the set of operations that can be performed on those values. Types include the elementary data types that are defined as part of the language, see A.11, as well as user defined types.

A.9 VARIABLE-DECLARATION

A *Variable-Declaration* defines the names of variables and associates a type with them.

Variable-Declaration   ⇨   VAR { *Identifier:46* : *Type:10; }*

All variables used in a program must be declared.

A.10 TYPE

Type   ⇨   *Simple-Type:11*
                                | *Array-Type:12*
                                | *Record-Type:13*
                                | *Pointer-Type:14*

Variables that are either of a *Simple-Type* or of a *Pointer-Type* hold only a single value at any one time. Variables that are either of an *Array-Type* or of a *Record-Type* hold composite values that are characterized by their structuring method and the types of their components.

A.11 SIMPLE-TYPE

.   *Simple-Type*   ⇨   INTEGER
                                | LONGINT
                                | CARDINAL
                                | LONGCARD
                                | REAL
                                | LONGREAL
                                | CHAR
                                | BOOLEAN
                                | (*Identifier:46* { , *Identifier:46* })
                                | [*Constant-Expression:35* . . *Constant-Expression:35*]

The predefined types INTEGER, CARDINAL, and REAL define sets of numeric values of implementation defined range. LONGINT, LONGCARD, and LONGREAL define wider ranges of the same kinds of numeric values. The type CHAR defines the set of ASCII characters, and the type BOOLEAN has the two values TRUE and FALSE.
   The form

   (*Identifier:46* { , *Identifier:46* })

defines an enumeration of constant values denoted by identifiers. These values must be unique and may not have any other use within their scope (see A.3). The order of the values follows the sequence in which the identifiers appear.

The form

    [*Constant-Expression:35* . . *Constant-Expression:35*]

defines a subrange of the type, the base type, of the values of the two *Constant-Expressions*. A value assigned to a variable of a subrange type must be in the specified interval.

A.12 ARRAY-TYPE

    Array-Type ⇨ ARRAY[*ConstantExpression:35* . . *ConstantExpression:35*] OF *Type:10*

An array is a named, ordered collection of elements, all of the same type defined by the *Type* immediately following the OF . . The number of elements is fixed and is defined by the sub-range of the index type given in brackets following ARRAY.

A.13 RECORD-TYPE

    Record-Type   ⇨ RECORD
                                     Identifier:46 : Type:10;
                      {   *Identifier:46 : Type:10;* }
                           END

A record is a named, ordered collection of components, which can be of different types. The number of components, called fields, of a record is fixed and each field is named.

A.14 POINTER-TYPE

    Pointer-Type   ⇨ POINTER TO *Type:10*

A pointer-type defines a set of values that refer to dynamic variables of a given base type. These dynamic variables are generated through the procedure ALLOCATE, which is imported from the module Storage. NIL is a pointer value constant that refers to no dynamic value and is compatible with all pointer types.

A.15 PROCEDURE-DECLARATION

    Procedure-Declaration   ⇨ *Procedure-Heading:16* ;
                                  { *Data-Declaration:06* }
                              BEGIN
                                  Statement-Sequence:19
                            END *Identifier:46* .

All objects, constants, types and variables, defined in the *Data-Declaration* are said to be local to the procedure. The values variables specified in the *Data-Declaration* are undefined at the start of execution of the *Statement-Sequence*. Objects defined in the containing module are also accessible in the procedure unless local objects have the same name.

A.16 PROCEDURE-HEADING

Procedure-Heading ⇨ PROCEDURE *Identifier:46* [*Parameter-List:17*] [: *Identifier:46*]

There are two kinds of procedures: normal procedures, which are invoked with a *Procedure-Call:22*, and function procedures, which are invoked by being referenced as a *Factor:33* in an expression. Function procedures are distinguished in their headings by having a : *Identifier* after the *Parameter-List*. This identifier specifies the type, which must be a *Simple-Type:11* or a *Pointer-Type:14*, of the value that will be returned by the procedure when it completes execution.

A.17 PARAMETER-LIST

Although I refer to them here as 'parameters', standard Modula-2 usage is to refer to them as 'formal parameters'.

Parameter-List ⇨ ([*Parameter:18* {; *Parameter:18* }])

Each parameter in the list is local to the procedure and must have a name that is distinct from all other objects referenced in the procedure. When the procedure is invoked, the values of the corresponding arguments in the *Procedure-Call:22* or *Factor:33* are evaluated and become the initial values of the parameters. The correspondence between a parameter and its argument is based on the parameter's position in the parameter list and is established at procedure invocation.

A.18 PARAMETER

Parameter ⇨ [VAR] *Identifier:46* : [ARRAY OF] *Identifier:46*

A *Parameter* associates the identifier by which the parameter is referenced with the type, named by the *Identifier* after the :, of values it may assume. A parameter that is introduced by VAR is a variable parameter and must correspond to an argument that is a variable. Changes to the value of a variable parameter during execution of the procedure also change the value of the corresponding argument. Thus a variable parameter can be thought of as a reference to the corresponding argument variable with the correspondence being established at the time the procedure is invoked and remaining in effect until execution of the procedure terminates. A parameter that is not introduced by VAR is a value parameter and may be thought of as a local variable that is initialized with the value of the corresponding argument. Changes to the value of a value parameter do not change the value of the corresponding argument.

If **ARRAY OF** appears in the *Parameter*, it indicates that the corresponding argument is an array with an index lower bound of 0 and an index upper bound of $N - 1$, where N is the number of elements in the corresponding argument array.

A.19 STATEMENT-SEQUENCE

Statement-Sequence: ⇨ *Statement:20 { ;*
                         Statement:20 }

Statements are separated by ;.

A.20 STATEMENT

Statement ⇨ [*Assignment:21*
            | *Procedure-Call:22*
            | *If-Statement:23*
            | *Case-Statement:24*
            | *While-Statement:27*
            | *Repeat-Statement:28*
            | *For-Statement:29*
            | RETURN [*Expression:30*]]

The return statement, introduced by **RETURN**, indicates the termination of a procedure. In the case of function procedures it must be followed by an expression that is evaluated to give the result value, which must have the same type as defined in the *Procedure-Heading:16*.

In addition to the types of statement shown, it is possible to have a null statement consisting of the absence of a statement. Thus, a semi-colon by itself serves as a null statement and it is also possible to treat the statements in a *Statement-Sequence:19* as though they were terminated by semi-colons instead of being separated by them.

A.21 ASSIGNMENT

Assignment ⇨ *Designator:34 := Expression:30*

The := is called the assignment operator. The type of variable referred to by the *Designator:34* must be *assignment compatible* with the type of the expression that follows the assignment operator. The proper definition of assignment compatibility goes beyond the scope of this synopsis but essentially means that no automatic conversion of values from one type to another takes place during the assignment.

A.22 PROCEDURE-CALL

Procedure-Call ⇨   [*Identifier:46* .] *Identifier:46* ([*Expression:30* {, *Expression:30*}])

If the corresponding *Procedure-Heading:16* has a list of parameters then the procedure call must have a matching list of expressions that form the argument list. Arguments and parameters are matched according to their positions in their list. If the *Procedure-Heading:16* has no parameters then an empty argument list, () must be provided in the procedure call. The optional *Identifier* . is provided for qualifying procedure names that have been imported without a FROM clause (see A.4).

A.23 IF-STATEMENT

If-Statement   ⇨   IF *Expression:30* THEN
                                       Statement-Sequence:19
                              {   ELSIF *Expression:30* THEN
                                       Statement-Sequence:19 }
                              [ELSE
                                       Statement-Sequence:19]
                                  END

The expressions following **IF** or **ELSIF** are usually called 'conditions' and must be of type BOOLEAN. The conditions are evaluated in sequence until one is found to be TRUE, at which point the associated *Statement-Sequence* is executed. If the **ELSE** is present, its associated *Statement-Sequence* is executed only if all the preceding conditions evaluated to FALSE.

A.24 CASE-STATEMENT

Case-Statement   ⇨   CASE *Expression:30* OF
                                       Case:25
                              { | *Case:25* }
                              [E̅LSE
                                       Statement-Sequence:19]
                                  END

The *Expression* following **CASE** is generally called the 'selector'. Its type must be a simple type, excluding REAL or LONGREAL, or an enumeration type, or a sub-range type. The execution of a *Case-Statement* is described in A.26. Again, the underlining of the | indicates the actual occurrence of the symbol.

A.25 CASE

Case   ⇨   *Case-Label:26* { , *Case-Label:26* } : *Statement-Sequence:19*

A.26 CASE-LABEL

Case-Label   ⇨ *Constant-Expression:35* [. . *Constant-Expression:35*]

The selector in the *Case-Statement* is first evaluated, then the *Statement-Sequence* whose *Case-Label* contains the selector value is executed. If the selector value does not appear in a *Case-Label*, then the ELSE clause must be present and its *Statement-Sequence* is executed.

A.27 WHILE-STATEMENT

The *While-Statement* controls, based on the value of a BOOLEAN expression, the repeated execution of a *Statement-Sequence*

While-Statement   ⇨ WHILE *Expression:30 DO*
                                   Statement-Sequence:19
                                   END

The *Expression* is evaluated before the *Statement-Sequence* is executed. The *Statement-Sequence* is executed repeatedly for as long as the *Expression* evaluates to TRUE.

A.28 REPEAT-STATEMENT

The *Repeat-Statement* controls, based on the value of a BOOLEAN expression, the repeated execution of a *Statement-Sequence*

Repeat-Statement   ⇨ REPEAT
                                   Statement-Sequence:19
                                   UNTIL *Expression:30*

The *Expression* is evaluated after the *Statement-Sequence* is executed. The *Statement-Sequence* is executed repeatedly until the *Expression* evaluates to TRUE. Thus, the *Statement-Sequence* is executed at least once.

A.29 FOR-STATEMENT

The *For-Statement* causes the repeated execution of a *Statement-Sequence* while a series of values is assigned to a variable called the 'loop control variable'.

For-Statement ⇨ FOR *Identifier:46* := *Expression:30* TO *Expression:30*
                                   BY *Constant-Expression:35* DO
                         Statement-Sequence:19
                         END

The *Identifier* names the loop control variable, which must have been declared as a regular variable – it cannot have been imported or be a parameter. Its type must be a *Simple-Type:11* excluding REAL or LONGREAL. The two *Expressions* are evaluated once at the beginning of the execution of the *For-Statement*. The value of the first expression is the initial value of the loop control variable and the value of second expression is the test value. The step value is given by the *Constant-Expression*. The statement sequence is executed repeatedly with the control variable taking successively the initial value, the initial value plus the step value, the initial value plus twice the step value, and so on. If the step value is positive, iteration continues until the control variable's value is greater than the test value. If the step value is negative, the test value should be less than the initial value and iteration continues until the value of the control variable is less than the test value.

A.30 EXPRESSION

Expression   ⇨ *Simple-Expression:31* [*Relation:39 Simple-Expression:31*]

A.31 SIMPLE-EXPRESSION

Simple-Expression   ⇨ [+ | –] *Term:32* { *Addition-Operator:40 Term:32* }

A.32 TERM

Term   ⇨ *Factor:33* [*Multiplication-Operator:41 Factor:33*]

A.33 FACTOR

Factor   ⇨   *Number:43*
           | *String:42*
           | *Designator:34*
           | [*Identifier:46* .] *Identifier:46* ([*Expression:30* {, *Expression:30*}])
           | (*Expression:30*)
           | NOT *Factor:33*

The form

[*Identifier:46* .] *Identifier:46* ([*Expression:30* {, *Expression:30*}])

represents the invocation of a function procedure with the optional *Identifier* . being provided for qualifying procedure names that have been imported without a FROM clause – see A.4. The *Expressions* are the arguments for the invocation, and obey the same rules as for a *Procedure-Call:22*.

A.34 DESIGNATOR

Designator ⇨ *Identifier:46* { . *Identifier:46* } [[*Expression:30* { , *Expression:30* }]] [^]

The { . *Identifier:46* } provides qualifiers for selecting fields in hierarchical order from a record. The [l *Expression:30* { , *Expression:30* }]] provides values for index selectors for specifying an element in an array of one or more dimensions. The [^] is a dereferencing operator for use when the previous part of the designator specifies a pointer value and it is the object that is referenced by the pointer value that is required.

A.35 CONSTANT-EXPRESSION

Constant-Expression ⇨ *Simple-Constant-Expression:36* [*Relation:39*
Simple-Constant-Expression:36]

A.36 SIMPLE-CONSTANT-EXPRESSION

Simple-Constant-Expression ⇨ [+ | −] *Constant-Term:37* { *Addition-Operator:40*
Constant-Term:37 }

A.37 CONSTANT-TERM

Constant-Term   ⇨ *Constant-Factor:38* { *Multiplication-Operator:41*
Constant-Factor:38 }

A.38 CONSTANT-FACTOR

Constant-Factor   ⇨ *Identifier:46*
                        | *Number:43*
                        | *String:42*
                        | (*Constant-Expression:35*)
                        | NOT *Constant-Factor:38*

A.39 RELATION

Relation   ⇨ =
                        | <>
                        | <
                        | >
                        | <=
                        | >=

A.40 ADDITION-OPERATOR

Addition-Operator   ⇨ +
                           | −
                           | OR

The + and − operators may only operate on numeric values and the OR operator may only operate on BOOLEAN values.

A.41 MULTIPLICATION-OPERATOR

MultiplicationOperator   ⇨ *
                                | /
                                | DIV
                                | MOD
                                | &

The * operator represents multiplication and may only operate on numeric values. The / operator represents division between REAL and LONGREAL values. The DIV and MOD operators represent division and remainder operations and may only operate on INTEGER, LONGINT, CARDINAL, and LONGCARD values. The & operator may only operate on BOOLEAN values.

A.42 STRING

String   ⇨ ' { *Character* } '
                | " { *Character* } "

A.43 NUMBER

Number   ⇨ *Integer:45*
                | *Real:44*

A.44 REAL

Real   ⇨ *Digit* { *Digit* } . { *Digit* } E *Integer:45*

A.45 INTEGER

Integer   ⇨ *Digit* { *Digit* }

A.46 IDENTIFIER

Identifier   ⇨ *Letter* { *Letter* | *Digit* }

A *Letter* consists of one of the 52 distinct upper and lower case letters.

A.47 COMMENT

Arbitrary sequences of characters enclosed in the comment brackets (* and *).

MODULA-2 IMPLEMENTATION
OF THE RUNNING EXAMPLE

This appendix contains a complete Modula-2 implementation of the Running Example together with the results it produced when run against the set of titles in the bibliography to this book.

Here, at last, is the complete listing of the Modula-2 implementation of the Running Example. The program was executed on a Macintosh™* using the Metrowerks™‡ Modula-2 compiler and supporting libraries. The course of this implementation of the Running Example was not smooth in that the Metrowerks compiler was the third version of the language that was used. The previous two compilers had to be abandoned because of bugs and lack of support. Moving the programs from one language implementation to another was difficult because of differences in the libraries. While the idea of a small programming language sounds wonderful, smallness is generally achieved by putting many of the things that make a big language big, into libraries. If the libraries are not standardized, then the programmer's interface varies from one implementation to another, for example, the arguments to the Concat procedure were in a different order and the file access procedures had different names. Moving from one implementation to another requires finding and changing all the changed library references. Two of the integrands in the implementation of the Running Example, FileInterface and String-Pack, arose out of the need to concentrate the library interfaces into two integrands. The alternative of standardizing the library interfaces, essentially makes them part of the language and one is back with a large language. There is no free lunch!

During the course of the implementation some problems with the design specifications had to be elucidated. Probably, the major clarification was required as a consequence of the designer's assumption that all the 'keywords' would start with letters. What is to be done with the title *Control Data 6400/6500/6600 Computer Systems Reference Manual*? I

---

*Macintosh is a registered trademark of Apple Computer, Inc.
‡Metrowerks is a registered trademark of Metrowerks, Inc.

decided that keywords that begin with non-alphabetic characters would be arbitrarily put into the 'A' bucket.

Presenting in this book the listing of an implementation is probably the supreme test of peer review (see Section 12.4). Of course, you will all find things that are wrong, contrary to your taste, or that you would have done better. Any programmer worthy of the title will. Finding such things will sharpen your critical faculties and help you think about your own style of programming in a more critical manner.

In the following listings, integrands are presented in a breadth-first ordering starting with: BuildPrintFile. The integrands are listed in the following order:

```
BuildPrintfile          Titles
InputMod                TitlePartDef
CSMod                   RefPartDef
Sortmod                 CSTitles
CvtMod                  BTListManager
OutputMod               Reporter
FileInterface           DateTime
TitleListMngr           StringPack
CSTListManager          FileNames
```

Each of these integrands contains one or more 'exported' procedures, which can be referenced by procedures in other integrands. The following is an alphabetical list of these exported procedures showing the name of the containing integrand:

List of exported procedures with name of containing integrand

Exported Procedure Name	Integrand Name	Exported Procedure Name	Integrand Name
AfterPattern	StringPack	Input	InputMod
AlignmentPointOfCSTitle	CSTitles	InputFileName	FileNames
AppendCST	CSTListManager	IsNullCShiftedTitle	CSTitles
AppendCSTToBucket	BTListManager	IsNullRefPart	RefPartDef
AppendTitle	TitleListMngr	IsNullTitle	Titles
BeforePattern	StringPack	IsNullTitlePart	TitlePartDef
BeginBucket	BTListManager	Length	StringPack
BeginCSTList	CSTListManager	LexiconFileName	FileNames
BeginTitleList	TitleListMngr	LowerCase	StringPack
BucketNameToChar	BTListManager	MakeCSTitle	CSTitles
CharsToRefPart	RefPartDef	MakeTitle	Titles
CharsToTitlePart	TitlePartDef	NullCShiftedTitle	CSTitles
CharToBucketName	BTListManager	NullifyCShiftedTitle	CSTitles
CharToString	StringPack	NullTitle	Titles
CircularShift	CSMod	OpenRead	FileInterface
CompareCShiftedTitles	CSTitles	OpenWrite	FileInterface
Concat	StringPack	Output	OutputMod
CopyCShiftedTitle	CSTitles	PrintFileName	FileNames
CreateBucketedCSTList	BTListManager	ReadLine	FileInterface
CreateCSTList	CSTListManager	RefPartToChars	RefPartDef
CreateTitleList	TitleListMngr	Report	Reporter
CShiftedTitleToChars	CSTitles	ShiftCSTitleOneWord	CSTitles
CvtToBucketedTitleList	CvtMod	Sort	Sortmod
DeleteSubstr	StringPack	StringAssign	StringPack
DumpCSTList	CSTListManager	StringCompare	StringPack
DumpTitleList	TitleListMngr	Substr	StringPack
ExtractChar	StringPack	TerminateReporter	Reporter
FromPattern	StringPack	TimeStamp	DateTime
GetFirstWord	CSTitles	TitlePartToChars	TitlePartDef
GetNextCST	CSTListManager	TitleToChars	Titles
GetNextCSTFromBucket	BTListManager	TraceFileName	FileNames
GetNextTitle	TitleListMngr	Translate	StringPack
GetRefPart	Titles	TrimBlanks	StringPack
GetTitle	CSTitles	UpperCase	StringPack
GetTitlePart	Titles	UpToPattern	StringPack
Index	StringPack	Verify	StringPack
InitializeReporter	Reporter	WriteLine	FileInterface

In presenting the listings, some of the techniques of using different type styles suggested in Baecker and Marcus (1990) have been adopted. These could be automated in a fairly simple software tool.

BuildPrintfile

```
MODULE  BuildPrintfile;

(* *N*  FUNCTION NAME: BuildPrintfile                                      *)
(* *N*                                                                     *)
(* *N*  AUTHOR: Michael Marcotty     DATE CREATED: 1990 May 03             *)
(* *N*                                                                     *)
(* *P*  PURPOSE: Build Printfile from the data contained in Titlestore and Lexicon.  *)
(* *P*           Each Title-Part of Titlestore contains keywords, that is words that *)
(* *P*           are not contained in Lexicon. For each keyword in the Title-Parts   *)
(* *P*           there will be an element in Printfile with a designation of the     *)
(* *P*           keyword.  The elements of Printfile are ordered alphabetically by   *)
(* *P*           designated keyword, the complete file being split into 26 parts     *)
(* *P*           according to the initial letter of the designated keyword, there being*)
(* *P*           one part for each letter of the alphabet.  The interface with these *)
(* *P*           data are handled by the Input, CircularShift, and Output procedures *)
(* *P*           respectively                                              *)
(* *P*                                                                     *)
(* *I*   INPUT: Titlestore: an ordered set of character strings consisting of words *)
(* *I*          separated by blanks.  Each string consists of two parts, a Title-Part *)
(* *I*          and a Reference-Part.  The Reference-Part is enclosed in brackets.  *)
(* *I*                                                                     *)
(* *I*          Lexicon: an ordered set of character strings, each string consists of *)
(* *I*          a single word.                                             *)
(* *I*                                                                     *)
(* *O*   OUTPUT: Printfile: an ordered set of representations of the elements of *)
(* *O*           of Titlestore, separated into 26 parts, see PURPOSE above. *)

    FROM InputMod         IMPORT Input;
    FROM CSmod            IMPORT CircularShift;
    FROM Sortmod          IMPORT Sort;
    FROM CvtMod           IMPORT CvtToBucketedTitleList;
    FROM OutputMod        IMPORT Output;
    FROM Reporter         IMPORT InitializeReporter, TerminateReporter, Report;
    FROM TitleListMngr    IMPORT TitleList;
    FROM CSTListManager   IMPORT CShiftedTitleList;
    FROM BTListManager    IMPORT BucketedCSTitleList;

    CONST
        MyName = "BuildPrintfile";

    VAR
        ListOfTitles:              TitleList;
        ExtendedListOfTitles:      CShiftedTitleList;
        SortedExtendedListOfTitles: CShiftedTitleList;
        BucketedListOfTitles:      BucketedCSTitleList;

BEGIN
    InitializeReporter(MyName);
    Report(MyName, "Started");

    Input(ListOfTitles);
    CircularShift(ListOfTitles, ExtendedListOfTitles);
    Sort(ExtendedListOfTitles, SortedExtendedListOfTitles);
    CvtToBucketedTitleList(SortedExtendedListOfTitles, BucketedListOfTitles);
    Output(BucketedListOfTitles);

    Report(MyName, "Completed");
    TerminateReporter;

    RETURN
END  BuildPrintfile.
```

InputMod

```
DEFINITION MODULE InputMod;
(* *N*   FUNCTION NAME:  InputMod                                          *)
(* *N*                                                                     *)
(* *N*   AUTHOR:  Michael Marcotty      DATE CREATED: 1990 May 08          *)
(* *N*                                                                     *)
(* *P*   PURPOSE: Read the input data consisting of lines containing a Title-Part  *)
(* *P*            followed by the reference marker [ and a Reference-Part terminated  *)
(* *P*            by ] and convert to internal format.                     *)

    FROM TitleListMngr IMPORT TitleList;

    PROCEDURE Input(VAR ListOfTitles: TitleList);

END InputMod.
```

```
IMPLEMENTATION MODULE InputMod;
    FROM Reporter       IMPORT Report;
    FROM TitleListMngr  IMPORT TitleList, CreateTitleList, AppendTitle, DumpTitleList;
    FROM FileInterface  IMPORT File, ReadLine, OpenRead, CloseFile;
    FROM TitlePartDef   IMPORT MaxTitleLength, CharsToTitlePart, TitlePart, TitlePartToChars;
    FROM RefPartDef     IMPORT MaxRefLength, CharsToRefPart, RefPart, RefPartToChars;
    FROM StringPack     IMPORT StringAssign, Concat, Substr, Length, Index,
                              BeforePattern, AfterPattern, TrimBlanks;
    FROM Titles         IMPORT MakeTitle, Title, TitleToChars;
    FROM FileNames      IMPORT InputFileName, MaxFileNameLength;

    PROCEDURE DeleteMultipleBlanks(VAR Text: ARRAY OF CHAR);
        CONST
            MyName            = "DeleteMultipleBlanks";
        VAR
            WorkingCopyOfText: ARRAY[0..(MaxTitleLength + MaxRefLength + 3)] OF CHAR;
            PieceOfTextToMove: ARRAY[0..(MaxTitleLength + MaxRefLength + 3)] OF CHAR;
    BEGIN
        StringAssign(Text, WorkingCopyOfText);
        StringAssign("", Text);
        WHILE Length(WorkingCopyOfText) > 0 DO
            BeforePattern("  ", WorkingCopyOfText, PieceOfTextToMove);
            Concat(Text, PieceOfTextToMove, Text);
            Concat(Text, " ", Text);
            AfterPattern("  ", WorkingCopyOfText, WorkingCopyOfText);
            TrimBlanks(WorkingCopyOfText);
        END;
        TrimBlanks(Text);
        RETURN;
    END DeleteMultipleBlanks;
```

InputMod

```
PROCEDURE Input(VAR ListOfTitles: TitleList);
   CONST
      MyName              = "Input";
   VAR
      TitleFile:          File;
      TitleFileName:      ARRAY[0..MaxFileNameLength] OF CHAR;
      InputLine:          ARRAY[0..(MaxTitleLength + MaxRefLength + 3)] OF CHAR;
      RefStart:           CARDINAL;
      TitleText:          ARRAY[0..MaxTitleLength] OF CHAR;
      RefText:            ARRAY[0..MaxRefLength] OF CHAR;
      CurTitlePart:       TitlePart;
      CurRefPart:         RefPart;
      CurTitle:           Title;

BEGIN
   InputFileName(TitleFileName);
   OpenRead(TitleFileName, TitleFile);

   ListOfTitles := CreateTitleList();
   ReadLine(TitleFile, InputLine);
   WHILE Length(InputLine) > 0 DO
      TrimBlanks(InputLine);
      DeleteMultipleBlanks(InputLine);
      RefStart := Index("[", InputLine);
      IF RefStart >= Length(InputLine) THEN
         Report(MyName, "Following title ignored because no [:");
         Report(MyName, InputLine);
      ELSE
         Substr(InputLine, 0, RefStart, TitleText);
          Substr(InputLine, RefStart, Length(InputLine) - RefStart, RefText);
         CharsToTitlePart(TitleText, CurTitlePart);
         CharsToRefPart(RefText, CurRefPart);
         CurTitle := MakeTitle(CurTitlePart, CurRefPart);
         AppendTitle(ListOfTitles, CurTitle);
      END;
      ReadLine(TitleFile, InputLine);
   END;
   CloseFile(TitleFile);
   RETURN;
   END Input;
END InputMod.
```

CSmod

```
DEFINITION MODULE CSmod;

(* *N* FUNCTION NAME: CSMod                                                    *)
(* *N*                                                                         *)
(* *N* AUTHOR: Michael Marcotty     DATE CREATED: 1990 May 08                  *)
(* *N*                                                                         *)
(* *P* PURPOSE: From the Title-Part of each title in the list of titles, construct all*)
(* *P*          possible titles consisting of circularly shifted Title-Parts followed *)
(* *P*          by copies of the Reference-Part from the original title.  Constructed *)
(* *P*          titles, and possibly the original title, that start with a word       *)
(* *P*          contained in the ListOfNoiseWords are discarded.              *)

   FROM TitleListMngr IMPORT TitleList;
   FROM CSTListManager IMPORT CShiftedTitleList;

   PROCEDURE CircularShift(ListOfTitles: TitleList;
                           VAR ExtendedListOfTitles: CShiftedTitleList);

END CSmod.
```

CSmod

```
IMPLEMENTATION  MODULE  CSmod;

FROM Reporter          IMPORT Report;
FROM FileNames         IMPORT LexiconFileName, MaxFileNameLength;
FROM StringPack        IMPORT Substr, Concat, Length, TrimBlanks, ExtractChar, StringAssign,
                              Index, BeforePattern, LowerCase, StringCompare;
FROM TitleListMngr     IMPORT TitleList, BeginTitleList, GetNextTitle, DumpTitleList;
FROM CSTListManager    IMPORT CShiftedTitleList, CreateCSTList, AppendCST, DumpCSTList;
FROM FileInterface     IMPORT File, OpenRead, CloseFile, ReadLine;
FROM Titles            IMPORT Title, NullTitle, TitleToChars, IsNullTitle;
FROM TitlePartDef      IMPORT MaxTitleLength;
FROM RefPartDef        IMPORT MaxRefLength;
FROM CSTitles          IMPORT CShiftedTitle, MakeCSTitle, ShiftCSTitleOneWord, GetFirstWord,
                              CopyCShiftedTitle, IsNullCShiftedTitle, CShiftedTitleToChars;

CONST
   MaxNoiseWordLength    = 10;
   MaxWordLength         = 20;
   MaxNumberOfNoiseWords = 100;
TYPE
   NoiseWord             = ARRAY[0..MaxNoiseWordLength] OF CHAR;

PROCEDURE  ReadAndStoreNoiseWords(VAR  NoiseWordArray:  ARRAY  OF  NoiseWord;
                                                     VAR WordCount: CARDINAL);
   CONST
      MyName             = "ReadAndStoreNoiseWords";
   VAR
      NoiseWordFile:        File;
      NoiseWordFileName:    ARRAY[0..MaxFileNameLength] OF CHAR;
      TooManyNoiseWords:    BOOLEAN;
      MessageText:          ARRAY[0..100] OF CHAR;
      CurrentNoiseWord:     NoiseWord;
BEGIN
   LexiconFileName(NoiseWordFileName);
   OpenRead(NoiseWordFileName, NoiseWordFile);
   WordCount         := 0;
   TooManyNoiseWords := FALSE;
   ReadLine(NoiseWordFile, CurrentNoiseWord);
   WHILE (Length(CurrentNoiseWord) > 0) & NOT TooManyNoiseWords DO
      LowerCase(CurrentNoiseWord);
      StringAssign(CurrentNoiseWord, NoiseWordArray[WordCount]);
      IF WordCount < MaxNumberOfNoiseWords THEN
         WordCount := WordCount + 1;
      ELSE
         StringAssign("Max number of noise words exceeded, last word read is ",
                                                              MessageText);
         Concat(MessageText, CurrentNoiseWord, MessageText);
         Report(MyName, MessageText);
         TooManyNoiseWords := TRUE;
      END;
      ReadLine(NoiseWordFile, CurrentNoiseWord);
   END;
   CloseFile(NoiseWordFile);
END  ReadAndStoreNoiseWords;
```

CSmod

```
PROCEDURE  CircularShift(ListOfTitles:  TitleList;
                            VAR ExtendedListOfTitles:  CShiftedTitleList);
   CONST
      MyName                  = "CircularShift";
   VAR
      NoiseWordArray:        ARRAY[0..MaxNumberOfNoiseWords] OF NoiseWord;
      TitleStored:           BOOLEAN;
      NoiseWordFound:        BOOLEAN;
      NoiseWordCount:        CARDINAL;
      NoiseWordIndex:        CARDINAL;
      CurrentTitle:          Title;
      FirstWord:             ARRAY[0..MaxWordLength] OF CHAR;
      TitleText:             ARRAY[0..(MaxTitleLength + MaxRefLength)] OF CHAR;
      MessageText:           ARRAY[0..100] OF CHAR;
      CurrentShiftedTitle:   CShiftedTitle;
      CopyOfShiftedTitle:    CShiftedTitle;
BEGIN
   ReadAndStoreNoiseWords(NoiseWordArray, NoiseWordCount);

   ExtendedListOfTitles := CreateCSTList();
   BeginTitleList(ListOfTitles);
   CurrentTitle := GetNextTitle(ListOfTitles);
   WHILE NOT IsNullTitle(CurrentTitle) DO
      TitleToChars(CurrentTitle, TitleText);
      CurrentShiftedTitle := MakeCSTitle(CurrentTitle);
      TitleStored := FALSE;
      WHILE NOT IsNullCShiftedTitle(CurrentShiftedTitle) DO;
         GetFirstWord(CurrentShiftedTitle, FirstWord);
         LowerCase(FirstWord);
         NoiseWordFound := FALSE;
         FOR NoiseWordIndex := 0 TO NoiseWordCount BY 1 DO
            IF StringCompare(FirstWord, NoiseWordArray[NoiseWordIndex]) = 0 THEN
               NoiseWordFound := TRUE;
            END;
         END;
         IF NOT NoiseWordFound THEN
            CopyCShiftedTitle(CurrentShiftedTitle, CopyOfShiftedTitle);
            AppendCST(ExtendedListOfTitles, CopyOfShiftedTitle);
            TitleStored := TRUE;
         END;
         ShiftCSTitleOneWord(CurrentShiftedTitle);
      END;
      IF NOT TitleStored THEN
         CurrentShiftedTitle := MakeCSTitle(CurrentTitle);
         AppendCST(ExtendedListOfTitles, CurrentShiftedTitle);
      END;
      CurrentTitle := GetNextTitle(ListOfTitles);
   END;

   Report(MyName, "Completed");
END  CircularShift;

END  CSmod.
```

Sortmod

```
DEFINITION MODULE Sortmod;

(* *N*  FUNCTION NAME:  Sortmod                                              *)
(* *N*                                                                       *)
(* *N*  AUTHOR: Michael Marcotty     DATE CREATED: 1990 May 11               *)
(* *N*                                                                       *)
(* *P*  PURPOSE: Sort the extended list of titles produced by CircularShift into *)
(* *P*           alphabetical order.                                         *)

   FROM TitleListMngr  IMPORT TitleList;
   FROM CSTListManager IMPORT CShiftedTitleList;

   PROCEDURE  Sort(ExtendedListOfTitles:  CShiftedTitleList;
                        VAR  SortedExtendedListOfTitles:  CShiftedTitleList);

END  Sortmod.
```

Sortmod

```
IMPLEMENTATION MODULE Sortmod;

   FROM Reporter       IMPORT Report;
   FROM CSTListManager IMPORT CShiftedTitleList, CreateCSTList, GetNextCST, DumpCSTList,
                             BeginCSTList, AppendCST;
   FROM CSTitles       IMPORT CShiftedTitle, NullCShiftedTitle, CompareCShiftedTitles,
                             CShiftedTitleToChars, IsNullCShiftedTitle;
   FROM TitlePartDef   IMPORT MaxTitleLength;
   FROM RefPartDef     IMPORT MaxRefLength;
   FROM Storage        IMPORT ALLOCATE, DEALLOCATE;
   FROM StringPack     IMPORT StringAssign, Concat, Substr, Length, TrimBlanks, ExtractChar;


   TYPE
      CSTitleTreePtr              = POINTER TO CShiftedTitleTreeElement;
      CShiftedTitleTreeElement = RECORD
                                    Left: CSTitleTreePtr;
                                    Right: CSTitleTreePtr;
                                    Value: CShiftedTitle;
                                 END;
   PROCEDURE  RemoveFromTreeInAscendingOrder(VAR  SubTreeRoot:  CSTitleTreePtr;
                                             OutputList: CShiftedTitleList);
   BEGIN
      IF SubTreeRoot <> NIL THEN
         RemoveFromTreeInAscendingOrder(SubTreeRoot^.Left, OutputList);
         AppendCST(OutputList, SubTreeRoot^.Value);
         RemoveFromTreeInAscendingOrder(SubTreeRoot^.Right, OutputList);
         DEALLOCATE (SubTreeRoot, SIZE(CShiftedTitleTreeElement));
         SubTreeRoot := NIL;
      END;
      RETURN;
   END  RemoveFromTreeInAscendingOrder;
```

Sortmod

```
PROCEDURE  Sort(ExtendedListOfTitles:  CShiftedTitleList;
                      VAR  SortedExtendedListOfTitles:  CShiftedTitleList);

    CONST
        MyName = "Sort";

    VAR
        TreeRoot:           CSTitleTreePtr;
        NewTreeElement:     CSTitleTreePtr;
        CurrentTreeElement: CSTitleTreePtr;
        ContinueClimbing:   BOOLEAN;
        CurrentCSTitle:     CShiftedTitle;
        SecondCSTitle:      CShiftedTitle;
        TitleText:          ARRAY[0..(MaxTitleLength + MaxRefLength)] OF CHAR;
        Message:            ARRAY[0..(MaxTitleLength + MaxRefLength)] OF CHAR;
BEGIN

    (*                  Put the CShifted Titles into a binary tree              *)
    BeginCSTList(ExtendedListOfTitles);
    TreeRoot        := NIL;
    CurrentCSTitle := GetNextCST(ExtendedListOfTitles);
    WHILE NOT IsNullCShiftedTitle(CurrentCSTitle) DO
        ALLOCATE(NewTreeElement, SIZE(CShiftedTitleTreeElement));
        NewTreeElement^.Left  := NIL;
        NewTreeElement^.Right := NIL;
        NewTreeElement^.Value := CurrentCSTitle;

        IF TreeRoot = NIL THEN
            TreeRoot := NewTreeElement;
        ELSE
            CurrentTreeElement := TreeRoot;
            ContinueClimbing   := TRUE;
            WHILE ContinueClimbing DO
                IF CompareCShiftedTitles(NewTreeElement^.Value, CurrentTreeElement^.Value)
                                                                              > 0 THEN

                    IF CurrentTreeElement^.Right = NIL THEN
                        CurrentTreeElement^.Right := NewTreeElement;
                        ContinueClimbing          := FALSE;
                    ELSE
                        CurrentTreeElement := CurrentTreeElement^.Right;
                    END;
                ELSE
                    IF CurrentTreeElement^.Left = NIL THEN
                        CurrentTreeElement^.Left := NewTreeElement;
                        ContinueClimbing         := FALSE;
                    ELSE
                        CurrentTreeElement := CurrentTreeElement^.Left;
                    END;
                END;
            END;
        END;
        CurrentCSTitle := GetNextCST(ExtendedListOfTitles);
    END;

    SortedExtendedListOfTitles := CreateCSTList();
    RemoveFromTreeInAscendingOrder(TreeRoot, SortedExtendedListOfTitles);
END Sort;

END Sortmod.
```

CvtMod

```
DEFINITION MODULE CvtMod;
(* *N*  FUNCTION NAME: CvtMod                                           *)
(* *N*                                                                  *)
(* *N*                                                                  *)
(* *N*  AUTHOR: Michael Marcotty      DATE CREATED: 1990 May 28         *)
(* *N*                                                                  *)
(* *P*  PURPOSE: Convert TitlePart in each Title in the SortedExtendedListOfTitles, *)
(* *P*           which is a circularly shifted Title, into an aligned Title for     *)
(* *P*           printing.                                              *)

    FROM CSTListManager IMPORT CShiftedTitleList;
    FROM BTListManager  IMPORT BucketedCSTitleList;

    PROCEDURE CvtToBucketedTitleList
                        (SortedExtendedListOfTitles: CShiftedTitleList;
                         VAR BucketedListOfTitles: BucketedCSTitleList);

END CvtMod.
```

```
IMPLEMENTATION MODULE CvtMod;

    FROM Reporter       IMPORT Report;
    FROM CSTListManager IMPORT CShiftedTitleList, CreateCSTList, GetNextCST, DumpCSTList,
                               BeginCSTList, AppendCST;
    FROM CSTitles       IMPORT CShiftedTitle, AlignmentPointOfCSTitle, GetTitle,
                               CShiftedTitleToChars, IsNullCShiftedTitle;
    FROM BTListManager  IMPORT BucketName, BucketedCSTitleList, CreateBucketedCSTList,
                               AppendCSTToBucket, CharToBucketName;
    FROM Titles         IMPORT Title, GetTitlePart, GetRefPart;
    FROM TitlePartDef   IMPORT MaxTitleLength, TitlePart, TitlePartToChars;
    FROM StringPack     IMPORT Substr, Concat, Length, TrimBlanks, ExtractChar, StringAssign,
                               Index, BeforePattern, LowerCase, StringCompare;

    PROCEDURE CvtToBucketedTitleList(SortedCSListOfTitles:  CShiftedTitleList;
                                     VAR BucketedListOfTitles: BucketedCSTitleList);
        CONST
          MyName = "CvtToAligned";
        VAR
          CurrentCSTitle:       CShiftedTitle;
          CurrentTitle:         Title;
          CurrentTitlePart:     TitlePart;
          TitleText:            ARRAY[0..MaxTitleLength] OF CHAR;
          CurrentBucketName:    BucketName;
          BucketLetter:         CHAR;
    BEGIN
        BucketedListOfTitles := CreateBucketedCSTList();
        BeginCSTList(SortedCSListOfTitles);
        CurrentCSTitle := GetNextCST(SortedCSListOfTitles);
        WHILE NOT IsNullCShiftedTitle(CurrentCSTitle) DO
          CShiftedTitleToChars(CurrentCSTitle, TitleText);
          AppendCSTToBucket(BucketedListOfTitles, CharToBucketName(ExtractChar(TitleText, 0)),
                                                                   CurrentCSTitle);
          CurrentCSTitle := GetNextCST(SortedCSListOfTitles);
        END;

        Report(MyName, "Completed");
        RETURN;
    END CvtToBucketedTitleList;

END CvtMod.
```

OutputMod

DEFINITION MODULE OutputMod;

```
(* *N*  FUNCTION NAME:  OutputMod                                           *)
(* *N*                                                                      *)
(* *N*  AUTHOR:  Michael Marcotty      DATE CREATED: 1990 May 08            *)
(* *N*                                                                      *)
(* *P*  PURPOSE: Format the Titles contained in the AlignedListOfTitles into the   *)
(* *P*           PrintFile.  In each Title, the TitlePart shown in its original form  *)
(* *P*           and occupies TitlePartLen characters and is to be aligned with the  *)
(* *P*           first word of its circularly shifted form starting at KeywordPosition *)
(* *P*           characters from the beginning of the printed line. Where a TitlePart *)
(* *P*           must be truncated at the beginning or end to fit into TitlePartLen  *)
(* *P*           characters after alignment, the truncation is shown by an ellipsis,  *)
(* *P*           (...). The Reference-Part is listed on the same line as the TitlePart *)
(* *P*           and starts TitlePartLen + TitleRefGap for printing.  The Title-Part is*)
(* *P*           characters from the beginning of the printed line.  If the Reference- *)
(* *P*           Part is too long to be printed on the line, it is truncated and this  *)
(* *P*           is marked with an ellipsis.                                 *)

    FROM BTListManager  IMPORT BucketedCSTitleList;

  PROCEDURE  Output(BucketedListOfTitles:  BucketedCSTitleList);
```

END OutputMod.

OutputMod

```
IMPLEMENTATION  MODULE  OutputMod;

FROM Reporter        IMPORT Report;
FROM FileInterface   IMPORT File, OpenWrite, WriteLine, CloseFile;
FROM TitlePartDef    IMPORT MaxTitleLength, TitlePart, TitlePartToChars;
FROM RefPartDef      IMPORT MaxRefLength, RefPart, RefPartToChars;
FROM CSTListManager  IMPORT CShiftedTitleList, CreateCSTList, GetNextCST, BeginCSTList;
FROM CSTitles        IMPORT CShiftedTitle, AlignmentPointOfCSTitle, GetTitle,
                            CShiftedTitleToChars, IsNullCShiftedTitle;
FROM StringPack      IMPORT Substr, Concat, Length, StringAssign, CharToString;
FROM FileNames       IMPORT PrintFileName, MaxFileNameLength;
FROM Titles          IMPORT Title, GetTitlePart, GetRefPart;
FROM BTListManager   IMPORT BucketName, BucketedCSTitleList, BeginBucket, BucketNameToChar,
                            GetNextCSTFromBucket;

CONST
   TextPartWidth           = 60;
   PrintAlignmentPoint     = 30;
   PrintLineLength         = TextPartWidth + MaxRefLength + 3;
   Ellipsis                = "...";
   LeftRightPartsSeparator = " ";
   TitleRefSeparator       = " : ";
   RightPartLength         = TextPartWidth - PrintAlignmentPoint - 1;
VAR
   Blanks:                 ARRAY[0..PrintLineLength] OF CHAR;
   BlankIndex:             CARDINAL;

PROCEDURE  PrintBucketHeader(NameOfBucket:  BucketName;  VAR  PrintFile:  File);
   VAR
      BucketLetter:        CHAR;
      BucketLetterStr:     ARRAY[0..1] OF CHAR;
      PrintLine:           ARRAY[0..PrintLineLength] OF CHAR;

BEGIN
   WriteLine(PrintFile, Blanks);
   Substr(Blanks, 0, PrintAlignmentPoint, PrintLine);
   Concat(PrintLine, "-", PrintLine);
   BucketLetter := BucketNameToChar(NameOfBucket);
   CharToString(BucketLetter, BucketLetterStr);
   Concat(PrintLine, BucketLetterStr, PrintLine);
   Concat(PrintLine, "-", PrintLine);
   WriteLine(PrintFile, PrintLine);
   WriteLine(PrintFile, Blanks);
   RETURN;
END  PrintBucketHeader;
```

OutputMod

```
PROCEDURE  PrepareLeftPartOfTitle(TitleText:  ARRAY  OF  CHAR;
                        AlignmentPoint: CARDINAL; VAR  PrintLine:  ARRAY  OF  CHAR);
    VAR
        SubstringLength:        CARDINAL;
        SubstringStartIndex:    CARDINAL;
        PartialPrintLine:       ARRAY[0..PrintLineLength] OF CHAR;
BEGIN
    IF AlignmentPoint > PrintAlignmentPoint THEN
        StringAssign(Ellipsis, PrintLine);
        SubstringStartIndex := AlignmentPoint - PrintAlignmentPoint +
                                                        Length(Ellipsis);
        SubstringLength      := PrintAlignmentPoint - Length(Ellipsis);
        Substr(TitleText, SubstringStartIndex, SubstringLength, PartialPrintLine);
        Concat(PrintLine, PartialPrintLine, PrintLine);
    ELSIF AlignmentPoint = PrintAlignmentPoint THEN
        Substr(TitleText, 0, PrintAlignmentPoint, PrintLine);
    ELSE
        SubstringLength := PrintAlignmentPoint - AlignmentPoint;
        Substr(Blanks, 0, SubstringLength, PrintLine);
        Substr(TitleText, 0, AlignmentPoint, PartialPrintLine);
        Concat(PrintLine, PartialPrintLine, PrintLine);
    END;
    RETURN;
END  PrepareLeftPartOfTitle;


PROCEDURE  PrepareRightPartOfTitle(TitleText:  ARRAY  OF  CHAR;
                        AlignmentPoint: CARDINAL; VAR  PrintLine:  ARRAY  OF  CHAR);
    VAR
        SubstringLength:        CARDINAL;
        SubstringStartIndex:    CARDINAL;
        PartialPrintLine:       ARRAY[0..PrintLineLength] OF CHAR;
        LengthOfTitleRightPart: CARDINAL;
BEGIN
    LengthOfTitleRightPart := Length(TitleText) - AlignmentPoint;
    IF LengthOfTitleRightPart > RightPartLength THEN
        SubstringLength := RightPartLength - Length(Ellipsis);
        Substr(TitleText, AlignmentPoint, SubstringLength, PartialPrintLine);
        Concat(PrintLine, PartialPrintLine, PrintLine);
        Concat(PrintLine, Ellipsis, PrintLine);
    ELSE
        SubstringLength := Length(TitleText) - AlignmentPoint;
        Substr(TitleText, AlignmentPoint, SubstringLength, PartialPrintLine);
        Concat(PrintLine, PartialPrintLine, PrintLine);
        SubstringLength := TextPartWidth - Length(PrintLine);
        Substr(Blanks, 0, SubstringLength, PartialPrintLine);
        Concat(PrintLine, PartialPrintLine, PrintLine);
    END;
    RETURN
END  PrepareRightPartOfTitle;
```

OutputMod

```
PROCEDURE  Output(BucketedListOfTitles:  BucketedCSTitleList);
  CONST
    MyName = "Output";
  VAR
    PrintFile:                File;
    PrintFileNameString:      ARRAY[0..MaxFileNameLength] OF CHAR;
    PrintLine:                ARRAY[0..PrintLineLength] OF CHAR;
    CurrentCSTitle:           CShiftedTitle;
    CurrentTitle:             Title;
    CurrentTitlePart:         TitlePart;
    CurrentRefPart:           RefPart;
    TitleText:                ARRAY[0..MaxTitleLength] OF CHAR;
    RefText:                  ARRAY[0..MaxRefLength] OF CHAR;
    AlignmentPointOfTitle:    CARDINAL;
    CharIndex:                CARDINAL;
    OK:                       BOOLEAN;
    BucketHeaderPrinted:      BOOLEAN;
    CurrentBucketName:        BucketName;
BEGIN
  PrintFileName(PrintFileNameString);
  OpenWrite(PrintFileNameString, PrintFile);

  FOR CurrentBucketName := MIN(BucketName) TO MAX(BucketName) BY 1 DO
    BucketHeaderPrinted := FALSE;
    BeginBucket(BucketedListOfTitles, CurrentBucketName);
    CurrentCSTitle := GetNextCSTFromBucket(BucketedListOfTitles, CurrentBucketName);
    WHILE NOT IsNullCShiftedTitle(CurrentCSTitle) DO
      IF NOT BucketHeaderPrinted THEN
        PrintBucketHeader(CurrentBucketName, PrintFile);
        BucketHeaderPrinted := TRUE;
      END;
      CurrentTitle     := GetTitle(CurrentCSTitle);
      CurrentTitlePart := GetTitlePart(CurrentTitle);
      TitlePartToChars(CurrentTitlePart, TitleText);
      AlignmentPointOfTitle := AlignmentPointOfCSTitle(CurrentCSTitle);

      PrepareLeftPartOfTitle(TitleText, AlignmentPointOfTitle, PrintLine);
      Concat(PrintLine, LeftRightPartsSeparator, PrintLine);
      PrepareRightPartOfTitle(TitleText, AlignmentPointOfTitle, PrintLine);
      Concat(PrintLine, TitleRefSeparator, PrintLine);

      CurrentRefPart := GetRefPart(CurrentTitle);
      RefPartToChars(CurrentRefPart, RefText);
      Concat(PrintLine, RefText, PrintLine);

      WriteLine(PrintFile, PrintLine);

      CurrentCSTitle := GetNextCSTFromBucket(BucketedListOfTitles, CurrentBucketName);
    END;
  END;
  CloseFile(PrintFile);
  RETURN;
END Output;

BEGIN
  StringAssign(" ", Blanks);
  FOR BlankIndex := 1 TO PrintLineLength BY 1 DO
    Concat(Blanks, " ", Blanks);
  END;
END OutputMod.
```

FileInterface

DEFINITION MODULE FileInterface;

```
(* *N* FUNCTION NAME: FileInterface                              *)
(* *N*                                                              *)
(* *N* AUTHOR: Michael Marcotty    DATE CREATED: 1990MAY15          *)
(* *N*                                                              *)
(* *P* PURPOSE: Provides the the interface between the application program and the  *)
(* *P*          file system on which the application is written.  Errors are either *)
(* *P*          reported through the Reporter module or on the screen if that is not *)
(* *P*          possible.                                           *)

    FROM FileIO   IMPORT FileDescr;

    TYPE File = FileDescr;

    PROCEDURE OpenRead(Name: ARRAY OF CHAR; VAR Fi: File);
(* *N* FUNCTION NAME: OpenRead                                    *)
(* *N*                                                              *)
(* *P* PURPOSE: The procedure OpenRead opens a file of the given name for reading.  *)
(* *P*          If the file does not exist, a new empty file is opened and an error is*)
(* *P*          reported.                                          *)

    PROCEDURE OpenWrite(Name: ARRAY OF CHAR; VAR Fi: File);
(* *N* FUNCTION NAME: OpenWrite                                   *)
(* *N*                                                              *)
(* *P* PURPOSE: The procedure OpenWrite opens a file of the given name for writing.  *)
(* *P*          If the file already exists, it is deleted and a new one is created.  *)
(* *P*          If the file does not exist, a new one is created.  *)

    PROCEDURE ReadLine(Fi: File; VAR Chrst: ARRAY OF CHAR);
(* *N* FUNCTION NAME: ReadLine                                    *)
(* *N*                                                              *)
(* *P* PURPOSE: The procedure ReadLine reads the given file character by character   *)
(* *P*          until an end of line character is reached.  As the reading takes place*)
(* *P*          the line read is built in Chrst.  The end of line character is not   *)
(* *P*          included in Chrst.  If the end of file is reached with no characters  *)
(* *P*          having been read, Chrst is set to be a null string. *)

    PROCEDURE WriteLine(Fi: File; Chrst: ARRAY OF CHAR);
(* *N* FUNCTION NAME: WriteLine                                   *)
(* *N*                                                              *)
(* *P* PURPOSE: The procedure WriteLine writes the given character string to the given*)
(* *P*          file and then writes an end of line character.      *)

    PROCEDURE CloseFile(Fi: File);
(* *N* FUNCTION NAME: CloseFile                                   *)
(* *N*                                                              *)
(* *P* PURPOSE: The procedure CloseFile closes the given file and the volume on  *)
(* *P*          which the file exists.                              *)

END FileInterface.
```

FileInterface

```
IMPLEMENTATION  MODULE  FileInterface;
    FROM FileIO   IMPORT accessPerm, accessMode, Open, Close, WriteMany, WriteCh, openError,
                         ErrNo, ReadCh, Eof, FileLength;
    FROM Strings  IMPORT Assign, Concat, Copy, Length, InitString;
    FROM InOut    IMPORT EOL;
    FROM SYSTEM   IMPORT ADR;
    FROM InOut    IMPORT ClearScreen, WriteString, WriteLn, HoldScreen;
    FROM Encode   IMPORT encFormat, GetEncodeFormat, SetEncodeFormat, EncodeInt;
    FROM Reporter IMPORT Report;

CONST
    EoFEncountered = -39;

    PROCEDURE  FileErrorHandler(Message:  ARRAY  OF  CHAR);
        CONST
            MyName = "FileErrorHandler";

        VAR
            OK:      BOOLEAN;
            TempStr: ARRAY[0..100] OF CHAR;
            Stop:    CARDINAL;

    BEGIN
        OK := EncodeInt(0, Stop, TempStr, ErrNo, 8);
        Concat(" error no = ", TempStr, TempStr);
        Concat(Message, TempStr, TempStr);
        Report(MyName, TempStr)
    END  FileErrorHandler;

    PROCEDURE  OpenRead(FileName:  ARRAY  OF  CHAR;  VAR  Fi:  File);
        CONST
            MyName = "OpenRead";
        VAR Access:       accessMode;
            TempStr:      ARRAY[0..100] OF CHAR;
            OK:           BOOLEAN;
            Stop:         CARDINAL;
    BEGIN
        Access := accessMode{readOnly};
        Fi     := Open(FileName, Access);
        IF Fi = openError THEN
            Concat("Error in opening file ", FileName, TempStr);
            Concat(TempStr, " for read access", TempStr);
            FileErrorHandler(TempStr);
        END
    END  OpenRead;
```

FileInterface

```
PROCEDURE ReadLine(Fi: File; VAR Chrst: ARRAY OF CHAR);
  CONST
     MyName = "ReadLine";
  VAR
     CurLen:      CARDINAL;
     MaxLen:      CARDINAL;
     CharRead:    CHAR;
     OK:          BOOLEAN;
     Truncate:    BOOLEAN;
     ReadingLine: BOOLEAN;
     OneChar:     ARRAY[0..1] OF CHAR;
BEGIN
  InitString(Chrst);
  Assign(OneChar, " ");
  MaxLen      := HIGH(Chrst);
  CharRead    := " ";
  CurLen      := 0;
  Truncate    := FALSE;
  ReadingLine := NOT Eof(Fi);
  WHILE ReadingLine DO
     OK := ReadCh(Fi, CharRead);
     IF OK THEN
        IF CharRead = EOL THEN
           ReadingLine := FALSE;
        ELSE
           IF NOT Truncate THEN
              IF CurLen = MaxLen THEN
                 Truncate := TRUE;
                 Report(MyName, "Line too long, truncated");
              ELSE
                 OneChar[0] := CharRead;
                 Concat(Chrst, OneChar, Chrst);
                 CurLen := CurLen + 1;
              END;
           END;
        END;
     ELSE
        IF ErrNo = EoFEncountered THEN
           ReadingLine := FALSE;
        ELSE
           FileErrorHandler("Error in reading line");
           Report(MyName, Chrst);
        END;
     END;
  END;
END ReadLine;
```

FileInterface

```
PROCEDURE OpenWrite(FileName: ARRAY OF CHAR; VAR Fi: File);
   CONST
      MyName = "OpenWrite";

   VAR Access:      accessMode;
       TempStr:     ARRAY[0..100] OF CHAR;
       OK:          BOOLEAN;
       Stop:        CARDINAL;
BEGIN
   Access := accessMode(writeOnly, create, erase);
   Fi     := Open(FileName, Access);
   IF Fi = openError THEN
      Concat("Error in opening file ", FileName, TempStr);
      Concat(TempStr, " for write access", TempStr);
      FileErrorHandler(TempStr);
   END
END OpenWrite;

PROCEDURE WriteLine(Fi: File; Chrst: ARRAY OF CHAR);
   CONST
      MyName = "WriteLine";
   VAR CharsWritten: LONGINT;
       LINoOfChars:  LONGINT;
BEGIN
   LINoOfChars  := Length(Chrst);
   CharsWritten := WriteMany(Fi, ADR(Chrst), Length(Chrst));
   IF CharsWritten = LINoOfChars THEN
      WriteCh(Fi, EOL)
   ELSE
      FileErrorHandler("Error in writing line");
      Report(MyName, Chrst)
   END;
END WriteLine;

PROCEDURE CloseFile(Fi: File);
   VAR OK: BOOLEAN;
BEGIN
   OK := Close(Fi);
   IF NOT OK THEN
      FileErrorHandler("Error in closing file")
   END

END CloseFile;

END FileInterface.
```

TitleListMngr

```
DEFINITION MODULE TitleListMngr;
(* *N*  FUNCTION NAME: TitleListMngr                                          *)
(* *N*  AUTHOR: Michael Marcotty      DATE CREATED: 1990 May 03               *)
(* *P*  PURPOSE: To implement the storage and manipulation of the TitleList data type  *)

   FROM Titles    IMPORT Title;

   TYPE TitleList;

   PROCEDURE CreateTitleList(): TitleList;
(* *N*  FUNCTION: NAME: CreateTitleList                                       *)
(* *P*  PURPOSE: Create an empty TitleList.                                   *)
(* *O*  OUTPUT: VAR:   TL - An empty TitleList                                *)

   PROCEDURE BeginTitleList(VAR TL: TitleList);
(* *N*  FUNCTION: NAME: BeginTitleList                                        *)
(* *P*  PURPOSE: Reset TitleList so that GetNextTitle will get the first      *)
(* *P*           title in the list.                                          *)
(* *I*  INPUT:   VAR   TL - TitleList to be reset                            *)
(* *O*  OUTPUT:  TL - TitleList reset so that next Title is its first Title   *)
(* *E*  ERROR ACTION: If the TitleList referenced by TL has not been created an error *)
(* *E*           is reported.                                                *)

   PROCEDURE GetNextTitle(TL: TitleList): Title;
(* *N*  FUNCTION: NAME: GetNextTitle                                          *)
(* *P*  PURPOSE: Get the title following the one obtained by the previous application*)
(* *P*           of this operation. If this is the first application since    *)
(* *P*           BeginTitleList was applied, the first title in the TitleList is *)
(* *P*           obtained. If the previous Title obtained was the last one in the *)
(* *P*           TitleList or if the TitleList is empty or has not been created, a *)
(* *P*           null Title is obtained.                                      *)
(* *I*  INPUT:   Value: TL-the TitleList from which the next title is to be obtained.*)
(* *O*  OUTPUT:  VAR:   The next title in the list or a null title.           *)

   PROCEDURE AppendTitle (VAR TL: TitleList;   T: Title);
(* *N*  FUNCTION: NAME: AppendTitle                                           *)
(* *P*  PURPOSE: Append the Title to the given TitleList.                     *)
(* *I*  INPUT:   Value: Title to be appended to the TitleList.                *)
(* *I*           VAR:   TitleList to which Title is to be appended            *)
(* *O*  OUTPUT:  VAR:   ListOfTitles to which the Title has been appended.    *)
(* *E*  ERROR ACTION: An error is reported if the TitleList referenced by TL has not *)
(* *E*           been created or if the Title cannot be appended.            *)

   PROCEDURE DumpTitleList(TL: TitleList);
(* *N*  FUNCTION: NAME: DumpTitleList                                         *)
(* *P*  PURPOSE: Produce a formatted dump of the Titles in the given TitleList. *)
(* *I*  INPUT:   Value: The TitleList to be dumped.                           *)
(* *O*  OUTPUT:  Character string representation of the titles in the TitleList *)
(* *O*           appended to the debugging file.                             *)

END TitleListMngr.
```

TitleListMngr

```
IMPLEMENTATION MODULE TitleListMngr;

    FROM Titles          IMPORT Title, NullTitle, TitleToChars;
    FROM Storage         IMPORT ALLOCATE, DEALLOCATE;
    FROM TitlePartDef    IMPORT MaxTitleLength;
    FROM RefPartDef      IMPORT MaxRefLength;
    FROM Reporter        IMPORT Report;

    TYPE
        ListElemPtr      = POINTER TO TitleListElement;
        TitleListElement = RECORD
                             Next: ListElemPtr;
                             Value: Title;
                           END;
        TitleListHead    = RECORD
                             ListStart:      ListElemPtr;
                             CurrentElement: ListElemPtr;
                           END;
        TitleList        = POINTER TO TitleListHead;

    PROCEDURE CreateTitleList(): TitleList;
        VAR
            NewList: TitleList;
    BEGIN
        ALLOCATE(NewList, SIZE(TitleListHead));
        NewList^.ListStart      := NIL;
        NewList^.CurrentElement := NIL;
        RETURN NewList;
    END CreateTitleList;


    PROCEDURE BeginTitleList(VAR TL: TitleList);
    BEGIN
        TL^.CurrentElement := NIL;
        RETURN;
    END BeginTitleList;

    PROCEDURE GetNextTitle(TL: TitleList): Title;
        CONST
            MyName           = "GetNextTitle";
        VAR
            OutTitle:   Title;
            TitleText:  ARRAY[0..(MaxTitleLength + MaxRefLength)] OF CHAR;
    BEGIN
        IF TL = NIL THEN
            OutTitle := NullTitle();
        ELSE
            IF TL^.CurrentElement = NIL THEN
                TL^.CurrentElement := TL^.ListStart;
            ELSE
                TL^.CurrentElement := TL^.CurrentElement^.Next;
            END;
            IF TL^.CurrentElement = NIL THEN
                OutTitle := NullTitle();
            ELSE
                OutTitle := TL^.CurrentElement^.Value;
            END;
        END;
        RETURN OutTitle;
    END GetNextTitle;
```

TitleListMngr

```
PROCEDURE AppendTitle (VAR TL: TitleList;    T: Title);
   VAR
      CurrentElementList: TitleList;
      NewTitleListElement: ListElemPtr;
BEGIN
   ALLOCATE(NewTitleListElement, SIZE(TitleListElement));
   NewTitleListElement^.Next  := NIL;
   NewTitleListElement^.Value := T;

   IF TL = NIL THEN
      TL := CreateTitleList();
   END;
   IF TL^.ListStart = NIL THEN
      TL^.ListStart := NewTitleListElement;
   ELSE
      TL^.CurrentElement^.Next := NewTitleListElement;
   END;
   TL^.CurrentElement := NewTitleListElement;

   RETURN;
END  AppendTitle;

PROCEDURE  DumpTitleList(TL:  TitleList);
   CONST
      MyName             = "DumpTitleList";
   VAR
      TitleText:              ARRAY[0..(MaxTitleLength + MaxRefLength)] OF CHAR;
      CurrentListElement:  ListElemPtr;
BEGIN
   IF TL = NIL THEN
      Report(MyName, "Title list is null");
   ELSIF TL^.ListStart = NIL THEN
      Report(MyName, "Title list is empty");
   ELSE
      Report(MyName, "Dump of Title list follows");
      IF TL^.CurrentElement = NIL THEN
         Report(MyName, "Current Element is nil");
      ELSE
         Report(MyName, "Current Element is:");
         TitleToChars(TL^.CurrentElement^.Value, TitleText);
         Report(MyName, TitleText);
      END;
      Report(MyName, "Dump of Title list follows");
      CurrentListElement := TL^.ListStart;
      WHILE CurrentListElement <> NIL DO
         TitleToChars(CurrentListElement^.Value, TitleText);
         Report(MyName, TitleText);
         CurrentListElement := CurrentListElement^.Next;
      END;
   END;
   RETURN;
END  DumpTitleList;

END  TitleListMngr.
```

CSTListManager

```
DEFINITION MODULE CSTListManager;
(* *N*   FUNCTION NAME: CSTListManager                                          *)
(* *N*   AUTHOR: Michael Marcotty     DATE CREATED: 1990 May 08                 *)
(* *P*   PURPOSE: To implement the storage and manipulation of the CShiftedTitleList *)
(* *P*            (Circularly Shifted Title Listdata type.                      *)
        FROM CSTitles    IMPORT CShiftedTitle;

        TYPE CShiftedTitleList;

        PROCEDURE CreateCSTList(): CShiftedTitleList;
(* *N*   FUNCTION: NAME: CreateCSTList                                          *)
(* *P*   PURPOSE:  Create an empty CShiftedTitleList                            *)
(* *O*   OUTPUT:   VAR:  CSTL - An empty CShiftedTitleList                      *)

        PROCEDURE DeleteCSTList(VAR CSTL: CShiftedTitleList);
(* *N*   FUNCTION: NAME: DeleteCSTList                                          *)
(* *P*   PURPOSE:  Delete the given CShiftedTitleList                           *)
(* *I*   INPUT:    VAR    CSTL - CShiftedTitleList to be deleted                *)
(* *O*   OUTPUT:   CSTL - CShiftedTitleList is set to NIL                       *)

        PROCEDURE BeginCSTList(VAR CSTL: CShiftedTitleList);
(* *N*   FUNCTION: NAME: BeginCSTList                                           *)
(* *P*   PURPOSE:  Reset CShiftedTitleList so that GetNextCST will get the first *)
(* *P*             Circularly Shifted Title in the List.                        *)
(* *I*   INPUT:    VAR    CSTL - CShiftedTitleList to be reset                  *)
(* *O*   OUTPUT:   CSTL - CShiftedTitleList reset so that next Title is its first Title*)
(* *E*   ERROR ACTION: If the CShiftedTitleList referenced by TL has not been created *)
(* *E*               an error is reported.                                      *)

        PROCEDURE GetNextCST(CSTL: CShiftedTitleList): CShiftedTitle;
(* *N*   FUNCTION: NAME: GetNextCST                                             *)
(* *P*   PURPOSE:  Get the title following the one obtained by the previous application*)
(* *P*             of this operation.  If this is the first application since   *)
(* *P*             BeginCSTList was applied, the first CShiftedTitle in the     *)
(* *P*             CShiftedTitleList is obtained.  If the previous CShiftedTitle *)
(* *P*             obtained was the last one in the CShiftedTitleList or if the *)
(* *P*             CShiftedTitleList is empty or has not been created, a null   *)
(* *P*             CShiftedTitle is obtained.                                   *)
(* *I*   INPUT:    Value: CSTL-the CShiftedTitleList from which the next title is to *)
(* *I*             be obtained.                                                 *)
(* *O*   OUTPUT:   VAR:  The next CShiftedTitle in the list or a null CShiftedTitle. *)

        PROCEDURE AppendCST (VAR CSTL: CShiftedTitleList;   CST: CShiftedTitle);
(* *N*   FUNCTION: NAME: AppendCST                                              *)
(* *P*   PURPOSE:  Append the CShiftedTitle to the given CShiftedTitleList.     *)
(* *I*   INPUT:    VAR:  CShiftedTitleList to which CShiftedTitle is to be appended *)
(* *I*             Value: CShiftedTitle to be appended to the CShiftedTitleList. *)
(* *O*   OUTPUT:   VAR:  CShiftedTitleList to which CShiftedTitle has been appended *)
(* *E*   ERROR ACTION:  An error is reported if the CShiftedTitleList referenced by *)
(* *E*                CSTL has not been created or if the CShiftedTitle cannot be *)
(* *E*                appended.                                                 *)

        PROCEDURE DumpCSTList(CSTL: CShiftedTitleList);
(* *N*   FUNCTION: NAME: DumpCSTList                                            *)
(* *P*   PURPOSE:  Produce a formatted dump of the CShiftedTitles in the given list. *)
(* *I*   INPUT:    Value: The CShiftedTitleList to be dumped.                   *)
(* *O* - OUTPUT:   Character string representation of the Circularly Shifted Titles *)
(* *O*             in the given list is appended to the debugging file.         *)

END CSTListManager.
```

CSTListManager

IMPLEMENTATION MODULE CSTListManager;

```
FROM Titles        IMPORT Title;
FROM CSTitles      IMPORT CShiftedTitle, NullCShiftedTitle, CShiftedTitleToChars;
FROM Storage       IMPORT ALLOCATE, DEALLOCATE;
FROM TitlePartDef  IMPORT MaxTitleLength;
FROM RefPartDef    IMPORT MaxRefLength;
FROM Reporter      IMPORT Report;


TYPE
   CSTListElementPtr        = POINTER TO CShiftedTitleListElement;
   CShiftedTitleListElement = RECORD
                                  Next:  CSTListElementPtr;
                                  Value: CShiftedTitle;
                              END;
   CSTListHead              = RECORD
                                  ListStart:      CSTListElementPtr;
                                  CurrentElement: CSTListElementPtr;
                              END;
   CShiftedTitleList        = POINTER TO CSTListHead;

 PROCEDURE CreateCSTList(): CShiftedTitleList;
   VAR
      NewList: CShiftedTitleList;
 BEGIN
   ALLOCATE(NewList, SIZE(CSTListHead));
   NewList^.ListStart      := NIL;
   NewList^.CurrentElement := NIL;
   RETURN NewList;
 END CreateCSTList;

 PROCEDURE BeginCSTList(VAR CSTL: CShiftedTitleList);
 BEGIN
   CSTL^.CurrentElement := NIL;
   RETURN;
 END BeginCSTList;

 PROCEDURE GetNextCST(CSTL: CShiftedTitleList): CShiftedTitle;
   VAR OutTitle:  CShiftedTitle;
 BEGIN
   IF CSTL = NIL THEN
      OutTitle := NullCShiftedTitle();
   ELSE
      IF CSTL^.CurrentElement = NIL THEN
         CSTL^.CurrentElement := CSTL^.ListStart;
      ELSE
         CSTL^.CurrentElement := CSTL^.CurrentElement^.Next;
      END;
      IF CSTL^.CurrentElement = NIL THEN
         OutTitle := NullCShiftedTitle();
      ELSE
         OutTitle := CSTL^.CurrentElement^.Value;
      END;
   END;
   RETURN OutTitle;
 END GetNextCST;
```

CSTListManager

```
PROCEDURE  DeleteCSTList(VAR  CSTL:  CShiftedTitleList);
   VAR
      ThisElement:  CSTListElementPtr;
      NextElement:  CSTListElementPtr;
BEGIN
   ThisElement := CSTL^.ListStart;
   WHILE ThisElement <> NIL DO;
      CSTL^.ListStart := ThisElement^.Next;
      DEALLOCATE(ThisElement, SIZE(CShiftedTitleListElement));
      ThisElement := CSTL^.ListStart;
   END;
   DEALLOCATE(CSTL, SIZE(CSTListHead));
   CSTL := NIL;
   RETURN;
END DeleteCSTList;

PROCEDURE  AppendCST (VAR  CSTL:  CShiftedTitleList;    CST:  CShiftedTitle);
   VAR
      CurrentElementList: CShiftedTitleList;
      NewCSTListElement:  CSTListElementPtr;
BEGIN
   ALLOCATE(NewCSTListElement, SIZE(CShiftedTitleListElement));
   NewCSTListElement^.Next  := NIL;
   NewCSTListElement^.Value := CST;
   IF CSTL = NIL THEN
      CSTL := CreateCSTList();
   END;
   IF CSTL^.ListStart = NIL THEN
      CSTL^.ListStart := NewCSTListElement;
   ELSE
      CSTL^.CurrentElement^.Next := NewCSTListElement;
   END;
   CSTL^.CurrentElement := NewCSTListElement;

   RETURN;
END AppendCST;

PROCEDURE  DumpCSTList(CSTL:  CShiftedTitleList);
   CONST
      MyName              = "DumpCSTList";
   VAR
      TitleText:              ARRAY[0..(MaxTitleLength + MaxRefLength)] OF CHAR;
      CurrentListElement: CSTListElementPtr;
BEGIN
   IF CSTL = NIL THEN
      Report(MyName, "Circularly Shifted Title list is null");
   ELSIF CSTL^.ListStart = NIL THEN
      Report(MyName, "Circularly Shifted Title list is empty");
   ELSE
      Report(MyName, "Dump of Circularly Shifted Title list follows");
      CurrentListElement := CSTL^.ListStart;
      WHILE CurrentListElement <> NIL DO
         CShiftedTitleToChars(CurrentListElement^.Value, TitleText);
         Report(MyName, TitleText);
         CurrentListElement := CurrentListElement^.Next;
      END;
   END;
   RETURN;
END DumpCSTList;
END  CSTListManager.
```

Titles

```
DEFINITION MODULE Titles;
    FROM TitlePartDef    IMPORT TitlePart;
    FROM RefPartDef      IMPORT RefPart;

    TYPE  Title;

    PROCEDURE MakeTitle(TP: TitlePart; RP: RefPart): Title;
(* *N*    FUNCTION: NAME: MakeTitle                                              *)
(* *P*    PURPOSE: Construct a Title from a RefPart and a TitlePart. If either part is *)
(* *P*             null, a null Title is constructed.                           *)
(* *I*    INPUT:   Value: TP-the TitlePart and RP-the RefPart, the TitlePart and RefPart*)
(* *I*             from which the Title is to be built.                         *)
(* *O*    OUTPUT:  VAR:   The constructed Title or null Title.                  *)

    PROCEDURE GetTitlePart(T: Title): TitlePart;
(* *N*    FUNCTION: NAME: GetTitlePart                                          *)
(* *P*    PURPOSE: Get the TitlePart of the given Title. If the Title is a null Title, *)
(* *P*             the TitlePart will be a null TitlePart.                      *)
(* *I*    INPUT:   Value: The Title from which the Title-Part is required.      *)
(* *O*    OUTPUT:  VAR:   The Title-Part of the Title or a null Title-Part.     *)

    PROCEDURE GetRefPart(T: Title): RefPart;
(* *N*    FUNCTION: NAME: GetRefPart                                            *)
(* *N*                                                                          *)
(* *P*    PURPOSE: Get the RefPart of the given Title. If the Title is a null Title, *)
(* *P*             the RefPart will be a null RefPart.                          *)
(* *P*                                                                          *)
(* *I*    INPUT:   Value: The Title from which the Reference-part is required   *)
(* *I*                                                                          *)
(* *O*    OUTPUT:  VAR:   The Reference-Part of the Title or a null Reference-Part. *)
(* *O*                                                                          *)

    PROCEDURE TitleToChars(T: Title; VAR ch: ARRAY OF CHAR);
(* *N*    FUNCTION: NAME: TitleToChars                                          *)
(* *P*    PURPOSE: Convert a Title to printable character string form.          *)
(* *I*    INPUT:   Value: The Title to be converted.                            *)
(* *O*    OUTPUT:  The character-string version of the Title.                   *)

    PROCEDURE NullTitle(): Title;
(* *N*    FUNCTION: NAME: NullTitle                                             *)
(* *P*    PURPOSE: Create a null title.                                         *)
(* *O*    OUTPUT:  A null title.                                                *)

    PROCEDURE IsNullTitle(T: Title): BOOLEAN;
(* *N*    FUNCTION: NAME: IsNullTitle                                           *)
(* *P*    PURPOSE: If the Title is a null Title, return the value TRUE otherwise *)
(* *P*             return FALSE.                                                *)
(* *I*    INPUT:   Value: The Title being tested.                               *)
(* *O*    OUTPUT:  The value of the function.                                   *)

END  Titles.
```

Titles

```
IMPLEMENTATION MODULE Titles;
   FROM StringPack    IMPORT StringAssign, Concat, Substr, Length, TrimBlanks, ExtractChar;
   FROM TitlePartDef IMPORT TitlePart, TitlePartToChars, MaxTitleLength;
   FROM RefPartDef   IMPORT RefPart, RefPartToChars, MaxRefLength;
   FROM Storage       IMPORT ALLOCATE, DEALLOCATE;
   FROM Reporter      IMPORT Report;
   TYPE
      TitleBody = RECORD
                     TitleField: TitlePart;
                     RefField:   RefPart;
                  END;
      Title    = POINTER TO TitleBody;

   PROCEDURE MakeTitle(TP: TitlePart; RP: RefPart): Title;
      VAR NewTitle: Title;
   BEGIN
      ALLOCATE(NewTitle, SIZE(TitleBody));
      NewTitle^.TitleField := TP;
      NewTitle^.RefField   := RP;
      RETURN NewTitle;
   END MakeTitle;

   PROCEDURE GetTitlePart(T: Title): TitlePart;
      VAR OutTitlePart: TitlePart;
   BEGIN
      OutTitlePart := T^.TitleField;
      RETURN OutTitlePart;
   END GetTitlePart;

   PROCEDURE GetRefPart(T: Title): RefPart;
      VAR OutRefPart: RefPart;
   BEGIN
      OutRefPart := T^.RefField;
      RETURN OutRefPart;
   END GetRefPart;

   PROCEDURE TitleToChars(T: Title; VAR CompleteTitleText: ARRAY OF CHAR);
      VAR
         RefTextChars:   ARRAY[0..MaxRefLength] OF CHAR;
         TitleTextChars: ARRAY[0..MaxTitleLength] OF CHAR;
   BEGIN
      TitlePartToChars(T^.TitleField, TitleTextChars);
      RefPartToChars(T^.RefField, RefTextChars);
      Concat(TitleTextChars, RefTextChars, CompleteTitleText);
   END TitleToChars;

   PROCEDURE NullTitle(): Title;
   BEGIN
      RETURN NIL;
   END NullTitle;

   PROCEDURE IsNullTitle(T: Title): BOOLEAN;
      VAR IsNullT: BOOLEAN;
   BEGIN
      IF T = NIL THEN
         IsNullT := TRUE;
      ELSE
         IsNullT := FALSE;
      END;
      RETURN IsNullT;
   END IsNullTitle;
END Titles.
```

TitlePartDef

```
DEFINITION MODULE TitlePartDef;

    CONST
        MaxTitleLength = 150;

    TYPE TitlePart;

    PROCEDURE CharsToTitlePart(ch: ARRAY OF CHAR; VAR TP: TitlePart);

    PROCEDURE TitlePartToChars(TP: TitlePart; VAR ch: ARRAY OF CHAR);

    PROCEDURE IsNullTitlePart(TP: TitlePart): BOOLEAN;

END TitlePartDef.
```

```
IMPLEMENTATION MODULE TitlePartDef;
    FROM StringPack    IMPORT StringAssign, Concat, Substr, Length, TrimBlanks, ExtractChar;
    FROM Storage       IMPORT ALLOCATE, DEALLOCATE;
    FROM Reporter      IMPORT Report;

    TYPE
        TitleText = ARRAY[0..MaxTitleLength] OF CHAR;
        TitlePart = POINTER TO TitleText;

    PROCEDURE CharsToTitlePart(ch: ARRAY OF CHAR; VAR TP: TitlePart);
    BEGIN
        ALLOCATE(TP, SIZE(TitleText));
        StringAssign(ch, TP^);
    END CharsToTitlePart;

    PROCEDURE TitlePartToChars(TP: TitlePart; VAR ch: ARRAY OF CHAR);
    BEGIN
        StringAssign(TP^, ch);
    END TitlePartToChars;

    PROCEDURE IsNullTitlePart(TP: TitlePart): BOOLEAN;
        VAR IsNullTP: BOOLEAN;
    BEGIN
        IsNullTP := TRUE;
        RETURN IsNullTP;
    END IsNullTitlePart;

END TitlePartDef.
```

RefPartDef

```
DEFINITION MODULE RefPartDef;
   FROM TitlePartDef IMPORT MaxTitleLength, CharsToTitlePart, TitlePart, TitlePartToChars;
   CONST
      MaxRefLength = 50;

   TYPE RefPart;

   PROCEDURE CharsToRefPart(ch: ARRAY OF CHAR; VAR RP: RefPart);

   PROCEDURE RefPartToChars(RP: RefPart; VAR ch: ARRAY OF CHAR);

   PROCEDURE IsNullRefPart(RP: RefPart): BOOLEAN;

END RefPartDef.
```

```
IMPLEMENTATION MODULE RefPartDef;
   FROM TitlePartDef IMPORT MaxTitleLength, CharsToTitlePart, TitlePart, TitlePartToChars;
   FROM StringPack  IMPORT StringAssign, Concat, Substr, Length, TrimBlanks;
   FROM Storage     IMPORT ALLOCATE, DEALLOCATE;
   FROM Reporter    IMPORT Report;

   TYPE
      RefText = ARRAY[0..MaxRefLength] OF CHAR;
      RefPart = POINTER TO RefText;

   PROCEDURE CharsToRefPart(ch: ARRAY OF CHAR; VAR RP: RefPart);
   BEGIN
      ALLOCATE(RP, SIZE(RefText));
      StringAssign(ch, RP^);
      TrimBlanks(RP^);
   END CharsToRefPart;

   PROCEDURE RefPartToChars(RP: RefPart; VAR ch: ARRAY OF CHAR);
   BEGIN
      StringAssign(RP^, ch);
   END RefPartToChars;

   PROCEDURE IsNullRefPart(RP: RefPart): BOOLEAN;
      VAR IsNullRP: BOOLEAN;
   BEGIN
      IF RP = NIL THEN
         IsNullRP := TRUE;
      ELSE
         IsNullRP := FALSE;
      END;
      RETURN IsNullRP;
   END IsNullRefPart;

END RefPartDef.
```

CSTitles

```
DEFINITION MODULE CSTitles;
    FROM Titles    IMPORT Title;

    TYPE   CShiftedTitle;

    PROCEDURE MakeCSTitle(T: Title): CShiftedTitle;
(* *N*   FUNCTION: NAME: MakeCSTitle                                          *)
(* *P*   PURPOSE: Construct a CShiftedTitle in its unshifted position from a Title   *)
(* *I*   INPUT:   Value: T the Titlefrom which the Title is to be built.  If the Title *)
(* *I*            is a null Title, the value of the function is a null CShiftedTitle. *)
(* *O*   VALUE:   The constructed CShiftedTitle or null CShiftedTitle.         *)

    PROCEDURE GetTitle(CST: CShiftedTitle): Title;
(* *N*   FUNCTION: NAME: GetTitle                                             *)
(* *P*   PURPOSE: Get the Title of the given CShiftedTitle.  If the CShiftedTitle is a *)
(* *P*            null CShiftedTitle, the Title will be a null Title.          *)
(* *I*   INPUT:   Value: The CShiftedTitle from which the Title is required.    *)
(* *O*   VALUE:   The Title of the CShiftedTitle or a null Title.             *)

    PROCEDURE ShiftCSTitleOneWord(VAR CST: CShiftedTitle);
(* *N*   FUNCTION: NAME: ShiftCSTitleOneWord                                  *)
(* *P*   PURPOSE: Circularly shift the CShiftedTitle by one word.  If the CShiftedTitle *)
(* *P*            has already been completely rotated, the result will be a null *)
(* *P*            CShiftedTitle.                                              *)
(* *I*   INPUT:   Var: The CShiftedTitle To be shifted.                        *)
(* *O*   VALUE:   The rotated CShiftedTitle or a null Title.                   *)

    PROCEDURE GetFirstWord(CST: CShiftedTitle; VAR Word: ARRAY OF CHAR);
(* *N*   FUNCTION: NAME: GetFirstWord                                         *)
(* *P*   PURPOSE: GEts the first word of the title part of a CShiftedTitle.  If the *)
(* *P*            CShiftedTitle is a null CShiftedTitle, the result will be a null *)
(* *P*            string.                                                     *)
(* *I*   INPUT:   Value: The CShiftedTitle from which the first word is required. *)
(* *O*   OUTPUT:  The first word of the title part of the CShiftedTitle or a null *)
(* *O*            string.                                                     *)

    PROCEDURE CShiftedTitleToChars(CST: CShiftedTitle; VAR ch: ARRAY OF CHAR);
(* *N*   FUNCTION: NAME: CShiftedTitleToChars                                 *)
(* *P*   PURPOSE: Convert a CShiftedTitle to circularly shifted character string form. *)
(* *I*   INPUT:   Value: The CShiftedTitle to be converted.                    *)
(* *O*   OUTPUT:  The character-string version of the circularly shifted title text. *)

    PROCEDURE AlignmentPointOfCSTitle(CST: CShiftedTitle): CARDINAL;
(* *N*   FUNCTION: NAME: AlignmentPointOfCSTitle                              *)
(* *P*   PURPOSE: Provide the alignment point of a CShiftedTitle.             *)
(* *I*   INPUT:   Value: The CShiftedTitle for which the alignment point is required *)
(* *O*   OUTPUT:  The number of characters from beginning of unshifted title at which *)
(* *O*            alignment occurs.                                           *)

    PROCEDURE CopyCShiftedTitle(SourceCST: CShiftedTitle;
                                VAR TargetCST: CShiftedTitle);
(* *N*   FUNCTION: NAME: CopyCShiftedTitle                                    *)
(* *P*   PURPOSE: Copy the given CShiftedTitle to the target CShiftedTitle.    *)
(* *I*   INPUT:   Value: The CShiftedTitle to be copied.                       *)
(* *O*   OUTPUT:  An independent copy of the given CShiftedTitle.             *)
```

CSTitles

```
'PROCEDURE  CompareCShiftedTitles(CSTOne:  CShiftedTitle;
                                  CSTTwo:  CShiftedTitle): INTEGER;
(* *N*   FUNCTION: NAME: CompareCST
(* *P*   PURPOSE:  Compares the circularly shifted title parts of two CShiftedTitles  *)
(* *P*             The comparison is intended to determine the alphabetical ordering  *)
(* *P*             of the two circularly shifted titles in a case independent manner. *)
(* *I*   INPUT:    Value: The two CShiftedTitles to be compared.                       *)
(* *O*   VALUE:    An integer value: - 1 if CSTOne > CSTTwo alphabetically             *)
(* *O*                               = 0 if CSTOne = CSTTwo                            *)
(* *O*                               =-1 if CSTOne < CSTTwo alphabetically             *)
(* *O*             Two NullCShiftedTitles compare as equals.  If only one of the two is*)
(* *O*             a NullCShiftedTitle, then the other will compare as greater.        *)

   PROCEDURE  NullCShiftedTitle():  CShiftedTitle;
(* *N*   FUNCTION: NAME: NullCShiftedTitle                                             *)
(* *P*   PURPOSE:  Create a null circularly shifted title.                            *)
(* *O*   Value:    A null CShiftedTitle.                                              *)

   PROCEDURE  NullifyCShiftedTitle(VAR  CST:  CShiftedTitle);
(* *N*   FUNCTION: NAME: NullCShiftedTitle                                             *)
(* *P*   PURPOSE:  Convert a valid CShiftedTitle to a null CShiftedTitle.             *)
(* *O*   OUTPUT:   A null CShiftedTitle.                                              *)

   PROCEDURE  IsNullCShiftedTitle(CST:  CShiftedTitle):  BOOLEAN;
(* *N*   FUNCTION: NAME: IsNullCShiftedTitle                                           *)
(* *P*   PURPOSE:  If the CShiftedTitle is a null CShiftedTitle, return the value TRUE *)
(* *P*             otherwise return FALSE.                                             *)
(* *I*   INPUT:    Value: The CShiftedTitle being tested.                              *)
(* *O*   OUTPUT:   The value of the function.                                          *)
```

END CSTitles.

CSTitles

```
IMPLEMENTATION MODULE CSTitles;
   FROM StringPack    IMPORT Substr, Concat, Length, TrimBlanks, ExtractChar, StringAssign,
                             Index, BeforePattern, LowerCase, StringCompare, DeleteSubstr,
                             Translate;
   FROM Titles        IMPORT Title, GetTitlePart, IsNullTitle;
   FROM TitlePartDef  IMPORT TitlePart, TitlePartToChars, MaxTitleLength;
   FROM RefPartDef    IMPORT RefPart, RefPartToChars, MaxRefLength;
   FROM Storage       IMPORT ALLOCATE, DEALLOCATE;
   FROM SYSTEM        IMPORT ADR;
   FROM Reporter      IMPORT Report;
   FROM Encode        IMPORT encFormat, GetEncodeFormat, SetEncodeFormat, EncodeInt;


   TYPE
      CSTitleBody    = RECORD
                            TitleField:  Title;
                            ShiftAmount: CARDINAL;
                       END;
      CShiftedTitle = POINTER TO CSTitleBody;

   VAR
      NullCSTitle: CShiftedTitle;


   PROCEDURE  NullCShiftedTitle():  CShiftedTitle;
   BEGIN
      RETURN ADR(NullCSTitle);
   END  NullCShiftedTitle;


   PROCEDURE  NullifyCShiftedTitle(VAR  CST:  CShiftedTitle);
   BEGIN
      DEALLOCATE(CST, SIZE(CSTitleBody));
      CST := ADR(NullCSTitle);
      RETURN;
   END  NullifyCShiftedTitle;


   PROCEDURE  IsNullCShiftedTitle(CST:  CShiftedTitle):  BOOLEAN;
      VAR IsNullT: BOOLEAN;
   BEGIN
      IF CST = ADR(NullCSTitle) THEN
         IsNullT := TRUE;
      ELSE
         IsNullT := FALSE;
      END;
      RETURN IsNullT;
   END  IsNullCShiftedTitle;


   PROCEDURE  MakeCSTitle(T:  Title):  CShiftedTitle;
      VAR NewCSTitle: CShiftedTitle;
   BEGIN
      IF IsNullTitle(T) THEN
         NewCSTitle := NullCShiftedTitle();
      ELSE
         ALLOCATE(NewCSTitle, SIZE(CSTitleBody));
         NewCSTitle^.TitleField  := T;
         NewCSTitle^.ShiftAmount := 0;
      END;
      RETURN NewCSTitle;
   END  MakeCSTitle;
```

CSTitles

```
PROCEDURE GetTitle(CST: CShiftedTitle): Title;
  VAR OutTitle: Title;
BEGIN
  OutTitle := CST^.TitleField;
  RETURN OutTitle;
END GetTitle;

PROCEDURE ShiftCSTitleOneWord(VAR CST: CShiftedTitle);
  VAR
    TitlePartText:  ARRAY[0..MaxTitleLength] OF CHAR;
    ShiftIncrease:  CARDINAL;
BEGIN
  IF NOT IsNullCShiftedTitle(CST) THEN
    CShiftedTitleToChars(CST, TitlePartText);
    Translate(TitlePartText, "-", " ");
    ShiftIncrease := Index(" ", TitlePartText) + 1;
    IF (ShiftIncrease + CST^.ShiftAmount) >= Length(TitlePartText) THEN
        NullifyCShiftedTitle(CST);
    ELSE
        CST^.ShiftAmount := CST^.ShiftAmount + ShiftIncrease;
    END;
  END;
  RETURN;
END ShiftCSTitleOneWord;

PROCEDURE GetFirstWord(CST: CShiftedTitle; VAR Word: ARRAY OF CHAR);
  VAR
    TitlePartText:  ARRAY[0..MaxTitleLength] OF CHAR;
BEGIN
  IF IsNullCShiftedTitle(CST) THEN
    StringAssign("", Word);
  ELSE
    CShiftedTitleToChars(CST, TitlePartText);
    BeforePattern(" ", TitlePartText, Word);
  END;
  RETURN;
END GetFirstWord;
```

CSTitles

```
PROCEDURE CShiftedTitleToChars(CST: CShiftedTitle; VAR ch: ARRAY OF CHAR);
   VAR
      TitlePartOfCST:          TitlePart;
      TitleTextChars:          ARRAY[0..MaxTitleLength] OF CHAR;
      ShiftedPartOfTitleText: ARRAY[0..MaxTitleLength] OF CHAR;
BEGIN
   IF IsNullCShiftedTitle(CST) THEN
      StringAssign("", ch);
   ELSE
      TitlePartOfCST := GetTitlePart(CST^.TitleField);
      TitlePartToChars(TitlePartOfCST, TitleTextChars);
      Substr(TitleTextChars, CST^.ShiftAmount, Length(TitleTextChars) - CST^.ShiftAmount,
                                                                              ch);
      Concat(ch, " ", ch);
      Substr(TitleTextChars, 0, CST^.ShiftAmount, ShiftedPartOfTitleText);
      Concat(ch, ShiftedPartOfTitleText, ch);
      TrimBlanks(ch);
   END;
   RETURN;
END  CShiftedTitleToChars;


PROCEDURE  CopyCShiftedTitle(SourceCST:  CShiftedTitle;
                                           VAR TargetCST: CShiftedTitle);
BEGIN
   IF IsNullCShiftedTitle(SourceCST) THEN
      TargetCST := NullCShiftedTitle();
   ELSE
      ALLOCATE(TargetCST, SIZE(CSTitleBody));
      TargetCST^.TitleField  := SourceCST^.TitleField;
      TargetCST^.ShiftAmount := SourceCST^.ShiftAmount;
   END;
   RETURN;
END  CopyCShiftedTitle;


PROCEDURE  AlignmentPointOfCSTitle(CST: CShiftedTitle): CARDINAL;
   VAR
      AlignmentPoint: CARDINAL;
BEGIN
   IF IsNullCShiftedTitle(CST) THEN
      AlignmentPoint := 0;
   ELSE
      AlignmentPoint := CST^.ShiftAmount;
   END;
   RETURN AlignmentPoint;
END  AlignmentPointOfCSTitle;
```

CSTitles

```
PROCEDURE  CompareCShiftedTitles(CSTOne:  CShiftedTitle;
                                          CSTTwo: CShiftedTitle): INTEGER;

   VAR
      ComparisonValue: INTEGER;
      TitleTextOne:    ARRAY[0..MaxTitleLength] OF CHAR;
      TitleTextTwo:    ARRAY[0..MaxTitleLength] OF CHAR;
      OK:              BOOLEAN;
      Stop:            CARDINAL;

   PROCEDURE DeletePunctuation(VAR Text: ARRAY OF CHAR);
      CONST
         Punctuation = ",.;:-""()?!";
         Blanks      = "             ";
         DoubleBlank = "  ";
   BEGIN
      Translate(Text, Punctuation, Blanks);
      WHILE Index(DoubleBlank, Text) < Length(Text) DO
         DeleteSubstr(Text, Index(DoubleBlank, Text), 1);
      END;
      RETURN;
   END DeletePunctuation;

BEGIN
   IF IsNullCShiftedTitle(CSTOne) & IsNullCShiftedTitle(CSTTwo) THEN
      ComparisonValue := 0;
   ELSIF IsNullCShiftedTitle(CSTOne) THEN
      ComparisonValue := -1;
   ELSIF IsNullCShiftedTitle(CSTTwo) THEN
      ComparisonValue := 1;
   ELSE
      CShiftedTitleToChars(CSTOne, TitleTextOne);
      LowerCase(TitleTextOne);
      DeletePunctuation(TitleTextOne);
      CShiftedTitleToChars(CSTTwo, TitleTextTwo);
      LowerCase(TitleTextTwo);
      DeletePunctuation(TitleTextTwo);
      ComparisonValue := StringCompare(TitleTextOne, TitleTextTwo);
   END;
   RETURN ComparisonValue;
END  CompareCShiftedTitles;

BEGIN
   ALLOCATE(NullCSTitle, SIZE(CSTitleBody));
   NullCSTitle^.TitleField  := NIL;
   NullCSTitle^.ShiftAmount := 0;

END  CSTitles.
```

BTListManager

```
DEFINITION  MODULE  BTListManager;
(* *N*  FUNCTION NAME: ATitleListManager                                    *)
(* *N*                                                                       *)
(* *N*  AUTHOR: Michael Marcotty    DATE CREATED: 1990 May 28                *)
(* *N*                                                                       *)
(* *P*  PURPOSE: To implement the storage and manipulation of the BucketedTitleList *)
(* *P*           data type, which is a sorted CShifted Title List separated into 26  *)
(* *P*           buckets, one for each letter of the alphabet.               *)

   FROM Titles     IMPORT Title;
   FROM CSTitles   IMPORT CShiftedTitle;

   TYPE BucketedCSTitleList;
        BucketName = (BucketA, BucketB, BucketC, BucketD, BucketE, BucketF, BucketG,
                   BucketH, BucketI, BucketJ, BucketK, BucketL, BucketM, BucketN,
                   BucketO, BucketP, BucketQ, BucketR, BucketS, BucketT, BucketU,
                   BucketV, BucketW, BucketX, BucketY, BucketZ);

   PROCEDURE  CreateBucketedCSTList(): BucketedCSTitleList;

   PROCEDURE  BeginBucket(VAR  BucketFile:  BucketedCSTitleList;
                                                     Bucket: BucketName);

   PROCEDURE  GetNextCSTFromBucket(BucketFile: BucketedCSTitleList;
                                   Bucket: BucketName): CShiftedTitle;

   PROCEDURE  AppendCSTToBucket(VAR  BucketFile:  BucketedCSTitleList;
                                   Bucket: BucketName; CST: CShiftedTitle);

   PROCEDURE  CharToBucketName(Letter:  CHAR):  BucketName;

   PROCEDURE  BucketNameToChar(Name:  BucketName):  CHAR;

END  BTListManager.
```

BTListManager

```
IMPLEMENTATION  MODULE  BTListManager;

FROM Titles            IMPORT Title;
FROM Storage           IMPORT ALLOCATE, DEALLOCATE;
FROM CSTitles          IMPORT CShiftedTitle, NullCShiftedTitle;
FROM CSTListManager    IMPORT CShiftedTitleList, CreateCSTList, BeginCSTList, GetNextCST,
                              AppendCST;
FROM StringPack        IMPORT Concat, StringAssign, Index, CharToString, Length, ExtractChar,
                              UpperCase;
FROM Reporter          IMPORT Report;

CONST
    Alphabet = "ABCDEFGHIJKLMNOPQRSTUVWXYZ";

TYPE
    BCSTListHead              = ARRAY BucketName OF CShiftedTitleList;
    BucketedCSTitleList       = POINTER TO BCSTListHead;

PROCEDURE  CreateBucketedCSTList(): BucketedCSTitleList;
    VAR
        NewSetOfBuckets: BucketedCSTitleList;
        BucketNameIndex: BucketName;
BEGIN
    ALLOCATE(NewSetOfBuckets, SIZE(BCSTListHead));
    FOR BucketNameIndex := MIN(BucketName) TO MAX(BucketName) BY 1 DO
        NewSetOfBuckets^[BucketNameIndex] := CreateCSTList();
    END;
    RETURN NewSetOfBuckets;
END  CreateBucketedCSTList;

PROCEDURE  BeginBucket(VAR  BucketFile:  BucketedCSTitleList;
                                                         Bucket: BucketName);
BEGIN
    BeginCSTList(BucketFile^[Bucket]);
END  BeginBucket;

PROCEDURE  GetNextCSTFromBucket(BucketFile:  BucketedCSTitleList;
                                             Bucket: BucketName): CShiftedTitle;
BEGIN
    RETURN GetNextCST(BucketFile^[Bucket]);
END  GetNextCSTFromBucket;

PROCEDURE  AppendCSTToBucket(VAR  BucketFile:  BucketedCSTitleList;
                                       Bucket: BucketName; CST: CShiftedTitle);
BEGIN
    AppendCST(BucketFile^[Bucket], CST);
END  AppendCSTToBucket;
```

BTListManager

```
PROCEDURE  CharToBucketName(Letter:  CHAR):  BucketName;
  CONST
    MyName    = "CharToBucketName";
  VAR
    BucketNameValue: BucketName;
    LetterOrdinal:   CARDINAL;
    Message:         ARRAY[0..100] OF CHAR;
    LetterStr:       ARRAY[0..1] OF CHAR;
BEGIN
  CharToString(Letter, LetterStr);
  UpperCase(LetterStr);
  LetterOrdinal := Index(LetterStr, Alphabet);
  IF LetterOrdinal >= Length(Alphabet) THEN
    StringAssign("Argument to CharToBucketName: ", Message);
    Concat(Message, LetterStr, Message);
    Concat(Message, " is not an uppercase alphabetic character, 'A' assumed.", Message);
    Report(MyName, Message);
    LetterOrdinal := 0;
  END;
  RETURN VAL(BucketName, LetterOrdinal);
END  CharToBucketName;

PROCEDURE  BucketNameToChar(Name:  BucketName):  CHAR;
BEGIN
  RETURN ExtractChar(Alphabet, ORD(Name));
END  BucketNameToChar;
```

END BTListManager.

Reporter

DEFINITION MODULE Reporter;

```
(* *N*  FUNCTION NAME:  Reporter                                              *)
(* *N*                                                                        *)
(* *N*  AUTHOR: Michael Marcotty     DATE CREATED: 1990 February 5           *)
(* *N*                                                                        *)
(* *P*  PURPOSE: To maintain an execution trace file that permits the application to  *)
(* *P*           write messages to this file during execution.  These messages are used*)
(* *P*           for logging or debugging purposes.  At the beginning of execution, the*)
(* *P*           Reporter subsystem must be initialized by executing InitializeReporter*)
(* *P*           and terminated through TerminateReporter.  Messages are logged through*)
(* *P*           the Report procedure.                                        *)
(* *P*           If an attempt is made to invoke Report without initializing Reporter  *)
(* *P*           the message is displayed on the screen and the program is aborted.    *)
(* *P*           If an attempt is made to invoke Report recursively, i.e. while it is  *)
(* *P*           already invoked, which could happen if an error is discovered by one  *)
(* *P*           of the FileInterface procedures, the message is displayed on the      *)
(* *P*           screen.                                                       *)
(* *P*           If the message is too long, it is split into segments at blanks.      *)

    PROCEDURE InitializeReporter(CallerName: ARRAY OF CHAR);
(* *N*  FUNCTION NAME:  InitializeReporter                                     *)
(* *N*                                                                        *)
(* *P*  PURPOSE: The procedure initializes the Reporter subsystem. The name of the file*)
(* *P*           used for logging messages is obtained by Reporter from the FileNames  *)
(* *P*           module.  The trace file is initialized with a date stamp, the screen  *)
(* *P*           is cleared and a message showing that execution has started displayed.*)

    PROCEDURE Report(CallerName: ARRAY OF CHAR; Message: ARRAY OF CHAR);
(* *N*  FUNCTION NAME:  Report                                                 *)
(* *N*                                                                        *)
(* *P*  PURPOSE: The procedure records the given message has having been written by the*)
(* *P*           named caller. If the message is longer than 80 characters, it is split*)
(* *P*           onto several lines.                                           *)

    PROCEDURE TerminateReporter();
(* *N*  FUNCTION NAME:  TerminateReporter                                      *)
(* *N*                                                                        *)
(* *P*  PURPOSE: To insert an ending time stamp into the trace file and to close it.   *)
```

END Reporter.

Reporter

```
IMPLEMENTATION MODULE Reporter;

    FROM InOut          IMPORT ClearScreen, WriteString, WriteLn, HoldScreen;
    FROM DateTime       IMPORT TimeStamp, DateTimeLength;
    FROM StringPack     IMPORT StringAssign, Concat, Substr, Length, TrimBlanks, ExtractChar;
    FROM FileNames      IMPORT TraceFileName, MaxFileNameLength;
    FROM FileInterface  IMPORT OpenWrite, WriteLine, CloseFile, File;
    FROM Encode         IMPORT encFormat, GetEncodeFormat, SetEncodeFormat, EncodeInt;
(*  FROM System         IMPORT Status, Terminate;*)

    CONST
        MsgLineMaxLen     = 80;
        MsgLeader         = "    ";
        MsgContLeader     = "        ";
        MaxLeaderLength   = 6;
        CallerNameLength  = 63;
        SeparatorLine     =
            "===========================================================================";

    VAR TraceFile:          File;
        InitCallerName:     ARRAY[0..CallerNameLength] OF CHAR;
        ReporterInitialized: BOOLEAN;
        ReporterBusy:       BOOLEAN;

    PROCEDURE GetMessageSegment(Message: ARRAY OF CHAR;
                                MaxSegmentLength: CARDINAL;
                                VAR MsgSegmentStart: CARDINAL;
                                VAR MsgSegment: ARRAY OF CHAR);
        VAR
            BlankIndex:     CARDINAL;
            SegmentLength:  CARDINAL;
            TempStr:        ARRAY[0..100] OF CHAR;
            OK:             BOOLEAN;
            Stop:           CARDINAL;
    BEGIN
        IF MsgSegmentStart >= Length(Message) THEN
            StringAssign("", MsgSegment);
        ELSE
            IF (Length(Message) - MsgSegmentStart) <= MaxSegmentLength THEN
                SegmentLength := Length(Message) - MsgSegmentStart;
            ELSE
                BlankIndex := MsgSegmentStart + MaxSegmentLength - 1;
                WHILE (ExtractChar(Message, BlankIndex) <> " ") &
                                                (BlankIndex > MsgSegmentStart) DO
                    BlankIndex := BlankIndex - 1;
                END;
                IF BlankIndex = MsgSegmentStart THEN
                    BlankIndex := MsgSegmentStart + MaxSegmentLength - 1;
                END;
                SegmentLength := BlankIndex - MsgSegmentStart;
            END;
            Substr(Message, MsgSegmentStart, SegmentLength, MsgSegment);
            MsgSegmentStart := MsgSegmentStart + SegmentLength;
        END
    END GetMessageSegment;
```

Reporter

```
PROCEDURE PutMessageOnScreen(Message: ARRAY OF CHAR);
   VAR
      MsgSegment:        ARRAY[0..MsgLineMaxLen] OF CHAR;
      MsgSegmentStart:   CARDINAL;
      MsgSegmentLength:  CARDINAL;
      Leader:            ARRAY[0..MaxLeaderLength] OF CHAR;
BEGIN
   StringAssign(MsgLeader, Leader);
   MsgSegmentStart := 0;
   GetMessageSegment(Message, MsgLineMaxLen - Length(Leader),
                                       MsgSegmentStart, MsgSegment);
   WHILE Length(MsgSegment) > 0 DO
      Concat(Leader, MsgSegment, MsgSegment);
      WriteString(MsgSegment);
      WriteLn;
      StringAssign(MsgContLeader, Leader);
      GetMessageSegment(Message, MsgLineMaxLen - Length(Leader),
                                       MsgSegmentStart, MsgSegment);
   END;
END PutMessageOnScreen;

PROCEDURE InitializeReporter(CallerName: ARRAY OF CHAR);
   VAR
      LogFileName: ARRAY[0..MaxFileNameLength] OF CHAR;
      Message:     ARRAY[0..MsgLineMaxLen] OF CHAR;
      DateTime:    ARRAY[0..DateTimeLength] OF CHAR;
BEGIN
   ReporterBusy := TRUE;
   ClearScreen;
   StringAssign(CallerName, InitCallerName);
   TraceFileName(LogFileName);
   OpenWrite(LogFileName, TraceFile);
   TimeStamp(DateTime);
   Concat("Trace of execution of ", CallerName, Message);
   Concat(Message, " begun at ", Message);
   Concat(Message, DateTime, Message);
   WriteLine(TraceFile, Message);
   Message := SeparatorLine;
   WriteLine(TraceFile, Message);
   ReporterInitialized := TRUE;
   ReporterBusy        := FALSE
END InitializeReporter;
```

Reporter

```
PROCEDURE Report(CallerName: ARRAY OF CHAR; Message: ARRAY OF CHAR);
   VAR
      TraceLine:        ARRAY[0..MsgLineMaxLen] OF CHAR;
      MsgSegmentStart:  CARDINAL;
      DateTime:         ARRAY[0..DateTimeLength] OF CHAR;
      Leader:           ARRAY[0..MaxLeaderLength] OF CHAR;
BEGIN
   IF NOT ReporterInitialized THEN
      ClearScreen;
      Concat("Reporter called by ", CallerName, TraceLine);
      Concat(Message, " before Reporter initialized. Message is:", TraceLine);
      WriteString(TraceLine);
      WriteLn;
      PutMessageOnScreen(Message);
      WriteString("Program execution will terminated.");
      WriteLn;
      WriteString("Press any key to return to main window.");
      WriteLn;
      HoldScreen;
(*       Terminate(killed)*)
   ELSIF ReporterBusy THEN
      Concat("Reporter called recursively by ", CallerName, TraceLine);
      Concat(". Message is:", CallerName, TraceLine);
      WriteString(TraceLine);
      WriteLn;
      PutMessageOnScreen(Message);
   ELSE
      ReporterBusy := TRUE;
      Concat(CallerName, "=>", TraceLine);
      WriteLine(TraceFile, TraceLine);
      StringAssign(MsgLeader, Leader);
      MsgSegmentStart := 0;
      GetMessageSegment(Message, MsgLineMaxLen - Length(Leader),
                                       MsgSegmentStart, TraceLine);
      WHILE Length(TraceLine) > 0 DO
         Concat(Leader, TraceLine, TraceLine);
         WriteLine(TraceFile, TraceLine);
         StringAssign(MsgContLeader, Leader);
         GetMessageSegment(Message, MsgLineMaxLen - Length(Leader),
                                          MsgSegmentStart, TraceLine);
      END;
      ReporterBusy := FALSE;
   END;
   RETURN
END Report;
```

Reporter

```
PROCEDURE  TerminateReporter();
   VAR
     Message:      ARRAY[0..MsgLineMaxLen] OF CHAR;
     DateTime:     ARRAY[0..20] OF CHAR;
     Ch:           CHAR;
BEGIN
   ReporterBusy := TRUE;
   TimeStamp(DateTime);
   Message := SeparatorLine;
   WriteLine(TraceFile, Message);
   Concat("End of execution of ", InitCallerName, Message);
   Concat(Message, " at ", Message);
   Concat(Message, DateTime, Message);
   WriteLine(TraceFile, Message);
   CloseFile(TraceFile);
   WriteString("Execution Terminated");
   WriteLn;
   WriteString("Press any key to continue");
   WriteLn;
   HoldScreen;
   ReporterInitialized := FALSE;
   ReporterBusy         := FALSE
   END  TerminateReporter;

BEGIN
   ReporterInitialized := FALSE;
   ReporterBusy         := FALSE

END  Reporter.
```

DateTime

```
DEFINITION  MODULE  DateTime;

(* *N*  FUNCTION NAME: DateTime                                          *)
(* *N*                                                                   *)
(* *N*  AUTHOR: Michael Marcotty      DATE CREATED: 1990 February 4      *)
(* *N*                                                                   *)
(* *P*  PURPOSE: Obtain the current date time as string of form yyyymmdd hh:mm:ss  *)
(* *P*           This is returned in Stamp.  If an error is detected, the value    *)
(* *P*           returned is the string "Error in date/time"            *)

   CONST DateTimeLength = 18;

   PROCEDURE  TimeStamp(VAR  Stamp:  ARRAY  OF  CHAR);

END  DateTime.
```

DateTime

```
IMPLEMENTATION  MODULE  DateTime;
    FROM Utilities      IMPORT GetDateTime, Secs2Date;
    FROM LUTypes        IMPORT DateTimeRec;
    FROM Encode         IMPORT encFormat, GetEncodeFormat, SetEncodeFormat, EncodeInt;
    FROM StringPack     IMPORT StringAssign, Concat, Substr;

    CONST Months = "JANFEBMARAPRMAYJUNJULAUGSEPOCTNOVDEC";

    PROCEDURE TimeStamp(VAR Stamp: ARRAY OF CHAR);
        VAR Secs:           LONGINT;
            DTR:            DateTimeRec;
            TempStr:        ARRAY[0..3] OF CHAR;
            MonInx:         CARDINAL;
            Format:         encFormat;
            Stop:           CARDINAL;
            ConversionOK:   BOOLEAN;
            OldPad:         CHAR;
    BEGIN
        (*      Set EncodeInt to make leading zeroes, zero instead of blank.      *)
        GetEncodeFormat(Format);
        OldPad          := Format.padChar;
        Format.padChar := '0';
        SetEncodeFormat(Format);

        GetDateTime(Secs);
        Secs2Date(Secs, DTR);
        (*              Convert year to 4 digit number string                 *)
        ConversionOK := EncodeInt(0, Stop, Stamp, DTR.year, 4);
        (*              Extract three letter month name from Months string    *)
        MonInx := (DTR.month - 1) * 3;
        Substr(Months, MonInx, 3, TempStr);
        Concat(Stamp, TempStr, Stamp);
        (*              Convert day to 2 digit number string                  *)
        ConversionOK := ConversionOK & EncodeInt(0, Stop, TempStr, DTR.day, 2);
        Concat(Stamp, TempStr, Stamp);
        (*              Convert hour to 2 digit number string                 *)
        Concat(Stamp, ' ', Stamp);
        ConversionOK := ConversionOK & EncodeInt(0, Stop, TempStr, DTR.hour, 2);
        Concat(Stamp, TempStr, Stamp);
        (*              Convert minutes to 2 digit number string              *)
        Concat(Stamp, ':', Stamp);
        ConversionOK := ConversionOK & EncodeInt(0, Stop, TempStr, DTR.minute, 2);
        Concat(Stamp, TempStr, Stamp);
        (*              Convert seconds to 2 digit number string              *)
        Concat(Stamp, ':', Stamp);
        ConversionOK := ConversionOK & EncodeInt(0, Stop, TempStr, DTR.second, 2);
        Concat(Stamp, TempStr, Stamp);

        IF NOT ConversionOK THEN
            StringAssign('Error in date/time', Stamp)
        END;
        (*                      Reset Padding                                 *)
        Format.padChar := OldPad;
        SetEncodeFormat(Format);
        RETURN

    END TimeStamp;

END DateTime.
```

StringPack

```
DEFINITION MODULE StringPack;

    PROCEDURE Length(S: ARRAY OF CHAR): CARDINAL;

    PROCEDURE StringAssign(Source: ARRAY OF CHAR;
                                        VAR Destination: ARRAY OF CHAR);

    PROCEDURE Substr(Source: ARRAY OF CHAR; StartIndex: CARDINAL;
                        Count: CARDINAL; VAR Destination: ARRAY OF CHAR);

    PROCEDURE Concat(String1: ARRAY OF CHAR; String2: ARRAY OF CHAR;
                                        VAR Destination: ARRAY OF CHAR);

    PROCEDURE Index(Pattern: ARRAY OF CHAR; Source: ARRAY OF CHAR): CARDINAL;

    PROCEDURE Verify(ValidChars: ARRAY OF CHAR;
                                  Source: ARRAY OF CHAR): CARDINAL;

    PROCEDURE TrimBlanks(VAR Text: ARRAY OF CHAR);

    PROCEDURE ExtractChar(Source: ARRAY OF CHAR; Index: CARDINAL): CHAR;

    PROCEDURE DeleteSubstr(VAR Source: ARRAY OF CHAR;
                                  Index: CARDINAL; Count: CARDINAL);

    PROCEDURE Translate(VAR Text: ARRAY OF CHAR; FromAlphabet: ARRAY OF CHAR;
                                        ToAlphabet: ARRAY OF CHAR);

    PROCEDURE UpperCase(VAR Text: ARRAY OF CHAR);

    PROCEDURE LowerCase(VAR Text: ARRAY OF CHAR);

    PROCEDURE StringCompare(String1: ARRAY OF CHAR;
                                        String2: ARRAY OF CHAR): INTEGER;

    PROCEDURE CharToString(Ch: CHAR; VAR Str: ARRAY OF CHAR);

    PROCEDURE BeforePattern(Pattern: ARRAY OF CHAR; Source: ARRAY OF CHAR;
                                  VAR Desgination: ARRAY OF CHAR);

    PROCEDURE AfterPattern(Pattern: ARRAY OF CHAR; Source: ARRAY OF CHAR;
                                  VAR Desgination: ARRAY OF CHAR);

    PROCEDURE UpToPattern(Pattern: ARRAY OF CHAR; Source: ARRAY OF CHAR;
                                  VAR Desgination: ARRAY OF CHAR);

    PROCEDURE FromPattern(Pattern: ARRAY OF CHAR; Source: ARRAY OF CHAR;
                                  VAR Desgination: ARRAY OF CHAR);

END StringPack.
```

StringPack

```
IMPLEMENTATION MODULE StringPack;

IMPORT Strings;

CONST
    UpperCaseAlphabet = "ABCDEFGHIJKLMNOPQRSTUVWXYZ";
    LowerCaseAlphabet = "abcdefghijklmnopqrstuvwxyz";


PROCEDURE Length(S: ARRAY OF CHAR): CARDINAL;
BEGIN
    RETURN Strings.Length(S)
END Length;

PROCEDURE StringAssign(Source: ARRAY OF CHAR;
                                        VAR Destination: ARRAY OF CHAR);

BEGIN
    Strings.Assign(Destination, Source);
    RETURN;
END StringAssign;

PROCEDURE Substr(Source: ARRAY OF CHAR; StartIndex: CARDINAL;
                          Count: CARDINAL; VAR Destination: ARRAY OF CHAR);

BEGIN
    IF Count <= 0 THEN
        Strings.Assign(Destination, "");
    ELSE
        Strings.Copy(Source, StartIndex, Count, Destination);
    END;
    RETURN;
END Substr;

PROCEDURE Concat(String1: ARRAY OF CHAR; String2: ARRAY OF CHAR;
                                        VAR Destination: ARRAY OF CHAR);

BEGIN
    Strings.Concat(String1, String2, Destination);
    RETURN;
END Concat;

PROCEDURE Index(Pattern: ARRAY OF CHAR; Source: ARRAY OF CHAR): CARDINAL;
    VAR
        PattIndex: CARDINAL;
BEGIN
    PattIndex := Strings.Pos(Pattern, Source);
    IF PattIndex > Strings.Length(Source) THEN
        PattIndex := Strings.Length(Source);
    END;
    RETURN PattIndex;
END Index;
```

StringPack

```
PROCEDURE Verify(ValidChars: ARRAY OF CHAR; Source: ARRAY OF CHAR):
                                                           CARDINAL;
   VAR
      SourceIndex:      CARDINAL;
      InvalidCharFound: BOOLEAN;
      TestPattern:      ARRAY[0..1] OF CHAR;
BEGIN
   SourceIndex      := 0;
   InvalidCharFound := FALSE;
   WHILE (SourceIndex < Strings.Length(Source)) & NOT InvalidCharFound DO
      Strings.ToString(Strings.FetchChar(Source, SourceIndex), TestPattern);
      IF Strings.Pos(TestPattern, ValidChars) >= Length(ValidChars) THEN
         InvalidCharFound := TRUE;
      ELSE
         SourceIndex := SourceIndex + 1;
      END;
   END;
   RETURN SourceIndex;
END Verify;


PROCEDURE DeleteSubstr(VAR Source: ARRAY OF CHAR; Index: CARDINAL;
                                                  Count: CARDINAL);
BEGIN
   IF Index = 0 THEN
      Strings.Copy(Source, Count, Length(Source) - Count, Source);
   ELSE
      Strings.Delete(Source, Index, Count);
   END;
   RETURN;
END DeleteSubstr;


PROCEDURE TrimBlanks(VAR Text: ARRAY OF CHAR);
BEGIN
   WHILE Strings.FetchChar(Text, 0) = " " DO
      Strings.Copy(Text, 1, Length(Text) - 1, Text);
   END;
   WHILE Strings.FetchChar(Text, Length(Text) - 1) = " " DO
      Strings.Delete(Text, Length(Text) - 1, 1);
   END;
   RETURN;
END TrimBlanks;


PROCEDURE ExtractChar(Source: ARRAY OF CHAR; Index: CARDINAL): CHAR;
BEGIN
   RETURN Strings.FetchChar(Source, Index);
END ExtractChar;
```

StringPack

```
PROCEDURE Translate(VAR Text: ARRAY OF CHAR; FromAlphabet: ARRAY OF CHAR;
                                              ToAlphabet: ARRAY OF CHAR);

    VAR
        CharPosition:    CARDINAL;
        CharIndex:       CARDINAL;
        CharAsString:    ARRAY[0..1] OF CHAR;
        ReplacementChar: CHAR;
BEGIN
    FOR CharIndex := 0 TO Strings.Length(Text) BY 1 DO
        Strings.ToString(Strings.FetchChar(Text, CharIndex), CharAsString);
        CharPosition := Strings.Pos(CharAsString, FromAlphabet);
        IF CharPosition < Strings.Length(FromAlphabet) THEN
            IF CharPosition < Strings.Length(ToAlphabet) THEN
                ReplacementChar := Strings.FetchChar(ToAlphabet, CharPosition);
            ELSE
                ReplacementChar := " ";
            END;
            Strings.AssignChar(ReplacementChar, Text, CharIndex);
        END;
    END;
    RETURN;
END Translate;

PROCEDURE UpperCase(VAR Text: ARRAY OF CHAR);
BEGIN
    Translate(Text, LowerCaseAlphabet, UpperCaseAlphabet);
END UpperCase;

PROCEDURE LowerCase(VAR Text: ARRAY OF CHAR);
BEGIN
    Translate(Text, UpperCaseAlphabet, LowerCaseAlphabet);
END LowerCase;

PROCEDURE CharToString(Ch: CHAR; VAR Str: ARRAY OF CHAR);
BEGIN
    Strings.ToString(Ch, Str);
    RETURN;
END CharToString;

PROCEDURE StringCompare(String1: ARRAY OF CHAR; String2: ARRAY OF CHAR):
                                                              INTEGER;

BEGIN
    RETURN Strings.CompareStr(String1, String2);
END StringCompare;

PROCEDURE BeforePattern(Pattern: ARRAY OF CHAR; Source: ARRAY OF CHAR;
                        VAR Destination: ARRAY OF CHAR);

    VAR
        PatternIndex: CARDINAL;
BEGIN
    PatternIndex := Strings.Pos(Pattern, Source);
    Strings.Copy(Source, 0, PatternIndex, Destination);
    RETURN;
END BeforePattern;
```

StringPack

```
PROCEDURE AfterPattern(Pattern: ARRAY OF CHAR; Source: ARRAY OF CHAR;
                                               VAR Destination: ARRAY OF CHAR);
    VAR
        PatternIndex: CARDINAL;
BEGIN
    PatternIndex := Strings.Pos(Pattern, Source);
    IF PatternIndex < Strings.Length(Source) THEN
        Strings.Copy(Source, PatternIndex + Strings.Length(Pattern),
                Strings.Length(Source) - Strings.Length(Pattern) - PatternIndex,
                                                                Destination);
    ELSE
        Strings.Assign(Destination, "");
    END;
    RETURN;
END AfterPattern;

PROCEDURE UpToPattern(Pattern: ARRAY OF CHAR; Source: ARRAY OF CHAR;
                                               VAR Destination: ARRAY OF CHAR);
    VAR
        PatternIndex: CARDINAL;
BEGIN
    PatternIndex := Strings.Pos(Pattern, Source);
    IF PatternIndex < Strings.Length(Source) THEN
        Strings.Copy(Source, 0, PatternIndex + Length(Pattern), Destination);
    ELSE
        Strings.Assign(Destination, "");
    END;
    RETURN;
END UpToPattern;

PROCEDURE FromPattern(Pattern: ARRAY OF CHAR; Source: ARRAY OF CHAR;
                                               VAR Destination: ARRAY OF CHAR);
    VAR
        PatternIndex: CARDINAL;
BEGIN
    PatternIndex := Strings.Pos(Pattern, Source);
    IF PatternIndex < Strings.Length(Source) THEN
        Strings.Copy(Source, PatternIndex, Strings.Length(Source) - PatternIndex,
                                                                Destination);
    ELSE
        Strings.Assign(Destination, "");
    END;
    RETURN;
END FromPattern;

END StringPack.
```

FileNames

```
DEFINITION MODULE FileNames;

(* *N*  FUNCTION NAME: FileNames                                              *)
(* *N*                                                                        *)
(* *N*  AUTHOR: Michael Marcotty      DATE CREATED: 1990 February 5           *)
(* *N*                                                                        *)
(* *P*  PURPOSE: Provide file names for application. This collects the names into one *)
(* *P*           place. If it were required, procedures in the implementation module  *)
(* *P*           could interrogate the user to obtain the name.               *)

  CONST
    MaxFileNameLength = 128;

  PROCEDURE TraceFileName(VAR NameOfTraceFile: ARRAY OF CHAR);
  PROCEDURE InputFileName(VAR NameOfInputFile: ARRAY OF CHAR);
  PROCEDURE LexiconFileName(VAR NameOfLexiconFile: ARRAY OF CHAR);
  PROCEDURE PrintFileName(VAR NameOfPrintFile: ARRAY OF CHAR);

END FileNames.
```

FileNames

```
IMPLEMENTATION MODULE FileNames;

  FROM Strings    IMPORT Assign;

  PROCEDURE TraceFileName(VAR NameOfTraceFile: ARRAY OF CHAR);
  BEGIN
    StringAssign("Macintosh HD:Modula-2:KWIC Source:AAALog", NameOfTraceFile);
  END TraceFileName;

  PROCEDURE InputFileName(VAR NameOfInputFile: ARRAY OF CHAR);
  BEGIN
    StringAssign("Macintosh HD:Modula-2:Refs", NameOfInputFile);
  END InputFileName;

  PROCEDURE LexiconFileName(VAR NameOfLexiconFile: ARRAY OF CHAR);
  BEGIN
    StringAssign("Macintosh HD:Modula-2:Lexicon", NameOfLexiconFile);
  END LexiconFileName;

  PROCEDURE PrintFileName(VAR NameOfPrintFile: ARRAY OF CHAR);
  BEGIN
    StringAssign("Macintosh HD:Modula-2:KWICOutput", NameOfPrintFile);
  END PrintFileName;


END FileNames.
```

The following is a listing obtained from running the BuildPrintFile program on a list of titles obtained directly through the use of a software tool from the text of the Bibliography in this volume.

−A−

...g: Concepts and Techniques	(Proceedings of the Nato C...	: [Naur et al. 1976]
Structured analysis	(SA): a language for commu...	: [Ross 1977]
Algorithms	+ Data Structures = Programs	: [Wirth 1976]
... Algorithms from ACM, Vol.	1, Algorithms 1-220	: [ACM 1980]
Programming in America in the	1950s—Some Personal Impres...	: [Backus 1980]
...om ACM, Vol. 1, Algorithms	1-220	: [ACM 1980]
Algorithm	201 Shellsort	: [Boothroyd 1963a]
Algorithm	207 Stringsort	: [Boothroyd 1963b]
A Primer of Algol	60 Programming Academic Press	: [Dijkstra 1962]
...Algorithmic Language Algol	60	: [Naur 1963]
Control Data	6400/6500/6600 Computer Sy...	: [CDC 1965]
Simula	67 Common Base Language	: [Dahl et al. 1970]
...hmetic, ANSI/IEEE Standard	754-1985	: [IEEE 1985]
...ng-point Arithmetic, Draft	8.0 of IEEE Task P754 with...	: [IEEE 1981]
Z—The	95% Program Editor	: [Wood 1981]
Algorithms + Data Structures	= Programs	: [Wirth 1976]
Programming Pearls—	Abstract Data Types	: [Bentley 1987]
...algebraic specification of	abstract data types	: [Guttag and Horning 1978]
...er of Algol 60 Programming	Academic Press	: [Dijkstra 1962]
Pinciples of Program Design,	Academic Press	: [Jackson 1975]
Collected Algorithms from	ACM, Vol. 1, Algorithms 1-220	: [ACM 1980]
...ming Considered as a Human	Activity	: [Dijkstra 1965]
Nesting in	Ada is for the birds	: [Clark et al. 1980]
The	Ada Language System	: [Wolfe et al. 1981]
...urus: a prototype advanced	Ada programming environment	: [Standish and Taylor 1984]
Stoneman: Requirements for	Ada Programming Support En...	: [Buxton 1980]
...Components and Packages in	Ada	: [Rice 1983]
Software Engineering with	Ada	: [Booch 1983]
...nguages Conference Keynote	Address	: [Hopper 1981]
... Problem Solving: The Next	Advance in Operations Rese...	: [Simon and Newell 1958]
Arcturus: a prototype	advanced Ada programming e...	: [Standish and Taylor 1984]
HIPO-A design	aid and documentation tech...	: [IBM 1974]
The	algebraic specification of...	: [Guttag and Horning 1978]
A Primer of	Algol 60 Programming Acade...	: [Dijkstra 1962]
...n the Algorithmic Language	Algol 60	: [Naur 1963]
Faults in Functions, in	Algol and Fortran	: [Hill 1971]
...verybody Should Know about	Algol	: [Higman 1963]
	Algorithm 201 Shellsort	: [Boothroyd 1963a]
	Algorithm 207 Stringsort	: [Boothroyd 1963b]
The Sachertorte	Algorithm and Other Antido...	: [Shore 1985]
Revised Report on the	Algorithmic Language Algol 60	: [Naur 1963]
	Algorithms + Data Structur...	: [Wirth 1976]
...gorithms from ACM, Vol. 1,	Algorithms 1-220	: [ACM 1980]
The Expression of	Algorithms by Charts	: [Bruno and Steiglitz 1972]
Collected	Algorithms from ACM, Vol. ...	: [ACM 1980]
The	Alphabet Effect	: [Logan 1986]
	Alphabet, mother of invention	: [McLuhan and Logan 1977]
Programming in	America in the 1950s—Some ...	: [Backus 1980]
...les of Information Systems	Analysis and Design	: [Mills et al. 1986]
An	Analysis of Some Commercia...	: [Elshoff 1976]
	Analysis of the Effects of...	: [Dunsmore and Gannon 1980]

APPENDIX C
EXAMINATION QUESTIONS

1. The PL/I program shown in Figure C.1 purports to find the number of elementary circuits in a complete directed graph with n vertices. A directed graph $G = (V, E)$ consists of a nonempty and finite set of vertices V and a set E of ordered pairs of distinct vertices called edges. A path in G is a sequence of vertices $p_{uv} = (v = v_1, v_2, \ldots, v_k = u)$ such that $(v_i, v_{i+1}) \in E$ for $1 \le i \le k$. A *circuit* is a path in which the first and last vertices are identical. A path is *elementary* if no vertex appears twice. A circuit is elementary if no vertex but the first and last appears twice. Two elementary circuits are distinct if one is not a cyclic permutation of the other. A directed graph is complete if all vertices are connected to all others. The definitions exclude graphs with loops (edges of the form (v, v)) and multiple edges between the same vertices. There are exactly

$$\sum_{i=1}^{n-1} \binom{n}{n-i+1}(n-1)!$$

elementary circuits in a complete directed graph with n vertices. The PL/I program is reproduced essentially as it appears in Auslander and Strong (1978) with a few syntactic corrections. This version of the algorithm was produced automatically from a recursive algorithm in Johnson (1975).

   This program is difficult to read and understand. Your first task is to convert it into a clear program. This requires restructuring it and choosing better names for its variables. The following clues to the way in which the algorithm works have been obtained from Johnson (1975). Elementary circuits are constructed from a root vertex s in the sub-graph induced by s and vertices 'larger than s' in some ordering of the vertices. To avoid duplicating circuits, a vertex, v is *blocked* when it is added to some elementary path beginning in s. It stays blocked as long as every path from v to s intersects the current elementary path at a vertex other than s. Furthermore, a vertex does not become a root vertex for constructing elementary paths unless it is the least vertex in at least one elementary circuit. The array A represents the graph as an adjacency matrix, where A(i, j) is '1'B if there is an edge from vertex i to vertex j. The vertices of the current elementary path are kept on a stack.

```
C_FIND:        PROCEDURE(N) RETURNS(FIXED BINARY);
               DECLARE N FIXED BINARY;
               DECLARE (A(N, N), B(N, N)) ALIGNED BIT(1);
               DECLARE BLOCKED(N) ALIGNED BIT(1), S FIXED BINARY;
               DECLARE (I, J) FIXED BINARY;
               DECLARE STACK(2*N) FIXED BINARY;
               DECLARE FSTACK(2:N+1) ALIGNED BIT(1);
               DECLARE STACK_INDEX FIXED BINARY INITIAL(1);
               DECLARE CIRCUIT_COUNT FIXED BINARY;
               /*        DECLARATIONS FOR CIRCUIT        */
               DECLARE F BIT(1), V FIXED BINARY;
               DECLARE XF BIT(1);
               DECLARE W FIXED BINARY;
               DECLARE K FIXED BINARY INITIAL(1);
               /*        DECLAREATIONS FOR UNBLOCK       */
               DECLARE U FIXED BINARY;
               DECLARE WU FIXED BINARY;
               DECLARE KU FIXED BINARY INITIAL(1);
               /*        MAIN BODY OF THE PROGRAM        */
               A = '1'B;
               STACK_INDEX = 1;
               CIRCUIT_COUNT = 0;
               S = 1;
               DO WHILE(S < N);
                DO I = S TO N;
                 BLOCKED(I) = '0'B;
                 DO J = 1 TO N;
                  B(I, J) = '0'B;
                 END;
                END;
L3:            V = S;
               K = 1;
CIRCUIT:       STACK(STACK_INDEX) = V;
               STACK_INDEX = STACK_INDEX + 1;
               F = '0'B;
               BLOCKED(V) = '1'B;
L1:            W = S - 1;
L1I:           W = W + 1;
               IF W > N THEN GO TO L2;
               IF A(V, W) THEN DO;
                IF W = S THEN DO;
                 CIRCUIT_COUNT = CIRCUIT_COUNT + 1;
                 F = '1'B;
                END;
                ELSE IF ^BLOCKED(W) THEN DO;
                 FSTACK(STACK_INDEX) = F;
                 K = K + 1;
                 V = W;
                 GO TO CIRCUIT;
                END;
               END;
               GO TO L1I;
```

FIGURE C.1 The PL/I program C_FIND.

```
L2:             IF F THEN DO;
                U = V;
                KU = 1;
UNBLOCK:        BLOCKED(U) = '0'B;
                WU = S - 1;
LUI:            WU = WU + 1;
                IF WU > N THEN GO TO LUE;
                IF B(U, WU) THEN DO;
                 B(U, WU) = '0'B;
                 IF BLOCKED(WU) THEN DO;
                  KU = KU + 1;
                  STACK(STACK_INDEX) = U;
                  STACK_INDEX = STACK_INDEX + 1;
                  U = WU;
                  GO TO UNBLOCK;
                 END;
                END;
                GO TO LUI;
LUE:            KU = KU - 1;
                IF KU > 0 THEN DO;
                 WU = U;
                 STACK_INDEX = STACK_INDEX - 1;
                 U = STACK(STACK_INDEX);
                 GO TO LUI;
                END;
                /*  END OF UNBLOCK              */
                END;
                ELSE DO W = S TO N;
                 IF A(V, W) THEN DO;
                  B(W, V) = '1'B;
                END; END;
                W = V;
                STACK_INDEX = STACK_INDEX - 1;
                V = STACK(STACK_INDEX);
                K = K - 1;
                IF K > 0 THEN DO;
                XF = F;
                F = FSTACK(STACK_INDEX);
                IF XF THEN F = '1'B;
                V = STACK(STACK_INDEX - 1);
                GO TO L1I;
                END;
                  /* END OF CIRCUIT */
                S = S+ 1;
                END;
                RETURN(CIRCUIT_COUNT);
     END C_FIND;
```

FIGURE C.1(CONTINUED) The PL/I program C_FIND.

Unfortunately, the program also has an error. The symptoms of this error are shown from the following table comparing the results produced by the program with the correct results obtained from evaluating the formula given above.

Number of vertices	Number of circuits from formula	Number of circuits found by program
6	409	414
7	2365	2371
8	16064	16071
9	125664	125672
10	1112073	1112082

Your second task is to find the error in the program and correct it.

2. If we consider a sequence of values $V[0]$, $V[1]$, $V[2]$, . . ., $V[n-1]$, and delete i (not necessarily adjacent) values from the list, we would have a subsequence of length $n - i$ . . . This subsequence is called an *upsequence* if its values are in non-decreasing order. We wish to write a program that, given a sequence $V[0 : n-1]$, where $n > 0$, calculates the length of the longest upsequence of $V[0 : n-1]$. A possible algorithm introduces an auxilliary array M such that during the execution of the program, M[j] contains the smallest value that ends an upsequence of length j in the part of V that has been examined. The array M is ordered. The algorithm is:

```
I    := 1;
K    := 1;
M[1] := V[0];
{Loop invariant:
     (0<=I<=N) & (K = length_of_upsequence(V[0 : I-1])) &
        (for all J: 1<=J<=K: M[J] is the smallest value that ends an
                                 upsequence of length J in V[0 : I-1])}
WHILE I <> N DO
   IF V[I] >= M[K] THEN
      K    := K + 1;
      M[K] := V[I];
   ELSE
      IF (V[I] < M[1]) THEN
         M[1] := V[I];
      ELSE
         {Use binary search to locate a value of J such that
                  M[J-1] <= V[I] < M[J]}
         M[J] := V[I];
      END;
   END;
   I := I + 1;
END;
```

Choose a better set of variable names than those used above. Write the code using the new names that you have chosen, for the binary search, together with the invariant relation for the loop. Show that, taking the invariant relation and the termination condition for the loop, the binary search algorithm finds the correct value for J. Show that the total algorithm indeed finds the longest upsequence in $B[0:n-1]$.

3. Give a brief definition of top-down design. What is the objective of this concept? List three difficulties that programmers might encounter when attempting to design their program in top-down fashion.

4. If you were to examine someone else's program, how would you determine whether it was modular? If you had to examine two programs A and B, how would you determine whether program A was more modular than program B?

5. Give a definition of structured programming in one or two brief paragraphs. What is the relationship between structured programming and the GO TO statement commonly found in high-level programming languages? Be specific: do not resort to the oversimplified statement that 'structured programming is programming without the GO TO statement'. Is it possible to write structured programs in Basic?

6. Several common programming languages allow the concept of 'global' variables, e.g., through the use of COMMON in Fortran, the LINKAGE SECTION in Cobol, and EXTERNAL variables in PL/1. Do you think the use of global variables makes it more difficult to understand the behavior of a program and, if so, why? What kind of restrictions should be placed on the issue of global variables. Does your conclusion have any consequences for the use of block-structured languages like PL/1 or Pascal?

7. The need for clear, precise, and unambiguous external specifications for a program is well known. How do you suggest that they should be written, bearing in mind that the specifications must be understandable by both the user and the programmers? Describe the criteria that you would use to judge the adequacy of specifications for a large project.

8. What kind of documentation do you think should be provided to assist the maintenance programmer in future maintenance of a program you have written? Do you think any standards can be developed in this area? Would it be possible to develop standards for comments in a program listing? How can we ensure that the comments are accurate and meaningful?

9. Give a definition of debugging. Why is it different from testing? Do you think that debugging is an art or a science? Why do you think some people are good at debugging and others are bad at it?

10. Why are human factors important in computer programming? What kinds of human factors should be considered? How can human factors be utilized more fully in all types of computer programming?

11. What is a reliable program? What are the characteristics of a structured program? How are the two related? What features of a language would make it easier to write reliable programs? Is it possible to write reliable programs in a language that does not encourage them?

12. Define and give examples of programming style. Give some advantages for following good programming style.

13. How would you approach development of a software product? Include the important steps and a description of each step.

14. The following are brief functional descriptions of integrands. Although the descriptions are terse and these modules are taken out of context, study each description and determine the probable unity of purpose: (functional, communicational, procedural, classical, logical, and coincidental) of each integrand.

   (a) Print and archive the output file.
   (b) Update, add, or delete a record in the database.
   (c) Sort the file of personnel records.
   (d) Read the next transaction, edit it, and display it to the user.
   (e) Write a message to the user (input is a message code number).
   (f) Allocate or free this area of storage.
   (g) Read or write an inventory record (two entry points).
   (h) Obtain the next L05 record.
   (i) Initialize the work areas needed to generate the object code.
   (j) Calculate the new arrival time and display it on the terminal.
   (k) Update record in database and read next transaction.
   (l) Print the next line, find the substring in second parameter, and convert the third parameter from character to floating-point.
   (m) Allocate a storage area (input specifies the amount to be allocated).
   (n) Read the next transaction or increment print-line count or initialize summary table (one of the arguments is a function code).
   (o) Find best potential date for this person (if there is none with consistent desires, return 'no date found' indicator).
   (p) Add a node to the tree, delete a node from the tree, search the tree for a node, or produce the postorder view of the tree (four entry points).
   (q) Initialize region table, close country file, open next transaction file, and print summary line.
   (r) Display shut-down message on all terminals.
   (s) Format screen for part display and read part record from data base.

(t) Mainline control module.

(u) Obtain first transaction, obtain lowest and highest keys in master file, and print page headings.

(v) Search region table, search salary table, or save employee list on spill file (three entry points).

15. Based on your experience and drawing on examples taken from existing programming languages, list four principles the language designers might adopt to make the programming process *as difficult as possible*. An example of such a principle is: *Make non-uniform use of keywords, parentheses, blanks and other special characters or constructs*.

   This principle is illustrated in Fortran by the two statements:

```
GOTO i (l1, l2, ..ln)
READ (u) v1, v2,..., vn.
```

16. The following is an example of a routine with side-effects:

```
MODULE SideEffects;
   VAR
       External:      INTEGER;

   PROCEDURE Effector(X: INTEGER): INTEGER;
      VAR
            ReturnValue: INTEGER;
   BEGIN
      ReturnValue := X + External;
      External    := External + ReturnValue;
      RETURN ReturnValue;
   END Effector;

BEGIN
   External := 1;
   Write(Effector(0));
   Write(Effector(0));
   Write(Effector(0));
   RETURN;

END SideEffects.
```

(a) What will be the sequence of values printed by the execution of this fragment?

(b) Would you expect there to be a difference between the execution of the following tests, assuming that External has the same value when the tests are made:

```
IF Effector(External) = External THEN
IF External = Effector(External) THEN
IF Effector(External) = (External + 0) THEN
IF (External + 0) = Effector(External) THEN
```

(c) What other difficulties might be expected from side effects like these?

(d) Under what situations might such a device be 'justified'?

17. List three things that would be more unwise for programmers to believe than that they have no need to interest themselves in management matters. (See Editor's Preface)

APPENDIX D
REFERENCES

Abrahams, Paul W., (1978), 'Review of Edsger W. Dijkstra *A Discipline of Programming*', Review #32,951, *ACM Computing Reviews*, vol. 19, no. 5, May.

Adams, R., (1972), *Watership Down*, Macmillan, New York.

Alexander, Christopher, (1964), *Notes on the Synthesis of Form*, Harvard University Press, Cambridge, Massachusetts.

Allworth, S. T., (1981), *Introduction to Real-time Software Design*, Macmillan, London and Basingstoke.

Allworth, S. T. and Zobel, Richard N., (1987), *Introduction to Real-Time Software Design*, Springer-Verlag, New York.

Andrews, Gregory R. and Schneider, Fred B., (1983), 'Concepts and notations for concurrent programming', *ACM Computing Surveys*, vol. 15, no. 1, March, pp. 3–43.

ANSI/IEEE 770 X3.97, (1983), *IEEE Standard Pascal Computer Programming Language*, American National Standards Institute and the Institute of Electrical and Electronic Engineers.

Appel, Kenneth and Haken, Wolfgang, (1977), 'Every planar map is four colorable', *Illinois Journal of Mathematics*, vol. 21, no. 3, September.

Aron, Joel D., (1974), *The Program Development Process*, Addison-Wesley, Reading, Massachusetts.

Ashby, W. Ross, (1963), 'Review of Feigenbaum's *Computers and Thought*', *Journal of Nervous and Mental Diseases*.

Ashcroft, E. A. and Manna, Z., (1971), 'The translation of GOTO programs to WHILE programs', *Proceedings of 1971 IFIP Congress*, August, pp. 250–5.

Augustine, Norman R., (1983), *Augustine's Laws*, Viking Penguin, Inc., New York.

Auslander, M. A. and Strong, H. R., (1978), 'Systematic recursion removal', *Communications of the ACM*, vol. 21, no. 2, February, pp. 127–34.

Backus, John, (1980), 'Programming in America in the 1950s – some personal impressions', in N. Metropolis, J. Howlett, and Gian-Carlo Rota (eds), *A History of Computing in the Twentieth Century*, Academic Press, New York.

Backus, John and Heising, W. P., (1964), 'Fortran', *IEEE Transactions on Electronic Computers*, vol. EC13, no. 4, August, pp. 382–5

Baecker, Ronald M. and Marcus, Aaron, (1990), *Human Factors and Typography for More Readable Programs*, Addison-Wesley, Reading, Massachusetts.

Baker, F. Terry, (1972), 'Chief programming team management of production programming', *IBM Systems Journal*, vol. 11, no. 1, January, pp. 56–73.

Barron, David W., (1977), *An Introduction to the Study of Programming Languages*, Cambridge University Press, Cambridge, England.

Beckermeyer, Robert, Dill, John, Elshoff, James, Marcotty, Michael and Murray, John T., (1974), 'Handling asynchronous interrupts in a PL/1-like language', *Software – Practice and experience*, vol. 4, no. 2, April–June, pp. 117–24.

Belady, Lazlos A. and Lehman, M. Manfred, (1979), 'The characteristics of large systems', in Peter Wegner (ed.), *Research Directions in Software Technology*, MIT Press, Cambridge, Massachusetts.

Ben-Ari, M., (1982), *Principles of Concurrent Programming*, Prentice Hall, Hemel Hempstead.

Bentley, Jon Louis, (1986a), *Programming Pearls*, Addison-Wesley, Reading, Massachusetts.

Bentley, Jon Louis, (1986b), 'Programming pearls – literate programming', *Communications of the ACM*, vol. 29, no. 5, May, pp. 364–9.

Bentley, Jon Louis, (1986c), 'Programming pearls – a literate program', *Communications of the ACM*, vol. 29, no. 6, June, pp. 471–83.

Bentley, Jon Louis, (1987), 'Programming pearls – abstract data types', *Communications of the ACM*, vol. 30, no. 4, April, pp. 284–90.

Bentley, Jon Louis, (1988), *More Programming Pearls*, Addison-Wesley, Reading, Massachusetts.

Berg, Helmut K., Boebert, W. E., Franta, W. R. and Moher, T. G., (1982), *Formal Methods of Program Verification and Specification*, Prentice Hall, Englewood Cliffs, NJ.

Bersoff, Edward H., Henderson, Vilas D. and Siegel, Stanley G., (1980), *Software Configuration Management*, Prentice Hall, Englewood Cliffs, NJ.

Blaauw, G. A., (1970), 'Hardware requirements for the fourth generation', in F. Gruenberger (ed.), *Fourth Generation Computers*, Prentice Hall, Englewood Cliffs, NJ.

Boehm, Barry W., (1973), 'The high cost of software', *Proceedings of a Symposium on the High Cost of Software*, Naval Postgraduate School, Monterey, California, September.

Boehm, Barry, (1976), 'Software engineering', *IEEE Transactions on Computers*, vol. C-25, no. 12, December, pp. 1226–41.

Boehm, Barry W., (1979), 'Software engineering: R&D trends and defense needs', in Peter Wegner (ed.), *Research Directions in Software Technology*, MIT Press, Cambridge, Massachusetts.

Boehm, Barry W., (1981), *Software Engineering Economics*, Prentice Hall, Englewood Cliffs, NJ.

Böhm, Corrado and Jacopini, Giuseppi, (1966), 'Flow diagrams, Turing machines, and languages with only two formation rules', *Communications of the ACM*, vol. 9, no. 5, May, pp. 366–71.

Booch, Grady, (1983), *Software Engineering with Ada*, Benjamin/Cummings Publishing Company, Menlo Park, California.

Boothroyd, J., (1963a), 'Algorithm 201, Shellsort', *Communications of the ACM*, vol. 6, no. 8, August, p. 445.

Boothroyd, J., (1963b), 'Algorithm 207, Stringsort', *Communications of the ACM*, vol. 6, no. 10, October, p. 615.

Brooks, Frederick P., (1975), *The Mythical Man Month*, Addison-Wesley, Reading, Massachusetts.

Bruno, J. and Steiglitz, K., (1972), 'The expression of algorithms by charts', *Journal of the ACM*, vol. 19, no. 3, July, pp. 517–25.

Buchanan, Bruce G. and Shortliffe, Edward H., (1984), *Rule-Based Expert Systems: The MYCIN experiments of the Stanford Heuristic Programming Project*, Addison-Wesley, Reading, Massachusetts.

Bunyan, John, (1678), *Pilgrim's Progress*.

Buxton, John, (1980), *Stoneman: Requirements for Ada programming support environments*, US Department of Defense, Advanced Research Projects Agency.

CDC, (1965), *Control Data 6400/6500/6600 Computer Systems Reference Manual*, Publication Number 60100000, Control Data Corporation, St Paul, Minnesota.

Cameron, John R., (1986), 'An overview of JSD', *IEEE Transactions on Software Engineering*, vol. SE-12, no. 2, February, pp. 222–40.

Chapin, Ned, (1974), 'Structured programming simplified', *Computer Decisions*, vol. 6, no. 6, June, pp. 28–31.

Clark, R. Lawrence, (1973), 'A linguistic contribution to goto-less programming', *Datamation*, vol. 19, no. 12, December, pp. 62–3; republished in *Communications of the ACM*, vol. 27 no. 4, April 1984, pp. 349–50.

Clarke, Lori A., Wiledon, Jack C. and Wolf, Alexander L., (1980), 'Nesting in Ada is for the birds', *ACM Sigplan Notices*, vol. 15, no. 11, November, pp. 139–45.

Cox, Brad J., (1986), *Object Oriented Programming*, Addison-Wesley, Reading, Massachusetts.

Dahl, Olle-Johann, Myhrhaug, B. and Nygaard, K., (1969), *Simula 67 Common Base Language*, Publication N.S.22, Norwegian Computing Center, Oslo, June.

Darnell, Peter A., and Margolis, Philip, (1988), *Software Engineering in C*, Springer-Verlag, New York.

DeMillo, Richard A., Lipton, Richard J. and Perlis, Alan J., (1979), 'Social processes and proofs of theorems and programs', *Communications of the ACM*, vol. 22, no. 5, May, pp. 271–80. See also *Communications of the ACM*, vol. 22, no. 11, November 1979, pp. 621–30 and vol. 23, no. 5, May 1980, pp. 307–8.

DeRemer, Frank and Kron, Hans H., (1976), 'Programming-in-the-large versus programming-in-the-small', *IEEE Transactions on Software Engineering*, vol. SE-2, no. 2, June, pp. 80–6.

Deutsch, Michael S., (1982), *Software Verification and Validation*, Prentice Hall, Englewood Cliffs, NJ.

Dick, Kay, (1963), *Writers at Work: The Paris Review interviews* (second series), Viking Press, New York.

Dijkstra, Edsger W., (1962), *A Primer of Algol 60 Programming*, Academic Press, London.

Dijkstra, Edsger W., (1965), 'Programming Considered as a Human Activity,' *Proceedings of the 1965 IFIP Congress*, Spartan Books, New York, pp. 213–17.

Dijkstra, Edsger W., (1968a), 'Goto statement considered harmful', *Communications of the ACM*, vol. 11, no. 3, March, pp. 147–8.

Dijkstra, Edsger W., (1968b), 'Cooperating sequential processes', in F. Genuys (ed.), *Programming Languages*, Academic Press, New York.

Dijkstra, Edsger W., (1969), 'Structured programming', paper delivered to *1969 NATO Conference: Software engineering techniques*, in Naur *et al.*, (1976) (eds), *Software Engineering: Concepts and techniques (Proceedings of NATO Conferences)*, Van Nostrand Reinhold, New York.

Dijkstra, Edsger W., (1972a), 'Notes on structured programming', in *Structured Programming* by Olle-Johann Dahl, Edsger W. Dijkstra and Charles Anthony Richard Hoare, Academic Press, New York.

Dijkstra, Edsger W., (1972b), 'The humble programmer', *Communications of the ACM*, vol. 15, no. 10, October, pp. 859–66.

Dijkstra, Edsger W., (1976), *A Discipline of Programming*, Prentice Hall, Englewood Cliffs, NJ.

Doherty, Walter J. and Kelisky, R. P., (1979), 'Managing VM/CMS systems for user effectiveness', *IBM Systems Journal*, vol. 18, no. 1, pp. 143–63.

Dreyfus, Hubert L., Dreyfus, Stuart E. with Athanasiou, Tom, (1986), *Mind Over Machine: the power of human intuition and expertise in the era of the computer*, Free Press, New York.

Dunsmore, H. E. and Gannon, John D., (1980), 'Analysis of the effects of programming factors on programming effort', *The Journal of Systems and Software*, vol. 1, pp. 141–53.

Elshoff, James L., (1976), 'An analysis of some commercial PL/1 programs', *IEEE Transactions on Software Engineering*, vol. SE-2, no. 2, June, pp. 113–20.

Elshoff, James L., (1978), 'An investigation into the effects of the counting method used on software science measurements', *ACM Sigplan Notices*, vol. 13, no. 2, February, pp. 29–46.

Elshoff, James L. and Marcotty, Michael, (1982), 'Improving computer program readability to aid modification', *Communication of the ACM*, vol. 25, no. 8, August, pp. 512–21.

Elson, Mark, (1973), *Concepts of programming languages*, Science Research Associates, Chicago.

Fairley, Richard E., (1985), *Software Engineering Concepts*, McGraw-Hill, New York.

Falkoff, Adin D. and Iverson, Kenneth E., (1978), 'The evolution of APL', in R. L. Wexelblat (ed.), (1981), *History of Programming Languages*, Academic Press, New York, pp. 661–74.

Fetzer, James H., (1988), 'Program verification: the very idea', *Communications of the ACM*, vol. 31, no. 9, September, pp. 1048–63.

Feuer, Alan R. and Gehani, Narain H., (1982), 'A comparison of the programming languages C and Pascal', *ACM Computing Surveys*, vol. 14, no. 1, March, pp. 73–92.

Fox, Geoffrey C., Johnson, Mark A., Lyzenga, Gregory A., Otto, Steve W., Salmon, John K. and Walker, David W., (1988), *Solving Problems in Concurrent Processors*, Prentice Hall, Englewood Cliffs, NJ.

Flon, Lawrence, (1975), 'On research in structured programming', *Sigplan Notices*, vol. 10, no. 10, October, p. 16.

Gane, Chris and Sarson, Trish, (1977), *Structured Systems Analysis: Tools and techniques*, Improved System Technologies, Inc., New York.

Ghezzi, Carlo and Jazayeri, Mehdi, (1987), *Programming Language Concepts 2/E*, John Wiley and Sons, New York.

Gleaves, Richard, (1984), *Modula-2 for Pascal Programmers*, Springer-Verlag, New York.

Gogol, Nikolai Vasilovich, (1835), 'The Tale of How Ivan Ivanovich Quarreled with Ivan Nikiforovich', in Leonard J. Kent (ed.), *The Complete Tales of Nikolai Gogol*, University of Chicago Press, Chicago.

Goldberg, Adele and Robson, D., (1983), *Smalltalk-80: The language and its implementation*, Addison-Wesley, Reading, Massachusetts.

Good, Donald I., Cohen, Richard M. and Hunter, Lawrence W., (1978), 'A report on the development of Gypsy', *Proceedings ACM National Conference*, vol. 1, December, pp. 116–22.

Goodenough, John B., (1975), 'Exception handling: issues and a proposed notation', *Communications of the ACM*, vol. 18, no. 12, December, pp. 683–96.

Gowers, Sir Ernest, (1973), *The Complete Plain Words*, revised by Sir Bruce Fraser, Her Majesty's Stationery Office, London.

Gries, David, (1976), 'An Illustration of current ideas on the derivation of correctness proofs and correct programs', *IEEE Transactions on Software Engineering*, vol. SE-2, no. 4, December, pp. 238–44.

Gries, David, (1981), *The Science of Programming*, Springer-Verlag, New York.

Guttag, John V. and Horning, James J., (1978), 'The algebraic specification of abstract data types', *Acta Informatica*, vol. 10, pp. 27–52.

Halmos, Paul R., (1970), 'How to Write Mathematics', *L'Enseignement Mathématique*, vol. 16, pp. 123–52. Also reproduced in Norman E. Steenrod, Paul R. Halmos, Manahem M. Schiffer and Jean A. Dieudonné, (1973), *How to Write Mathematics*, American Mathematical Society, Rhode Island, pp. 19–48.

Halstead, Maurice H., (1974), *Elements of Software Science*, Elsevier/North-Holland, New York.

Hanson, David R., (1981), 'Is block structure necessary?' *Software – Practice and Experience*, vol. 11, pp. 853–66.

Harbison, S. P. and Steele, G. L., Jr, (1984), *A Reference Manual*, Prentice Hall, Englewood Cliffs, NJ.

Hardy, G. H., (1928), 'Mathematical proof', *Mind*, vol. 38, pp. 1–28.

Harland, David M., (1986), *Concurrency and Programming Languages*, Ellis Horwood, Chichester.

Hatley, Derek J. and Pirbhai, Imtiaz A., (1987), *Strategies for Real-Time System Specification*, Dorset House Publishing, New York.

Higman, Bryan, (1963), 'What everybody should know about Algol', *Computer Journal*, vol. 6, no. 1, February, pp. 50–6.

Higman, Bryan, (1977), *A Comparative Study of Programming Languages*, Elsevier North-Holland, New York.

Hill, I. David, (1971), 'Faults in functions, in Algol and Fortran', *The Computer Journal*, vol. 14, no. 3, August, pp. 315–16.

Hoare, Charles Anthony Richard, (1973), *Hints on Programming Language Design*, Technical Report STAN-CS-73-403, Computer Science Department, Stanford University, Palo Alto, California, December. Also in (1974), *Computer Systems Reliability*, Infotech State of the Art Report no. 20, Infotech, Maidenhead, England.

Hopper, Grace Murray, (1978), 'History of Programming Languages Conference, keynote address', in R. L. Wexelblat (ed.), (1981), *History of Programming Languages*, Academic Press, New York, pp. 7–20.

Hopper, Grace Murray, (1981), 'The first bug', *Annals of the History of Computing*, vol. 3, no. 3, July, pp. 285–6.

Horning, James and Wortman, David, (1977), 'Software hut: a computer program engineering project in the form of a game', *IEEE Transactions on Software Engineering*, vol. SE-3, no. 4, July.

Horowitz, Ellis, (1984), *Fundamentals of Programming Languages* (2nd edn), Computer Science Press, Rockville, Maryland.

IBM, (1974), *HIPO – A Design Aid and Documentation Technique*, Form GX20-1851, IBM, White Plains, NY.

IEEE, (1981), 'A proposed standard for binary floating-point arithmetic, draft 8.0 of IEEE Task P754 with introductory comments by David Stevenson', *IEEE Computer*, vol. 14, no. 3, March, pp. 51–62.

IEEE, (1985), *IEEE Standard for Binary Floating-point Arithmetic*, ANSI/IEEE Standard 754-1985, IEEE, New York, August.

Iverson, Kenneth E., (1962), *A Programming Language*, John Wiley, New York.

Jackson, Michael A., (1975), *Principles of Program Design*, Academic Press, London.

Jackson, Michael A., (1983), *System Development*, Prentice Hall, Hemel Hempstead.

Jensen, Randall W. and Tonies, Charles C., (1979), *Software Engineering*, Prentice Hall, Englewood Cliffs, NJ.

Johnson, Donald B., (1975), 'Finding all the elementary circuits of a directed graph', *SIAM Journal of Computing*, vol. 4, no. 1, March, pp. 77–84.

Jones, Capers, (1986), *Programming Productivity*, McGraw-Hill, New York.

Jones, Clifford B., (1980), *Software Development: A rigorous approach*, Prentice Hall, Hemel Hempstead.

Keller, Daniel, (1990), 'A guide to natural naming', *ACM Sigplan Notices*, vol. 25, no. 5, May, pp. 95–102.

Kelly-Bootle, Stan, (1981), *The Devil's DP Dictionary*, McGraw-Hill New York.

Kelly-Bootle, Stan, (1987), *Modula-2 Primer*, Howard W. Sams, Indianapolis.

Kemeny, John G. and Kurtz, Thomas E., (1964), *BASIC Instruction Manual*, Dartmouth College, Hanover.

Kernighan, Brian W. and Plauger, P. J., (1976), *Software Tools*, Addison-Wesley, Reading, Massachusetts.

Kernighan, Brian W. and Plauger, P. J., (1978, first edition 1974), *The Elements of Programming Style*, McGraw-Hill, New York.

Kernighan, Brian W. and Ritchie, Dennis M., (1978), *The C Programming Language*, Prentice Hall, Englewood Cliffs, NJ.

Kline, Morris, (1980), *Mathematics*, Oxford University Press, Oxford.

Knuth, Donald Ervin, (1972), 'Ancient Babylonian algorithms', *Communications of the ACM*, vol. 15, 1972, pp. 671–7. Errata in *Communications of the ACM*, vol. 19, 1976, p. 108.

Knuth, Donald Ervin, (1974), 'Structured programming with goto statements', *ACM Computing Surveys*, vol. 6, no. 4, December, pp. 261–301.

Knuth, Donald Ervin, (1983), *The WEB System of Structured Documentation*, Stanford Computer Science Technical Report 980, Stanford University, California.

Knuth, Donald Ervin, (1984), 'Literate programming', *Computer Journal*, vol. 27, no. 2, May, pp. 97–111.

Knuth, Donald Ervin and Pardo, Luis Trabb, (1976), *The Early Development of Programming Languages*, Report STAN-CS-76-562, Stanford University, Computer Science Department, August.

Kurtz, Thomas E., (1963), *Background for the Time Sharing System*, Dartmouth Computation Center Time Sharing Project, Memo no. 1, Hanover, New Hampshire.

Kurtz, Thomas E., (1978), 'Basic', in R. L. Wexelblat (ed.), (1981), *History of Programming Languages*, Academic Press, NY, pp. 515–37.

Lavington, Simon H., (1975), *A History of Manchester Computers*, National Computing Centre Publications, London.

Lavington, Simon H., (1980), *Early British Computers*, Manchester University Press, Manchester; published in United States by Digital Equipment Corporation, Bedford, Massachusetts.

Ledgard, Henry F., (1987), *Software Engineering Concepts*, vols 1 and 2, Addison-Wesley, Reading, Massachusetts.

Ledgard, Henry F. and Marcotty, Michael, (1975), 'A genealogy of control structures', *Communications of the ACM*, vol. 18, no. 11, November, pp. 629–39.

Lientz, Bennet P. and Swanson, E. Burton, (1980), *Software Maintenance Management*, Addison-Wesley, Reading, Massachusetts.

Linger, Richard C., Mills, Harlan D. and Witt, Bernard I., (1979), *Structured Programming: Theory and practice*, Addison-Wesley, Reading, Massachusetts.

Liu, Chester C., (1976), 'A look at software maintenance', *Datamation*, vol. 22, no. 11, November, pp. 51–5.

Logan, Robert K., (1986), *The Alphabet Effect*, William Morrow and Company, New York.

MacLennan, Bruce J., (1983), *Principles of Programming Languages: Design, evaluation, and implementation*, Holt, Rinehart, and Winston, New York.

Macro, Allen, (1990), *Software Engineering: Concepts and management*, Prentice Hall, Hemel Hempstead.

Macro, Allen and Buxton, John, (1987), *The Craft of Software Engineering*, Addison-Wesley, Reading, Massachusetts.

Malengé, Jean-Pierre, (1980), *Critique de la Physique du Logiciel*, Publication Informatique, Université de Nice.

Mantei, Marilyn, (1981), 'The effect of programming team structures on programming tasks', *Communications of the ACM*, vol. 24, no. 3, March, pp. 106–13.

Marcotty, Michael and Ledgard, Henry, (1986), *Programming Language Landscape: Syntax, semantics and implementation*, (2nd edn), Science Research Associates, Chicago, Illinois. A slightly abbreviated version of this book is *The World of Programming Languages*, Springer-Verlag, New York, 1987.

McCabe, Thomas, (1976), 'A complexity measure', *IEEE Transactions on Software Engineering*, vol. SE-2, no. 6, December, pp. 308–20.

McCarthy, John, (1963), 'A basis for a mathematical theory of computation', in P. Braffort and D. Hirshberg, *Computer Programming and Formal Systems*, North-Holland, Amsterdam, pp. 33–7.

McCarthy, John, (1978), 'History of Lisp', in R. L. Wexelblat (ed.), (1981), *History of Programming Languages*, Academic Press, NY, pp. 661–74.

McGehee, Brad Michael, (1984), *Writing Software User Manuals*, Writer's Digest Books, Cincinnati, Ohio.

McLuhan, H. Marshall and Logan, Robert K., (1977), 'Alphabet, mother of invention', *Et Cetera*, vol. 34, December, pp. 373–83.

Mehlmann, Marilyn, (1981), *When People Use Computers*, Prentice Hall, Englewood Cliffs, NJ.

Miller, George A., (1956), 'The magical number seven, plus or minus two: some limits on our capacity for processing information', *Psychological Review*, vol. 63, no. 2, March, pp. 81–97.

Miller, Robert B., (1968), 'Response time in man–computer conversational transactions', *American Federation of Information Processing Societies Conference Proceedings, Fall 1968*, vol. 33 (pt. 1), pp. 267–77.

Miller, Webb, (1980), *Collected Algorithms from ACM, vol. 1, Algorithms 1–220*, Association for Computing Machinery, New York.

Miller, Webb, (1987), *A Software Tools Sampler*, Prentice Hall, Englewood Cliffs, NJ.

Mills, Harlan D., (1972), *Mathematical Foundations for Structured Programming*, IBM Corporation Report FSC 71-6012, Gaithersburg, Maryland, February.

Mills, Harlan D., (1986), 'Structured programming: retrospect and prospect', *IEEE Software*, vol. 3, no. 6, November, pp. 58–66.

Mills, Harlan D. and Baker, F. Terry, (1973), 'Chief programmer teams', *Datamation*, vol. 19, no. 12, December, pp. 58–61.

Mills, Harlan D., Linger, Richard C. and Hevner, Alan R., (1986), *Principles of Information Systems Analysis and Design*, Academic Press, Orlando, Florida.

Morrison, Philip and Morrison, Emily, (1961), *Charles Babbage and his Calculating Engines*, Dover Publishing Company, New York.

Myers, Glenford J., (1975), *Reliable Software Through Composite Design*, Petrocelli/Charter, New York.

Myers, Glenford J., (1978), 'A controlled experiment in program testing and code walkthroughs/inspections', *Communications of the ACM*, vol. 21, no. 9, September, pp. 760–8.

Myers, Glenford J., (1979), *The Art of Software Testing*, John Wiley, New York.

Myhill, John, (1952), 'Some philosophical implications of mathematical logic: three classes of ideas', *Review of Metaphysics*, vol. 6, no. 2, December, pp. 165–98.

Nassi, Isaac and Schneiderman, Ben, (1973), 'Flowcharting techniques for structured programming', *ACM Sigplan Notices*, vol. 8, no. 8, pp. 12–26.

Naur, Peter (ed.), (1963), 'Revised report on the algorithmic language Algol 60', *Communications of the ACM*, vol. 3, no. 1, January, pp. 1–17.

Naur, Peter, Randell, Brian and Buxton, John N., (1976), *Software Engineering: Concepts and Techniques (Proceedings of the Nato Conferences)*, Van Nostrand Reinhold, New York.

Nicholls, John E., (1975), *The Structure and Design of Programming Languages*, Addison-Wesley, Reading, Massachusetts.

Oman, Paul W. and Cook, Curtis R., (1990), 'Typographic style is more than cosmetic', *Communications of the ACM*, vol. 33, no. 5, May, pp. 506–20.

Organick, Elliott I., Forsythe, Alexandra I. and Plummer, Robert P., (1978), *Programming Language Structures*, Academic Press, New York.

Orr, Kenneth T., (1977), *Structured Systems Development*, Yourdon Press, New York.

Overgaard, Mark, (1980), 'UCSD Pascal™: a portable software environment for small computers', *AFIPS Conference Proceedings*, vol. 49, AFIPS Press, Arlington, Virginia, pp. 747–54.

Parnas, David L., (1971), 'Information distribution aspects of design methodology', *IFIP Congress Proceedings*, Ljubljana, Yugoslavia, pp. 339–44.

Parnas, David L., (1972), 'On the criteria to be used in decomposing systems into modules', *Communications of the ACM*, vol. 15, no. 12, December, pp. 1053–8.

Parnas, David L., (1977), 'The use of precise specifications in the development of software', in B. Gilchrist (ed.), *Information Processing 77*, IFIP, North-Holland, Amsterdam, pp. 861–7.

Peterson, J., (1977), 'Petri nets', *ACM Computing Surveys*, vol. 9, no. 3, September.

Pratt, Terrence, (1984), *Programming Languages: Design and implementation* (2nd edn), Prentice Hall, Englewood Cliffs, NJ.

Punch, (1845), vol. viii, p. 1.

Putnam, L. H., (1982), *Software Cost Estimating and Lifecycle Control*, IEEE Catalog, Los Alamitos, California.

Quine, Willard V. O., (1951), *Mathematical Logic*, (rev. edn), Harvard University Press, Cambridge, Massachusetts.

Reps, Thomas William, (1984), *Generating Language Based Environments*, The MIT Press, Cambridge, Massachusetts.

Reynolds, John C., (1981), *The Craft of Programming*, Prentice Hall, Hemel Hempstead.

Rice, John R., (1983), 'Remarks on software components and packages in Ada', *ACM Sigsoft Software Engineering Notes*, vol. 8, no. 2, April, p. 8.

Rochkind, Marc J., (1975), 'The source code control system', *IEEE Transactions on Software Engineering*, vol. SE-1, December, pp. 364–70.

Rosenberg, Ronni Lynne, (1980), *Incomprehensible Computer Systems: Knowledge without wisdom*, MIT Report MIT/LCS/TR-227, Massachusetts Institute of Technology, Cambridge, Massachusetts.

Ross, Douglas, (1977), 'Structured analysis (SA): a language for communicating ideas', *IEEE Transactions on Software Engineering*, vol. SE-3, no. 1, January.

Ross, Douglas T., Goodenough, John B. and Irvine, C. A., (1975), 'Software engineering: process, principles, and goals', *IEEE Computer*, May 1975.

Rubinstein, Richard and Hersh, Harry M., (1985), *The Human Factor*, Digital Press, Burlington, Massachusetts.

Rubin, Frank, (1987), '*GOTO Considered Harmful* Considered Harmful', *Communications of the ACM*, vol. 30, no. 3, March, pp. 195–6. See also No. 7, July, pp. 632–4, No. 8, August, pp. 659–62, and No. 12, December, pp. 997, 1085.

Russell, Bertrand, (1903), *The Principles of Mathematics*, Cambridge University Press, Cambridge.

Russell, Bertrand, (1945), *A History of Western Philosophy*, Simon & Schuster, New York.

Sackman, H., Erikson, W. J. and Grant, E. E., (1968), 'Exploratory experimental studies comparing online and offline programming performance', *Communications of the ACM*, vol. 11, no. 1, January, 1968, pp. 3–11.

Sammet, Jean E., (1969), *Programming Languages: History and fundamentals*, Prentice Hall, Englewood Cliffs, NJ.

Sammet, Jean E., (1978), 'The early history of Cobol', in R. L. Wexelblat (ed.), (1981), *History of Programming Languages*, Academic Press, NY, pp. 199–243.

Schneider, M. L., (1984), 'Ergonomic considerations in the design of text editors', in Y. Vassiliou (ed.), *Human Factors and Interactive Computer Systems*, Ablex Publishers, Norwood, NJ, pp. 141–61.

Schneiderman, Ben, (1986), *Designing the User Interface: Strategies for effective human–computer interaction*, Addison-Wesley, Reading, Massachusetts.

Shaw, Mary, Almes, Guy T., Newcomer, Joseph M., Reid, Brian K. and Wulf, Wm A., (1981), 'A comparison of programming languages for software engineering', *Software – Practice and Experience*, vol. 11, pp. 1–52.

Shore, John, (1985), *The Sachertorte Algorithm and Other Antidotes to Computer Anxiety*, Penguin, New York.

Shortliffe, Edward H., (1976), *Computer-Based Medical Consultations: MYCIN*, Elsevier, New York.

Simon, Herbert A. and Newell, Alan, (1958), 'Heuristic problem solving: the next advance in operations research', *Operations Research*, vol. 6, Jan.–Feb., p. 8.

Spencer, Herbert, (1852), 'The philosophy of style', *Westminster Review*, pp. 435–59.

Stallman, Richard M., (1981), 'Emacs: the extensible, customizable, self-documenting display editor', *ACM Sigplan Notices*, vol. 16, no. 6, June, pp. 147–56.

Standish, Thomas A. and Taylor, Richard N., (1984), 'Arcturus: a prototype advanced Ada programming environment', *ACM Software Engineering Notes*, vol. 9, no. 3, May, pp. 57–64.

Stevens, Wayne, (1981), *Using Structured Design*, John Wiley, New York.

Stevens, Wayne, Myers, Glenford J. and Constantine, Larry L., (1974), 'Structured design', *IBM Systems Journal*, vol. 13, no. 2, pp. 115–39.

Stoy, Joseph E., (1977), *Denotational Semantics: The Scott–Strachey approach to programming language theory*, MIT Press, Cambridge, Massachusetts.

Stroustrup, Bjarne, (1986), *The C++ Reference Manual*, Addison-Wesley, Reading, Massachusetts.

Strunk, William and White, Elwyn Books, (1979), *The Elements of Style* (3rd edn), Macmillan, New York.

Taylor, Richard N., Baker, Deborah A., Belz, Frank C., Boehm, Barry W., Clarke, Lori A., Fisher, David A., Osterweil, Leon, Selby, Richard W., Weiden, Jack C., Wolf, Alexander L. and Young, Michael, (1987), *Next Generation Software Environments: Principles, problems, and research directions*, Coins Technical Report 87-63, Department of Computer and Information Science, University of Massachusetts, Amherst, July.

Teitelbaum, Tim and Reps, Thomas, (1981), 'The Cornell Program Synthesizer: a syntax-directed programming environment', *Communications of the ACM*, vol. 24, no. 9, September, pp. 563–73.

Teitelman W. and Masinter, L., (1981), 'The Interlisp programming environment', *IEEE Computer*, vol. 14, no. 2, April, pp. 25–33.

Tennen, Richard D., (1981), *Principles of Programming Languages*, Prentice Hall, Hemel Hempstead.

Thomas, Edward J. and Oman, Paul W., (1990), 'A bibliography of programming style', *ACM Sigplan Notices*, vol. 25, no. 2, February, pp. 7–16.

Trainor, W. L., (1973), 'Software: from satan to saviour', *Proceedings of the NAECON*, May.

Tymoczko, Thomas, (1980), 'Computers, proofs and mathematicians: a philosophical investigation of the four-color proof', *Mathematics Magazine*, vol. 53, no. 3, pp. 131–8.

Ullman, J. D., (1982), *Principles of Database Systems* (2nd edn), Computer Science Press.

Walston, C. E. and Felix, C. P., (1977), 'A method of programming measurement and estimation', *IBM Systems Journal*, vol. 16, no. 1, pp. 64–5.

Warnier, Jean Dominique, (1974), *Logical Construction of Programs*, H. E. Stenfert Kroese B.V., Leiden, Holland.

Warnier, Jean Dominique, (1978), *Program Modification*, Martinus Nijhoff Social Sciences Division.

Weinberg, Gerald M., (1971), *The Psychology of Computer Programming*, Van Nostrand Reinhold Company, New York.

Weinberg, Gerald M., (1982), *Understanding the Professional Programmer*, Little, Brown, Boston, Massachusetts.

Weinberg, Gerald M., (1983) 'Kill that code!', *Infosystems*, August, pp. 48–9.

Weiss, Eric A., (1972), 'Review of *The Psychology of Computer Programming*, by Gerald M. Weinberg', *ACM Computing Reviews*, vol. 13, no. 4, #23,001, April, pp. 175–6.

Weizenbaum, Joseph, (1976), *Computer Power and Human Reason: From judgment to calculation*, W. H. Freeman, San Francisco.

Wexelblat, Richard L., (1976), *Maxims for Malfeasant Designers, or How to Design Languages to Make Programming as Difficult as Possible*, Second International Conference on Software Engineering, pp. 331–6.

Wexelblat, Richard L. (ed.), (1981), *History of Programming Languages*, Academic Press, New York. (Papers from a conference held in 1978.)

Whorf, Benjamin, (1956), *Language, Thought and Reality*, MIT Press, Cambridge, Massachusetts.

Wirth, Niklaus, (1969), 'On multiprogramming, machine coding, and computer organization', *Communications of the ACM*, vol. 12, no. 9, September, pp. 489–98.

Wirth, Niklaus, (1971), 'Program development by stepwise refinement', *Communications of the ACM*, vol. 14, no. 4, April, pp. 221–7.

Wirth, Niklaus, (1976), *Algorithms + Data Structures = Programs*, Prentice Hall, Englewood Cliffs, NJ.

Wirth, Niklaus, (1977), 'Modula: a language for modular multiprogramming', *Software – Practice and Experience*, vol. 7, pp. 3–35.

Wirth, Niklaus, (1983), *Programming Modula-2* (2nd edn), Springer-Verlag, Berlin.

Wolfe, Martin I., Babich, Wayne, Simpson, Richard, Thall, Richard and Weissman, Larry, (1981), 'The Ada language system', *IEEE Computer*, June, pp. 37–45.

Wood, Steven R., (1981), 'Z – The 95% program editor', *ACM Sigplan Notices*, vol. 16, no. 6, June, pp. 1–7.

Wulf, William and Shaw, Mary, (1973), 'Global variables considered harmful', *ACM Sigplan Notices*, vol. 8, no. 2, February, pp. 28–34.

Yourdon, Edward, (1977), *Structured Walkthroughs*, Yourdon, New York.

Yourdon, Edward and Constantine, Larry L., (1979), *Structured Design: Fundamentals of a discipline of computer program and systems design*, Prentice Hall, Englewood Cliffs, NJ.

Zave, Pamela, (1982), 'An operational approach to requirements specification for embedded systems', *IEEE Transactions on Software Engineering*, vol. SE-8, no. 3, May, pp. 250–69.

INDEX